A CITY DIVIDED

A CITY DIVIDED

RACE, FEAR, AND THE LAW IN POLICE CONFRONTATIONS

DAVID A. HARRIS

ANTHEM PRESS

Anthem Press
An imprint of Wimbledon Publishing Company
www.anthempress.com

This edition first published in UK and USA 2020
by ANTHEM PRESS
75–76 Blackfriars Road, London SE1 8HA, UK
or PO Box 9779, London SW19 7ZG, UK
and
244 Madison Ave #116, New York, NY 10016, USA

British Library Cataloguing-in-Publication Data
A catalogue record for this book is available from the British Library.

Library of Congress Cataloging-in-Publication Data
A catalog record for this book has been requested.

ISBN-13: 978-1-78527-300-1 (Pbk)
ISBN-10: 1-78527-300-0 (Pbk)

This title is also available as an e-book.

To
Ruben Harris
of blessed memory

and

Levi Ruben Blythe Harris
Beginning a life filled with joy and love

CONTENTS

ACKNOWLEDGMENTS

Anyone who thinks that writing a book is a one-person task—the scholar toiling in a lonely garret, turning out a finished product for others to read—is sadly mistaken. While it is the author who conceives of the ideas and puts fingers to keyboard or pen to paper, any book that makes it to a reader owes its existence to an entire cast of people.

For those who encouraged me to write this book and who helped me get back on track when the effort seemed derailed, I cannot thank them enough. Among those who played these key roles for me were Sam Walker, Kathleen Clark, Richard Leo, Jeff Shook, Ralph Bangs, Eric Miller, Rachel Harmon, Seth Stoughton, Barry Friedman, John Wallace, Richard Garland, and especially Tamara Lave. I also thank Kerry Lewis and Bryan Campbell, who supplied me with much of the basic information and documents I needed to get the job done.

The brilliant and encouraging editorial assistance of Kate Scheinman was absolutely key to the quality of the finished product. Law librarians Linda Tashbook and Karen Shepard, Research Fellow Joey Maguire, and the entire library staff of the University of Pittsburgh School of Law all have my gratitude as well.

For the many people who talked to me about the case, granted interviews, and gave me background, I am deeply appreciative. Some of you were directly involved in some of the events; others had a particular professional take on what occurred. Some were current or former officials or officers; others were advocates, either part of the case or outside it. Some of your comments and thoughts appear in the book; for others, your discussions with me are not quoted but nonetheless helped guide me in important ways. I am especially grateful to Jordan Miles and to the members of his family, whose help and cooperation were a key element in allowing this project to come to fruition.

Throughout the years that I worked on this project, I had the support of the Dean's Scholarship funding from the University of Pittsburgh School of Law.

I was also gratified to have been awarded the Buchanan Ingersoll & Rooney Faculty Scholar Award for support of this project. My appointment as the Sally Ann Semenko Endowed Chair also supported my efforts. Former Pitt Law Deans Mary Crossley and Chip Carter and current Dean Amy Wildermuth did all that I asked to facilitate and support this work. I cannot thank them enough.

Last, I cannot adequately express my thanks to my family, friends, and colleagues who helped me through some of the most difficult times in my life as I worked on this project over almost eight years. Your encouragement and support meant everything to me. This book would never have come to be without all of you.

CHAPTER 1

THE INCIDENT

MICHAEL SALDUTTE, RICHARD EWING, AND DAVID SISAK

They had all applied for the assignment: plainclothes anti-crime patrol in one of the city's most dangerous and violent neighborhoods. That's what put Pittsburgh Police officers Michael Saldutte, Richard Ewing, and David Sisak together in an unmarked "99" car on the night of January 12, 2010, rolling slowly through the city's Homewood neighborhood.

Year in and year out, Homewood—a residential enclave of mostly poor residents in the city's East End—had the most homicides of any neighborhood in Pittsburgh, and it usually led in other violent crimes, like aggravated assault and robbery. All three men had significant experience as active officers; for example, David Sisak had made about 1,000 arrests over the prior four years. These kinds of records—actions showing a "go get the bad guys" attitude—undoubtedly helped the officers get the coveted assignment to a 99 car: an unmarked anti-crime vehicle that roamed the vicinity at will, looking for signs of trouble—especially crime involving guns and violence—instead of waiting to answer calls like a regular patrol car. Each of the officers stood about six feet tall and weighed around 200 pounds.

Richard Ewing, a former Marine who had earned a brown belt in martial arts, drove the dark-colored, two-door 99 car; Michael Saldutte, sitting in the front passenger seat, had trained in martial arts and what he called "grappling." David Sisak rode in the back seat, operating the police computer. All three had taken defensive tactics training as police recruits. Saldutte served as an instructor in defensive tactics for the whole police department, and he had had special training in spotting people carrying concealed weapons. The clear winter night had brought frigid temperatures, and a thick coating of snow and ice already

1

covered streets and sidewalks. The officers all wore dark, plain clothes in layers against the bitter cold and heavy boots. Their police badges hung on cords around their necks.

A few minutes after 11:00 p.m., the 99 car drove down residential Tioga Street. Ewing drove slowly, only about 15 miles per hour, to allow the officers to look for anything unusual. As they passed a small white house at 7940 Tioga, Saldutte saw something: a male figure "standing up tight against [the corner of a] house"; the man faced away from the street. Saldutte told his partners that he saw someone, and he asked Ewing to turn the car around to get a better look. Ewing continued a short way down Tioga (he did not want the person near the house to notice them), turned around, and then pulled the 99 car even with the white house. As they came to a stop, with the white house on the driver's side of the car, the officers saw that while they had been turning around and coming back, the man had begun to walk away from the house, toward the sidewalk, and was walking toward the street. The man "seemed not to have noticed" the 99 car until it stopped in the street in front of him. When he saw the unmarked car, the man—young, small in stature, and wearing a heavy coat against the cold—stopped dead in his tracks and thrust his right hand into his coat pocket.

Officer Ewing immediately opened the driver's door window all the way, held up the badge hanging around his neck for the man to see, and identified himself with the words "Pittsburgh Police." Officer Saldutte, on the passenger side, opened his door, got halfway out—one leg on the street, the other still inside—and leaned over the car. Showing the badge around his neck and identifying himself as a Pittsburgh Police officer, Saldutte said to the man, "Hold up—do me a favor and take your hand out of your pocket." All of the officers understood that, in an encounter with an unknown person, officers needed to get the person to make his or her hands visible. Requiring a display of empty hands meant the subject could not harm them with a weapon. The man immediately obeyed: he pulled his hand out of his pocket.

Even so, the officers became suspicious: they already suspected that the man had a gun. According to Saldutte, "I felt at this point he could be carrying a weapon." Sisak concurred, "We thought he had a gun from the get-go." The man had behaved suspiciously by standing next to a house at night and then putting his hand in his pocket when he saw the police. Saldutte, still leaning over the car, asked the man, "Is that your house?" The man replied, "No, I live down the street," pointing down Tioga. Saldutte then asked the man why he was "creeping" around the white house if he did not live there. The young man did not answer. Instead, he began to walk away, slowly, in the direction he had pointed. As he walked, Saldutte and his partners noticed that the right pocket of the man's coat—the same pocket into which he had initially thrust his hand—sagged noticeably lower than the other side of the coat, as if it contained a heavy object. And the man's right hand seemed to touch the pocket and cradle the heavy object against him from the outside, in an effort to keep it from swinging with his gait. Saldutte, still half in, half out of the car, said to Ewing and Sisak, "He has something on him—I think he's going to go on us." According to Saldutte, what he saw—the suspicious activity by the house, the hand automatically thrust into the pocket, the hand trying to keep a heavy object in the pocket from moving—was "consistent with a firearm" in the right pocket. These cues fit perfectly into his training to spot concealed firearms and into all of his experiences on the street.

After walking away a few steps, the man broke into a run. As he did, the officers noticed that the heavily weighted right coat pocket was swinging, out of rhythm with the man's steps, while he tried to steady it with his right hand. Despite—or maybe because—he went into a full run, the man did not get far. After just a few yards, he slipped on the ice and fell heavily, face down.

Saldutte, Ewing, and Sisak swung into action.

Saldutte, now out of the car, ran toward the man, yelling "Pittsburgh Police! Stay on the ground!" The man attempted to push himself up, but Saldutte grabbed him from behind and put his arms all the way around the man's lower chest, to keep him from standing up and getting to the gun in his coat pocket. As Saldutte attempted to establish control, the man's right arm came loose from the bear hug and swung back; his elbow caught Saldutte on the side of the head, causing the officer to lose his balance and fall back. Ewing and Sisak had gotten out of the car, yelling that they were police and ordering the man to stop. As the man attempted to get to his feet, Sisak pulled out his Taser and shot the man in the back, but the Taser had no effect—probably because of the man's winter coat—and he kept struggling to get off the ground. Sisak charged at him, grabbing him from behind, and pushed him down through the hedges separating the yard of the white house from the one next to it. Sisak rode him through the hedge to the ground, putting all of his weight into it, and Ewing and Saldutte ran around the bushes to the yard of the next house to help. But the man would not stop struggling, fighting the officers hard, even when Sisak had him down.

With this kind of battle, the officers began to suspect the influence of drugs. As the officers knew, suspects who took certain drugs could engage in prolonged intense physical struggles. Sisak, in particular, felt that the man "was going to die" because of excited delirium, defined by the FBI as "a serious and potentially deadly medical condition involving psychotic behavior, elevated temperature,

and an extreme fight-or-flight response by the nervous system," which Sisak had
learned about in training. The man kept fighting, and he kicked with one of his
legs straight back—the officers called it a "donkey kick"—hitting Sisak directly
in the knee. In immediate and intense pain, Sisak lost his grip; the man was now
trying to get up, but Ewing and Saldutte would not allow it. Ewing took the man
down to the ground again, using the weight of his body.

With Ewing on the man's left side and Saldutte on his right, they tried to
handcuff him, as he yelled, "Don't take me to jail, just let me go home!" Saldutte
got a cuff on the man's right wrist. Sisak managed to get up again despite the hard
kick he had taken to the knee, and he now knelt in front of the man's head. But
as the struggle continued, the man pulled his cuffed right hand out of Saldutte's
grip and moved it directly toward his own right coat pocket. Saldutte, working
to get the arm back, felt a hard object in the area of the man's coat pocket, and
the officer was sure that the man was going to pull out a gun. Saldutte called out,
"I lost the cuff—he's going for it!" Sisak, kneeling directly in front of the man,
felt he was about to be shot to death. Ewing and Saldutte kneed and punched
the man repeatedly, trying to get him to protect himself from the pain with his
hands so that he could not grab for the gun. Sisak hit the man with several hard
blows to the head and face, with no effect. Saldutte delivered a hard knee strike
to the man's head—and finally the man stopped struggling. Quickly, the officers
cuffed him. The fight was over; the man lay face down in the snow. The whole
incident ended just a couple of minutes after it started.

With the man now securely cuffed and face down in the snow, Saldutte
reached into the man's right coat pocket to retrieve the heavy object. He pulled
out—not a gun but a bottle of Mountain Dew soda. Ewing remembered later
that it was a regular size bottle that would have come out of a vending machine.
Finding the bottle seemed to upset Saldutte, who tossed it into the snow in the
yard. Saldutte then searched the man thoroughly, but he did not find a gun.

Saldutte had had the man in view the whole time, from initially spotting
him to seeing him walk away from the white house, until snapping the cuffs on
him. The other officers also had their eyes on him continuously, at least since
Ewing pulled the car next to him, and none of the officers had seen the man
discard anything. They figured that the gun had fallen out of the man's pocket
during the struggle, and they began a thorough search of the yards of both
houses where the struggle had taken place. Ewing checked the whole area with
his flashlight, he said, but he found no gun, and nothing associated with one,
such as a magazine or ammunition. Saldutte searched single-mindedly, with one
objective: "I kept looking for a gun." They searched carefully enough to find
other items: the Taser cartridge and a set of handcuffs one of the officers had

dropped during the fight. The three officers searched methodically, as they had learned to do, looking through the snow and the bushes and everything else to find the gun. But they did not find one.

A short time later, a police transport wagon arrived to take the handcuffed man away. Since the man had visible injuries to his face, department protocol dictated that the two uniformed officers in charge of the wagon, Darren Fedorski and David Horak, take the injured man to a hospital for medical treatment and then to the county jail for booking. As the officers walked the handcuffed man to the door of the transport wagon, a woman opened a second floor window of the house at 7940 Tioga, where the police had originally seen the man. The woman, Monica Wooding, stuck out her head to ask what was going on. The police asked if she knew the man in handcuffs and if he had permission to be next to her house. When Wooding said she could not see the man well enough, Fedorski and Horak moved him back from the wagon toward the house and shined a flashlight on his face. Wooding told the officers she did not know him and that he did not have her permission to be on her property. Fedorski and Horak then locked the man in the wagon. They drove to West Penn Allegheny Hospital. While waiting for treatment in the emergency room, the man "spontaneously uttered" to Officer Fedorski, "I'm glad it was the police I fought with, and not some gang banger, because I would have got shot."

After completing the necessary medical treatment, the officers transferred the man to jail. He faced two counts of aggravated assault (one each involving the blows to Officers Saldutte and Sisak) and also charges of loitering, resisting arrest, and escape.

The officers did not keep the Mountain Dew bottle. They felt no need to do so, because "It wasn't evidence."

During the struggle that night, the three police officers never had any doubts that they were dealing with an armed man; they believed their lives were in grave danger. None of them found a gun at the scene, despite the painstaking searches of the area that the officers performed, and later searches by other officers yielded no gun either. Nevertheless, months—even years— later, the officers remained convinced that the man had had a gun and that he had come within seconds of killing them. As Officer Sisak said, "I still believe he had a gun on him that night." Despite never finding a weapon and not having seen the man discard or throw anything, "Nothing has changed my mind. I'm one hundred percent positive he had a gun." Sisak says that, "He had to have a gun" because "he had no other reason to run from us. He knew who we were."

JORDAN MILES

On January 12, 2010, a little past 11:00 p.m., Jordan Miles left his mother's house on Tioga Street in Pittsburgh's Homewood neighborhood. He walked toward his grandmother's house, just around the block on Susquehanna Street. He had been staying overnight at his grandmother's for years, because she had a spare room, and with Jordan's younger siblings at home, space at his mom's was tight. Jordan attended Creative and Performing Arts (CAPA) High School in Pittsburgh. He was a senior and played the viola, majoring in music and performing with the school's orchestra and other classical music ensembles. The following year, he was to attend Penn State University, which had awarded him a scholarship. A shy young man, Jordan stood five feet six inches tall and weighed about 150 pounds. He had just turned 18.

Jordan went down the four steps of his mom's house toward the street, wearing his new winter coat (a birthday gift from his grandmother) against the cold. He was talking on his cell phone as he left, continuing the conversation he had begun inside with his friend, Jamiah. He walked out into the middle of the empty street because the ice on the sidewalks and the heavy slush at the sides of the street made it hard to walk anywhere else. No one was out on that very cold night. Jordan noticed a car—just a regular vehicle—sitting in the middle of the intersection of Tioga and Pitt Streets, down the block, but he gave it no thought. It seemed to be waiting to give someone a ride from the bus stop at that corner.

When Jordan had walked about three or four houses down from his mother's place, the car suddenly moved, speeding toward him. It swerved and stopped in front of him, making the young man jump back off the street, "almost [to] the sidewalk." Before Jordan could think, one of three men in the car jumped out and began to yell at him—very loudly: "Where's your gun? Where's the money? Where's the drugs?" The other men jumped out of the car too, also yelling these things; all were wearing dark civilian clothes. Jordan had no idea who they were.

Jordan became frightened. He and his family lived in Homewood and knew it as their home, but he also understood that Homewood had a high rate of violent crime, including robberies. Instantly he panicked. "I thought I was gonna be robbed," if not worse. He reacted, instantly, by trying to flee, running back toward his mother's house. But the ground had a thick coat of ice and snow, and after just a few steps, he fell forward.

Almost immediately, one of the men—Jordan thought it was the driver, but he was not sure—jumped on top of him, trying to pull off his coat. The other two men started to beat him, and Jordan was terrified. Eventually, the men forcibly pulled off his coat and got him on the ground, face down in the snow.

The beating continued. Several times Jordan attempted to lift up enough to get his face out of the snow, but this led to more blows. One of the men pressed his knee hard into Jordan's back, resulting in terrible pain in his neck. He did not understand who these men were or why they were beating him. He attempted to pull his hands underneath himself to try to push off the ground, but when he did this, the men hit him more. Every attempt to move or raise his head resulted in more blows. Jordan remembers yelling, "Oh my God, please don't kill me." The men eventually put handcuffs on him. Another attempt to get his face out of the snow brought more beatings.

At this point, Jordan thought the men planned to abduct and kill him. "I really thought I was going to be killed or abducted," he said later, because "I didn't know these were cops." He did know how dangerous the neighborhood was, and the men were demanding money and drugs; the handcuffs made him think that they were going to rob, abduct, and kill him, and then throw his body into the freezing river.

Jordan started to pray aloud. One of the men choked him until he could not breathe and told Jordan to shut up, and when he continued to pray under his breath, the man slammed him back into the snow. Jordan then made a last attempt to get his face out of the snow so that he could breathe—and suffered a powerful blow from a hard, heavy object to the right side of his face. The impact left him dazed, and he lay still for a couple of minutes. His face felt numb, and he noticed blood, dripping fast from his mouth. At that point, Jordan said later, "I gave up, thinking that it was my time to die."

The men asked him where he had been going, and he told them. They searched his pockets, finding his wallet with his identification, his iPod, and his keys. He was carrying nothing else. One of them asked where his money was, since his wallet contained no cash. Jordan told them he never carried money on the street. But he told them he had just had a birthday and had received some money as a gift and would go home to get it for them, if they would let him live. The men seemed uninterested. One of them said, "What are you talking about? We're not going to hurt you."

He saw that the men walked around the area, searching for something. Without moving first, he asked the men if they would take his face out of the snow. They finally sat him up.

Jordan saw a small truck stop in front of the scene. When Jordan saw that it was a police truck, he felt immediate relief: "I was happy to see the police." He thought that one of his neighbors must have seen what happened and called 911 and that these officers were here to arrest the men who tried to rob and kill him. But when two uniformed police officers got out of the truck, they walked calmly over to the three men who had beaten him. One of the three men who had hit him told the police officers with the truck that he, Jordan, had a gun and that they were searching for it. As one of the officers in uniform lifted him and escorted him to the truck, Jordan realized for the first time that the men who had beaten him were also police officers. In all of this time, they had never identified themselves as police or shown their badges.

The two uniformed officers in the truck took Jordan to West Penn Allegheny Hospital for treatment of the injuries to his face. Riding in the truck, handcuffed, Jordan said aloud that he was glad to learn that the three men in plain clothes had been police rather than gang members or robbers, because "Nothing would have held (gang members) back from killing me, abducting me ...." After that, the police took Jordan to the Allegheny County Jail, where he remained for 22 hours until his mother secured his release.

ONE VIOLENT INCIDENT, TWO DIFFERENT STORIES

We know that Officers Richard Ewing, Michael Saldutte, and David Sisak and high school student Jordan Miles were involved in a violent incident in the Homewood neighborhood of Pittsburgh on the night of January 12, 2010. But, in crucial respects, the officers and the student tell two very different versions of the story. The officers say they identified themselves as police, multiple times; Jordan says this never happened and he did not know they were police. The officers say Jordan had a gun, but they found only a Mountain Dew bottle. Jordan says he never had a gun, or a bottle of anything, in his pocket. These two stories resonated with different groups of people and had a huge impact on the city of Pittsburgh—then and now.

Days after Jordan's arrest, when a picture of his injured and swollen face appeared all over the city's media, the case exploded. It angered many and quickly polarized the city. Community members held demonstrations against the police; counter-demonstrations soon occurred in support of the officers. The criminal case against Jordan—for aggravated assault on two of the officers and for resisting arrest, escape, and loitering—began, and community outrage about the actions of the police officers grew. Soon after, prosecutors began federal and state criminal investigations of the police officers, centering on claims of false arrest, excessive force, and violations of Jordan's federal civil rights. Then months later, Jordan Miles filed a civil rights lawsuit against the officers. The case did not settle before trial as some cases like this do; instead, it went through not one but two long trials in federal court. When the legal actions finally ended, no one felt fully satisfied or vindicated by the outcome—not Jordan Miles, or the three police officers, or supporters of either side.

This book tells that whole story, which is important and compelling in itself, and because there is something larger here than just this one terrible incident in Pittsburgh. Jordan Miles's violent struggle with the three officers occurred more than four years *before* the day in August of 2014 when a young man named Michael Brown died in a struggle with a police officer in Ferguson, Missouri. The incident involving Jordan Miles and the Pittsburgh Police officers foreshadowed what would happen with Michael Brown, and with Eric Garner in Staten Island, New York; Tamir Rice in Cleveland, Ohio; Philando Castille in Falcon Heights, Minnesota; Alton Sterling in Baton Rouge, Louisiana; and so many others. *The story of the Jordan Miles case is the story of all of these cases that followed.* There is, thankfully, one crucial distinction for which everyone can feel grateful: Jordan Miles did not die in the struggle. He lived and can tell his own story. The case involving Jordan Miles gives us an opportunity to see what happens on the streets of violent urban neighborhoods—how these incidents occur and how things can go terribly wrong so quickly. It gives us a way to see how officers and the people they encounter react to one another, and why. We can see the outsized influence of race and fear. And since Jordan's case ultimately involved both the criminal and civil aspects of the legal system, it shows us how the law and the courts in these cases succeed—or fail. With the chance to look back on the full picture, in the context of a case that has not received the kind of exhaustive national examination that some other cases have, we get a fresh look at why these kinds of incidents keep occurring and, in turn, what we might do to avoid them in the future.

RACE, FEAR, AND THE LAW

The clear differences in the stories of the incident, as recounted by Jordan and the three officers to investigators, lawyers, and the courts, could lead a dispassionate observer to say, "Someone's lying here," and throw up his or her hands. This book will confront those differences head-on, without covering them up. The commonalities in the stories, however, may tell us even more than the differences. First, fear played a primary role in the incident—both for Jordan and for the three officers. These officers, who had the courage to take on a dangerous job in an area with a reputation for violence, feared that Jordan Miles had a gun and he therefore had to be disarmed. When Jordan tried to get away and struggled when the officers attempted to subdue him, they feared death at his hands. Their training and the culture of policing constantly reemphasized that fear. For Jordan, it is understandable that he tried to get away from men who he thought were robbers assaulting him. He didn't know that these were police officers. But what many people do not realize is that for African Americans like Jordan, running from the police under almost any circumstance can make all the sense in the world.

Second, the case forces us to think about race. The issue shows itself at many points in this story, and it pervades our thinking about crime, about violence, about our urban environment, and about policing. Racial differences cause us to interpret ambiguous situations and clues differently than we might otherwise. Solid science proves that when people get racial cues, such as seeing black faces, we fill in blank spots with perceptions of fear and danger more readily than when those cues do not appear. We may even read race and our assumptions about danger into situations where race does not actually show up. (In fact, if you reread the stories of the incident at the beginning of this chapter, you will not find the race of any of the four people mentioned—not once. Yet more than a few readers probably assumed that the incident involved white officers and a young black male.) Nothing about the presence of racial issues should surprise anyone; race pervades American life in a thousand ways, even if most white people do not think about it at all. Telling this story, without discussing how race may have contributed to the incident itself, and how it raised its head any number of times in the months and years that followed, would not make for a true and full presentation of what happened.

And we also cannot understand what happened without an examination of a crucial aspect of the training that police receive today. In almost every jurisdiction in the United States, but especially in any large city or metropolitan area, police receive months of training. The practice of the old days—recruits were sworn in; given a badge, a gun, and a uniform; and then told to go do the job—passed long ago, and good riddance. Much of the training that officers receive today focuses on the issue of assuring officer safety. And somewhere between the old days and now, we began to teach officers that every encounter with a civilian is a potential threat—that every traffic stop and every face-to-face exchange of words has the potential for deadly violence. To be sure, the police officer's job includes an element of danger and the possibility of violence that most jobs simply do not. But when we train our officers that the possibility for deadly violence exists always and everywhere, they will inevitably begin to see it where it does not lie, and any effort by reformers to throttle back that impulse— to slow down the process to create time and distance for safety—begins to seem like a recipe for increased danger and threat.

All of these factors—along with the shortcomings of the legal system—will lead us to ask what we can change to prevent these calamities from happening on the street and how we might better handle them in the aftermath. *A City*

Divided: Race, Fear, and the Law in Police Confrontations ends with a comprehensive set of recommendations geared toward strengthening public safety through a new approach to policing, rebuilding the relationships necessary for that to happen, and changing our laws and legal processes to do a better job when incidents occur.

In the end, we have this certainty. Something went terribly wrong on Tioga Street. Somehow, an 18-year-old, 150-pound high school viola player, who had made the honor roll and was headed to college, a kid who had never crossed paths with law enforcement and was just a few steps from his mother's house and around the block from his bedroom at his grandmother's house, ended up in a nearly fatal encounter with three much larger police officers who still swear that the young man had a gun and who believe that he almost shot them. The high schooler and two of the officers suffered injuries; the city became divided; and anger poured out against the police, from those who live in the neighborhoods that need police help the most. The officers would continue to say that they did nothing wrong, that they did their jobs as they should have, and that whatever went wrong lay at the feet of Jordan Miles. Jordan would surely say something different. But put blame aside. Events careened toward disaster, a near catastrophe was narrowly averted, and no matter who we think should accept fault, the questions this book tries to answer are, "What happened? Why? How can we do better?"

PART I

WHAT HAPPENED?

The incident on Tioga Street on January 12, 2010, involving high school student Jordan Miles and Pittsburgh Police Officers Michael Saldutte, David Sisak, and Richard Ewing, became a defining moment for the city of Pittsburgh and influenced the relationship between the Pittsburgh Police and the city's African American community for years after. This incident had an impact far greater than any "typical" arrest in the city would, and it changed the course of a young man's life. And yet, the whole encounter lasted but a few minutes. No doubt the officers thought of it as a routine part of their usual duties, and they likely imagined they would hear very little about it going forward. This was just another arrest, although one that included a lot of physical force.

But the incident—which quickly became known as the Jordan Miles case—proved anything but routine. To understand what happened that night, and to fully grasp the events that followed, we must begin with a deep grounding in the most basic question: What happened?

For this case, understanding what happened begins with knowing who the people in this story are. Who is Jordan Miles? He had reached the age of 18 the day before this happened, but what can we know about him and his life? Who are Officers Saldutte, Sisak, and Ewing? What brought them to police work and how long had they served? We also must know something about the place where the incident occurred. Homewood is a Pittsburgh neighborhood with a rich history and serves as the physical context for all that Jordan and the officers thought about that night.

Answering what happened also means we must know what occurred when the case burst into the public sphere in Pittsburgh, and we must see the almost instantaneous reactions it engendered. And we also need to understand the beginnings of the legal process in a criminal court against Jordan. All of these events came in the first two months following the incident.

Finally, we need to understand the investigations of the police actions—one by the city's internal affairs office, another by the federal government, and a third by the county prosecutor's office. Understanding how these investigations played out is essential to an appreciation of how the case divided the city—and how it ultimately resulted in not one but two civil trials in federal court.

Part I of the book will answer those questions.

A NOTE FROM THE AUTHOR

In a perfect world, I would have had the chance to conduct personal interviews of the three police officers involved. However, my requests for interviews, made through their attorneys, did not produce that opportunity. Of course, declining to speak to me or to anyone else about the case is the absolute right of the officers. Fortunately, from my point of view, all three of the officers had spoken about the case, on the record, in multiple legal proceedings, police reports, and elsewhere, personally and through representatives. In those statements, they discussed not just the basic facts of what happened that night in January of 2010 but their thought processes, objectives, fears, and beliefs. They talked about what happened in personal terms, and they discussed what they thought when the incident ended, and many months after. They discussed some aspects of their personal backgrounds and their experience and training. Using these materials, I did my best to capture their actions, thoughts, and perspectives as they described them, as well as their professional backgrounds and training. I have added to this the thoughts and perspectives of other police officers who have deep experience in the realities of urban policing and have endeavored at every turn to give the officers' perspectives its due, despite not having direct access to the three officers themselves. The fact that I did not have the chance to conduct personal interviews does appear in the notes at the end of Chapter 2, but I wanted readers who might miss those notes to know this.

This book is written in a style accessible to a general audience. Given the nature of the material, however, a glossary of legal- and police-related terms appears after the final chapter.

CHAPTER 2

THE PEOPLE AND THE PLACES

The incident on Tioga Street in Pittsburgh, in January of 2010, lasted just minutes. But it sparked a series of events—a criminal case against Jordan Miles, internal investigations of the three police officers, federal and state investigations of police use of force, and a long civil trial—that spanned years. The story of these events will follow, but to fully understand, we must know something about the people involved[1] and the place where it all happened.

OFFICER MICHAEL SALDUTTE

Michael Saldutte[2] came to the Pittsburgh Bureau of Police[3] from Bethel Park, a borough of approximately 30,000 people, southwest of Pittsburgh. During high school, Saldutte participated in football and track and field. After high school, he worked for a tree service and then became a farm laborer. He lived in New Wilmington, Pennsylvania, a town of about 2,500, located approximately 65 miles north of Pittsburgh. When he read an ad in the *Pittsburgh Post-Gazette* seeking recruits for the Pittsburgh Police, Saldutte applied and was accepted; by the time of the Tioga Street incident, he had been with the Pittsburgh Police for about six years. He lived in the city's Brookline neighborhood.

Since becoming an officer, Saldutte worked hard on his physical conditioning and fighting skills. During their training, all Pittsburgh Police recruits take classes in defensive tactics including the basics of self-defense and proficiency in hand-to-hand combat. Saldutte went further. After becoming an officer, he began martial arts training. He also worked out regularly at a gym, using weight training and other methods to maintain his physical conditioning, and also trained in what he called "grappling or wrestling." In addition, he had experience in Jiu-Jitsu and became involved (first as a student and then as an instructor) in the self-defense system called Krav Maga, associated with the Israeli military. Saldutte eventually became an instructor in defensive tactics for the Pittsburgh Police, teaching other officers these skills. In connection with becoming an instructor, he completed a course in "Pressure Points and Control Tactics." At the time of the incident on Tioga, Officer Saldutte stood about five feet ten inches tall and weighed a little over 200 pounds. He was 28 years old.

In late summer 2009, less than six months before the incident on Tioga Street, Saldutte—still a patrol officer—applied for and received an assignment to the 99 car. As part of his application for the position, Saldutte noted that he had "received training from the ATF" (the federal agency now called the Bureau of Alcohol, Tobacco, Firearms and Explosives) "on characteristics of an armed individual, which I use on a daily basis." The training—Saldutte recalled its title as "Understanding the Characteristics of an Armed Individual"—formed a key part of how Saldutte would do the work involved in the 99 car assignment. (Saldutte noted that Officer Ewing attended the training as well.) Recalling the daily use of the training, Saldutte said that a police officer looks "for numerous indicators, whether it be their characteristics, body movement, subconscious actions, demeanor, reactions to you as a police officer." Among the subconscious reactions is the "security pat" or "security feel," in which a suspect confronted by a police officer would pat or touch the clothing over the area of the body where a gun is concealed.

But Officer Saldutte's thinking about the possible presence of a weapon went beyond what he learned in the ATF training. During proceedings in the Jordan Miles case, one of the lawyers asked the officer about his mind-set when patrolling Homewood:

Q: When you're on patrol, let's say you're in a "99" car, and you purport or contend to see somebody engaged in what you believe to be a suspicious activity for some reason and it's at night, do you presume ... that the person may have a weapon?

A: I presume that everyone that I come in contact with is a potential threat and could be armed until I know otherwise.

Saldutte made it clear that he held this belief separate and apart from the "Characteristics of an Armed Individual" observations that he might make; if he saw any suspicious person—in fact, anyone he had contact with—he would presume that person had a gun and posed a threat.

OFFICER DAVID SISAK[4]

David Sisak was 34 years old when the incident on Tioga Street occurred. Sisak had a bachelor's degree in criminology from a local university. He had taken the traditional police academy training and other law enforcement training as well, in what he called a "trade-related school" setting. At the time of the incident, Officer Sisak stood six feet one inch tall and weighed roughly 215 pounds. He lived in the Westwood neighborhood of Pittsburgh; before that, he lived in Brookline, the same neighborhood as Officer Saldutte.

After graduating from Kiski Area High School located in a suburban area about 30 miles from Homewood, Sisak went directly to college. Around the time he graduated from college, Sisak saw an advertisement for positions with the Ocean City, Maryland Police Department. He qualified and trained at Maryland's Eastern Shore Criminal Justice Academy, in Salisbury, Maryland. He joined the Ocean City police force as a patrol officer. Illegal drugs formed a main focus of both Sisak's training and the activity of the Ocean City department. After a year, Sisak left the department and returned to the Pittsburgh area for family reasons. He took a job at Summit Academy, a privately owned "juvenile facility" in Butler, Pennsylvania, about an hour's drive north of Pittsburgh, and after that he worked for private security companies. He then joined the Pittsburgh Police, beginning with police academy training in September 2005.

Officer Sisak's first permanent duty assignment as a patrol officer put him in Zone 5—the same zone where Officer Saldutte worked. Up until Sisak's full assignment to the 99 car in August 2009 with Saldutte and Ewing, Sisak worked as a regular patrol officer, in uniform, and in a marked police car. When the opportunity to fill the 99 car assignment came up, Sisak applied, and he made sure that the command officer making the assignment knew what an active officer he was. In his memo applying for the position, Sisak pointed out that he had made more than 1,000 arrests in the prior four years, and—according to statistics compiled every month—he led his shift and his zone in gun arrests. Unlike Officer Saldutte, Officer Sisak did not attend or receive special training on spotting the characteristics of armed persons. He attributed his unusual degree of success at making gun arrests to his "attention to detail" and to the area in which he worked: "It's a high crime area. There's a lot of people out there committing crimes with guns." Based on his success, the commander picked him for the 99 car assignment. Officers Sisak, Saldutte, and Ewing would have the autonomy to plan and execute their actions on each shift, based on any instructions given to them by their commander.

More than a year and a half after the incident, when asked if he had been back to the scene on Tioga Street, Officer Sisak said that he had not. "I'm actually a lot safer not going out to that neighborhood, so I do my best to stay away from there," he said. "It's such a high crime area. Anything can happen to you there."

OFFICER RICHARD EWING[5]

Richard Ewing joined the military out of high school, enlisting in the U.S. Marines at the age of 18. He did his basic training at Parris Island, South Carolina, and left the Marines as a sergeant after four years. During his time in the Corps, he received the standard training, including hand-to-hand combat skills; he became a certified brown belt in Marine Corp martial arts training, doing approximately eight hours of training and practice a week. Training included kicks, knee and elbow strikes, punches, various defense strategies, and also "leg sweeps," arm bars, takedowns, choke holds, and the application of force to "pressure points" on the body. Ewing's training also included the use of weapons in hand-to-hand combat, such as pugil sticks and bayonets. The idea, he said, was to be able to defend yourself and your fellow soldiers, and to kill if necessary to do that. Assigned to anti-terrorism fleet protection work, Ewing served in the Middle East.

After his discharge from the Marines, Ewing returned to the Pittsburgh area. He worked for an asphalt company while attending school at the Community College of Allegheny County, and he eventually entered the police academy. When he joined the police force in September 2005, Ewing lived in Pittsburgh's Carrick neighborhood; he then moved to Lincoln Place, also in the city. After completing his field training, Ewing was stationed in Zone 5, which included Homewood. At the time of the incident on Tioga Street, Ewing stood six feet two inches tall and weighed over 200 pounds. He was in his late twenties, married, and a father.

JORDAN MILES[6]

Jordan Miles was born in Pittsburgh on January 11, 1992. He grew up on Tioga Street in the Homewood neighborhood and had celebrated his 18th birthday just one day before the incident. His mother, Terez Miles, worked as an interior designer, and his father, Otis Williams, lived in Sweetwater, Texas, where he worked with machines. In addition to Jordan and his mother, the household included Jordan's 17-year-old sister, Kielan, and one of his two brothers, Brandon; another brother, Dorian, was in the U.S. Army. Ms. Miles raised the four children as a single parent. Fortunately, she had the help of her own mother, Patricia Porter, a retired Pittsburgh Public Schools teacher, who lived around the block on Susquehanna Street. The two women—Jordan's mother Terez and his grandmother Patricia, who Jordan called Nanna—served as the two most important adults in Jordan's life, and together they worked to raise four well-behaved and grounded children. Ms. Miles's house was solid and well-kept but not large, and when all three boys were living at home, they shared one bedroom. Around the time that Jordan started middle school, an idea emerged. Grandmother Patricia Porter, who lived just around the block, had a room to spare; Jordan could sleep there. From that point on, Jordan had his own room. He kept his clothes at his grandmother's, sleeping, eating breakfast, and leaving for school from that residence. He spent much of the rest of his time at home with his mother, sister, and brothers in the family's house on Tioga.

At the time that Jordan was growing up in Homewood, the neighborhood was mostly African American. Like most other American cities, Pittsburgh had long been segregated. But it was not uncommon to see white people in Homewood during the day or night. According to Terez Miles,[7] while Homewood has mostly black residents, whites frequent the area too—sometimes as residents, and also as visitors, such as those who have family members in Homewood, or as business or tradespeople. Sometimes, the white people in Homewood committed crimes—in fact, that explained why some of them came to the area. Jordan remembered that when he was young—perhaps 9 or 10 years old—one of the older homes on his block became a "drug house" run by a white couple. People came and went day and night, in cars and on foot; many were white. Jordan did not fully understand the nature of what went on in and around the house at the time, but he remembered that a mix of white and black people showed up. He recalled that he would see the white people and he knew they were up to no good but "they were presentable and they would even say hi."

Around the time that Jordan was 9, he came home from school with a form for his mother to look at. The form asked if the student had an interest in learning to play a musical instrument. Jordan really wanted to learn to play, but he had not yet decided what instrument to try. He wanted to play "something manly, like a trumpet or a trombone," so he selected the viola, because he thought it was "some kind of horn." When he got the instrument and realized that it was a slightly larger version of a violin, it surprised him; it seemed like "a sissy thing." But Jordan found that he had a knack for the viola. He could play it almost immediately and soon found himself playing with kids above his grade level. Like other children who discover a connection to the arts in their early years, Jordan fell in love with the viola, and it became "my life—I loved playing that instrument." It set the stage for his progress into middle and high school. "I absolutely adored playing," he said.

Beginning in junior high, Jordan attended Pittsburgh's Creative and Performing Arts (CAPA) schools. He first attended the junior high CAPA program, which was housed at Rogers Middle School in the Garfield neighborhood of Pittsburgh. Then when he reached ninth grade, he attended Pittsburgh CAPA High School (then and now simply known as CAPA) in its sparkling new facility in downtown Pittsburgh. The school gave students the full slate of college preparatory courses, taught in 80-minute "blocks" through the morning. After lunch, each student spent the rest of the school day engaged in one of six "majors"—instrumental music, vocal music, theater, dance, visual arts, or writing. Many people in Pittsburgh regard CAPA—sometimes referred to as a magnet school or specialty school—as the crown jewel of the Pittsburgh Public Schools system. When the G-20 Summit meeting came to Pittsburgh in September 2009, First Lady Michelle Obama took the other spouses of the gathered world leaders to two places: the Warhol Museum and CAPA High School, where select students performed for the dignitaries.[8] Admission to the school was competitive, and students had to audition or present their work to a panel of faculty. Moving from the familiar setting of the junior high at Rogers to the downtown showcase building, Jordan did not know if he would like CAPA at first. His friends from the neighborhood had all gone to other high schools, and CAPA seemed like "a nerd school" and maybe not for him. But within a few weeks, Jordan says "it grew on me," and he began to enjoy it there. And every day, Jordan was able to spend half the day playing the viola—in the string orchestra, the small ensembles, and the jazz band. He was happy. He thrived at CAPA, and he had a good circle of friends.

As much as he enjoyed being at CAPA, in his first couple of years Jordan did not apply himself as a student. He described himself then as young and immature, and was content earning C grades—a scenario completely familiar to the parents of legions of high school students. In his junior year, however, his mind-set began to change. Suddenly it seemed that "adulthood was approaching very quickly." He began to think about what he would do with himself. "I needed a plan. I didn't want to spend the rest of my life working at, like, McDonald's. I wanted to make something of myself." So he began to buckle down and became more serious about his studies. His grades began to rise, semester by semester, and by the first semester of his senior year, Jordan had become a much stronger student. That semester, he received two Bs, and the rest were As. He made the school honor roll, a real point of pride. That fall, he was admitted to Penn State University, with a scholarship.

Prior to the night of January 12, 2010, Jordan Miles had never been arrested. He had had no negative interactions with the police—really, very few interactions at all. He did not yet drive, so he had never been stopped by the police while driving—an experience virtually all young black drivers have, much more often than their white peers. He had been taught to respect the police. His grandmother told him to "just call [the police] if there is an emergency. They will be there to help ... I respected them." His grandmother had instructed him to honor the police because "they're here to serve and protect us." If he were to have any encounter with them, she said, Jordan was "not to give them any type of trouble." He should not "withhold anything from them and should just be cooperative" with them. He remembers that when he was 9 or 10 years old, his mother had a friend who was a police officer who sometimes visited their home. Jordan respected him and thought the man was "like a superhero and nothing could stop him."

Growing up in Homewood, Jordan knew there was crime there, and some of it was violent. He was not naïve about the neighborhood because growing up there, one could not be. He'd seen crime committed in the open, especially drug-related crime such as drug use and what looked like person-to-person sales. He had also witnessed other more serious crimes such as when a group of whites jumped a black kid and beat him. Jordan and one of his friends witnessed the incident and went to help the victim, which caused the assailants to run. He knew about gun violence too. "I know there is shootings in that part of town where I am. It is a very high [crime] neighborhood. I hear gun shots every day ...." But even if it sounds strange to those living elsewhere, Jordan and his family felt safe on their block. It was home. He did not leave his mother's house on January 12, 2010 at 11:00 p.m. feeling afraid. In fact, he walked out the door, bound for his grandmother's, with his cell phone glued to his ear, talking to his friend Jamiah—just like any other kid his age. Jordan's mother was not afraid for her son, either. He was only going around the block, and he would be at her mother's door in just a couple of minutes. Nothing could happen in such a short time.

HOMEWOOD: FROM COUNTRY TO STREETCAR SUBURB TO DANGER ZONE

As previously noted, Jordan Miles had lived most of his life in the Homewood neighborhood of Pittsburgh—one of the city's 93 distinctive enclaves. Located in Pittsburgh's "East End"—the part of the city situated between the Monongahela and Allegheny Rivers, beginning from the point of land where the two rivers form the Ohio River—Homewood (or Homewood-Brushton, as it has sometimes been known) began in the 1860s as a country refuge for the city's wealthiest residents. By 2010, however, it had become a neighborhood of concentrated poverty, vacant lots, boarded up buildings, and criminal violence.

Pittsburgh's early growth owes everything to its location around the area of land where the three rivers converge.[9] This location made for an ideal transportation hub, and with the advent of coal and steel making, the advantages of location became abundantly clear. By the mid-1800s, as industrialization took over the area at the confluence of the rivers, the environment became dirty, filled with noxious pollution. But everyone lived there, both the people who worked in the mills and the business owners who ran the mills, the rich and the poor alike.

The coming of rail transportation in the mid-nineteenth century changed things. In 1852, the Pennsylvania Railroad ran trains into the downtown Pittsburgh area and from there through the flat land toward the east. The rural area just a few miles from the industrialized downtown—country in every sense—could now be reached by train. One of the first Pittsburghers to recognize the possibilities of this change was a 25-year-old man named Andrew Carnegie, who had already made a successful start in business.[10] Carnegie soon moved away from the smoke, up to "the country life" not far from the railroad station. In the area that would become Homewood, he could commute on the train from his large estate to the downtown business area, and later he had a telegraph line directly connected to his house. Homewood soon became the country retreat for the wealthy of Pittsburgh, filled with great homes and estates owned by some of the industrial titans of the era, such as George Westinghouse, Henry Clay Frick, and John Heinz. Homewood thus began as an elite community: white, Protestant, and wealthy.

With another innovation in transportation infrastructure, Homewood changed again. Between 1892 and 1893, four electric trolley lines were laid on four of the main streets of Homewood, making the area instantly accessible not just to the wealthy but also to the middle class. With the ability to commute on the trolley to downtown jobs, the "streetcar suburb" was born—and Homewood became a desirable place to live. By 1910, roughly 30,000 people lived in Homewood, making it "one of the largest and most populated neighborhoods in Pittsburgh."[11] The residents—with a wide variety of occupations but mostly white Protestant Northern Europeans—built a bustling community, with its own business district. Eventually, Andrew Carnegie, who had long before moved from Homewood and Pittsburgh to New York City, built one of the largest of his many Carnegie libraries in Homewood.

In 1911, one of the first middle-class black families moved to Homewood.[12] Robert Vann was the publisher of the *Pittsburgh Courier* newspaper, one of the most widely read publications in black communities across the nation, and he moved his new family to Monticello Street. He faced some opposition from white neighbors, but little came of it. In 1917, he bought the house next to his and rented it to another black family. This time Vann faced more hostility from whites; some of them moved away, but Vann did not back down, and his block became the beginnings of Homewood's first black area. By the 1930s and 1940s, Homewood had about 40,000 residents living in a densely populated area, many preserving their own cultures and traditions even as they lived close together with people of other backgrounds. Though whites and blacks tended to move in separate social worlds, and some restaurants and bars would not serve blacks, the neighborhood maintained a cooperative and calm atmosphere. It helped that many of the white immigrant families shared with their black neighbors a history as victims of discrimination; like blacks, Irish and Italians had also felt the bite of exclusion from jobs, educational institutions, and neighborhoods. All in all, Homewood formed a more diverse and tolerant community than many others in Pittsburgh in this period.

By the 1950s, circumstances changed yet again. With World War II and its aftermath, black Americans from elsewhere migrated to Pittsburgh for job opportunities. Many of the newly developed areas outside the city would not accept black residents, and Homewood was therefore one of the few housing options available for black newcomers and for African Americans returning from the war. Black people remained a minority in Homewood, where white families—mostly Irish and Italian—dominated. Thus Homewood's integrated population made the neighborhood a place where many types of people felt welcome and could afford to live.

However, several trends began to encourage a white exodus from Homewood. According to Steven W. Sapolsky and Bartholomew Roselli, actions by Pittsburgh's civic leaders in the mid-1950s in another Pittsburgh neighborhood had grave consequences for the city's entire black population. The largest and perhaps most important African American neighborhood in Pittsburgh, dating back decades, was called The Hill. Close to downtown and its jobs and industry, The Hill hosted the largest concentration of black families, black businesses, and black culture in the city. In fact The Hill had given the nation many of the greatest black cultural figures in the first half of the twentieth century. For example, the great playwright August Wilson, who chronicled the history of twentieth-century African American culture in his cycle of 10 plays, came from The Hill and set all but one of the plays there.[13] The Hill was also the home of a vibrant jazz performance culture, including clubs such as the legendary Crawford Grill. Jazz musicians traveling from Chicago to Philadelphia and New York always stopped and played in the clubs of Pittsburgh. The constant presence of the greatest jazz musicians of the time led to the discovery of many Pittsburgh artists; it was here that Duke Ellington discovered his lifelong collaborator, Billy Strayhorn. Nevertheless, Pittsburgh's city leaders decided, in the 1950s, to build an igloo-shaped "Civic Arena" stadium in the lower portion of The Hill. Using the power of eminent domain, the city condemned and destroyed an entire section of this vibrant black neighborhood and used it for the stadium and parking facilities. This development resulted in the displacement of 4,000 black families and 400 black-owned businesses and the destruction of an immeasurable amount of black culture. Many of these businesses and cultural venues simply disappeared. With limited options for where they might go to live, African American residents faced a real housing crisis. Homewood remained one of the few areas in which blacks were accepted, but even there, the shortage of housing immediately became acute.

The local real estate and rental industry, however, saw this as an opportunity—for themselves. According to John Brewer, Jr., one of the most well-respected local historians and head of the Trolley Station Oral History Center in Homewood,[14] with the housing crisis of the 1950s, real estate agents and rental operators pushed out white residents by any means they could. They turned around and, with no additional investment in or improvement of the properties, rented them to the housing-starved black population, at twice or even three times the prior prices. Brewer says that when he was a boy in the early 1950s, Homewood had a black population of only 15 to 20 percent; most of the people who lived there were Italian and Irish. By the end of the 1950s, when he entered high school, "the neighborhood was 55 or 60 percent black" after the demolition of the lower Hill and the displacement of those black families into Homewood.

In the 1960s, the real estate industry continued to engage in "blockbusting"— again encouraging white residents to flee the neighborhood by using a fear of blacks moving in. These realtors would then scoop up homes from the white owners at a fraction of their value and resell them at higher prices to black people needing housing. Whites, with federally subsidized home loans and new interstate highways, moved to commuter suburbs. Blacks were legally or illegally restricted from buying in these newer areas, while banks would often refuse to make housing loans in majority-black neighborhoods (a practice known as redlining). With the white flight to the suburbs came the rise of suburban malls, which then led to the collapse of business districts in Homewood and nearby East Liberty.

In the aftermath of the assassination of Dr. Martin Luther King, Jr., in 1968, riots occurred in Pittsburgh (as in many other American cities), and

Homewood took many of the blows in Pittsburgh. According to John Brewer, the neighborhood experienced significant property loss. Nearly all of the remaining white-owned businesses closed afterward, and the remaining black middle-class families moved away. "The riots," Brewer says, "provided the final nail in the coffin. Homewood passed on" for all practical purposes. The vibrant, solid neighborhood, with its many small homes, apartments, and businesses, had vanished. Homewood was now majority black and poor. Along with the loss of steel industry jobs in the 1980s across the region, chronic poverty enveloped many neighborhoods, including Homewood.

Then in the late 1980s, crack cocaine arrived in Homewood, along with gangs and drug dealers. Crack, the smokable form of cocaine, ravaged many urban communities in the United States. In Homewood, small "crews" and local neighborhood gangs claimed affiliation with bigger gangs from elsewhere, like the Los Angeles–based Crips and Bloods. Brewer remembers that the presence of drug activity and gang members, with "their Crips and Bloods gang colors," tended to "promote a quiet terror" among residents in the area, which began to feel hostile and unsafe to many of the long-time residents. With the continued physical deterioration of housing and businesses and structures of all kinds, even those living in Homewood, who knew it had not always seemed a "bad area," began to think of it that way.

By the beginning of the twenty-first century, Homewood had become one of the most dangerous of the city's 93 neighborhoods. According to data from the Criminal Intelligence Unit of the Pittsburgh Bureau of Police,[15] in 2003, more than 10 percent of all homicides in Pittsburgh took place in Homewood, and with just a few exceptions, this would remain the pattern every year through 2016. In 2013 and 2014, a whopping 18 percent of all homicides in Pittsburgh occurred in this one neighborhood. In other categories of violent crime, the neighborhood also saw outsized activity, with approximately 5 percent of all robberies and aggravated assaults in the city occurring within Homewood.

In 2009, the Pittsburgh Police initiated a city-wide reorganization, and Homewood became part of Zone 5,[16] along with other higher-crime neighborhoods such as Larimer, parts of East Liberty, Lincoln-Leamington-Belmar, and East Hills. In 2010, the year that Jordan Miles and the three officers fought on the ground in Homewood, 37 percent of homicides and 24 percent of robberies took place in Zone 5. In 2012 and 2013, 46 and 49 percent, respectively, of all homicides and 22 and 21 percent of all robberies occurred there.

PATROLLING HOMEWOOD: A VIEW FROM A VETERAN

Maurita Bryant[17] knows the Homewood neighborhood far better than most residents of Pittsburgh, and better than most Pittsburgh Police officers. Bryant grew up in Homewood; she graduated from Westinghouse High School, where Homewood's teens have attended school for decades. Throughout her adult life and into the present, Bryant has lived in Homewood; her daughter also attended Westinghouse. What makes her point of view truly unique is that, since 1977, Maurita Bryant has served in law enforcement. That year, she joined the Pittsburgh Police; her 38 years there found her in almost every job in the department, and for 23 of those years, she served in a variety of command and supervisory positions. She served as the commander in Zone 5, which included Homewood, from 1995 to 2000; for approximately six years after that, she headed the department's Major Crimes unit. The department promoted her to assistant chief in 2006, and she held that rank until she left the agency. She then joined the Allegheny County Police Department, where she is currently assistant superintendent.

As a young person in Homewood, Maurita Bryant recalls living in a vibrant place that was also racially and ethnically diverse. There were stores and commercial activity. The neighborhood was dense but lively. But she remembers that things changed with the rioting in the neighborhood in 1968. When the National Guard arrived, they put up cement barriers to the main streets to control access to the neighborhood; the Guard left when the worst was over and eventually the physical barriers disappeared. But, as Bryant sees it, metaphorical barriers to the neighborhood soon replaced those made of cement. After the riots, any remaining white residents and white-owned businesses fled; little in the way of resources, money, or new activity flowed into Homewood again. The stores that had burned down or that left the area after these events were never replaced; city resources did not return, and schools and other infrastructure deteriorated. The condition of housing and other infrastructure declined. In the 1980s, drug activity on the street became much more visible, and the invasion of crack in the late 1980s and early 1990s broke things open. Small gangs or "sets" began to dominate the increasingly brazen drug activity, and by the time she arrived as Zone 5 commander in 1995, drug sales and associated violence were "rampant." By the 2000s, Homewood was "really bad"—it had become a high-crime area. Drugs and guns go hand in hand, Bryant says; and shooting in Homewood, especially in an area she calls the Race Street corridor, became routine. The sets would get into "beefs" (disputes or grudges) with each other over drug sales or territory, disrespect shown to each other's members, or almost anything else, and they would shoot at each other, even across the streets in daylight, indifferent to the presence of civilians and vehicle traffic. The reaction of Pittsburgh patrol units assigned to the area, she said, did not help things. Patrol officers would often just drive past illegal activity, such as drug sales or prostitution, and do nothing; patrol officers in uniform were no longer proactive in places like Homewood. Bryant said that when the gangbangers would see this, they felt empowered—they figured they could do what they wanted. There was "shooting left and right." And the good people in Homewood would not cooperate with the police. This was not because the people did not like police; rather, Bryant said, they saw that the police did nothing when they themselves witnessed crime on the corners—they just drove by—so residents thought the police would not protect them.

Bryant said she (and others) went to then Chief of Police Nathan Harper about the lack of proactive police action in Homewood. Eventually, the department created the Street Response Units (SRUs)—48 officers, working undercover, surveilling criminal activity and then actively pursuing (even physically chasing suspects, when necessary) and arresting street criminals in Homewood and other high-crime areas. This aggressive approach brought crime down in Homewood and in other neighborhoods. However, not all of the department's zone commanders liked the SRU approach. SRU officers were not attached to any zone or command, and the zone commanders wanted more control over them. According to Bryant, this was the origin of the 99 cars: they were small roving anti-crime units, but they operated within and were attached to one zone command. They would work in plain clothes and unmarked cars and were tasked with preemptively seeking out drugs and guns. To suppress drug and gun activity, she said, "you needed the more aggressive officers, who were not afraid to do the police work" of pursuing and catching those with drugs, which inevitably meant guns. Those units required supervision, she said—a leader in the unit who would keep it on the straight and narrow. Unfortunately, that was not always the case. Instead, the department "gave out awards, recognizing officers for the largest number of guns seized" in a month. But this was a mistake; she said it made the officers in these units competitive. This encouraged some officers to "cut corners." (Bryant specified no particular officer; it was, she said, a general problem with this awards-for-guns-seized approach.)

According to Assistant Superintendent Bryant, this was the Homewood of early 2010: high crime, homicides, guns, and danger, along with a resident population with a mistrust of the police. "You always had to watch your back" there, she said. "It was then still one of the most violent neighborhoods" in the city. Officers patrolling there did not have it easy, and in specialty units, like the 99 cars, officers rarely encountered anyone except the criminals they were seeking out; they would likely have had little contact with the great majority of Homewood residents who were just regular civilians, trying to get by in a challenging and difficult environment. This could lead to officer thinking becoming "blurred," Bryant said; it would be easy to fall into thinking that everyone in the neighborhood is a suspect.

These facts formed the background to the incident of January 12, 2010: Homewood was an area of high crime, including outsized rates of homicide, robbery, and aggravated assault. Jordan Miles would have had some intuitive grasp of these facts; the police officers involved would certainly have known them too.

CHAPTER 3

THE IMMEDIATE AFTERMATH

A MOTHER FINDS OUT

Terez Miles[1] had no concerns as her son Jordan left the house to walk around the corner to his grandmother's on the night of January 12, 2010. She had no premonition of danger, no dim realization that anything about that evening seemed different. On the contrary, everything seemed fine—just routine. She recalled later that when Jordan got ready to leave, he put on his new coat, a birthday gift from his grandmother, and Ms. Miles stopped him to admire the coat. As the young man left the house, he was on his cell with one of his friends, something almost every parent with teenage children has seen. "He goes out the door, I think nothing of it." She was tired and started to think about getting ready for bed.

She was aware, of course, of Homewood's reputation as a neighborhood with higher than normal rates of crime and violence. If a person wanted to find trouble in the neighborhood, she said, they could; but for Ms. Miles, her mother, and their family, those concerns did not enter into their thinking very often. The Miles home and the 7900 block of Tioga usually seemed calm and quiet; the city had demolished the few drug houses some years back—one run by white people, with many white customers. The Miles family had no involvement in the petty crime in the area, let alone any of the violence; their only personal experience with crime had occurred several years before when someone broke into their home and stole video game equipment. Terez Miles's mother's home, around the block on Susquehanna Street, sat on another relatively quiet stretch. A bar, on one of the corners of Tioga and the nearest cross street, catered not to the young and rowdy but to an older, quiet crowd of men. Even so, Ms. Miles had trained her children to walk to their grandmother's house in the direction that would keep them from running into the drinkers who occasionally stumbled out of the bar. All in all, their group of streets did not look rich and vacant lots and abandoned buildings did not help its appearance, but Ms. Miles always felt reasonably safe, as long as she and her family maintained the level of awareness and care appropriate for city dwellers in an area that did have crime.

Ms. Miles had been asleep for at least an hour or two when her phone rang. It was her mother, Patricia Porter, asking if she knew where Jordan was. "I said, 'he should have been at your house by now.' She said, 'well, he never showed up.'" Her mother wondered if Jordan might have gone over to a friend's house. Terez assured her that Jordan would not have done that without at least saying something. Both mother and grandmother knew that the young man would not go off somewhere like this, late at night, without telling one of them, especially because Jordan knew that his grandmother would wait up for him before locking her doors for the night.

In that instant, with that call from her mother, everything changed in Terez Miles's mind. As comfortable as she had been in her home, and on her couple of blocks in Homewood, she knew—as every parent in Homewood knew—that life could change very quickly and drastically. "Every horrible thought went through my mind," she said. "If he's not at my mother's house … there's only one thing that could have happened. He met with some kind of danger. He's been killed." She could hardly think. "All the horror of a parent losing a child— I went through that night." She cried, feeling paralyzed—not knowing what to do—and also not wanting to call anyone who would tell her that they'd found Jordan's body in some alley. During those hours, Ms. Miles remembered later, she experienced a parent's worst nightmare: she was certain that her child had come to great harm—that he was dead.

She finally dozed off, and then with the daylight, her mother called again. "She told me, 'Jordan has been arrested,' and she said he might have gotten a little scratched up because he'd been in some kind of a scrape." Ms. Miles felt immediate relief: Jordan was alive. Even if he'd somehow gotten arrested and a bit banged up, he was not dead. She could not imagine how this had happened—"how does he get arrested and get into a fight, just walking around our block?"—but she felt glad. A bit later, her mother called again, saying she'd had a call from Jordan, who told his grandmother, "Nanna, I got arrested. They beat me, but I don't know why."

A short time later, Jordan's mother and grandmother found themselves in downtown Pittsburgh, at the city courts building adjacent to the Allegheny County Jail. Everyone taken into police custody in Pittsburgh (and in any of the more than one hundred other separate municipalities in the county) ended up in the same county jail. Jordan's grandmother put up the money for Jordan's bail, and a court employee told them that the jail would release him in due course. This person also said that Jordan had some "scratches." The two women waited all day, and into the night. At around 9:30 or 10:00 p.m., court personnel told them that the jail would soon release a group of men from the front entrance to the jail, up the hill and around the corner on Second Avenue. Ms. Miles and her mother pulled their car onto Second, directly in front of the entrance, to wait for Jordan. Finally, men started to come out, singly and in small groups. Ms. Miles got out of the car to wait on the sidewalk, so Jordan would see her. A man came toward her—"he looked unsavory, like a street person." She was afraid, thinking maybe she should get back into her car. The man's face was terribly swollen, with one eye shut, and she remembers thinking he looked like "an elephant man." Then the man said, "Mom!" Terez stopped—he sounded like her son Jordan, but he certainly didn't look like him. But the voice—she knew it was him, although he was unrecognizable. Ms. Miles broke down. She tried to hug her son, but he made her stop because it hurt too much.

With Jordan in the car, they drove toward the hospital, even though he said the police had already taken him to one. She looked at Jordan and simply could not believe it. "His face was terribly swollen—both his eyes were black, and there were broken blood vessels in both eyes." Jordan had loved wearing his hair in dreadlocks; now she could see that some of his dreads had been pulled out, leaving a bloody, bald patch on his scalp. At some point between the jail, the hospital, and their home, Ms. Miles bought a disposable camera. "I just thought I needed to take pictures of how he looked that night." Otherwise, she thought, people would not believe what she had seen.

When Ms. Miles and her mother finally got Jordan home, "we were all just speechless, silent." The worst of the swelling in Jordan's face took some days to go down; his swollen eyes, with blood turning the whites a frightening red shade, took longer. What could have happened, she wondered, to precipitate the kind of beating her son had taken? Looking at him, she felt "surprised that they did not kill him, but so grateful" that he had lived.

And still, years later, she could not understand how such a thing could have happened to Jordan, just going around his own block to his grandmother's house. "How would I have guessed," she said, "going up the street, the quiet way, around the corner to my mother's house, would be a danger? It just didn't make sense."

Jordan was home, but the ordeal was just beginning. He faced five criminal charges: two felony charges of aggravated assault (one for hitting Officer Saldutte with his elbow, another for kicking Officer Sisak in the knee); a charge of resisting arrest; an escape charge, for trying to get away; and a count of "loitering and prowling at night," for his lurking in the shadows next to Monica Wooding's house, at 7940 Tioga.

THE POLICE REPORT

With the man subdued, arrested, and transported from the scene, Officers Saldutte, Ewing, and Sisak wound up their search of the area in front of the houses on Tioga where the altercation had taken place. Despite a careful search, they never found a weapon. In some cases like these, follow-up searches could be done the next day, during daylight hours; sometimes, subsequent searches would include dogs trained to locate firearms or other contraband, or mobile banks of ultrabright lights, like the ones used by road repair or utility repair crews. With no gun recovered, the officers eventually ended their efforts. And the police did not attempt these follow-up efforts with dogs or lights, that night or any other.

With the events concluded, the next day the officers sat down to write their report of the incident. Both Saldutte and Ewing have their names on the report as "reporting officer." Ewing wrote it and it references Ewing as "I," but it clearly represented all three officers. Sisak's name appears as a victim, referencing his injured knee, and as an "additional reporting officer." (Saldutte is also listed as a victim due to the elbow he took to the head, but the report says he suffered no injury.) The other victim listed in the report is Sarah Henderson, the resident of 7940 Tioga—the home beside which Officer Saldutte saw the man lurking. While the report used the correct address, Sarah Henderson did not live there; Monica Wooding did. The report lists the arrestee as "Miles, Jordan, Sex M, Race Black, Age 18" and lists him as five feet seven inches tall, weighing 180 pounds (making him an inch taller and 30 pounds heavier than he actually was). The listed evidence consists of one spent Taser cartridge, with its serial number, and nothing else. The officers list themselves as working in Zone 5, with "Vehicle/Assignment 3599"—the designation for the department's crime-hunting 99 cars. The report tells the basics of the story from the police point of view:

> On the above date and time, officer's [sic] Saldutte, Sisak, and I (Ewing) were working in plain-clothes capacity, and traveling in an unmarked vehicle. Officers were conducting a proactive patrol in the Homewood section of the City.
>
> While traveling outbound on Tioga St., we observed a male (later identified as Miles, Jordan) standing on the left side of 7940 Tioga Street. As we drove

past this location, PO Saldutte observed that the male was standing up against the side of the house as if he was trying to avoid being seen. This was at 2300 hours [11 p.m.] with no street lights, or house lights in this area.

Finding this males [sic] actions suspicious, we turned out [sic] vehicle around and returned to 7940 Tioga St. As I pulled up in front of the house, Miles began walking toward the street along the side of the house. I stopped our vehicle in-front [sic] of 7940 Tioga St., and I watched as Miles placed his right hand in the right front pocket of his jacket. PO Saldutte exited the passenger side of our vehicle and identified himself as a Police Officer and displayed his badge around his neck. PO Saldutte told Miles to take his hand out of his pocket, which he did. PO Saldutte asked Miles if he lives at the house that he just came from, and Miles stated, "no, I live down the street" and started to walk inbound on Tioga St. PO Saldutte asked, "then why are you sneaking around someone else's house?" Miles did not answer PO Saldutte and continued to walk. PO Saldutte told Miles to stop as he [Saldutte] began to walk towards him [Miles]. As Miles was walking away, we noticed that he had a large, heavy object in the front right pocket of his coat. Miles [sic] right coat pocket was hanging much lower than the left side, and the size of the object in his pocket was pulling the pocket open.

Believing that Miles was involved in criminal activity and possibly armed, PO Saldutte again ordered Miles to stop. At that time, Miles looked back at PO Saldutte and began to run inbound on Tioga as he grabbed his right pocket, holding it tightly against his body to prevent it front [sic] swinging. PO Saldutte began to pursue Miles a short distance while giving him commands "Stop Pittsburgh Police." Miles attempted to run between 7940 and 7938 Tioga but slipped on ice and fell to the ground face first on the front sidewalk of 7940 Tioga. PO Sisak and I exited out [sic] vehicle at that time and gave verbal commands to Miles of "Pittsburgh Police stay on the ground." PO Saldutte was approaching Miles as he began he was getting [sic] off of the ground. PO Saldutte Miles commands [sic] to "stay on the ground" but Miles continued to get back to his feet. When PO Saldutte grabbed Miles from behind by his jacket, Miles immediately swung his right elbow backwards striking PO Saldutte in the right side of his head, causing him to lose his grasp. PO Sisak and I observed Miles assault PO Saldutte as PO Sisak stated "stop your [sic] under arrest" as he deployed his Taser at Miles who was running around hedges in the front of 7938 Tioga St.

The Taser probes struck Miles in the back, but due to his thick winter coat, the Taser was not effective. PO Sisak was able to push Miles to the ground.

PO Sisak told Miles to places his hands behind his back as he grabbed his right arm to handcuff him, when Miles donkey kicked PO Sisak in his right knee causing PO Sisak to fall to the ground in severe pain. Miles began to get back up when I took hold of his left arm and tried to perform an arm-bar to force him back to the ground. Miles was able to get to his feet and again tried to flee. I performed a leg sweep and took Miles to the ground. Once on the ground PO Saldutte was able to grab Miles's right arm and tried to pull it behind his back to place him in custody. As PO Saldutte was trying to gain control of Miles's right arm, he felt a large heavy object which he thought was a firearm in Miles's front right pocket (same pocket that we observed a large heavy object earlier). PO Saldutte stated that he believed that Miles was armed. I was able to take hold of Miles left arm, but due to Miles actively resisting, PO Saldutte and I were unable to get Miles's arms behind his back.

With Miles having assaulted 2 police officers, believing that he was armed, unable to handcuff him, and Miles not following any commands, PO Saldutte and I began to deliver knee strikes to both sides of Miles's body in an attempt to get his hands behind his back, as we both had Miles in an arm-bar. PO Sisak was able to push Miles body against the ground, and PO Saldutte was able to get a handcuff on Miles's right wrist. Once PO Saldutte got the handcuff on wrist, Miles began yelling "your [sic] not taking me to jail, just let me go home!" and started fighting again. Miles began rolling onto the left side of his body and was able to get his handcuffed right arm back underneath his chest, causing PO Saldutte to lose his grasp. PO Saldutte told PO Sisak and I [sic] that he had lost control of Miles right hand. Miles then reached for what we believed was a weapon in his right coat pocket, as PO Saldutte held onto the pair of handcuffs attached to his right wrist. At this point PO Sisak delivered 2–3 closed fist strikes to Miles [sic] head/face with still no effect. I then delivered 1 knee strike to Miles head causing him to momentary [sic] stop resisting, allowing PO Saldutte and I [sic] to place him in handcuffs.

At this time we have been trying to take Miles into custody for over 1 minute. Miles appeared to be under the influence of controlled substance due to him not complying with pain compliance techniques.

Search incident to arrest, PO Saldutte discovered the hard object in Miles coat pocket was a bottle of mountain dew [sic].

Miles was transported to West Penn hospital by 3502 where he was treated ... and released by doctor Martin [sic].

Officer Sisak was transported to Mercy Hospital by Sgt. Lee for treatment.

The resident of 7940 Tioga St. stated that they did not know Miles and that he did not have permission to be on their property or around their house.

It should be noted that the incident took place in a front yard that had approximately 4 to 6 inches of snow.[2]

The report goes on to list the "date/time original offense occurred" as 01/12/2010 at 2308 hours—11:08 p.m.—and the time of arrest as 2315 hours—11:15 p.m., just seven minutes later, with the struggle occupying "over one minute."[3]

Several pieces of the report merit special attention. In the second paragraph, we see the first major inconsistency with Jordan's own account: "Saldutte observed that the male was standing up against the side of the house as if he was trying to avoid being seen." Jordan says he never stood against the side of any house. On the contrary, to avoid the icy sidewalks, he walked in the street where the snow and ice had at least been tamped down somewhat by passing vehicles. And note that from the beginning, Saldutte stated his belief that the person he saw was trying to avoid detection—and thus became worthy of police attention and suspicion. Second, as Jordan emerged from the side of the house to the street, Ewing said (in the third paragraph) that he "watched as Miles placed his right hand in the right front pocket of his jacket." So according to the report, this one movement raised suspicion that Jordan Miles had a weapon in his pocket. Saldutte first made sure to identify himself and then "told Miles to take his hand out of his pocket, which he did." Note both the precise command Saldutte gave and that Jordan instantly complied. Saldutte then asked Jordan where he lived, and hearing it was not the house by which Jordan stood, asked him, "then why are you sneaking around someone else's house?" It did not seem to occur to the officers—already suspicious that the unidentified man lurking next to a house had a gun—to order the man to halt and put his hands in the air, and then to immediately perform a frisk—something they would have had the legal right to do. The same paragraph goes on to say that Miles took immediate action by walking away, which is when the officers made the assumption that the young man was armed and they again ordered him to stop.

As for the description of the struggle, which differs greatly from that given by Jordan Miles, Officer Ewing's report says that "[a]s PO Saldutte was trying to gain control of Miles's right arm, he felt a large heavy object which he thought was a firearm in Miles's front right pocket (same pocket that we observed a large heavy object earlier). PO Saldutte stated that he believed that Miles was armed." In the police narrative, Saldutte's feeling of the "large heavy object" in the same pocket into which Jordan put his hand, and which the officers saw sagging down as Jordan started to try to escape, confirmed for the officers that they had it right: the man had a gun. The officers then got a handcuff on Jordan's right wrist, but he somehow pulled it free and was able to move his hand underneath his prone body, toward that heavy pocket with the gun. According to later statements, this was the moment when Saldutte yelled that Jordan was going for a gun—when Sisak, kneeling in front of Jordan at his head, says that he felt that Jordan would shoot him. But Ewing got to him first by kneeing Jordan in the head, which momentarily stunned him, allowing the officers to put on both handcuffs.

Saldutte then searched Jordan, beginning with that all-important right coat pocket, and "discovered the hard object in Miles coat pocket was a bottle of mountain dew [sic]"—not a gun. Then, as the police searched the area for a gun or anything else on the ground and got a police wagon to transport the arrested man, the narrative says that they got a lucky break: They spoke with Monica Wooding, the person who lived in the house where they had seen Jordan lurking. (Wooding is not named in the report, but everyone agrees that she was indeed the "resident of 7940 Tioga St." they talked with that night.) According to later reports, the officers had her take a look at Jordan from the window of her house. Ewing's report says that Wooding "stated that [she] did not know Miles and that he did not have permission to be on [her] property or around [her] house."

The violent encounter between Jordan Miles and the three police officers on January 12 turned into a legal case in which the facts mattered a great deal, and few of the facts turned out to be as important as these: the soda bottle and the gun (Jordan says he had neither one that night), his hiding himself between the houses, the men identifying themselves as officers, and Monica Wooding's viewing of a man in police custody whom she told police she did not recognize. But when Officer Ewing wrote the report, it surely did not seem like the case would amount to anything more than a host of similar encounters in any given year. The officers had a confrontation with a citizen; often (though not always), those facing the police in these instances were young black men. Sometimes these encounters included violence, and almost always the police would file charges. A criminal case would then work its way slowly through the long body of the criminal justice system, like a large snake swallowing a small animal whole, slowly digesting it. This case, however, did not follow the usual path. It became something different—something much greater. But on the night of January 12, 2010, no one could have known what would happen.

JORDAN AT THE HOSPITAL

After the arrest, uniformed police transport officers, Darren Fedorski and David Horak, took the injured Jordan to West Penn Hospital's emergency room for a medical check and any necessary treatment[4] before going on to the jail. A doctor examined Jordan noting head injuries; facial injuries and abrasions (especially to the right side of his face and his eyes); and pain in his head, neck, and body. Under "context" the doctor noted, "18 y.o. … stuck [sic] in the face during arrest by police," presumably as reported by Jordan. The records also indicate that the doctor found a "stick embedded in [Jordan's] gum," which was removed. A CT scan indicated head and facial trauma, but no evidence of any "acute intracranial trauma" (e.g., skull fracture or intracranial hemorrhage) or facial fracture. A full drug screening showed no traces of any drugs of abuse. The medical staff also checked Jordan for neurological deficits and similar problems. Eventually, they cleared him, saying that Jordan could go on to the jail for booking.

While in the ER at West Penn Hospital, Jordan had two conversations that would become important later on. First, while waiting for medical attention, the two transport officers stayed with Jordan, since the police had arrested him. As they waited, Jordan spoke. According to a supplemental report by Officer Fedorski: "While Miles was waiting for medical treatment inside the emergency room, Miles spontaneously uttered, 'I'm glad it was the police I fought with, and not some gang banger, because I would have got shot.'"[5] The odd phrase "spontaneously uttered" jumps out; one might expect something more common, like "said." But the use of "spontaneously uttered" here is no accident. Legally, it denotes a statement made without any police questioning—and that means the person in custody need not have received Miranda warnings in order for the state to use the statement against him. A suspect need only receive Miranda warnings when police ask questions to a suspect in custody; if a suspect says something without a question, or any statement that functions as a question, posed by the police—a spontaneous utterance—the Miranda warning rules don't apply. Lawyers for the officers would attempt to use the statement later.

Jordan also had a visitor in the ER. Pittsburgh Police Sergeant Charles Henderson,[6] one of the supervisors on duty that evening in Zone 5, had gotten word of the altercation and arrest on Tioga and that the transport officers had taken the arrested man to West Penn Hospital for treatment. Henderson first reviewed the events of the evening with the officers and then went to see the suspect for himself. He found Jordan being treated in the ER and was able to observe the young man's swollen face and multiple abrasions. He then went into the room to speak to Jordan, with a particular plan for doing so: "I did not give him Miranda Warnings, as our conversation was not part of the criminal prosecution, it was merely administrative"—another legal justification for "no Miranda required." In answer to Henderson's questions, Jordan said that he had been in a fight with the police. What Henderson really wanted to know, however, concerned what Jordan had done: Why had he run from the police, if he had not done anything wrong? "He said that he thought he was going to be robbed." Henderson's report makes clear that he did not believe this, since he already believed that Jordan *knew* the men had worn badges and identified themselves as officers. Jordan confirmed that he had, indeed, grown up in Homewood, which sealed it for Henderson. "I asked him when was the last time he was aware of three white males with badges, verbally identifying themselves as police having been known to commit robberies in this area? Before he answered, I stated that his story didn't make sense to me …."

The conversation soon ended. Like the conversation with Officer Fedorski, lawyers would attempt to use it later, trying to show that Jordan had always known the men he fought with were officers. Jordan always denied this, from the very first statement he made in the case until the last time he spoke about it, and the hospital statements do not prove otherwise. From Jordan's point of view, his statement to Fedorski meant that he learned the men were police officers *after the fact* and was glad. Sergeant Henderson's supplemental report shows that he spoke with the officers first, before talking to Jordan, and Henderson appears to have accepted everything his officers told him. Walking in to see Jordan later, under arrest, happened only after Henderson had absorbed what his fellow officers had told him. Henderson's report of his conversation with Jordan assumed that the young man must have known he was facing police officers rather than unknown civilians.

The conversation with Sergeant Henderson highlighted another important issue that would factor into virtually all of the perceptions of the case and in all the proceedings that would follow: the role played by race. For Henderson, the question of race did not arise because a young black man, in a majority black neighborhood, had a confrontation with three white police officers. Rather, it took the form of: "Who could imagine three white men in Homewood, confronting a young black man at night in a robbery? How could three white men in Homewood be anything other than police officers? Surely, they could not be criminals," as Jordan had believed. Of course, Henderson also brought the "facts" he carried from the three officers: that they had identified themselves verbally and with badges, but as we already know, Jordan has denied this, unequivocally. But the assumptions about race—that whites in black neighborhoods could only be police and could not be criminals—would reverberate throughout the case.

ANGRY PUBLIC, DEFENSIVE POLICE

As noted previously, the officers filed a five-count criminal complaint against Jordan, charging two counts of aggravated assault (for the blows suffered by Ewing and Saldutte), as well as resisting arrest and attempted escape. The court scheduled an initial hearing for January 21, but when the officers failed to appear in court as scheduled, the judge postponed it.[7] But something else did happen that day: news of the incident hit the media.

The Media

Pittsburgh's daily newspapers, the *Post-Gazette* and the *Tribune Review*, began to run multiple stories about the case, as did local television stations. According to the *Post-Gazette*'s January 22 story, Jordan Miles showed up for the hearing before the judge postponed it, ready to "defend himself from the charges by describing the beating he took from the police," including multiple blows to the head, a chunk of hair pulled out of his scalp, and other injuries.[8] Kerry Lewis, an attorney for Jordan, said that based on what he had seen, "I can't see any justification for the extreme force used."[9] According to a police department spokeswoman, the city's Office of Municipal Investigations— Pittsburgh's internal affairs unit, with jurisdiction over the police department and other municipal agencies—had already begun an investigation.[10] The next day, Pittsburgh Mayor Luke Ravenstahl said that Jordan's claims that he had suffered an unjustified beating by the police left him "very troubled." He said that "we'll take it very seriously" and that the officers had been reassigned from their undercover work and would work in full uniform.[11] The case also hit the national media on January 22, with a story on CNN under the headline "Brutality Charged as Pittsburgh Police Defend 'Fist Strikes' on Teen."[12] The CNN story contained quotes from both the police report and from Jordan's mother Terez Miles, giving very different versions of what happened and repeating the mayor's expression of concern.

Then on January 25, the Associated Press, whose stories appear in media outlets across the country, ran a story about the case. Under the headline "Pittsburgh Police Accused of Brutality in Jordan Miles Beating," the story reports that the police said they arrested Miles "after a struggle they say revealed a soda bottle under his coat, not the gun they suspected."[13] Terez Miles said she felt that her son had been "racially profiled" because "it's a rough neighborhood" and the police "assumed he was up to no good because he's Black." Mayor Ravenstahl repeated that the city investigation continued and that if the officers' actions did not meet professional standards, "they will be held accountable for those actions."[14] Jordan would await a doctor's approval before returning to school; he reported "suffering from nightmares and flashbacks."[15]

The FBI

By January 26, reports began to surface in the media that the FBI had begun a federal investigation into the incident. According to the *Post-Gazette*, Jeffrey Killeen, of the Pittsburgh office of the FBI, "confirmed that agents are looking into allegations that city police officers brutally beat an 18-year-old CAPA student earlier this month."[16] According to Killeen, the investigation had begun with a first-stage assessment—not a full investigation—but the inquiry had started. Killeen said that the assessment had nothing to do with a request from a Miles family lawyer to open an investigation. "There's been a great deal of publicity about this" and "we can open up cases on our own. We don't have to have an allegation from outside .... We take action on our own if it is warranted."[17]

The Photos

While the written reports in these news stories may have disturbed readers and viewers, the real outrage came from the accompanying photos, which were the images of Jordan, taken by his mother, after she picked him up at the County Jail. These pictures accompanied almost all of the news reports, and they remain hard to look at, even for those who saw them years ago. The photos also ran on local television news broadcasts—then and now, the major source of local news for most people—as well as in the newspapers. On January 21, just nine days after the incident, WTAE television in Pittsburgh ran its first story that included the pictures. The anchor, with a concerned and serious look on her face, began the story by saying, "We're getting our first look at photos showing injuries a local teenager says ... are the result of police brutality. We want to warn you— these are disturbing."[18] In television station KDKA's story on the case featuring the photos, the anchor also described the pictures as viewers saw them: "The pictures are shocking ... a teenager's face is cut, bruised, and swollen—his hair ripped from his scalp."[19] The Pittsburgh *Post-Gazette's* first story containing one of the photographs ran in the paper on January 27, accompanying a story about the deep community anger the case had provoked.[20]

The photos of Jordan taken by his mother after his release from the county jail appeared in almost every subsequent television news story as the case became a staple of news coverage for the next several years, and even after. Sometimes the photos were featured items in the report, and other times they were part of a story logo shown behind the anchor as the story began. Jordan's face, seen from the right side, looks misshapen—it is swollen, with the cheek and lower forehead a grotesque shape. Along his hairline, one sees that his dreadlocks, which cover the rest of his head, are torn out, leaving a bald area spotted here and there with bloody patches. His right eye is swollen shut, a puffy pillow shape with a slit across the middle where the eye would usually open. A second photo, taken straight on, shows small bloody wounds all over his face; one side of his upper lip is so enlarged that it completely covers half of his lower lip. A third photo, taken as Jordan lay in a hospital bed, shows more wounds, with the blood visible across his swollen right eye. The Associated Press report, which carried one of the photos, described them this way:

> The photos taken by Jordan Miles' mother show his face covered with raw, red bruises, his cheek and lip swollen, his right eye swollen shut. A bald spot mars the long black dreadlocks where the 18-year-old violist says police tore them from his head.[21]

By the end of just one week after the first media reports, the images of Jordan's brutalized face had appeared countless times in newspapers and on television; no one in Pittsburgh paying the least bit of attention to local news could have missed them. Those images, along with the story of what Jordan said had happened, ignited a deep well of rage at the police.

On January 26, a group of students from CAPA High School, where Jordan attended, left their downtown school building during the school day. Accompanied by their principal and some other adults, they marched through the streets to the city's municipal building, carrying handmade signs and chanting, "Justice for Jordan!" The students and representatives of the Black Political Empowerment Project and its leader, Tim Stevens, marched into the City Council chambers and to the mayor's office, to demand an investigation. Many of the students spoke, and some fought back tears.[22] Stevens, speaking during the demonstration, referred to the photographs and said, "I cannot fathom how the Pittsburgh police, could in any reasonable way, defend the beating, stomping, choking and kicking of an unarmed, 5–7, 150-pound teenager by three armed police officers."[23] With the photos of Jordan Miles and his battered face "stirring tears" throughout the day in City Council chambers, even members of the Council appeared moved. Doug Shields, then a member of the Council, told the chamber, "Something's wrong here .... If it makes us uncomfortable, then maybe we should quit the job." Holding up a photo of Jordan, Shields said, "I wonder how much we're going to have to pay for this."[24]

The photos of Jordan's brutalized face remained an indelible image. A poster for a demonstration in May 2011 paired one of those photos with another showing Jordan's smiling, handsome face in a senior-year picture taken before the incident. The caption accompanying the two images read, "The Photos Make Everyone an Eyewitness."[25]

The Police

The reaction from the police side was quite different—ranging from simple denial, to caution, to outrage. For their part, Officers Saldutte, Sisak, and Ewing did not speak publicly, but their report and/or the criminal complaint against Jordan (the document charging Jordan with crimes for his conduct in the incident) did become public. Thus their version of events on the night of January 12 accompanied Jordan's in many of the media reports, including the first reports in the Pittsburgh *Post-Gazette* on January 21 and the reports by CNN and the Associated Press. All of these stories reported that the officers (1) had seen Jordan on Tioga Street, (2) considered his behavior suspicious, (3) suspected that he might have a gun because of the signs that he had a large heavy object in his coat, and (4) had to subdue him in a struggle when he ran after they warned him that they were police. The reports completely denied the truth of what Jordan said. Thus Jordan's version of what happened did not appear in the media unchallenged; from the beginning, the police version also received coverage, often right alongside Jordan's own account.

Pittsburgh Police Chief Nathan Harper, a veteran officer who had spent his entire career with Pittsburgh's police force, issued a statement that urged caution and care before coming to any conclusion about what happened. Harper said he would wait for the "complete, formal and independent" investigation by the Office of Municipal Investigation before making any statement. "We understand the concern from the family, the community and the school children. However, there is a due process for both Mr. Miles and the arresting officers. To some the process may seem slow," he said, but it would move as rapidly as possible and "it will be thorough, and it will reveal the facts."[26]

The city's police union, the Fraternal Order of Police (FOP) Lodge No. 1, did not show any similar reluctance to tell the public what had happened. Charles Hanlon, then the FOP's vice president, called the three officers the most effective in the city at removing guns from Pittsburgh's streets. "These guys have stellar records. They're decorated for the job that they do," he said, noting that the officers had had special training to recognize the presence of guns in situations like the one they faced that night. "Their actions were correct and law abiding by everything they have received in their training." As for calls by members of the public for the police officers to not remain on duty during the investigation, Hanlon dismissed these comments as "demand[s] by special interest groups," and "an insult to [the officers'] hard work."[27]

Just days later, on February 2, the Associated Press reported that the Pittsburgh Police had suspended the three officers, but details remained thin. The officers would reportedly continue to receive their pay but would no longer work on the streets of the city—at least for the time being.[28] The city remained tense, with dozens of news articles and opinion posts on blogs and elsewhere; several investigations began to churn forward. The next major event in the case would occur a month later, at the beginning of March—a preliminary hearing into the case of *Commonwealth of Pennsylvania v. Jordan Miles.*

THE PRELIMINARY HEARING

What Is a Preliminary Hearing?

When the police arrest someone and take that person into custody, he or she first undergoes an arraignment. The arraignment usually occurs quickly after the police bring the arrested person to the jail—the same day, that night, or the next morning. The arrested person—now called a "defendant"—receives a copy of the charges, hears about the right to counsel (to have a lawyer), and may have a bail amount set. The arraignment does not look at the evidence in the case. The judge then sets a date for a preliminary hearing, which is the next step in the process.

A preliminary hearing serves as a screening stage for a case, with a specific standard set by law. According to Pennsylvania Code Rule 542, the court determines "from the evidence presented whether there is a *prima facie* case that (1) an offense has been committed and (2) the defendant has committed it."[29] This does not mean that the prosecution must prove the case beyond a reasonable doubt—the traditional criminal law standard of proof. Rather, the idea of a prima facie case (the Latin phrase means "on its face" or "at first appearance") relies on a much lower standard: Looking at the evidence, does it convince the judge that enough proof exists just to send the case to the next stage for a possible trial?

Attorney Paul Boas, one of the best-known practitioners of criminal law in the Pittsburgh area, who has tried cases in the city for decades, explains that the preliminary hearing standard of a prima facie case does not function as a trial does, with the court weighing evidence from both sides. Rather, a judge must look at the evidence from the point of view most favorable to the Commonwealth (i.e., to the state of Pennsylvania), usually without any defense evidence presented at all, and ask: Does the evidence reach the level that a reasonable juror *could* believe it—not would believe it or should believe it, but *could* believe it?[30] The defense may not use the preliminary hearing to pry into the details of the prosecution's case. Rather, the court simply looks at whether the prosecution has brought forward enough evidence that, on its face, the court should allow the case to proceed to trial.[31] Other states often call their preliminary hearing standard "probable cause," and Pennsylvania's prima facie standard basically works the same way, says Boas. More than nine out of ten times, the defense presents no evidence at the preliminary hearing. The prima facie legal standard, so easy for the Commonwealth to meet in the overwhelming number of cases, means that the defense has little to gain by putting witnesses on the stand. Moving forward with defense testimony at the preliminary hearing would just tip off the prosecution to the defense strategy, witnesses, and evidence. The only exceptions, Boas says, would come in cases in which a lawyer had very strong evidence—strong enough that the attorney could make a plausible argument that the judge should throw the case out— something very rare indeed.[32]

The preliminary hearing takes place in a court. In Pittsburgh, that court is usually the Pittsburgh Municipal Court, located adjacent to the Allegheny County Jail on First Avenue near the city's downtown. Like many states, Pennsylvania has a multitiered court system, and trials in regular criminal cases usually take place in the Court of Common Pleas, the state's trial court of general jurisdiction. Preliminary hearings in Pittsburgh and across Pennsylvania occur in what the state calls its "minor judiciary" courts. The judges (who are referred to as "magisterial district judges") in these minor judiciary courts preside at preliminary hearings. They become judges by election (though they may also "take the bench"—become a judge—first through an appointment to fill the remaining term of a judge who has left the office). Pennsylvania does not require a legal education, admission to the bar, or experience in law practice to serve as a magisterial district judge;

those taking the office need only take a one-month training class and then pass a certification test. Some of these magisterial district judges do have law degrees; many, however, do not.

Commonwealth of Pennsylvania v. Jordan Miles

On March 4, 2010, after two continuances, the clerk of the court called to order a preliminary hearing in the case of the *Commonwealth of Pennsylvania v. Jordan Miles*. This hearing would constitute the first formal in-court examination of the evidence supporting the five criminal counts that the police had filed against Jordan.

Before the proceedings began, many people came to the courtroom including the police officers involved and, of course, Jordan Miles and his mother. Kerry Lewis, Jordan's attorney, was also there. While waiting for the hearing to start, Ms. Miles noticed something out of the corner of her eye.[33] Two of the police officers waved at Jordan, signaling that he should follow them into the hallway. Before Ms. Miles could react, she watched her son follow the officers toward the door. Jordan's mother did not like what she saw and she got up to follow. When she got to the hallway, she found the two officers speaking to Jordan in a tone that she characterized as harsh and intimidating, asking him, "Why did you run from us?" She heard Jordan reply, "because I didn't know you were cops!" Ms. Miles immediately walked up to them and stopped everything. She asked the officers "how dare they try to intimidate my son" like this, and she turned Jordan around and marched him back into the courtroom. Jordan had a lawyer, and ethics rules would not permit a prosecutor to speak directly with Jordan, requiring that all communication come through his lawyer, in order to protect him. This rule protects the parties to the case who have made the wise choice to have their interests represented by lawyers because lawyers from the other side cannot just contact the client directly.[34] But those rules do not bind the police. If Jordan had said something inadvisable or wrong or naïve, nothing would have prevented the officers from putting those statements into evidence.

Magisterial District Judge Oscar Petite, Jr., took the bench for the preliminary hearing. Unlike some of the other magisterial district judges in Pittsburgh, Judge Petite had a full legal education and a license to practice law in Pennsylvania—and that may have mattered. Graduating from Duquesne University School of Law, after obtaining a Bachelor of Science from Carnegie Mellon University, Judge Petite had served since 1995. Before becoming a judge, he had worked in the county probation department and before that at an agency serving the aged.[35] The district in which he served as a judge covered parts of Pittsburgh's downtown core and other nearby areas—all of it completely within the city.

When Judge Petite took the bench in the small courtroom of the Pittsburgh Municipal Court, he found a substantial crowd with many spectators standing. Large numbers of police officers, members of the public, Jordan's family, and the press competed for space. Usually, those standing would have to find a seat or leave. But Judge Petite made an exception. "Because of the number of people in this courtroom—I would presume everybody wants to hear—I'm going to allow everybody to remain standing because of the interest in this case."[36] But, he said, "you must stand quietly, I don't want to hear any comments from anybody on either side," referring to the police and supporters of Jordan. "I don't want to hear any coughing, or sneezing, or any guffaws, or anything. I want complete quiet on this particular case." If he didn't get it, he said, "I will clear this courtroom in a heartbeat." With a serious tone set, Judge Petite said to the prosecutor, "You may call your first witness."

Before any witness took the stand, however, the prosecutor, Assistant District Attorney Steven Stadtmiller of the Allegheny County District Attorney's Office, moved to have the escape charge dropped, for lack of evidence. Neither the defense nor Judge Petite had any objection. Then came a motion from Jordan's defense attorney, Kerry Lewis, asking the court to dismiss the entire complaint—all of the charges—because of what he called a "defect in the sworn statement by the police supporting the charges." Lewis told Judge Petite that the defense wanted to present evidence that the sworn police statement (a sworn version of the police report, for purposes of filing charges) "contains a statement amounting to perjury and it relates directly to the charge of loitering and prowling," which he called the "pretext" for Jordan's arrest and the struggle that followed. Lewis told Judge Petite the defense would present a witness to prove his assertions. Assistant District Attorney Stadtmiller objected, but Lewis persisted, telling the judge that his witness, the person living in the home at 7940, would contradict an important part of what the police statement said. Judge Petite said that while he would "note" Lewis's motion, the hearing would proceed, and if Lewis wanted to call his witness later in the hearing when appropriate, he could ask to do so then.[37] With that, Stadtmiller called his first witness: Officer Michael Saldutte.

Witnesses for the Prosecution

Officer Saldutte's testimony followed closely the contents of the police report he and Officer Ewing had written. The officers, in plain clothes and an unmarked car, saw a man behaving suspiciously up against a house on Tioga Street. On doubling back, the man behaved in ways that caused the officers to believe he had a gun. They stopped him, identified themselves as police officers, verbally and with badges, at every point, but the man ran from them, compounding their suspicions. They tackled him, fought him, and—fearing for their lives because of the presence of a gun—they finally handcuffed him.[38] The whole encounter, Saldutte said, took about a minute and a half. In this particular telling, Saldutte omitted all of the other details, such as feeling the hard object in the defendant's pocket, yelling to his partners that the man was going for a gun, and striking the man in the head to get him, finally, to stop struggling and into the handcuffs. Saldutte did say that, once the first handcuff snapped around the man's right wrist, the man began to yell, "don't take me to jail, just let me go home!"—a sure sign that the man knew the three men on top of him were police.[39]

Saldutte then testified to another aspect of the incident. When the fight had finished, a resident of 7940 Tioga—a woman—raised one of the second floor windows and looked outside. "She said, 'Are you guys all right out there?' And I said, 'Yes, ma'am, Pittsburgh Police.' And she said, 'I know who you are.' I said, 'We arrested a male for sneaking around the side of your house. Was anybody trying to get inside your house?' And she stated, 'I heard noises, and I thought they were mice or mices.' Then she said, 'I wanted to let my dogs out, but I was scared.' And she continued to have a small conversation." Prosecutor Stadtmiller continued with this line of questioning.

Q [Stadtmiller]:	Was Mr. Miles ever exhibited to her?
A [Saldutte]:	Yes he was.
Q:	Did you ask her if she knew him?
A:	Yes.
Q:	What was her response?
A:	She stated she didn't know and no one should be around her house or on her property.

The prosecutor's questions wound up with testimony about how the man, now known to the officers as Jordan Miles, was transported from Tioga Street in a marked police wagon summoned to the scene. The wagon, operated by a pair of uniformed officers, took Jordan to a hospital because Jordan was injured, before taking him to the county jail.[40] The prosecutor also called one of the uniformed officers, Darren Fedorski, as a witness, but not for the mundane details of hospital and jail transportation. While at the hospital with Jordan, Fedorski testified about Jordan's statement to him.

Q [Stadtmiller]:	And while you were present at the hospital, did he make any statement to you about this incident?
A [Fedorski]:	Yes, he did.
Q:	Did you write a report?
A:	Yes.
Q:	Did you put it in quotes in your report?
A:	No, sir.
Q:	Do you remember what it is without looking at it?
A:	Yes.
Q:	What was it he said?
A:	"I'm glad I fought the police because if it was some gangbanger, I would have got shot."

One can easily understand why the prosecution would want the statement in evidence; it might show Jordan knew from the beginning that he was fighting with police. Of course, it did not prove that. The statement, made after the fight, proved only that *at some point* (perhaps well after the struggle), Jordan was relieved to learn that he'd struggled with police and not with gang members who might have done worse than the officers did.

Lewis took the opportunity to cross-examine Saldutte at the preliminary hearing. Any lawyer would have done this, but most judges would limit the scope of cross-examination at a preliminary hearing. After all, the preliminary hearing has a limited purpose, which, as noted earlier, is to determine whether a prima facie case exists and that the defendant had some involvement in it. Most courts will keep defense counsel from exploring other aspects of the case, but Judge Petite gave Lewis wide latitude. Lewis took Saldutte through the details of the fight, establishing (1) that the man putting his hand in his pocket and (2) the sight of the man putting his hand around the sagging coat pocket as he started to move away led the officer to believe the man had a weapon. Lewis then added that, if one believed the officers' report, the man had "vigorously" protected the bottle of Mountain Dew soda later found in that sagging pocket.[41] Lewis then focused on the Mountain Dew bottle itself—the heavy object that caused the officers to believe that Jordan had a gun.

Q [Lewis]:	You searched Miles and discovered that the object that he was reaching for, when he was down on the ground, in his right-hand pocket was a bottle of Mountain Dew; is that correct?
A [Saldutte]:	Yes, sir.
Q:	Do you know what size that bottle was?

A: No, I do not.

Q: Did you bother saving that bottle?

A: No sir, we did not.

Q: Well, you searched around the scene to get the Taser cartridge. You put that in evidence, didn't you?

A: Yes, we did.

Q: Why didn't you put the bottle in evidence?

A: It's not evidence.

Q: Well, the main reason you had to use the degree of force you were using was because you thought he was armed, isn't that right?

A: We believed he was armed. He assaulted two police officers and resisted arrest, yes.

Q: I'm asking you, Officer, you stated in your Affidavit that he was armed, is that right?

A: Yes, we believed he was armed.

Q: And your use of force is dictated on the basis that the suspect could be armed; isn't that right?

A: Yes, sir.

Q: Nobody ever pulled their guns in this incident, did they?

A: No, sir.

Q: And nobody bothered to retrieve the bottle and put it into evidence, is that correct?

A: Like I said, it's not evidence.

Q: It's not evidence. Well, if Jordan wanted to test the bottle for finger prints or DNA to show that it was never in his pocket—

The prosecutor objected, and Judge Petite soon cut off this line of questioning. The exchange about the bottle had revealed nothing new. The assertion of the presence of the bottle of Mountain Dew in Jordan's pocket came straight from the police report. But it previewed the position of the police officers all the way through the case: They found the bottle, which had made it appear that the pocket contained a gun, but they hadn't kept the bottle because "it wasn't evidence" of the crimes for which they had arrested Jordan. The exchange also previewed much of the response to this assertion as the case went forward: If the officers believed that Jordan had a gun that night because of the large heavy object that made his coat sag, saving the bottle as a piece of evidence would have proved their assertion. Of course, Jordan has always denied he had any bottle that night. But if the police were telling the truth about the presence of the bottle—that a bottle was present—not keeping it would have deprived Jordan of the chance to test it so as to prove he had never touched or possessed it.

Lewis did get to ask another direct question about the presence of a weapon: "There was no weapon, was there?"—to which Saldutte answered "no sir."

In any run-of-the-mill case, the testimony of Officers Saldutte and Fedorski would have been enough to establish a prima facie case. The testimony of Saldutte showed at least the reasonable suspicion necessary to suspect a crime might be afoot—lurking near a house, perhaps with an intent to burglarize it,[42] and that the person observed had some level of involvement. Fedorski added the statement by Jordan, which a judge could view as an admission of guilt in the fight. And the low legal standard used at a preliminary hearing—whether a judge believes the prosecution has made a prima facie case that a crime had occurred and the defendant had participated—should have made it easy for the prosecution to succeed. In short, the prosecution seemed to have presented enough evidence to move the case to the next stage: a formal trial of the charges against Jordan. But this hearing would not follow the usual pattern. If defense attorneys rarely presented witnesses at a preliminary hearing, this case became an exception. Attorney Lewis called Monica Wooding, the woman who lived at 7940 Tioga Street, who Saldutte described as raising her window and talking with the police the night of the incident.

Witness for the Defense

Wooding took the stand. Instead of starting directly with his questions, Lewis asked the judge to explain to this witness that she had a right to her own lawyer to advise her before she testified. Any witness in any case, let alone a defendant in a criminal case, has a right to consult a lawyer, if he or she had one, before testifying. Lewis wanted that fact put to the witness and put on the record.[43] To call Lewis's request unusual understates the situation. But Judge Petite granted the request and spoke directly to Wooding. He asked her if she understood that Lewis did not represent her and that she had a right to her own attorney to protect her own interests.[44] Wooding said she understood and that she would go ahead and testify without consulting an attorney. She took the oath and Lewis himself warned her, asking if she realized she was "under oath and any statements that you make here that would perjure you [sic], you could be prosecuted and arrested."[45] Wooding said, again, that she understood, and Lewis began his questioning.

Monica Wooding said that on January 12, at 11:00 p.m., she and her 14-year-old son sat in her bedroom, on the second floor of her home at 7940 Tioga, watching television. She told Lewis that she had known Jordan Miles, "since he was a little kid," and that her son played basketball in the neighborhood with Jordan and some of the other boys.[46] On the night in question, she first sensed something was amiss when, "I looked outside and seen the cops outside in front of my house." The police wagon had already arrived. Lewis then directed his questions at the testimony given by Officer Saldutte and the statements in the police report about Wooding's interactions with the police:

Q [Lewis]: Did you tell the police that you did not know Jordan Miles?
A [Wooding]: No, I did not.
Q: Did you tell the police that Jordan did not have permission to be around your house or on your property?
A: No, I didn't.[47]

Wooding said the police never asked her any of those things. She said that she'd gone to her bedroom window and saw the police outside.

A [Wooding]: I looked outside and I seen the cops out there. So I didn't know what was going on, but the police van was in the process of leaving with whoever was in there. The officers were outside in front of my house, and I proceeded to say to one of the officers, because he looked like another officer, did he know Officer Konackj. Then he asked me was anybody trying to get in my house. I said no....
Q [Lewis]: Did he ask you that more than one time?
A: Like two or three times, and the third time of saying no, I let him know if somebody was trying to get in my house, I would let my dogs out ....
Q: Do you ever recall telling—did you tell Saldutte that there were mice?
A: I hear my dog bark because I thought she would have been barking at a mouse. That is what I said.

Lewis then showed Wooding the sworn police statement that said that Wooding told the officers that she did not know the person they showed her, and he had no permission to be on her property.

Q: You are saying in court under oath today that you never
                said that?
A: Correct, I never said that.

Monica Wooding's testimony denied, in the most direct way possible, what the
police officers said that she had told them. She had indeed talked to them, and
she had mentioned both her dogs and mice. But she contradicted the core of
what the officers had sworn to in their statement: They had not shown the man
to her, and she had never told them that Jordan had no right to be around
her house.

The Judge's Ruling

Anyone accustomed to observing preliminary hearings in Pittsburgh or anywhere else might simply say, so? What Wooding said seemed unusual in the
context of a type of hearing that usually saw no defense witnesses at all, but
Saldutte's testimony still established the prima facie case needed. The brief conversation between the police officers and Monica Wooding, through her bedroom window, whatever its substance, did not change that. Perhaps Assistant
District Attorney Stadtmiller agreed; he declined to cross-examine Wooding.
In his closing statement, Stadtmiller said only that "all five police officers were
present when the woman stated she didn't know the person and that is what they
put in the report." In short, five officers said differently, and in the end what she
had said did not matter. The observations of Saldutte and then the other police
officers upon seeing Jordan, and their actions, constituted more than enough
evidence to satisfy the low bar of proof required at a preliminary hearing.[48]

But when the end of the hearing came, Wooding's testimony did matter.
Judge Petite began his decision by restating the legal standard: "was a prima
facie crime committed and is he the one that did it." From there, he set out his
reasoning:

> We have a young man walking in his own neighborhood, a high crime
> neighborhood or whatever you want to call it. I guess it is around eleven
> o'clock at night. This man is walking through his neighborhood and
> approached by an undercover police officer who was not either in uniform
> or in a marked police vehicle. And from that particular point, this whole
> thing begins to go down hill.

... I'm not sure there was truly a crime committed here. The court has to take into consideration testimony by all of the witnesses, particularly the lady, I believe, at 7940, and one of the officers was saying he had a conversation with her. While the lady is actually here in court today testifying, and gave a statement, and knows she could be possibly charged with perjury, she decided to waive her rights to an attorney today while she made those statements. This court has to take that into consideration when making a determination as to whether or not there is a prima facie case here, because but for him being found on the side of that house late at night at the time when the officers were going through the community, I don't think we would be here today.

I also have to take careful consideration to realize that officers are witnesses just like everybody else. This court has the job of making the determination, not based on a position, but based on the testimony. One witness is no more important than the other ....

Lastly, when you look at the Commonwealth of Pennsylvania and they say the totality of the circumstances, and when I look at everything involved in this case, I'm left with no other alternative but to dismiss all charges against Jordan Miles. If the Commonwealth wishes to present this case again, there are certain rules that you have to follow. Certainly you cannot present the same [sworn statement.] Fix it and I will take another look.

Judge Petite said that the district attorney's office could also take the case to a judge of the Court of Common Pleas, which "can overrule me." But, given what he had heard, "I'm dismissing the case."[49]

For those in attendance, "surprise" does not convey strongly enough the emotions of the moment. Judges rarely dismiss cases at the preliminary hearing phase; the low legal standard requiring minimal evidence and the usual benefit of the doubt police get from judges and prosecutors made it uncommon indeed. For a judge to throw out a case that had captured so much public attention, with police testimony that seemed to establish the required prima facie case, was totally out of the realm of what participants and observers might expect to happen at the hearing. And the judge had said what judges usually never say, even if they think it. Judge Petite simply did not believe the testimony of Officer Saldutte or the contents of the police documents, given the contradictory testimony of Monica Wooding. The judge also seemed to harbor grave doubts about the truth of what the police said happened before Wooding stuck her head out of her bedroom window, implying that police might see suspicion and wrongdoing much too readily when a young black man walked, at night, in his own neighborhood, an African American neighborhood—high-crime area though it might be.

As of 11:50 a.m. on March 4, two things had become certain. Judge Petite had freed Jordan Miles from the charges against him. While the prosecution could refile the charges or appeal his decision, the case against Jordan had ended for the present. And the police did not like it at all. They were furious.

AN ANGRY POLICE DEPARTMENT

The police reaction to Judge Petite's decision dismissing all charges did not take long to surface in public. The chatter among police officers in e-mails and in public statements began immediately, and such communication lacked any nuance: The police officers were outraged, angry, and felt disrespected.

As noted earlier in this chapter, police officers in Pittsburgh belong to the FOP, a national organization with union locals in many cities throughout the United States. Pittsburgh has a long history with the FOP; its local, called "Fort Pitt Lodge No. 1," was formed in 1915 and is said to be the first unit of what was to become the national FOP. With this long history, the FOP local in Pittsburgh had long played a key role in Pittsburgh on all police and public safety issues.[50] This was still the case in 2010, and much of the sentiment of police officers about the Jordan Miles case emerged on the FOP website's news pages. The FOP news from Pittsburgh in March 2010 began with a report that the city faced a state of emergency due to a forecast of imminent flooding. But the coverage quickly turned to officers' anger over the case against Jordan Miles and the investigations of the three police officers who had arrested him, over allegations that they had used excessive force against Jordan.[51] According to the FOP news report, nearly three months after the incident involving Jordan and the three officers, the city's Office of Municipal Investigations had still made "no decision" about the officers' conduct, "raising concern among street cops they may be fired."[52] Marty Griffin, a Pittsburgh journalist and radio talk show host, questioned Officer Dan O'Hara, the president of Pittsburgh's FOP local, asking if he thought there are "a lot of angry police officers." O'Hara replied, "Oh, I absolutely agree there's a lot of upset police officers, no doubt."[53]

The brunt of the anger focused, first and foremost, on Judge Petite's decision to dismiss the charges against Jordan Miles at the preliminary hearing. The FOP news report attacked the propriety of Judge Petite's hearing ruling, saying it had caused "outrage" among police. Bill Diffenderfer, one of the attorneys then retained by the FOP to represent one of the three officers, demanded that the district attorney refile the charges against Jordan, so a "neutral, detached party"—another judge—would hear the case.[54] Diffenderfer's comment strongly implied not only that Judge Petite had not decided the case correctly, but that Petite had, in fact, shown bias toward one side and a lack of fairness. This was an attack that went to the heart of what the law requires of a judge. Diffenderfer did not explain why Judge Petite was both wrong and had violated the core tenet of fairness and neutrality; after all, judges in other settings decide whether or not to believe witnesses all the time. Taking the word of Wooding, over that of a police officer, somehow went beyond the pale.

The FOP news reports also discussed what the outrage among officers might motivate officers to do. It said that "emails ... circulating through the police department" openly discussed actions that officers would take to express their displeasure with the court or the investigation. Officers reportedly had begun to talk of "boycotting public events"—that is, refusing optional extra duty or secondary employment in which officers opted to work as private security for public functions such as festivals or parades. A big public event, the city's St. Patrick's Day parade, would occur in just a few days. According to the FOP news report, the e-mails claimed that "60 officers have already dropped out of St. Patrick's Day duties." Others had even discussed refusing extra work "if needed for flooding patrols."[55] Even more important, officers had begun discussing a broader work slowdown by calling in sick—a tactic sometimes called the "Blue Flu."[56] Some of the messages had a more precise target. According to a report in the *New Pittsburgh Courier*, the city's African American newspaper, two police officers said that "a text message blast went out some time on March 5"—the day after the dismissal of charges against Jordan Miles—"calling for officers to either refuse to patrol Homewood and [sic] to 'take their time' responding to any calls there."[57] If true, this call to fail to protect the residents of one African American neighborhood surely represented an immoral response to an action of a sitting judge and was a threat to the safety of an entire neighborhood.

Any broad work slowdown would disrupt police operations all over the city. Such action could cause major problems not just with immediate public safety concerns but also with police investigation of crimes that had already occurred, with vehicle traffic and accidents, and with other routine aspects of police work. The department's leadership did not regard discussion of a sick-out as an idle threat or something to ignore; they knew how enraged many officers were, and they could not take the chance that this anger would lead to damaging action. Deputy Chief Paul Donaldson, the second-ranking command officer in the department, wrote a department-wide e-mail, addressing the threats head on. He said he had heard "disturbing rumors" that some police officers "are contemplating a work slowdown or diminished patrols" in response to the dismissal of charges in the case against Jordan Miles.[58] Donaldson did not mince words when he described his view of a police work slowdown. "Any such actions are forbidden and would be detrimental to the involved officers and the entire" police department, he said. Donaldson went on to say that the department should not read the dismissal of the charges as a judgment on the conduct of the three police officers who arrested Jordan Miles. "There is no correlation between the resolution of the criminal charges in this case and the professional behavior of these individuals." Deputy Chief Donaldson then went on to address the court's dismissal of charges and the proper view of the workings of the justice system:

> Not every police encounter ends with an arrest and not every arrest results in a conviction. Nor would we want it to …. Decisions are made by magistrates, judges and juries that we do not agree with, but must accept …. This does not give us cause to personally attack those who are tasked with making those decisions. At times like these you should perform in such a way that if people say unflattering or negative things about us, that no one will believe them.[59]

Donaldson added that a work slowdown in protest of Judge Petite's decision "would tarnish our image." He felt certain, he said, that talk of a slowdown was "merely rumors, but felt a need to address it."[60]

Perhaps heeding the warning from Deputy Chief Donaldson, the "Blue Flu" never materialized. But officers did find a way to show their displeasure with the decision in the preliminary hearing, their support of their three fellow officers, and their absolute denial that anyone could view the incident on Tioga Street on January 12 as a grave injustice with the infliction of unjustified violence against Jordan Miles. This demonstration of extreme displeasure by police came during the St. Patrick's Day parade—always one of the city's signature public events and often described as one of the nation's largest. Rather than boycotting any extra service for the security of the event, the police decided to come out with their supporters and make their feelings known. In advance of the parade, which would occur on Saturday, March 13 (the city often held its parade on a designated weekend day instead of March 17, to minimize disruption and traffic problems on business days), the FOP Fort Pitt Lodge No. 1 exhorted its members to attend the parade in "unprecedented" numbers and to purchase and wear specially made T-shirts for the occasion.[61] The shirts, green with white lettering, had "3599" on the front—the police department designation for the

99 car in which Saldutte, Sisak, and Ewing patrolled that night. On the back, the shirt read, "We Support our THREE BROTHERS" with the last two words in large block capital letters. Between the words "THREE" and "BROTHERS," which were stacked on top of one another, ran a black horizontal stripe. In the middle of the black stripe ran a thin blue line—graphically capturing the phrase that police serve as the "thin blue line" protecting civilized citizens from the chaos and disorder that would otherwise overrun society.[62] FOP local president Dan O'Hara told the Pittsburgh *Tribune Review* that the union meant the shirts to show that "we fully support these three officers and brothers and we want the entire city of Pittsburgh to know that." In case the shirts sold out, the union would provide posters with the message, "Support Your Police" so "every member can show that we are one strong union who backs each other up."[63] Local vice president Charles Hanlon added that only officers planning to march in the parade could buy the shirts.

When the parade occurred, about 75 police officers and supporters marched, most wearing the shirts, some carrying signs, and some doing both.[64] Television footage from station KDKA, captured by a citizen who posted the images on YouTube, shows a group of officers walking down the street and receiving cheers from some in the crowd. FOP local president Dan O'Hara said the reaction of the people proved that Pittsburgh supported its police. "Pittsburgh supports their police. We always knew that—we still know it."[65] A civilian watching the parade, who wore one of the shirts, explained that he wore it because "we support the police. We're 100 percent behind them."[66]

This reaction—that the city of Pittsburgh supports the police—was not shared by everyone across the city. Many in the African American community had a strongly negative reaction to the police show of solidarity at the parade, an event that everyone in town typically celebrated together. The *New Pittsburgh Courier* asked some black Pittsburghers what they thought.[67] Shabaka Wilkins told the paper, "I think that it is ridiculous. I also believe that the officers made it clear how they really feel about what happened with Miles. They think it is okay and they are sticking by each other." Monique Wynn, who said she lived in Homewood, noted, "the whole department is a disgrace, supporting the officers after what they did. They believe in sticking up for the blue and it is unfair. Even if Jordan was in the wrong for resisting, you could see that the abuse was beyond justifiable." According to Stacy Fincer, "it was disrespectful and should not have been permitted. For the fact that they are public servants, they should show their support to each other behind the scenes since there is still an open investigation." Vendetta Jackson told the paper, "I am livid about it. When I saw it on TV, I thought that it was the 2010 Klan without the white robes. It is support of an unjust beating …. Where are humanity, morality, and integrity?" Perhaps Greg Fincher captured these sentiments the best. "I don't think they should have worn those shirts," he said. "It was blatantly sending a message that they don't think that what happened to Jordan Miles was wrong. It is understandable why young Black men don't trust the police."[68]

The case of Jordan Miles and Officers Saldutte, Sisak, and Ewing would grind on for years. But by St. Patrick's Day, just two months after the events of January 12, the wounds had become both visible and deep. Jordan's face, swollen, cut, and bruised, had startled the public and angered many, but others— police officers and many other residents—felt differently: They unequivocally supported the police. The lack of trust in police by many in the African American community had reached a low point—and it would only get worse.

CHAPTER 4

INVESTIGATIONS AND DECISIONS

With the charges against Jordan Miles dismissed at the preliminary hearing and the city divided in its reactions to the incident itself and to the dismissal, the case began to unfold in multiple, related directions. The incident spawned several investigations including (1) an internal affairs investigation of the officers, by the Office of Municipal Investigations (OMI), aimed at looking into whether the officers had violated police policy or disciplinary rules; (2) a federal investigation of the officers' conduct, by the U.S. Department of Justice, for civil rights violations; and (3) an investigation of whether the officers had violated Pennsylvania law, by the district attorney of Allegheny County (the county that includes Pittsburgh). Early on, the district attorney, Stephen Zappala, announced that he would wait until the federal authorities completed their investigation before making any decision about state charges against the police.[1] In the meantime, Zappala had another decision to make: would he recharge Jordan Miles for the crimes that the police had alleged he had committed? Those charges included two counts of aggravated assault on police officers (for striking Saldutte with an elbow and for injuring Sisak's knee with a kick), each carrying a possible sentence of up to 20 years.[2] Zappala's spokesperson did not immediately commit to recharging Jordan, saying that the office would "have to take a close look" at the case because the judge seemed to have based his decision largely on "the testimony of the victim of the prowling charge," Monica Wooding.[3] Despite the significance of Wooding's testimony, Pittsburgh Police clearly expected that Zappala would refile the charges. "We firmly believe there was enough evidence" to go forward, said Chuck Hanlon, a Pittsburgh Police officer who then served as vice president of Pittsburgh's Fraternal Order of Police union lodge. "We plan to lobby the district attorney pretty hard to re-file those charges."[4] Bill Difenderfer, an attorney then representing one of the three officers, said that since the law allowed the district attorney to refile, "the district attorney's office absolutely has to re-file these charges" because the case made prosecution "compelling."

59

Ultimately, District Attorney Zappala decided not to refile the charges against Jordan. According to Zappala, the facts alleged by the police officers in their reports and testimony justified the initial charges. Nevertheless, Judge Petite "was responding to public pressure" when he dismissed the charges. This would, of course, offend basic principles of justice if true. Still, Zappala thought, the community "owns" the criminal justice system, and he asked himself, "is the community best served if we [re-filed charges and] put this [case] back through a preliminary hearing. And the conclusion I reached was that it was not."[5]

With spring turning toward summer in 2010, the case assumed what would become a familiar pattern. The three police officers remained on paid administrative leave, collecting their base salaries plus court-related overtime, as they had been since February 1.[6] Jordan Miles, freed of criminal charges, finished the school year and graduated from Pittsburgh High School for the Creative and Performing Arts.[7] The focus shifted from allegations of crimes committed by Jordan to allegations of criminal behavior committed by the three officers.

THE INVESTIGATIONS

In any case of alleged police misconduct in Pittsburgh, four different types of investigations may take place. Two of them—by (1) the Office of Municipal Investigations (OMI) and (2) the Citizens Police Review Board (CPRB)—aim primarily at determining whether officers committed professional misconduct by violating departmental rules or policy. Investigations by (3) the district attorney and (4) the U.S. Department of Justice determine whether the officers violated state or federal criminal laws.

The OMI

The OMI examines all complaints of misconduct made against employees of the City of Pittsburgh.[8] These include complaints against the police and also, for example, against employees of the Fire, Emergency Medical Services, and Building Inspections bureaus OMI's jurisdiction includes complaints of both civil and criminal conduct. In an administrative (i.e., noncriminal) investigation, city employees must cooperate with the inquiry; failure to do so may result in disciplinary proceedings independent of whatever misconduct the complaint originally alleged.

OMI claims complete independence from the city's agencies whose employees it investigates; it does not function as part of the police department. In fact, the Pittsburgh Police has no internal affairs unit, the way many modern departments do; OMI fills that role. Nevertheless, OMI remains part of

Pittsburgh's city government and is not independent of it. According to its own documentation, "its authority is drawn from the Public Safety Director, to whom it reports."[9] The Mayor appoints the Public Safety Director, who oversees the city's fire, EMS, and police agencies. In other words, while OMI stands apart from the police department, it exists as part of city government. Its staff includes "a civilian Assistant Chief, civilian Coordinator, detective, and civilian clerk."[10] The OMI says that it "acts solely as a fact-finder and does not make disciplinary decisions or recommendation." This, it says, is a good thing: "by staying removed from the disciplinary process, OMI ensures citizens and employees a fair, thorough investigation."[11] "Any person involved in an incident" can file a complaint with OMI, and it accepts anonymous complaints and those made by third parties on behalf of someone else, as long as "corroborative evidence can be obtained."[12] According to OMI's website, it will close a case with a finding that falls into one of four "possible closing categories": *sustained* (i.e., OMI finds the complaint true), *not sustained* (the opposite), *exonerated* (the employee, not the complainant, is correct), or *unfounded* (the complaint has no basis).[13]

According to published reports,[14] OMI began investigating the incident on Tioga Street, just weeks after it occurred. An OMI investigator interviewed all three officers and Jordan, as well as others. Pittsburgh's Mayor, Luke Ravenstahl, promised to have the investigation completed by the end of February 2010, but no announcement of a conclusion or OMI's findings occurred then—or for months afterward. When a member of the City Council asked the Mayor about the delay in late April of 2010, claiming that OMI investigators had actually finished and that the Mayor and the city's Department of Public Safety were simply withholding the report,[15] he received a reply from the City Solicitor indicating that the OMI investigation "is not complete and remains open." One reason for this, the Solicitor said, was "the initiation of a federal investigation" that might "reveal additional or new evidence" that would help the investigation. Prudence dictated that "the City act in [a] manner that respects the integrity of the federal investigation."[16] This contradicted earlier statements from the city that "OMI review does not depend on the outcome of any other pending investigation."[17] Nothing in the city's laws or regulations required slowing or holding up the investigation; the city simply decided to do so.

The CPRB

OMI's online materials note that its jurisdiction and investigation may overlap with another agency: the CPRB. Like OMI, the CPRB investigates allegations against Pittsburgh Police officers, and those allegations come in the form of citizen complaints. OMI notes that the CPRB "is an independent agency that is empowered to investigate allegations of police misconduct and hold public hearing at which complainants, witnesses and police officers must appear."[18] OMI and CPRB may investigate complaints about the same incident, and nothing prohibits parallel investigations from going forward.[19] Though separate, the agencies may share investigative information.

The CPRB exists because of historic dissatisfaction with police oversight through OMI, which—for all its claims of independence—still remains part of Pittsburgh's city government, just like the police department. That dissatisfaction has its roots in Pittsburgh's history of police mistreatment of African Americans, especially in lethal police actions that have ended in the deaths of African Americans. This history is many decades long, but for most black Pittsburghers, the modern era starts with a black man named Jerry Jackson. On April 5, 1995, Jackson, 44 years old, drove a suspected stolen car the wrong way on a one-way street. He fled as Pittsburgh Housing Police Department Officer John Charmo gave chase. Charmo chased Jackson into the narrow Armstrong Tunnel and killed him with 13 shots,[20] using unauthorized Black Talon hollow-point bullets.[21] The Pittsburgh Police Department—a separate agency from the Housing Authority Police—had responsibility for the investigation. Charmo claimed that Jackson had managed to turn his vehicle completely around, twice, in the tight confines of the tunnel, driving toward Charmo and threatening his life. This seemed implausible, and when Pittsburgh Police investigators confirmed his story, many suspected a cover-up. Nevertheless, with only this evidence in hand, a coroner's inquest (an archaic procedure then still existing to hear cases in such settings in Pennsylvania) recommended no charges. Four years later, new evidence surfaced of a videotape made by Pittsburgh investigators on the scene, showing "wheel markings in the Armstrong Tunnel from Jackson's car that contradicted Charmo's claim that Jackson turned his car around" and caused Charmo to fire in self-defense.[22] The tape came to light through a civil lawsuit filed by Jackson's family.[23] After a second coroner's inquest that included the new evidence, a relatively new district attorney—Stephen Zappala, the same district attorney who would later find his office involved in Jordan Miles's case— brought in an independent investigator, and in 1999, Charmo faced homicide charges. In the end, however, Charmo agreed to plead guilty on exceedingly favorable terms: He went to prison but served only 11 months.[24]

Another case of the death of a black man at the hands of the police quickly followed. On October 12, 1995, a police officer from the Pittsburgh suburb of Brentwood stopped Jonny Gammage, a black man in his thirties, for a traffic offense. Four other officers from suburban jurisdictions quickly arrived after the first officer called for backup. The car that Gammage was driving that night, a Jaguar, belonged to Ray Seals, then a defensive end for the Pittsburgh Steelers. Seals had loaned the car to Gammage, his cousin, who was a businessman visiting from Syracuse, New York. Within just seven minutes of the traffic stop, an altercation resulted in all five of the officers taking Gammage to the ground, with at least two of the officers on top of him. Gammage died, and an autopsy determined the cause of death to be asphyxiation caused by pressure applied to his chest and neck.[25] Only three of the officers involved faced charges of involuntary manslaughter. Ultimately, a jury acquitted one of the officers, and the other two walked free after two mistrials.[26]

The Gammage cases involved suburban officers (although the traffic stop actually occurred just inside Pittsburgh's city limits), but with Jerry Jackson's death so recent, the issues of police mistreatment of African Americans in Pittsburgh came to a head. In March of 1996, the American Civil Liberties Union (ACLU) filed a class action lawsuit against Pittsburgh and its police department; 66 individual plaintiffs alleged that the police had victimized them in a variety of ways. In addition to the city and the department, the suit named 121 individual officers as defendants.[27] Allegations included unlawful searches and seizures, use of excessive force, and unlawful arrests. The next month, the U.S. Department of Justice began an investigation of the Pittsburgh Police Department to ascertain whether the department engaged in patterns or practices of unconstitutional policing, under a new federal law enacted in 1994.[28] The investigation represented the first time the Justice Department had used this statute, and it would result in the first-ever "consent decree" to reform a police department the following year.[29]

With the start of the investigation, a prominent African American member of the Pittsburgh City Council, Sala Udin, introduced a bill to create a civilian review board. Udin's bill, 1996-397, had seven public hearings and ultimately went down to defeat.[30] Undeterred, citizen activists and some members of the Council petitioned for a ballot measure that would create a civilian review board. Successive challenges to petition signatures by the Fraternal Order of Police and other actions failed to defeat the petition drive. On primary election day, May 22, 1997, the measure passed, with nearly 58 percent of the vote, garnering support from almost all communities and neighborhoods in the city and formally amending the city's home rule charter to create a free-standing, independent civilian review authority: the CPRB.

The CPRB would have its own board, with members appointed by the Mayor and the city council; its own staff and budget; its own investigators; and the power to hold hearings and issue subpoenas for testimony and evidence. It could make findings, deciding whether officers had committed misconduct or not, in individual cases based on complaints or based on investigations started on its own initiative. It could not impose discipline on officers, but it could recommend discipline to the chief of police, who would then have to accept, reject, or modify those findings. Whatever its powers and place in the city's government, the CPRB represented a rejection of the status quo regarding police misconduct, discipline, and the judicial system's seeming inability to come to grips with what, for African Americans, had become an untenable situation. It represented a concrete answer to the deaths of Jerry Jackson and Jonny Gammage, with the most democratic pedigree imaginable: a body created by citizens, through the vote, over the opposition of the police and others, to address a problem that the police and elected leaders of the city could not or would not fix.

Thus, in 2010, the CPRB seemed like a logical alternative for an investigation into the incident involving Jordan Miles, even as OMI—perhaps with its investigation completed—remained silent. But it turned out that the CPRB's own rules prevented this from happening. A federal investigation had begun, and that stopped any action by the CPRB. According to the CPRB's bylaws,

> Should the Review Board or its staff learn at any time that the District Attorney, the State Attorney General's office or the Department of Justice has initiated criminal proceedings against a Subject Officer, the Review Board shall defer any preliminary inquiry and/or investigation until such criminal proceedings have been withdrawn or concluded.[31]

This meant the CPRB, an agency uniquely suited and even created to investigate incidents like the one in Homewood on January 12, 2010, would have to stay on the sidelines until the conclusion of the criminal investigations. Jordan Miles did file a complaint with the CPRB, and it held a hearing on the use of "99 cars," the assignment of Officers Saldutte, Sisak, and Ewing when they encountered Jordan Miles on Tioga Street on that cold January night.[32] CPRB records indicate that the Jordan Miles matter was "removed from suspension" (reactivated) in May of 2012, but public files show no other actions on the case by the CPRB.

District Attorneys and Prosecution of Police Use-of-Force Cases

Beyond the investigations by OMI, two other investigations (one state and one federal) would probe whether the officers violated criminal law in the incident in which they arrested Jordan Miles. The question, in other words, would involve whether the officers committed crimes in how they arrested and apprehended Jordan.

As the prosecuting authority closest to the ground—the local authority with responsibility for charging crimes in the vast majority of incidents—the office of the elected district attorney of the county in which an alleged criminal activity took place would usually investigate and make charging decisions first. The district attorney's office would decide whether to bring charges against the suspected police officers, just as that office would do in any case involving civilians. The local police department would usually run the investigation, but when their own employees became the subject of the investigation, sometimes officers from the district attorney's own staff or from other law enforcement authorities might handle the investigation. The district attorney would then decide whether or not to bring charges by evaluating the charge-worthiness of the case under the law of the individual state. In the case involving the three officers and Jordan, the criminal laws of Pennsylvania would govern. The main crimes likely under consideration would include false arrest. Whatever additional charges the prosecutor might bring, such as assault—for the injuries inflicted on Jordan and the amount of force the officers used to inflict those injuries—would form the centerpiece of the case. Given this, understanding several aspects of the law that apply only to police officers becomes crucial.

Civilians—nonpolice officers—have no right to use force on others in the normal course of life. Other people may annoy us, do things we do not like, even steal from us and deprive us of our property,[33] and still we would have no right to use force on them. We would have to call the police. Using force, or even threatening to do that, would put a civilian in danger of a charge of assault.[34] The great exception to this rule is self-defense. Under the laws of Pennsylvania (and all other U.S. states), a person under unjustifiable and illegal attack may exercise the ancient, deeply rooted right of self-defense. Pennsylvania's self-defense law reads: "The use of force upon or toward another person is justifiable when the actor believes that such force is immediately necessary for the purpose of protecting himself [or herself] against the use of unlawful force by such other person on the present occasion."[35] The use of force in defense may also extend to defending others in some limited circumstances, such as defending one's children, close relatives, or spouse.[36]

Police officers operate in an entirely different legal universe when it comes to the use of force. The criminal law allows the police to use force to carry out the legal and justifiable aspects of their job. This includes using force to effectuate an arrest or to prevent the escape of an arrested person. On its face, this would cover exactly the situation that Officers Saldutte, Sisak, and Ewing said they faced the night that they encountered Jordan Miles. They suspected him of criminal activity and felt that they had the requisite probable cause (or at least reasonable suspicion) for an arrest or at least to command Jordan to stop and account for his actions. When he fought their efforts to detain him and hit one and then kicked another, they would have the right to use force to subdue him and make an arrest. Pennsylvania's law explicitly gives officers this right. Section 508 (a) of Title 21 of the Pennsylvania Code says that a police officer

> [N]eed not retreat or desist from efforts to make a lawful arrest because of resistance or threatened resistance to the arrest. He is justified in the use of any force which he believes to be necessary to effect the arrest and of any force which he believes to be necessary to defend himself or another from bodily harm while making the arrest.[37]

This ability of police to use force in the course of carrying out their legal duties constitutes the central purpose of this law, but note this key phrase: "force which he believes to be necessary ...." First, the law commands us to look to what the officer believed, not to our own reactions later, reading a report or viewing a video. The officer's belief about this is paramount. Second, and perhaps even more important, the officer may *only* use the amount of force *necessary* to carry out the arrest or defend himself or herself. And, by implication, the officer *cannot use more force than necessary*. If the suspect resists arrest by running away, tackling the suspect to the ground would seem necessary. Beating the suspect in order to teach him or her a lesson obviously exceeds any necessity.

This variation in legal standards for civilians and for police in using force explains why prosecutors face different decisions in civilian and police use-of-force cases. In the case of a civilian, the questions line up straightforwardly: Did the civilian defendant assault the victim by using force? Did the civilian have any conceivable legal justification for the use of force, such as self-defense or the defense of another person? In the case of a police officer engaged in his or her duties, the case only begins with the question of whether the officer used force. The prosecutor must also ask whether the officer did this because the officer believed it necessary to carry out official duties and, even if so, whether the officer used excessive force, that is, more force than necessary. This explains why cases in which police use force or violence often carry the term "excessive force."

But Stephen Zappala, the Allegheny County District Attorney, did not confront these questions immediately. They would all wait for another day. Because the federal investigation into the incident had already begun, with FBI agents actively looking at whether or not the three police officers had violated federal criminal laws, the decision was made[38] to defer the state investigation and possible prosecution until the completion of the federal investigation. Zappala did not have to defer; nothing prohibited his going forward at the same time, either separately or in coordination with the federal effort. But he decided to wait the feds out. This meant that, for the foreseeable future, the action in the case would focus on the federal side.

Federal Investigations: "Willful" Violations of the Constitution

The federal government has a body of criminal law, like the states, but these federal laws have a more limited scope and jurisdiction. For these laws to apply, they must pertain to a federal interest. For example, the federal penal code contains laws against murder, theft, and robbery, but prosecutors working for the federal government would not use these laws unless the alleged crime happened on federal land, such as a national park. The local district attorney's office would handle almost all garden-variety criminal offenses in a jurisdiction, such as retail theft or burglary. Federal crimes, on the other hand, such as interstate drug trafficking, mail and wire fraud, and racketeering, would find their way to the desk of a federal prosecutor, an employee of the U.S. Department of Justice. Federal law divides the United States into 93 federal districts, and each district has its own chief federal prosecutor, called the United States Attorney for that particular district. The U.S. Attorney, along with his or her staff of prosecutors (called assistant U.S. Attorneys), decides which federal criminal cases to charge and bring to trial.

For most cases, a U.S. Attorney confronts questions very much like those asked in any state prosecutor's office: Exactly what proof does this crime require me to have? Can the available witnesses testify in a convincing way? What about the strength of the other evidence, such as physical or forensic evidence? But some federal crimes require proof of a special element not found in state crimes. Cases involving the prosecution of police officers for excessive force in incidents like the one involving Jordan Miles come up under one such federal statute. This law gives federal authorities jurisdiction to prosecute such cases by virtue of the fact that they involve possible violations of federal civil rights. The law, Section 242 of Title 18 of the U.S. Code, reads:

> Whoever, under color of any law, statute, ordinance, regulation, or custom, willfully subjects any person in any State, Territory, Commonwealth,

Possession, or District to the deprivation of any rights, privileges, or immunities secured or protected by the Constitution or laws of the United States, or to different punishments, pains, or penalties, on account of such person being an alien, or by reason of his color, or race, than are prescribed for the punishment of citizens, shall be [punished] ....[39]

Section 242 goes on to describe the escalating types of punishment that a court may impose, depending on the severity of the conduct, whether injury or death of the victim resulted, and the like.

This statute would form the legal basis for any federal prosecution of the three police officers who had taken Jordan Miles down on the night of January 12, 2010. The U.S. Attorney for the Western District of Pennsylvania, whose jurisdiction covered Pittsburgh, Allegheny County, and 25 other counties on the western side of the state, would have to decide whether the evidence he or she had could prove that the officers had violated the terms of that statute, in order to go forward with the case.

The U.S. Attorney would have to try to prove the officers guilty of using excessive force to a jury that would give the police the benefit of the doubt, with police officers seen as the good guys[40]—just as the local district attorney would have to do in a state court case. But the U.S. Attorney would face another burden, unique to federal law. The U.S. Attorney, working under the federal statute, would also have to show that the police used excessive force for the purpose of depriving the victim of his or her "rights, privileges or immunities secured or protected by the Constitution or the laws of the United States."

The obligation to prove a willful violation of the Constitution or U.S. law represents the highest burden of proof in American criminal law. Proof for conviction under Section 242 requires proving everything that a state criminal case would take, grappling with every extralegal issue with which a prosecutor would contend (e.g., the jury's natural sympathy for police officers), plus the additional burden of showing that a police officer had acted willfully when he or she violated the Constitution or federal law. The U.S. Supreme Court defined "willfully" for purposes of Section 242 in a case in 1945 called *Screws v. United States*.[41] In *Screws*, Justice Douglas declared that "willfully" meant that the statute required proof that the defendant had a "specific intent" to deprive the victim of his or her constitutional right. For example, to beat the victim without justification would not be enough. To violate the federal *statute*, the officer would have to beat the victim without justification with the *additional intention* of violating the victim's constitutional rights—as Justice Douglas put it, with "a purpose to deprive a person of a specific constitutional right."[42] Prosecutors at every level use facts and inferences drawn from these facts in virtually every kind of case to prove required mental states in criminal cases, for example, to show that a defendant acted intentionally or recklessly. But federal prosecutors using Section 242 have to do that, and more: They have to prove that the bad intentions of the defendant went as far as intending to violate the constitutional rights of the victim—not just to intentionally or recklessly break the law.

There is disagreement about what the specific "intent requirement" in Section 242 means in federal criminal cases against police officers. For its part, the Department of Justice itself seems to play down the specific proof needed to meet the burden. Citing the *Screws* opinion, the Department says that:

> [T]he statute does not require the Government to show the defendants were thinking in constitutional terms at the time of the depravations .... A person may be guilty of a violation of Section 242 without any familiarity with the Constitution. If the defendant intended to deprive the victim of a right, such as, for example, intending to use more force than is necessary, or intending to steal money, he need not "recognize the unconstitutionality of his acts."[43]

This characterization of the proof required by the law, as interpreted in the *Screws* case—requiring little more than proof that the defendant had the intention to do what he or she did and that what he or she did violated the Constitution—leaves one asking what more the law demands for proof of the extra, specific intent. Critics of the Department of Justice say that it performs badly in this area because it brings so few cases under Section 242, and they point to the specific intent standard as one of the chief reasons. These critics say the Department acts as if the *Screws* standard is actually much higher than what the Department says in the statement just quoted. For example, a report by the nongovernmental organization Human Rights Watch said that the Department of Justice's "poor performance" stems from a variety of factors (e.g., unsympathetic victims, witnesses with poor credibility, and "the public's predisposition to believe police officers"), but especially from "the added requirement, as interpreted by the courts, that prosecutors prove the accused officer's 'specific intent' to deprive an individual of his or her civil rights." Because of this and other "stringent standards," the group said, "federal prosecutors—who like their local counterparts are interested in winning cases, not merely trying them—may be less than eager to pursue cases against police officers."[44] The report goes on to note that the Department of Justice only brings charges in a small percentage—as low as 1 or 2 percent—of all such cases investigated.[45]

Regardless of these disagreements, the proof of mental state required by Section 242 remains a significant burden for federal prosecutors to meet. Thus any decision to go forward with a federal charge requires strong evidence, just as a starting point. But even solid evidence might not prove sufficient. Besides judging compliance with Section 242, U.S. Attorneys must look to the Department of Justice's own internal standards, found in a comprehensive, highly detailed set of rules. According to those rules, bringing federal criminal charges requires more than a strong suspicion that the defendant violated the law. A prosecutor's instincts, even if seasoned and honed over decades of trial work, would not supply a basis for going forward with charges. A prosecutor who could only say, "I've got some evidence here—let's throw it up against the wall and see what sticks,"[46] would have no business bringing federal charges. The *U.S. Attorneys' Manual*, the book of guiding principles and regulations for federal prosecution,[47] articulates the governing rule in Standard 9-27.220:

> The attorney for the government should commence or recommend federal prosecution if he/she believes that the person's conduct constitutes a federal offense, that the admissible evidence will probably be sufficient to obtain and sustain a conviction, and that a substantial federal interest would be served by the prosecution ....[48]

Commentary in the *Manual* explains the meaning of the idea that the "evidence will probably be sufficient" to get a conviction:

> [B]oth as a matter of fundamental fairness and in the interest of the efficient administration of justice, no prosecution should be initiated against any person *unless the attorney for the government believes that the admissible evidence is sufficient to obtain and sustain a guilty verdict by an unbiased trier of fact.*[49]

In other words, the U.S. Attorney has to believe that he or she has the evidence to convict. And conviction in a criminal case, in the United States, requires a finding of guilt beyond a reasonable doubt. Without enough evidence to believe the prosecution could convince a judge or jury to that standard, the U.S. Attorney should not bring charges.

All of this would make any decision to go with federal criminal charges against the three officers difficult and complicated. In the case of Jordan Miles, that decision fell to the new U.S. Attorney, David J. Hickton.[50]

A new president routinely replaces nearly all U.S. Attorneys in all of the 93 districts around the country, usually with nominees from his or her own party.

President Obama nominated Hickton, a Pennsylvania native, to the position of U.S. Attorney for the Western District of Pennsylvania in May of 2010, and the Senate confirmed him on August 5, 2010—nearly eight months after the events involving Jordan Miles and the three Pittsburgh Police officers on Tioga Street. David Hickton graduated from the University of Pittsburgh School of Law in 1981. His law practice centered on civil (noncriminal) matters, including civil litigation, transportation issues, and commercial law, with a few forays into white-collar criminal defense. He was active in civic affairs, though not through elected or appointed office.[51] He had long aspired to serve as the U.S. Attorney, as a way to do work that would benefit the citizens of the region, especially in the area of civil rights law. Visitors to his office could not help but notice Hickton's affection for Robert F. Kennedy, the former U.S. Attorney General and a storied figure in the fight for racial equality and civil rights. Kennedy was Hickton's personal and professional role model, whose picture hung on Hickton's office wall. As Hickton took office as the new U.S. Attorney, he found waiting for him, courtesy of his predecessor, a file on the Jordan Miles case, containing a completed investigation and a fully prepared recommendation regarding whether or not he should bring charges against the officers. His predecessor as U.S. Attorney had deferred the decision to Hickton, since he would have to live with it.

The Federal Case against the Officers

The federal investigation of the case, now complete, contained all of the information gathered by the assigned FBI agents. It also contained a full legal analysis by veteran assistant U.S. Attorneys—career members of the staff who had supervised the investigation and delved deeply into the facts uncovered and the law involved. Looking over the full set of facts, the applicable law, and how those facts—in the form of evidence in court—would or would not prove the case, the assistant U.S. Attorneys had concluded that the evidence could not prove the case beyond a reasonable doubt under the high federal "willfully" standard. They recommended[52] that the U.S. Attorney decline to prosecute the officers and allow any further investigation and prosecution, if warranted, to come from the office of the county's district attorney, under Pennsylvania law. The final decision would come from Hickton himself.

The assistant U.S. Attorneys who had handled the case within his office, who had recommended not bringing charges, explained to Hickton why they believed he should decline to prosecute. Hickton remembers, however, that the investigating FBI agents had a different take. They wanted charges brought against the officers, because they thought the evidence sufficient to support the case and to result in a guilty verdict. Hickton "immediately ordered that [the investigation] be re-opened." He knew that the attorneys on his staff had already reached a conclusion, that they felt much of the investigative work had already finished. But Hickton wanted to start over from scratch. "I was extremely determined that we would look at all aspects of the case."

When the reopened investigation concluded, his staff recommended again that he not prosecute. The evidence in the case, they said, simply could not meet the law's willfulness standard. They said that the evidence might show, at most, a bad mistake about the amount of force used, which would not prove a crime under the federal law. Moreover, they told Hickton that evidence of the beating of Jordan—that is, the young man's actual injuries—"looked worse than" they actually were. The swelling of Jordan's face, as it appeared in that "horrible picture" so widely circulated in the media, "actually went down rather quickly," and Jordan thankfully had no broken bones and had required no further hospitalization after that night. The facts showed no permanent injury, and that would make it tough to prove the necessary intent.

Hickton remained unsatisfied. He ordered a third look at the evidence, but the attorneys on his staff came to the same conclusion: The evidence simply would not support a decision to charge and try the three police officers under federal law. Hickton eventually met with two top lawyers from the Civil Rights Division of the Department of Justice about the case. Both had served as part of, or supervisors on, hundreds of such investigations at the Department of Justice, and they reviewed the case in detail at his request. Hickton had deep respect for their experience, and he was disappointed when they told him they'd come to the same conclusion as his own staff: The evidence would not support federal criminal charges. When Hickton pushed back at their conclusion, the lawyers told him that the Department of Justice could not support him if he went forward. Hickton remembers raising his voice in anger and frustration before walking out of his office to the street and then walking for hours, trying to blow off steam.

He made his decision unhappily, knowing it would please no one: certainly not Jordan and his family and supporters, and not Hickton's own friends, allies, and colleagues in the African American community and the civil rights organizations in Pittsburgh. The police would also find his actions wanting; even with no charges brought, they would no doubt feel that the process had taken far too long. Nevertheless, with the evidence he had, the U.S. Attorney decided that he could not bring charges when there was uncertainty about whether he could prove them beyond a reasonable doubt.

Hickton decided to meet with Jordan Miles and his mother to inform them of his decision before making the public announcement. He felt that they should not find out in the press, that they had a right to know up front and to hear the reasons behind it. Hickton asked to meet with the family, and he also asked the two Department of Justice lawyers to return to Pittsburgh to participate in the meeting, which they did. Hickton and the two lawyers told Jordan and his mother that the government would not file federal charges against the officers and explained the reasons why, including the high standard they would have to meet in order to show a willful violation of the Constitution and the difficulty of proving the case beyond a reasonable doubt. Hickton remembers it as "a very tough meeting." He said that he did not know what the family expected coming into the meeting, "but I think they were surprised … they were shocked and speechless."

After this meeting, Hickton sent advance word of the decision to Nathan Harper, then Chief of Police in Pittsburgh, to leaders in the African American community, and to the lawyers for the three officers. Then, on May 4, 2011, almost 16 months after the incident on Tioga Street, U.S. Attorney Hickton read a statement that he had carefully written with his top staff in a news conference:

> Today, we announce that no federal criminal charges will be brought in the Jordan Miles matter.
>
> We just met with Jordan Miles and his family and informed them of our decision. We have also communicated our decision to the attorneys for the officers. This was a difficult and troubling case. The public, understandably, has many questions regarding what occurred. However, the narrow question before us is whether there is sufficient evidence to prove beyond a reasonable doubt that a crime was committed.
>
> Senior members of my staff, seasoned civil rights prosecutors from the Civil Rights Division and the FBI have conducted a thorough and independent review of this matter. I have also personally invested a great deal of time reviewing all aspects of the investigation into this incident.
>
> After this review, we have decided that we lack sufficient evidence to seek federal charges against the three police officers who were involved in the incident with Mr. Miles. In order to prevail in court on a criminal civil rights charge, the government must prove that the law enforcement officer willfully deprived a person of a federally protected right. I have concluded that the evidence in this case will not support the heavy burden of a criminal

charge against the officers. The conclusion I have reached is consistent with the conclusion reached by the Civil Rights Division of the United States Department of Justice.

After some explanation about why he could not say more, the statement concluded with a message for the Miles family and the community at large.

I understand that Mr. Miles, his family, and members of the community may be greatly disappointed by the news ..., while others may support the decision not to prosecute. Be assured that the United States Attorney's Office, the Civil Rights Division of the Department of Justice and the Federal Bureau of Investigation conducted a complete and thorough review and investigation of the events surrounding this matter. Our decision not to pursue federal charges is based upon a review of all of the facts developed by that extensive investigation and specific to this case. While no criminal indictment could be brought here, let me be clear about this: we will diligently investigate reports of illegal stops, detention and excessive force incidents, and stand ready to devote the resources required to ensure that all allegations of civil rights violations are fully investigated, and where appropriate, prosecuted.[53]

As planned, Hickton took no questions. The U.S. Department of Justice issued its own statement, which closely paralleled Hickton's.[54] The media reported Hickton's decision, and if they could get nothing more from him, they got plenty of comment from others, such as Dan O'Hara, then president of the Fraternal Order of Police lodge in Pittsburgh. "They're vindicated," he said of the officers. "This was a good day for the officers and the department. The system works. It leaves very little to the imagination that these guys were doing what they're trained to do."[55] Others felt much differently. "I disagree with their assessment that they don't have a case to prove beyond a reasonable doubt," said Kerry Lewis, the attorney who had already represented Jordan on the criminal charges against him and also retained to represent Jordan and his family in a separate federal civil lawsuit (discussed in Chapter 5). "The findings are quite simple and straight-forward. He was beat to a pulp." Lewis called the decision not to prosecute the officers "ridiculous."[56] Tim Stevens, chairman of the Black Political Empowerment Project and one of the city's preeminent civil rights leaders, took pains to point out that Hickton's decision not to prosecute did not vindicate the officers at all. "Allegations of police misconduct and brutality were not proven baseless against these three officers," he said. "If one reads this statement very carefully, it does not say a crime was not committed." All Hickton's statement really said was that the federal prosecutors couldn't prove that a crime had been committed.

For David Hickton himself, the decision left him unsettled and unsatisfied. Years later, the case still pulled at him. "I made a decision, and I would stand by it. It was not the decision I emotionally wanted to make, but it was the correct legal decision ... based on good advice by good people," he says. But "it is still a raw point with me, all these years later." He is not alone in his dissatisfaction. Brandi Fisher, who created Pittsburgh's Alliance for Police Accountability because of the Jordan Miles case, understood that the evidence had to meet the high burden of proof.[57] But years later, she still feels the officers should have faced charges. "I thought it was bullcrap. I thought it was a cop out."[58] And Sala Udin, one of the most prominent members of the city's African American community, a former member of Pittsburgh City Council, and an ally of Hickton, still feels the sting of the decision. Years later, he cannot understand why Hickton did not file federal charges. "I am left really disappointed that [Hickton] could not seek justice in a more assertive way," he said. "I don't believe it was a legally justifiable reason. It had to do with politics."[59]

OTHER DECISIONS IN THE WAKE OF THE FEDERAL INVESTIGATION

On May 5, 2011, one day following Hickton's announcement, came another official statement. At a news conference, Pittsburgh's Chief of Police, Nathan Harper, and the city's Mayor, Luke Ravenstahl, stood together to declare that the city would immediately reinstate Officers Michael Saldutte, Richard Ewing, and David Sisak. They would return to work from their paid administrative suspensions, and the police department would not discipline them. They would receive not so much as a reprimand for their conduct in the case.

Luke Ravenstahl, the young, inexperienced "boy mayor" who took office at 26 when the incumbent mayor died,[60] attempted to sound a conciliatory note. "I don't believe there is anybody in Pittsburgh, especially myself as the leader of this great city, who doesn't wish that the events of January 12, 2010 did not occur," he said. But with the officers cleared by the federal government, reinstating the officers constituted the correct action. The incident was "thoroughly investigated by the Department of Justice and the FBI," and with no basis for charges, the officers needed to return to work.[61] The Mayor said that the time had come for the city to try to heal, and allowing the officers to resume work was part of that.[62] Chief Harper, a Pittsburgher who had come up through the ranks to become chief in 2006 and the first African American to hold the top job since Chief Earl Buford served from 1992 to 1995,[63] said that he wanted the officers reinstated because of the federal findings and because of the findings of the OMI. OMI had not released the findings of its investigation to the public. But according to Harper, OMI had concluded that its investigation had failed to "prove or disprove" allegations against the officers,[64] and these conclusions "matched the federal findings."[65] The city had therefore closed the OMI investigation.

The statement about OMI came as a surprise. Jordan, his family, and the many observers of the case still awaited OMI's findings, so to hear that the city had closed the OMI matter shocked them. It turned out that the city closed the OMI investigation and finalized the report *on the same day* as Chief Harper's reinstatement announcement—May 5, 2011. While the city never released the OMI report, Harper's statements were factually correct. Based on interviews with Jordan, all three officers, at least nine other witnesses, and review of a considerable amount of other evidence, OMI had looked at the case from the points of view of the officers and of Jordan.[66] The separate versions of the story, OMI said, "could not be more different," and so "each version of this incident will be analyzed as if it were true to determine whether the officers violated Bureau of Police rules and regulations." After a thorough review of the "Police Version" and the "Jordan Miles Version," if the officers' version was correct, "it is hard to understand why Jordan"—who the report characterized as "a fine young man" who had "resisted the easy temptations of the street" and had a "bright future"—would have run and then "engage(d) in a violent struggle" with the officers if he had not committed a crime. On the other hand, if the officers had not identified themselves, as Jordan said, "Jordan's reaction would be understandable." In addition, "resolving this case also comes down to the Mountain Dew bottle," which OMI called "the catalyst for every action the police took, including their belief that Jordan may have been armed. If there was no Mountain Dew bottle, the officers' actions were unjustified." But "if the Mountain Dew bottle existed, we are sure the officers now wish they would have sent it to the property room." The report stated that it had found no "neutral evidence," despite the testimony of Monica Wooding at the preliminary hearing directly contradicting the police version of events. Wooding's testimony had caused Judge Oscar Petite to dismiss the charges against Jordan. But the OMI report dismissed the significance of this evidence. In short, the case came down to the word of Officers Saldutte, Sisak, and Ewing, on the one hand, and Jordan Miles on the other. "It is OMI's policy not to take the word of the officers over the word of the complainant and vice versa," the report said; therefore, "the allegations against the officers are closed as NOT RESOLVED."

Chief Harper admitted that the incident had left Jordan physically injured,[67] and he appeared to concede that Jordan had committed no crime when the police stopped him. He even said that officers need to realize that a person may run from them out of fear and not because they had committed a crime.[68] But that did not mean the officers had done anything wrong. Put simply, he said, "there is no evidence to show [Jordan's injuries were] the result of wrongful conduct by the officers."[69] He took a soft tone, discussing the incident as a "teachable moment" for the city. But in the end, he left little question where he believed the blame should lie for what happened. "From this, we would hope that the young people realize that when a police officer approaches them, and if they've done nothing wrong, to see what the police officer wants instead of running away from the police officer," adding "we aren't the enemy out there."[70] Translation: Jordan suffered injuries, and the officers might even have made a mistake in thinking he was up to something. But, bottom line, Jordan caused this; it was his fault. If he hadn't done anything wrong, he had no reason to run. And no one—not even someone who had done nothing—should run from the police when ordered to stop.

THE FALLOUT

If Hickton's announcement had deeply disappointed Jordan and his family and supporters, the reinstatement of the officers landed like a hard kick in the gut. Jordan, now 19 and more than a year removed from the incident, could hardly grasp what had happened in 24 hours. "Emotionally, it's really, really hard to understand everything that went on, to try to make sense of everything that's going on," he said.[71] His mother, Terez Miles, said that the decisions not to prosecute and then to reinstate the officers were "unfortunate because I think the officers are clearly guilty of wrongdoing." The U.S. Attorney's office, she said, "went out of (its) way to say they didn't think the police did anything right here or that Jordy did anything wrong," so the lack of charges reflected not vindication or lack of misconduct but the lack of enough evidence to prove a case. And as far as the reinstatement of the officers, she called it "bad news for the city. I don't feel any safer with them out there."[72] The president of the Pittsburgh chapter of the NAACP, M. Gayle Moss, characterized her organization as "outraged," calling the incident "a modern-day lynching."[73] Elizabeth Pittinger, the long-time executive director of the CPRB, said simply, "it sucks."[74]

But amidst the celebration, on one side, and anger on the other over these two crucial decisions, the many voices seemed to overlook an important fact. Federal authorities had concluded their investigation, and they would not file criminal charges; the City of Pittsburgh's own internal investigation, conducted by OMI, had also ended without any findings of misconduct. But the district attorney's office would investigate the officers under the laws of the state of Pennsylvania. Having insisted that they would await the end of the federal probe because "we don't do simultaneous investigations,"[75] the district attorney's office now became the central focus of the question of whether the officers would face criminal charges.

On May 5, 2011, as the city and the police department reinstated the three officers, the possibility of criminal charges remained unresolved. Federal charges would not follow, but charges under Pennsylvania's law remained a real possibility. Of course, convicting police officers of criminal conduct would not be easy in state court where a jury would still give officers the benefit of the doubt. But Pennsylvania's law—*any* state's law, for that matter—would pose a lower burden of proof than would the federal statute. The district attorney would have to prove misconduct, excessive force, or the like but would not have to prove that the officers did these things in an effort to willfully deprive Jordan of his constitutional rights; the enormous burden of proof under federal law would not stand in the district attorney's way. Put simply, a case against the officers in state court would undoubtedly prove easier than trying to do so in a federal court. And here lies an unanswered question: Why did the city and the police department seemingly have no hesitation about reinstating the officers, *with an active state criminal investigation against all three still underway?* Chief Harper said in his comments concerning the reinstatement that "we spoke to [the District Attorney's office] this morning" and the office had asked for some documents, but after that conversation, "I am very comfortable bringing the officers back."[76] One might wonder whether Chief Harper knew something the public did not. But perhaps he just knew the way things worked in Pittsburgh.

A month went by, and the district attorney neither made any determination nor issued any statements. A group of citizens gathered signatures and delivered a petition to the district attorney's office, "asking him to prosecute."[77] Brandi Fisher, the chair of the Alliance for Police Accountability, which helped shepherd the signature gathering, said that "what charges [Zappala] brings, we leave to him. But we'd expect assault, false arrest and perjury to be among them." Tim Stevens, the leader of the Black Political Empowerment Project, said that the case "has provoked outrage across all racial and economic lines" in the city. "Charge them," he said, and "let a jury decide." Jordan's mother, Terez

Miles, said that "I pray the District Attorney will do the right thing" because "for him to allow this to continue is unacceptable."[78] When the petitions with thousands of signatures were delivered to the district attorney's office, Zappala did not emerge from the office to accept the petitions. His spokesman would only say that the matter was "still under review" and would give no timetable for the completion of the investigation.

Another month went by, then another, and many more. On May 16, 2012— a full year after the federal authorities declined to prosecute and handed their investigation findings over to the district attorney's office—the other shoe dropped. District Attorney Zappala announced that he would not charge the three officers involved in the altercation with Jordan Miles. The district attorney said that there was "not a prosecutable case" against Officers Sisak, Saldutte, and Ewing, because he did not have sufficient evidence.[79] To make their decision, the district attorney said that he and his investigators read the depositions taken in the separate civil case filed by Jordan Miles against the officers; they also relied on the reports of four expert consultants, particularly a report by Clifford W. Jobe, Jr., a retired state police officer who trains police officers. In his report, Jobe said the three officers used tactics "consistent with accepted law enforcement practices, training and standards" to subdue Jordan.[80] (Jobe's report also made clear that he accepted the officers' version of the events of January 12 and not Jordan's version.[81]) District Attorney Zappala made a point of saying that he agreed with the federal government, and he defended his office's record in prosecuting cases against police officers accused of misconduct involving African Americans and other minorities. He'd prosecuted John Charmo and Jeffrey Cooperstein, two white officers involved in separate instances in the killings of black men, and had even sought a new opportunity to try the officers involved in the death of Jonny Gammage. In the prior 18 months, he said, he had investigated 13 other cases involving allegations of police misconduct.[82] But this case would not see charges from his office. Asked whether he should have allowed this case to go to trial and let a jury decide, Zappala replied that if he had, a judge would throw the case out for lack of evidence before a jury could decide. "The case wouldn't get to a jury."[83]

Little about the reactions to the decision not to prosecute would surprise anyone who had followed the case. Jordan Miles told KDKA-TV that he was "a little disappointed" but not surprised.[84] Ms. Miles said that, after the long period of waiting, she felt "not surprised at all" and only felt shocked that "it took him this long to come out and admit it."[85] Supporters of Jordan Miles condemned the decision, but Sergeant Mike LaPorte, then president of the Pittsburgh Fraternal Order of Police lodge, lauded it. "It is reassuring that

District Attorney Zappala's office did a thorough and impartial investigation the results of which proved what we knew all along." LaPorte praised Zappala for "not bowing to self-interest groups who fueled unrest over this incident," though he also complained that the investigation took far too long. "[T]his is police work 101, and anyone who knows what happened would be able to see that."[86]

Zappala's announcement marked the end of the criminal investigations of the officers for their conduct on January 12, 2010, on Tioga Street. This meant that neither the three officers nor Jordan himself would face the possibility of criminal convictions. This left many in Pittsburgh unsatisfied, feeling that the officers, or Jordan, should face a jury for criminal conduct. With both federal and state prosecutors declining to charge the officers because of lack of evidence, and with District Attorney Zappala not refiling the charges against Jordan after Judge Petite threw them out, the only forum left for a full hearing about what had happened, in front of a jury of citizens, would be a civil trial in federal court, in a case filed by Jordan against the city and the three officers.

CHAPTER 5

THE REMAINING ARENA: CIVIL LITIGATION

With the criminal investigations closed and no decision on responsibility for the events of January 12 by either the Office of Municipal Investigations (OMI) or the Citizen Complaint Review Board (CCRB), a civil lawsuit remained the only path for Jordan Miles to take to claim his rights—or from the point of view of the officers, to show that they had done nothing wrong. And that direction, while the only alternative left, would prove long, difficult, and expensive.

SECTION 1983: THE ESSENTIAL TOOL OF CIVIL RIGHTS LITIGATION

Like most people suing over police misconduct, Jordan's lawyers brought his case under the federal Civil Rights Act of 1871,[1] known as Section 1983. Congress created the law, one of a group of statutes[2] enacted after the American Civil War, to protect freed black people from actions by the former Confederate states and lower-level governments in those states. This statute creates a basis for a lawsuit for those who have suffered a particular kind of legal deprivation at the hands of governments or their officials. The applicable parts of Section 1983 read as follows:

> Every person who, under color of any statute, ordinance, regulation, custom or usage, of any state or territory ... subjects ... any citizen of the United States or other person within the jurisdiction thereof to the deprivation of any rights, privileges or immunities secured by the Constitution and laws, shall be liable to the party injured in an action at law, suit in equity, or other proper proceeding for redress ....[3]

The idea behind Section 1983 was that persons suffering the loss of their rights at the hands of governments or government officials could use a federal court action to assert and insist upon those rights and obtain damages. Since the law's passage, Section 1983 has served as "the statutory basis for ... police abuse actions" brought in federal court against state or local police officers.[4] The U.S. Supreme Court has stated multiple times that the law itself does not create any new rights. Rather, it gives people a way to uphold their existing rights when state agents (like police officers) violate those rights.[5] Jordan's lawyers used a Section 1983 complaint, filed well before the outcomes of the criminal investigations against the police, to defend his constitutional rights against illegal arrest and excessive use of force.

In order to grasp the discussion of civil litigation, we need a few definitions. With a civil case, we move out of the realm of thinking about crimes, for which the person charged might go to prison, and instead we think about assessment of liability and damages—who, if anyone, might be to blame (i.e., be liable) for an injury (physical, legal, economic, or otherwise) to another, and the cost (i.e., the damages) of those injuries. Unlike criminal law, a civil lawsuit is brought by the person who alleges that he or she suffered injuries; we call that person the plaintiff. The plaintiff sues the person who supposedly caused the injuries; that person is the defendant. We refer to both the plaintiff and the defendant in civil cases as parties to the civil lawsuit. At least four significant barriers face plaintiffs suing police under Section 1983. Jordan's case met the criteria to overcome the first three barriers, but we must understand what they look like if we want to comprehend fully the difficulties faced by people suing the police. The fourth barrier would play a major role in Jordan's case.

1. First, a Section 1983 plaintiff would need to show that the actions taken by the defendants in the case met the statute's requirements as "under color of" the law of any state's "statute, regulation, custom, or usage ..." (i.e., actions they took as part of their duties under the authority of state law). In his case, Jordan's attorneys alleged that the police officers, as employees of the Pittsburgh Bureau of Police, violated the Fourth Amendment of the U.S. Constitution. They acted in their positions as police officers, carrying out the duties and priorities of the police department; under any reasonable definition, they acted "under color of" law for purposes of Section 1983.

2. Second, a plaintiff in a case brought under Section 1983 must show a deprivation of "a right secured by the U.S. Constitution or a federal statute."[6] Jordan alleged that the police deprived him of his constitutional

rights in three ways. First, Jordan's lawyers alleged abuse of the constitutional legal process for arrest, seizure, and prosecution, carried out by the three officers. Second and third, Jordan alleged false arrest and use of excessive force; both of these allegations, if true, would violate Jordan's rights under the Fourth Amendment to the U.S. Constitution, which guarantees that "the right of the people to be secure in their persons, houses, papers, and effects, against unreasonable searches and seizures, shall not be violated ...."[7] Fourth Amendment history makes clear that both an arrest and any use of force by a police officer qualify as a seizure of the person. In an arrest, the officer takes the person into custody; an officer uses force correctly only to make an arrest or other legitimate and constitutional police business. Performing an arrest falsely, or using more than the allowed and proper amount of force, violates the guarantee in the Fourth Amendment against "unreasonable" seizures.

3. The third hurdle posed in Section 1983 cases makes it difficult and sometimes impossible for those wronged by the police to hold officers accountable. When police action results in damage, injury, or death, and the injured party brings a lawsuit, police may assert a defense called *qualified immunity*. In practical terms, a successful qualified immunity defense means that the police officer may have violated the Constitution, but nevertheless has a complete legal shield from any consequences for those actions if the constitutional right in question is not "clearly established"—meaning that the right "must be sufficiently clear that a reasonable official would understand that what he is doing violates that right."[8] To laypeople, this may seem bizarre. But the Supreme Court has reaffirmed the qualified immunity doctrine for decades, and it certainly constitutes the most substantial legal barrier to bringing Section 1983 suits against police. In Jordan's case, the rights against illegal arrest and excessive use of force have long been "clearly established," so the three officers would not have the qualified immunity that has caused many police cases to fail before they get to court.

RIGHTS MATTER AND SO DOES MONEY

The fourth and final hurdle all Section 1983 plaintiffs must deal with concerns economics—having the resources necessary to litigate the case and to pay the lawyers for the years of work involved. A Section 1983 lawsuit resembles a *tort* suit, which is a lawsuit that one private party files against another, for damages due to negligence in, for example, an automobile accident. The difference, of course, is that Section 1983 cases concern damages allegedly caused by state agents (police officers, prison guards, and so on) acting "under color of" state law.

In tort cases, American law allows attorneys to take these cases on a *contingency-fee basis*: The attorney represents the plaintiff without a paid fee or retainer at the beginning, on the clear understanding that the lawyer will receive payment if and when the case produces a verdict and damages for the plaintiff, or when the parties enter into a settlement. (One-third of the settlement or verdict usually goes to the lawyer, but the plaintiff doesn't pay the lawyer anything unless and until the settlement or verdict payment is received from the defendant.) In such cases, the attorney typically pays for all costs of the litigation up-front, with those costs reimbursed out of the eventual settlement or verdict. Costs often include not just filing fees but the cost of pretrial discovery (the work done to prepare for the eventual trial) such as depositions and the retention of expert witnesses necessary for the case. Lawyers foot the bills for the costs, in expectation of recouping them down the road when the defendant pays. While most tort suits for damages eventually result in recovery of some money for the plaintiff, some of these cases come with the risk that no money will be recovered, or the money that does come will not cover costs, let alone pay for the attorney's time and work. This means that lawyers won't take cases with so high a risk that they may never receive payment, resulting in the fact that some cases will attract no lawyer interest.

However, if most tort cases eventually result in recovery of some money, this does not necessarily follow for most Section 1983 cases. And therefore most lawyers—even those with the appropriate background and skill—face a daunting choice when agreeing to represent a Section 1983 plaintiff.

1. These cases have always been notoriously difficult to win. Few juries wish to side against a police officer.
2. While some Section 1983 cases could involve serious injuries and even deaths—generating the possibility of significant damages—for most civil rights cases, it is difficult to decide how much these types of damages are "worth." For example, imagine a person illegally searched on a city sidewalk by a police officer during an illegal detention that lasts 25 minutes; the officer finds no contraband, and no charges result. The detention and the search may have no legal basis, but how can a jury put a value to this 25 minutes of lost time and invasion of personal space? Do the damages amount to $10,000 or $100,000? Or just $1?

3. Civil rights cases tend to last many years—much longer than typical tort suits—and civil rights cases often involve difficult issues that many lawyers do not have the experience to take on and that require a specialized set of skills.

In all, this means that most people with civil rights claims will have nowhere to turn because "some civil-rights violations would yield damages too small to justify the expense of litigation ...."[9]

The U.S. Congress attempted to address some of these economic issues more than four decades ago. In a law passed in 1976, called the Civil Rights Attorneys' Fees Awards Act,[10] Congress declared that the prevailing plaintiff in a Section 1983 civil rights lawsuit could obtain attorney's fees and costs from the other side in the litigation (in other words, the municipality or its agencies such as a police department) in cases that "would yield damages too small to justify the expense of litigation."[11] Congress passed the Fees Act as a way to make more civil rights claims economically viable.[12] The world before the Fees Act had shown a "well-documented" lack of civil rights lawyers willing to take these cases; the Fees Act aimed to change this by "making more lawyers available for private enforcement of the nation's public interest."[13] In other words, the Fees Act would correct the legal market's understandable failure to take on these cases because of their lack of economic viability—and to supply the funds for vindication of federal civil rights through a law that required losing parties—governments and their agencies, who had violated constitutional rights—to pay for it.

The U.S. Supreme Court has made repeated decisions that weaken the Fees Act, defeating Congress's intentions. In *Marek v. Chesney*, decided in 1985, the Court approved an interpretation of Rule 68 of the Federal Rules of Civil Procedure that allowed it to apply to civil rights cases. Rule 68, which had existed for decades, allowed a defendant to make an offer to settle a case "on specific terms, with costs accrued." Under Rule 68, if the final judgment (the amount of money) the plaintiff eventually receives in the case turns out to be "not more favorable than the unaccepted offer, the offeree must pay the costs incurred after the offer was made."[14] In other words, if the judgment the plaintiff is actually awarded at the end of the trial is less than what the defendant had offered earlier on, the plaintiff has to pay all of the costs the defendant accrued in fighting the case after the defendant made the offer, and the plaintiff cannot recover any costs incurred by the plaintiff after the offer. Thus (1) if the defendant city or police agency makes an offer of settlement to the plaintiff in a police misconduct case, and (2) if the plaintiff rejects this offer and (3) the final judgment amount in the plaintiff's favor does not exceed the earlier offer, then (4) the plaintiff's lawyers can receive no attorney's fees (cannot be paid) for any work done after the date of the rejection of the offer, and (5) the plaintiff has to pay the defendant's costs and fees after the settlement is made. If the offer is made early in the pretrial litigation phase, considerable resources would still need to be expended in moving the case forward after the offer, if it is rejected. *Marek* gave defendants in police misconduct cases a powerful and effective tool: By making an early, low offer to settle, defendants had the opportunity "to create leverage on plaintiff's counsel to settle early and perhaps for less than the claim seems to be worth, for fear of missing out on fees almost entirely."[15]

In a second action that weakened the Fees Act, the Supreme Court approved a move by defendants in a civil rights case that seemed calculated to drive a wedge between civil rights plaintiffs and their lawyers. In *Evans v. Jeff D.*, in 1986, the Court sustained the terms of a settlement offer in which the acceptance of the offer by the plaintiff required that the plaintiff waive all claims to attorneys' fees under the Fees Act. The plaintiff would receive an amount to settle the claim, but defendants would pay nothing for the legal work required to bring the claim. The plaintiff's lawyers would find themselves in the position where they would have to advise the client to accept the settlement if the settlement best served the client's interest, but doing so would go directly against the lawyers' interests. Accepting the settlement would mean that the lawyers, who had taken the case and invested time and money into it (perhaps for many years), would receive nothing and would lose everything they had paid up-front to support the case. The Supreme Court found the arrangement unobjectionable, saying that it did not violate the Fees Act.

THE DISCOVERY PROCESS

In the case of *Jordan Miles v. City of Pittsburgh*, the discovery process created the first window into what the evidence in the civil cases would look like, in particular the identities of the likely witnesses and what they would say. The discovery process occurs after the case begins and prior to trial; during this phase, both parties attempt to flesh out the facts of the case by using depositions (the taking of sworn testimony prior to trial outside of court, with lawyers asking questions and a word-for-word record of the proceedings created), written questions and answers called interrogatories, and other tools. The idea is to uncover the facts before going to trial, so that the parties will have the full facts of the case either for a settlement or for a trial. Discovery revealed a case in which the police officers would contest the main facts with vigor and also the fact that two key law enforcement players would give crucial evidence that would support Jordan's case. Neither side emerged from discovery holding all the cards, making the case likely to go to trial.

The depositions (sworn statements, taken through pretrial questioning by the lawyers that resembles what will go on in trial as witnesses testify) of the three police officers tracked the contents of the initial police report almost to the letter. These statements added context and depth to the officers' training and experience. For example, Officer Saldutte had training (given by a former agent of the Bureau of Alcohol, Tobacco, Firearms, and Explosives) in recognizing the traits of someone who has a concealed weapon[16]; Officer Sisak had performed over 1,000 arrests in four years, and he had made a kind of specialty of gun arrests, although he did not have the special training in spotting concealed guns that Saldutte had; Sisak attributed his success to his own "attention to detail" and the types of high-crime areas he patrolled.[17] The stories of all three officers on the core event were consistent with one another and closely matched the original police report and Officer Saldutte's testimony at the preliminary hearing.

Two things stood out in the depositions. First, the officers absolutely believed that they were engaged in a life or death struggle with an armed man who had a gun in his right coat pocket. For example, Officer Sisak testified in his deposition that he saw a weapon "right off the bat .... When he grabbed his jacket, I believed he had a gun."[18] And Sisak still believed it on the day of his deposition, over 18 months later, despite the fact that multiple searches never turned up a gun and the pocket allegedly contained a soda bottle. Asked if not finding a gun or anything he had learned since had caused him to change his mind, Officer Sisak said "absolutely not." Just because a gun had not been found did not mean one had not been in Jordan's pocket: "I'm still 100 percent certain he had a gun."[19]

Second, the presence of fear in the situation is real. In the officers' telling, they follow their observations, their training, and their experience, and it leads them to think that the man they saw had a gun, and for that reason, they must arrest him. They use that training and experience and their familiarity with hand-to-hand fighting to bring the man down, and they struggle to disarm him. Despite the training, the experience, and the advantages of both size and numbers, they believe that death or serious injuries are real possibilities. As they struggle with the handcuffs, Officers Ewing and Saldutte are on either side of the man, who is prone and face down, and Officer Sisak is positioned on his knees, facing the man's head. The man pulls his right hand away, and under him, toward that pocket, and Sisak hears Saldutte say, "I lost the cuff, he's going for it"—the gun. Sisak sees the man's right hand go toward his waist, underneath him. He feels the danger in that moment; he's the one positioned where he'd be facing the gun barrel, if the man got it out of his pocket: "I just remember seeing his hand go down. I thought he was going to shoot me."[20] With a blow to the man's head, he stopped trying to move, and the click of the handcuffs on both his wrists ended the struggle. But the certainty that the officers were facing a man with a gun who was fighting them—and for Sisak, that he was about to be shot—never left; this certainty shows up in the deposition testimony as if it had happened only the day before.

Jordan's deposition testimony also did not vary significantly from the statements he had made earlier. As he had then, he recounted leaving his mother's home for this grandmother's house around the block and his bedroom there. As he walked in the street in order to avoid the icy sidewalks, an unmarked car drove up to him, very close, and three large men came out all at once, yelling at him: Where are the drugs, the money, the guns? Surprised, not knowing who the men were, he was scared. These men never identified themselves as police officers and wore no uniforms or badges. Jordan attempted to run, but fell on the ice almost immediately, and the men jumped on him and began a sustained beating. He thought the men wanted to rob him; he struggled, tried to get up but failed. And as with the officers, fear hit him hard. "I was terrified," said Jordan, thinking he would be shot. He lived in the neighborhood and was well aware that there is "shooting in that part of town where I am." He said he screamed, pleading with the officers, "please don't kill me, please don't shoot, me, oh my God." He thought the men were going to abduct him: "I thought they would put me in the car and kill me and throw me in the river."[21] He recalls struggling for his life and beginning to pray out loud—until he was hit, hard, with some kind of object on the right side of his head.

Thus, the depositions of the three officers and of Jordan showed, just as the initial reports and statements had, that the two stories—the officers' and Jordan's—had crucial differences. Was Jordan lurking by the side of the building? Did the police ever identify themselves? But one could find commonalities, too. The most important of these was something none of them could see, but all of them felt: fear.

The depositions of two other witnesses would attract the most attention, and both came from the Pittsburgh Police Department. The first witness, RaShall Brackney, had attained the rank of commander in 2000, at just 39 years old. A product of the very Homewood neighborhood where Jordan lived and a graduate of Pittsburgh's Carnegie Mellon University, Brackney had joined the department in 1984.[22] She rose rapidly, from patrol officer to sergeant, worked as assistant to the chief, and started and ran the department's crime analysis program. In 1996, the department promoted her to lieutenant, where she oversaw patrol in the city's Hill District, and from there, Brackney moved to the Training Academy, overseeing all training for recruits. In 2000, upon promotion to commander, she oversaw operations at the Municipal Courts Building and then moved to the Special Operations Division, in 2001. That assignment included oversight of SWAT teams, hostage negotiation work, the bomb squad, motor and motorcycle patrol, and even river rescues.

Commander Brackney became a witness in the case of *Jordan Miles v. City of Pittsburgh* because before the events of January 12, 2010, she had done two stints as commander of Zone 5—the police zone covering Homewood and much of the surrounding area. During her second command there, two of the officers involved in the case (David Sisak and Richard Ewing) worked under Brackney in Zone 5. (Michael Saldutte did not serve under her.) Brackney gave deposition testimony about the disciplinary records of both of the officers. Also, although she had not been in command of Zone 5 on January 12, 2010, Commander Brackney also testified in her deposition about some aspects of the incident because the Chief of Police had asked her to look at the case. The Mountain Dew bottle became one focus of questioning in the deposition. Brackney described herself as a stickler for detail in police work, and with a person arrested for aggravated assault on a police officer—as Jordan had been—having the evidence to show exactly what started the fight would make a big difference. "If there was a bulge" in the person's clothing, and that formed the basis for the encounter, "we should be able to identify the bulge." She got more specific, stating, "If the bulge was a Mountain Dew bottle, if we weren't going to keep it, we should have photographed it. There should have been some evidence that it existed."[23]

The other witness from the police department was Chief of Police Nathan Harper. Harper had monitored the case from the beginning; he had ordered the OMI investigation, and he had had extensive discussions about the case with Deputy Chief Paul Donaldson[24] and with Commander Brackney, among others.[25] By the time of his deposition, on June 16, 2011, Harper knew the case and its details well—well enough to have reinstated the three officers the previous month, after the U.S. Attorney's Office ended the federal investigation. Chief Harper said that, given what the officers reported—seeing a bulge in the unidentified man's pocket, the pocket hanging down as if containing something heavy, and the man touching the pocket with one of his hands—he felt that they had probable cause to stop the man.[26] As for Jordan Miles's assertion that the officers had not identified themselves as police, Chief Harper said that "we'll never know the truth of that"—strikingly, Harper did not call Jordan's statement wrong or untrue. If Jordan did tell the truth, then his detention and the use of force by the officers that followed was, indeed, wrong.[27] But at the same time, Harper said he had "no reason" not to accept the officers' version of events (in which they asserted that they had clearly and repeatedly identified themselves).[28] The blame for the whole incident, Harper said, lay with Jordan. "What troubles me is the fact that this all could have been avoided by just the fact that Miles lived in the neighborhood, could have answered the officers' questions, and conducted himself where he wouldn't have run." This answer could not have come as a surprise because it tracked the Chief's statement at the May 5 news conference, a little over a month earlier, during which he had announced that he had reinstated the three officers to duty.[29]

Despite taking the expected road of supporting his officers, one surprise did emerge. The Chief stated unequivocally that the now-infamous Mountain Dew bottle, allegedly found in the pocket of Jordan Miles when the officers finally subdued him, "should have been retained for purposes of evidence."[30] Officer Saldutte had made a mistake in tossing it away. In fact, Chief Harper went further than Commander Brackney, who had testified that the officers might have photographed the bottle; according to Harper, the officers should have saved it. Failing to preserve this piece of evidence, he said, violated police department policy.[31]

SHAPING THE CASE FOR TRIAL

The creation of a factual record through the discovery process set the stage to get the case ready to go to trial. First came pretrial efforts to settle. On June 13, 2011, the defendants made an offer to settle the whole case. Formally called an Offer of Judgment, under Federal Rule of Civil Procedure 68,[32] it offered Jordan Miles $180,000 to close the case.[33] But Jordan and his family rejected the offer.[34] Speaking well before the deadline to accept or reject the city's proposal, attorney Kerry Lewis, one of two lawyers who would represent Jordan Miles in the trial, said the question went beyond whatever money the city offered. "This case is about the policies in place that we believe have to be changed." The dismissal of the offer did more, of course, than simply say no to the city's bid to get the case settled. It also engaged the gears of Federal Rule 68: if the case later resulted in a verdict or settlement less than the offered $180,000, Jordan's lawyers could recover no costs and fees that they incurred later than the offer was made, and Jordan would also be liable for the defendants' costs and fees after that date. As explained earlier, this made litigating the case riskier. Attorney Lewis told the media he understood the risks: "If our verdict does not exceed $180,000, then we would not be entitled to counsel fees as awarded by the government," he said.[35]

Approximately 10 months later, word came on April 24, 2012, that the City of Pittsburgh, a defendant in the case along with the three officers, had agreed to a settlement with Jordan.[36] The settlement of $75,000 released the city from the case but did not alter the case against the individual officers; those claims stayed in place and unchanged. The city would also remain obligated to pay any damages or fees assessed against the officers.[37] With any claims against the city resolved, the case would proceed in a legal context that accurately reflected everything about the facts that had come to light in the media after the incident and in the discovery process: two different stories with many points of agreement. The settlement with the city meant that no issues of the city's responsibility for the conduct of the officer would distract attention from those core issues.

That left pretrial motions, common to any case that would go to trial.[38] The subject of most of these motions related directly to what would happen at the trial, such as which witnesses would and would not testify, in certain instances what the court would allow the witnesses to testify about, and whether certain pieces of evidence or lines of testimony would come before the jury at all. These arguments would come before Federal District Judge Gary L. Lancaster, who would preside over the case. Judge Lancaster, who then served as Chief Judge of the U.S. District Court for the Western District of Pennsylvania (covering Allegheny County, which encompasses Pittsburgh, and 24 other counties in the western part of the state), had served on the court since December of 1993. The first African American ever to serve as Chief Judge in the Western District of Pennsylvania,[39] Judge Lancaster had graduated from the University of Pittsburgh School of Law. He had served as regional counsel to the state's Human Relations Commission and then as an Assistant District Attorney, after which he entered private practice for nine years. He returned to public service as a U.S. Magistrate (an appointed judicial officer, not a full judge, who does certain judicial work) and then became a full-fledged judge in 1993. Thus when Judge Lancaster took up the pretrial motions in the case, he had years of experience on the bench. He also had a reputation for showing all who appeared before him fairness and respect, as well as the ability to handle any kind of case. A fellow judge described him as "the Walter Payton of the federal bench—he was tough but he was a sweet guy."[40] He had a keen intellect and an ability to cut through the issues with fairness[41]; those two qualities came to the fore in a conference with the lawyers in Jordan's case on July 9, 2012,[42] during which Judge Lancaster decided the large number of motions still pending on the witnesses and the testimony.

In typical business-like fashion, Judge Lancaster greeted the lawyers and got right to it: "We have a number of things we have to get through, I'm thinking to do it rather quickly." The first matter concerned a piece of evidence. Witness Monica Wooding had spoken with the three officers through her window on the night of January 12; the struggle between the officers and Jordan had happened outside her house. She had testified at the preliminary hearing in the state's case against Jordan Miles that she had *not* said what the officers attributed to her in their report and in their testimony, and this caused Judge Oscar Petite to dismiss the charges against Jordan. However, two months after the initial incident, something else had happened: Ms. Wooding had discovered an ammunition clip in her yard. She called law enforcement, and they came and retrieved it. The defense now wanted to use that ammunition clip to argue that it showed that Jordan did in fact have a gun with him on the night of the altercation (although it also could have come from one of the officers fighting with Jordan or from someone else entirely). Jordan's lawyer's moved to exclude the ammunition clip from evidence, and Judge Lancaster agreed, calling its proposed use by the defense "speculative."[43]

After deciding several other minor matters, Judge Lancaster moved on to a crucial issue. Jordan's lawyers wanted to use information from the officers' disciplinary history and history of complaints by civilians as "prior bad acts" evidence—proof that the actors (in this case, the officers) had done particular bad actions in the past, in order to prove in the current case the person's "motive, opportunity, intent, preparation, plan, knowledge, identity, absence of mistake, or lack of accident."[44] Judges tend to exercise caution in allowing the use of "prior bad acts" evidence; in particular, they prohibit the use of this kind of proof as character evidence to show that the person involved had a bad character and "on a particular occasion the person acted in accordance with the character or trait."[45] The judge has discretion to allow the use of "prior bad acts" but only to prove motive or other things that do not imply that the person acted because of his or her flawed character. For example, the actions show an overall plan or way of proceeding, or the actions did not result from a mistake but from intention. Judge Lancaster ruled that Jordan's lawyers could use this disciplinary evidence, but only for purposes of impeaching the officers—attacking their credibility—or for rebutting their testimony.[46]

Tim O'Brien, who had joined Kerry Lewis as one of Jordan's lawyers, had considerable experience at litigating civil rights cases against police, and he understood the stakes. O'Brien pushed back against Judge Lancaster, arguing that the disciplinary evidence would become necessary to prove that the officers had not, in fact, identified themselves—a key part of Jordan's case. "The defendants have universally and consistently contended that they identified themselves as police officers in this case, that they did so pursuant to the standard procedure and they always do it. We have witnesses who will testify of instances where [these officers] did not identify themselves and we're offering … them for purposes of impeachment." Judge Lancaster said again he would allow the evidence, but only for impeachment—attacking credibility—and not for the "prior bad act" category. This ruling would limit the use that Jordan's lawyers could make of the witnesses of which Mr. O'Brien spoke; it also limited the same kind of testimony from Commander RaShall Brackney, who had a direct hand in supervising two of the three officers and who would have handled any disciplinary actions that might have been taken against them.[47]

With those rulings, and a few more minor ones, Judge Lancaster had the case ready for trial. This case that had divided the city sharply, and was still subject to wide public discussion, would come before a federal jury on July 16, 2012[48]— more than two-and-a-half years after the confrontation on Tioga Street.

PART II

WHY DID THIS HAPPEN?

The story of Jordan Miles and the three Pittsburgh Police officers who fought on the snowy ground on January 12, 2010, painted a vivid picture of the basic mechanics of policing in twenty-first century America. It also showed how the public and the media reacted and how political and law enforcement leaders behaved when faced with these challenges. In earlier chapters, we saw the case begin to advance through the legal system. We also looked at how that system does, or does not, work to find the truth and rectify the wounds inflicted by the incident and its aftermath. Later in this book, we will continue to look at the specifics of this case.

First, let us look at a basic question—a question so simple that we might easily move past it, amidst critique and discussion of the law and policing, of policy and history. Why did this happen? How could a walk around the block for an African American high school senior go so terribly wrong? How could a group of experienced police officers patrolling a neighborhood for guns and crime end up in what they believed to be a life-or-death struggle with a teen who had just left his house? How could this happen to a young person who had never had so much as a scrape with the law, who was an honors student in the city's premier arts academy—a kid who loved playing the viola?

One can argue that the police simply reacted to what they saw and what the young man did—and therefore, the officers did their jobs accordingly; the incident happened because Jordan ran when he should not have. Others will say that Jordan could not have acted any other way when faced with three men in dark clothes in a dark car, suddenly converging on him at night in Homewood. Putting that important disagreement aside for the moment, surely we can all agree that this incident should never have happened. A young man who was living his life, going to school, and headed to college on a scholarship, with a squeaky-clean record and a talent for playing a string instrument, should not have ended up on the ground, fighting with police officers. So, again, why did this happen?

The answer requires that we step back from the story of what happened, and for the next several chapters look for answers in an understanding of fundamental aspects of our society that have special resonance in the relationship between police officers, on the one hand, and black people and their communities on the other. First among these forces, race *plays a central role in how police and members of the African American community react to each other. Second,* fear *pushes these kinds of confrontations into the danger zone; when fear combines with the difficulties that race creates, we end up with a toxic mixture. We associate our police officers with bravery and courage, and for good reasons; but, without a doubt, fear constantly haunts their world, and this fear afflicts all sides in any interaction. Black Americans experience real fear at the hands of police, during every contact they have with officers, no matter the person of color's age, gender, education, or station in life. These two forces—race and fear—can help explain why, on that January night, Jordan chose to run and seek to escape—*even if we assume *he knew that the three men were police officers.*

CHAPTER 6

THE POISON OF RACE

Given even the barest specifics of what happened between Jordan Miles and the three Pittsburgh Police officers on January 12, 2010, race would quickly emerge as a central issue in the case and in public reactions to the incident. After all, the encounter involved three white police officers and one young black man, in an African American neighborhood. For members of Pittsburgh's black community, the Jordan Miles case hit a very specific, and familiar, nerve. Incidents of police violence and injustice against blacks in and around Pittsburgh have occurred for decades, with Jonny Gammage and Jerry Jackson just two of the most prominent examples.[1] But understanding the problem requires going beyond history. Understanding necessitates grasping what lies in the minds of those who encounter black people in America, below the surface of conscious beliefs. Research over the last 25 years has exposed much of this landscape for the first time. We know now that race—particularly the perception of a person as African American—includes stereotypes and unconscious biases that cause most Americans to view virtually all black Americans as threats. Some of this research reinforces the very thoughts and actions that the officers reported in those few minutes that Jordan and the police officers encountered each other, that is, the association of black people, particularly men, with danger, violence, and guns. The research proves that seeing a black person causes us to perceive weapons, especially guns, more readily; to sense greater danger and see violence in an ambiguous situation; and to feel threatened more readily. This noxious combination of fear and race creates the conditions for a possible disaster every time an officer, whether white or black, and a black person encounter one another. Let us take this general statement to the realm of specifics: Our unconscious racial biases reinforced (or, perhaps, even created) the perfect conditions for the mistakes of that terrifying and perilous January night, when Jordan Miles almost died.

RACE, RACISTS, AND RACISM TODAY IN THE
UNITED STATES

Almost two decades into the twenty-first century, a simple question about race in the United States still proves worth asking: How do Americans today think of racism in society, or in the criminal justice system in particular? For a lot of Americans—especially those of a certain age, old enough to have watched network television in the 1960s and 1970s—racism has a face and a name: Archie Bunker.

Archie Bunker was the central character of a weekly comedy called *All in the Family*.[2] A native of Queens, New York, and a white blue-collar working man in middle age, Archie reigned as the proudly prejudiced patriarch of his family. He had opinions on women, on anti–Vietnam War protesters, and on racial and ethnic minorities, all of which would be seen today as strongly politically incorrect. He never hesitated to loudly express these bigotries. Archie expressed these conscious beliefs about the inferiority of others relative to his own white male peers, and he did so not in careful whispers designed to expose his beliefs only to other racists, but openly and proudly. Even for those who have never seen the program, Archie-like behavior and speech still stand as the point of reference for many people: Racism means outward bigotry; consciously held and expressed attitudes of prejudice against racial, ethnic, or gender groups; and the use of racial slurs.

The scientific work of the last several decades, however, tells us that out-loud, in-your-face bigotry, even if disturbingly resurgent since the 2016 presidential election,[3] does not constitute the most pervasive manifestation of racism in American culture. The real answer to the question of how race manifests, especially in the criminal justice system, does not involve overt racism. Rather, race manifests in unconscious bias or, to use the terminology of social psychology, *implicit bias*. We see the effects of implicit bias not as *attitudes* but as *behaviors*.

A definition of implicit bias is a good place to start. "Implicit" in this context means something very much like "unconscious," in other words, the thoughts or feelings below the level of conscious awareness. "Bias" in this context denotes a preference for, or an aversion to, a particular group. To say that someone has implicit biases makes no judgment about the person's character, and having implicit biases does not make someone a bad person. Since implicit biases have nothing to do with conscious beliefs or intentions; they cannot serve to challenge, or increase, one's integrity or honor. Nevertheless—and this is what makes them significant—*implicit biases can have an impact on behavior*, even though they do not enter our conscious awareness. At bottom, implicit bias is about the roots of human behavior, that is, what we do and what motivates and shapes what we do, even if we do not know it. And when it comes to action, the situations in which we find ourselves matter more than our conscious attitudes, because situations allow our implicit biases to direct our behavior—even though this happens outside of any conscious awareness.

What we know about implicit biases comes, first and foremost, from a test called the Implicit Association Test (IAT). A full discussion of how the IAT works and why would take us well beyond the scope of this book; suffice it to say that the IAT—available to anyone with a computer and an internet connection, for approximately two decades, and administered many millions of times—has become a well-validated measure of the pervasiveness of racial bias.[4] The IAT has its critics, certainly, who have mounted valid challenges, chief among them that the existence of implicit biases in a person against a particular racial or ethnic group cannot predict whether that biased person may act in a biased way toward someone in any given situation.[5] But the IAT does tell us that pervasive implicit bias favoring whites and disfavoring blacks permeates American society as a whole. Overall, approximately 75 percent of the millions of people who have taken the IAT exhibit some preference for whites in contrast to blacks—a preference that may be slight, moderate, or strong. This figure includes 88 percent of whites and well over 40 percent of African Americans, and these implicit biases show up even in people who hold conscious beliefs in the importance of racial and ethnic equality.

Other prominent researchers have shown how implicit racial bias influences behavior in important everyday interactions. For example,

- In a 2005 study by Marianne Bertrand and Sendhil Mulainathan, potential employers received resumes from applicants (actually fake applicants—which the potential employers did not know about—as part of the study).[6] All of the resumes were identical, save one detail: some of the resumes used a stereotypically African American name (e.g., Lekisha, Jamal), while others used a stereotypically Caucasian name (e.g., Emily, Greg). Resumes with recognizably white names received one employer callback for every 10 resumes sent out; those with African American–sounding names received one callback for every 15 resumes.
- In "Written in Black and White: Exploring Confirmation Bias in Racialized Perceptions of Writing Skills," researchers presented 60 law firm partners with a memorandum for each of them to review. (A memorandum is a document a lawyer writes on a legal question, typically discussing research into the topic, conclusions, and recommendations.) The partners were a mixed group from 22 different law firms, with a little more than 40 percent female and 40 percent from racial and

ethnic minority groups. All received the same memorandum to assess, as they would do with a junior associate at their law firms. All of the memoranda contained the same number of identical grammatical, factual, and technical errors. Half of the memoranda came from "third-year associate Thomas Meyer, graduate of New York University Law School, identified as Caucasian" and the other half came from "third-year associate Thomas Meyer, graduate of New York University Law School, identified as African American." The results dovetail neatly with the presence of implicit bias in any random group of people. The lawyers found greater numbers of grammatical, technical, and factual errors for "black Thomas Meyer" than for "white Thomas Meyer"; they made 11 edits in "white Thomas Meyer's" memorandum and 29 in "black Thomas Meyer's."

Research results from the IAT and other measures of implicit bias confirm that unconscious racial bias exists and has real-world impacts. It cannot be disregarded as a fad or junk science or just the flavor of the month in the media. And if it permeates American society, it also permeates law enforcement. Police departments draw their recruits from society, and these agencies themselves have deep roots in that same society. There is therefore every reason to expect these same implicit attitudes among departments and their officers.

This leads to a question closer to the point of the Jordan Miles story: Do we know anything about the implicit biases and associations against African Americans that could have direct impacts on policing, public safety, and the interactions between black people and police officers? The answer, in short, is yes: We now know a lot about the psychology of race and how it might impact police work, and much of what we know is alarming. Robust and replicated evidence, from decades of science, tells us that whites, and even other black people, may see blacks as violent, involved in crime, and dangerous. The particulars are stunning—and they coincide almost eerily with the events of January 12, 2010, on Tioga Street.

BLACK MEANS DANGER, VIOLENCE, AND CRIME

For more than half a century, social psychologists and other scientists have found evidence of widely held American stereotypes about African Americans that associate them with violence and crime. The work of these scientists has varied in experimental format, subject, and theoretical approach, but it has all arrived at the same destination. Stanford University professor and MacArthur

Fellow Jennifer Eberhardt and Professor Philip Atiba Goff and their colleagues commented on this in 2004:

> The stereotype of Black Americans as violent and criminal has been documented by social psychologists for almost 60 years. Researchers have highlighted the robustness and frequency of this stereotypic association by demonstrating its effects on numerous outcome variables .... Not only is the association between Blacks and crime strong (i.e., consistent and frequent), it also appears to be automatic .... The mere presence of a Black man, for instance, can trigger thoughts that he is violent and criminal.[7]

B. Keith Payne, professor of psychology and neuroscience at the University of North Carolina, has said much the same thing. "Violent traits such as hostility, aggression, and criminality are consistently included in white Americans' stereotypes of Black Americans."[8] In a study published in 1980, two other scholars came to a similar finding, concerning students observed in desegregated schools: "both black and white students tend to link blacks with concepts of threat, aggression and violence," with white students showing a stronger link.[9] In 1976, another researcher commented that "one of the stereotypes frequently applied to blacks is that they are impulsive and given to crime and violence."[10] All of this work comes to mind when remembering a statement not from a white public figure but from an African American icon of the civil rights era, the Reverend Jesse Jackson. Jackson memorably said that "there is nothing more painful for me at this stage of my life than to walk down the street and hear footsteps and start to think about robbery and then look around and see it's somebody white and feel relieved."[11]

We can now draw on a body of knowledge that will give us much more specific information about these stereotypes and inform us about the unconscious concepts at play in our minds as well. The question no longer need stop at the general stereotype of blacks as violent, dangerous, and crime prone. We now know much more about how these processes work and what behavior we might expect to see as a result.

THE EFFECTS OF BLACK STEREOTYPES ON VISUAL PROCESSING

In a series of five collected studies, Professors Eberhardt and Goff and their colleagues tested the effect of the black/crime association on the ways that people see.[12]

- In their first study, these researchers exposed people, very quickly, to images of black male faces, white male faces, or no faces. This process is called "priming." After doing this, they showed the subjects a series of deliberately degraded, poor quality images of crime-related objects, such as a gun, in a series in which the images become a little clearer each time (with 41 total images in the series). The subjects were asked to push a button when they could make out what the image was. Those initially primed with black male faces could see the gun earlier in the series of images than those who were shown white faces or no faces at all. The subjects who were primed with white faces detected the object later in the series of images. Priming the subjects with black faces sharpened perceptions of objects related to crime; priming them with white faces inhibited detection.

- In the second study, the researchers primed the subjects with images of crime-related objects, which caused them to pay more attention to black male faces than to other faces. Thus the association between blacks and crime, the researchers wrote, is "bidirectional"—that is, "just as Black faces and Black bodies can trigger thoughts of crime, thinking of crime can trigger thoughts of Black people ...."

- Using volunteer police officers as subjects and using crime-related words and images of black and white faces, the researchers demonstrated that bringing crime concepts to mind caused the officers to pay more attention to black male faces and also to misremember black faces as more stereotypically black than was actually the case.

- Then they also showed police officer subjects different male faces, some black and some white. The researchers then asked the officers the question, "Who looks criminal?" The officers chose more black faces than white faces, and the more stereotypical the black face, the more likely that officers would report that the face looked criminal.

Eberhardt and Goff's groundbreaking work gives us considerable insight into why black people so often feel that they receive extra and unwarranted attention from police. The bidirectional association it reveals—(1) seeing black people brings to mind crime and violence and (2) crime and violence brings to mind black people—shows that these associations "function as visual tuning devices— directing people's eyes, their focus, and their interpretations of stimuli with which they are confronted," with this happening "despite individual difference in explicit racial attitudes."[13] Thus the fact that we live in a "crime-obsessed culture" means that just thinking about crime would happen frequently and doing so would lead people to "conjure up images of black Americans that 'ready' [them] to register and selectively attend to black people who may be present in the actual physical environment."[14]

The implications pull us directly into a consideration of how police do their work and behave toward the public. Officers have the task of detecting criminal actions and responding to them; they probably think about violent crime more often than the rest of us. This would likely cause officers to focus on black people, as compared to whites, especially on black people who have the most stereotypically black features. This may create a public perception of harassment of black citizens; note that it may also *inhibit* the observation of white criminals and criminality. In fact, the researchers point out that "police officers may face elevated levels of danger in the presence of white armed suspects in comparison with Black armed suspects" because they may have delayed and had less accurate responses to possible threats presented by armed white suspects, in terms of recognizing weapons. In contrast, "unarmed, innocent Blacks may easily become the targets of intense visual surveillance by both police officers and the lay public .... Racial profiling may be rooted in more fundamental perceptual processes than previously recognized."[15]

With this bidirectional connection between the stereotypes of blacks and crime, the danger—to black people *and* even to police officers—is both real and obvious. In the particular scenario in which Jordan Miles, a black male, faces three police officers who already have the task of looking for guns and signs of criminal conduct, just seeing Jordan and his black skin would increase their focus on crime and guns. Seeing him would also make it more likely that an officer would read ambiguous clues—the way a coat pocket looks on a dark night, or (to use the language of the experiment) a degraded image—as a gun.

AN AUTOMATIC PROCESS

Another important piece of research extends the idea that mere exposure to the faces of black people can change police behavior significantly. In a study published in 2001, researcher B. Keith Payne looked at how priming subjects with a brief glimpse at a face—some black, some white—not only changed the results of the responses but also illuminated the thinking process of people seeing those faces.[16]

The rapid priming of subjects with black or white faces can trigger stereotypes, and those stereotypes may impact a person's thinking and reactions. The question for Payne was whether those impacts happened on the conscious level (and could therefore be subjected to some type of control) or whether they operated automatically (meaning that we do not have the ability to consciously rein them in). Payne's study showed that the process at work was largely, if not entirely, automatic. Previous work, Payne said, had noted that "group stereotypes may be activated outside of awareness and may influence behavior without the knowledge or intent" of the person involved.[17] So, he asked, "what are the causes" of the psychological state of the person with the unconscious bias who then follows that bias in his or her behavior? According to Payne, his results showed that using the racial priming of black and white faces "exerted an automatic influence, independent of controlled processing" and that the automatic influence on the tasks, which showed evidence of racial biases, "was not directly related to explicit racial attitudes."[18] Payne said that his results provided strong support for the idea that Americans' exposure to black faces created a racially biased response through an automatic process in thinking. The importance of the finding is that automatic processes operate outside of our conscious knowledge, and unlike conscious thoughts or processes, we cannot consciously change these perceptions.

RACE AND (THE PERCEPTION OF) SIZE, FORMIDABILITY, AND THREAT

Even with the disproportionately large number of killings of unarmed black men at the hands of the police, the death of Tamir Rice in 2014 stands out. Tamir was *12 years old* when two Cleveland police officers pulled up to where he stood in a park, playing with a toy gun, and within several seconds, one of the officers had shot the boy. The officers went to that location based on a civilian's call to 911, in which the caller described the gun Tamir had as probably a toy; that last piece of information never made it to the officers. Almost as soon as the squad car arrived, police gunshots took Tamir down.[19]

In the aftermath, the public heard many theories for why this tragedy occurred. Most appallingly, perhaps, another police department in Ohio had let the officer who killed Tamir go; they did not consider him temperamentally suitable for the job.[20] But something else showed up in some of the explanations that came from the police. Tamir, they said, was no ordinary 12-year-old playing in the park. A representative of the Cleveland Police Department explained the killing of the boy this way. "Tamir Rice is in the wrong. He's menacing. He's 5-feet-7, 191 pounds. He wasn't that little kid you're seeing in pictures. He's a 12-year-old in an adult body."[21] In other words, people should not blame the officer who shot this young boy less than five seconds after the police car pulled within feet of where the boy stood; rather, the officer saw a large man, felt threatened, and acted appropriately, given that threat.

This explanation of Tamir Rice's death does not stand alone. In April of 2014, seven months before Tamir was killed, a police officer in Milwaukee, Wisconsin, shot a man named Dontre Hamilton 14 times, killing him. The officer later testified that Hamilton seemed very strong, with a "muscular build" and that the officer feared a physical confrontation with him. Hamilton "most definitely would have overpowered ... me or pretty much any officer I can think of .... He was just that big, that muscular."[22] The medical examiner who conducted Hamilton's autopsy said he was five feet seven inches tall (shorter than the average American man by two inches) and weighed 169 pounds (more than 20 pounds lighter than the average). The same type of thing has surfaced in other cases as well, in which black victims of police violence have been portrayed as being larger than they actually are.

These statements do not arise randomly; rather, they arise from the way that people—particularly white people—perceive black men. A team of three psychologists, led by John Paul Wilson of Montclair State University, investigated this phenomenon. In a series of seven insightful experiments, Wilson and his colleagues found that biased perceptions account for these consistent overestimates of the size and formidability of black men.[23] They also found that these biases account for other important judgments. They set out to test the hypothesis that "people would misperceive young Black men as physically larger and more formidable than young White men" of strictly comparable size. They also wanted to know if these race-based misperceptions could lead to race-based decisions about the use of force. The seven careful studies they conducted yielded clear results. People "perceive young Black men as taller, heavier, more muscular, more physically formidable, and more capable of physical harm than young White men of the same actual size; and that this bias in physical size perception can influence the decision to use force against them."[24] The data, they say, "strongly suggest some amount of racial bias in perceptions of formidability,"[25] which has significant downstream consequences in that participants judged blacks "as more capable of harm" than physically comparable whites.

As in perception of size and strength, participants in the study "showed a robust race-based bias, perceiving Black men as more capable of harm than White men," controlling carefully for any actual size differences.[26] (Interestingly, while both white and black test subjects perceived black men as being larger and more muscular than white men, the black test subjects showed a weaker effect, and black test subjects did not share the further effect of seeing black men as more capable of harm.) Moreover, Wilson and his colleagues also found that test subjects were more likely to judge use of force against young black men to be appropriate than against similar-sized young white men. According to the researchers, "[I]ncreased justification of force ... was strongly associated with racially biased judgments of overall size and formidability. People judged Black men as larger and more harmful than White men, thus rendering them more suitable recipients of physical force."[27] And the more stereotypically Afrocentric the physical features of black men (e.g., darker complexion or skin tone), the more pronounced the effects observed became.[28]

These researchers caution, appropriately, that "it cannot be concluded from these data that the process that we have observed necessarily unfolds in real world force decisions" or motivates the use of force by any particular officer. But the implications are too dramatic to miss. In a country in which police have the legal privilege to use an appropriate level of force to carry out their lawful duties, the appropriateness of any use of force lies in an assessment of the individual circumstances, and one of the most important factors in this judgment will be the perceived threat posed by the person facing the police. If racial biases will cause people—including police officers—to consistently overestimate the physical size, muscularity, and potential for harm of black men, this helps explain why black men find themselves confronted with greater fear on the part of both civilians and police and with more frequent uses of force by police. To the extent that these incidents arise and thereafter find their way into courts of law, it could surprise no one familiar with the research of Wilson and his team if judges and jurors seem to give the benefit of the doubt to claims of threat and the need to use force against a black man.

RACE AND GUNS: SEEING AND SHOOTING

The research discussed so far tells us that race serves unconsciously as a bidirectional visual tuning device, focusing on the presence, faces, and bodies of black people. The presence of black people brings to mind thoughts of crime and violence, and thoughts of crime turn our attention to blacks. By now, we should understand that racially biased thinking processes operate automatically—that is, not on the level of conscious thinking, which we could perhaps influence and control. We also know that racial biases cause those of us looking at physically matched young black men and young white men to view the young black men as larger, more muscular, and stronger; more threatening and more likely to do harm; and therefore more appropriate as targets for the use of force and for greater levels of force. With guns ever present in the United States, and with the danger that guns pose to police officers, researchers have also asked about the effects of racial biases on our perception of guns and our perception of armed people. The results of these studies, especially combined with those already mentioned, further explain why black men end up on the wrong end of police gunfire.

First, let us return to the study by B. Keith Payne, discussed above,[29] which found that racially biased thinking operates automatically. In that study, Payne primed people—showed them very quickly—images of black or white faces. After seeing the faces, observers saw images of either handguns or hand tools and had to identify which type of object they had seen by pressing particular keys. Because existing stereotypes associate blacks with crime and violence, Payne hypothesized that seeing a black face as a priming device would cause the people in the experiment to "respond faster to guns." Payne found that, when nonblack participants saw a black face as a priming device, they were faster in picking out the gun as compared with the tool. Seeing a white face introduced almost no difference in speed between recognizing the gun and the tool. Error rates remained low for both conditions. The difference in speed for recognizing the gun over the tool had no relation to explicit racial attitudes of the participants, which Payne also measured. When Payne speeded up the process by requiring participants to respond quickly, in a limited amount of time, to the question, "gun or tool?", the error rates (in which participants misidentified a tool as a gun) increased for people who saw the prime of the black face, as compared to people who saw the prime of the white face.

Among the most important research on weapons and race, the work of Joshua Correll and various colleagues stands out. A professor of social psychology at the University of Colorado at Boulder, Correll began studying the relationship between race and the decision to shoot by utilizing a simple setup that resembled a videogame. Test subjects would observe a scenario on a video screen. The scenario always involved a man in a public place, such as a parking lot, park, or city street. Two factors would vary in these scenarios. First, the male would be either black or white. Second, the male, moving forward toward the test subject, would grasp an object, which was either a gun or another small object, like a wallet or cell phone. Test subjects would view each scenario and were faced with two buttons to push: one for "shoot" and the other for "don't shoot." The task allowed the test subjects to see the man, his race, and the object simultaneously. The test subject would then choose to shoot or not. The device would measure both the speed of the reaction and its accuracy—in other words, how fast the test subject pressed a button and whether the person pressed the right button ("shoot" for armed men and "don't shoot" for unarmed men) or made an incorrect response (shot an unarmed man or failed to shoot an armed man). The question was whether the data would show evidence of a "shooter bias," that is, was the shoot/don't shoot decision influenced by the race of the man in the video?

In the first published research in the series in 2002,[30] Correll and his colleagues used both college undergraduates and community members as test subjects. The studies showed clear evidence of racial bias by both the college students and community members. The research showed bias in the speed with which the test subjects responded correctly to the targets. They were faster to "shoot" the armed black men than the armed white men. They also pressed "don't shoot" more quickly for unarmed white men than for unarmed black men. The participants showed racial bias in the accuracy of their responses: They were more likely to shoot an unarmed black man than an unarmed white man, and they were more likely to not shoot an armed white man than to not shoot an armed black man. Forcing test subjects to make the choice (to shoot or not shoot) faster increased errors and the influence of bias. "In essence," Correll and a colleague said, "participants were faster and more accurate when responding to targets that fit the kinds of stereotypes that … are prevalent in U.S. society (armed blacks and unarmed whites), but they were slower and more likely to make mistakes in response to targets that deviated from these stereotypes (unarmed blacks and armed whites)."[31]

Correll's 2002 work raised an obvious question: Would the same biases appear in a population of police officers? A subsequent study tested this very issue.[32] Correll and colleagues used the same testing protocols, but this time their subjects fell into three groups. The first consisted of people from Denver (the community group), the second consisted of police officers from Denver, and the third consisted of police officers from other parts of the country. The opportunity to compare police officers to members of the community they served might generate especially important insights, since all of the individuals in Denver shared the same broad environment, and having non-Denver officers participate would illuminate whether Denver officers responded in a way that was different than American police generally. For all three groups, researchers took the same kinds of measurements that they had in the 2002 study—reaction time and accuracy.

All three groups—Denver community, Denver officers, and officers from elsewhere—showed the same significant biases in reaction time. Participants in all three groups shot faster at armed black men than at armed white men in the video. They also hit "don't shoot" faster for unarmed white men than for unarmed black men. In other words, all three groups responded more rapidly to images that conformed to dominant racial stereotypes (blacks/armed and dangerous, whites/unarmed and not dangerous).

For the measurement of error—hitting "shoot" for an unarmed man or "don't shoot" for an armed one—the researchers looked to measure not just the rate of error but the criteria of judgment each group used.[33] Correll and his colleagues found that Denver community members—nonlaw enforcement Denver residents—showed a "pronounced" racial bias; they set a low standard for the decision to shoot black men versus white men. The police officers (both the Denver and non-Denver groups) did not show evidence of this kind of bias; they used the same standard in the decision to shoot when seeing either black or white men in the video. The officers were "no more likely to shoot a black target than a white target."[34] The results, Correll and his colleagues said, were "particularly provocative." Although officers show the same biases affecting the speed of their response—that is, both police and civilians have difficulty processing images inconsistent with dominant stereotypes, making them slower with those than with stereotype-consistent images—officers did not show any impact on their ultimate decision to shoot. Civilians, however, did. Put another way, racial biases slowed both civilians and police officers, and these biases also seemed to make civilians more "trigger happy." Police officers did not show such biasing effect on the decision to shoot; they did not become trigger happy. "Inasmuch as it is the ultimate decision to shoot (and not the delay in making that decision) that carries life or death consequences for the suspect," this result should command the "greatest interest" of both police and community.[35]

The researchers then repeated the testing, this time using just Denver officers and Denver community members, and this time cutting back the amount of time allowed for participants to choose either shoot or don't shoot. The same pattern emerged: Racial biases slowed down both police and civilians, but only civilians showed racial biases in the ultimate decision of whether or not to shoot; police did not. This, the researchers said, might mean that police expertise, imparted through training, "improves the outcomes of the decision process ...." In the next phase, researchers gave the civilian participants practice on the shoot/don't shoot task as a way of simulating the training that police receive, and the civilians improved their accuracy. The bias existing in their unconscious decision-making lessened and with it the level of error. Training, it seems, *can* make a difference (even if the "practice" given to the civilians was only a pale imitation of the many hours that police officers spend in firearms training). The bottom line of the 2007 study by Correll and his colleagues requires attention: While a race-based "shooter bias" exists, and while it affects the speed of judgments of both police officers and civilians, it influenced the ultimate decision to shoot only in civilians; police officers, in Denver and elsewhere, did not exhibit the same bias. Police "officers were ultimately able to overcome the influence of race" in the decision to shoot, "something community members simply could not do."[36]

In a further study, attempting to examine whether training could supply the answer to racial bias in police shootings of African Americans, Correll and colleagues Jessica J. Sim and Melody S. Sadler looked at the question of whether training might either decrease or increase the influence of anti-black racial bias in shoot/don't shoot decisions.[37] The bottom line is that not all training has the same effect. When the training used race as a seemingly relevant factor—for example, when the training material that made up the test contained far more armed blacks than armed whites (i.e., a ratio of three to one), training would not help overcome bias. When either the simulated training or the police officers' on-the-job experience pointed to blacks as a source of danger, training no longer reduced bias. "When race is diagnostic of danger … in a sense, when race becomes a task-relevant cue, even experts may rely on it to facilitate weapons detection."[38] Thus any training or experience that "reinforces the utility of race information" will mean that "even highly trained individuals show racial bias …."[39] Thus we must not only train officers (and perhaps civilians who wish to carry firearms for self-defense) thoroughly but also ensure that the training does not inadvertently reinforce the stereotypes that already exist. For those police officers practicing their craft in environments in which they consistently encounter a considerable number of violent criminals who happen to be black, due to the geographic focus of where the officers are assigned to work, a police department wishing to avoid racial bias should consider rotating officers into other social contexts.

POLICE SHOOTINGS OF OTHER OFFICERS
AND OF CIVILIANS

We can see that the science on the effect of race on our thinking has an impact in the way people—and particularly police officers—make judgments on crim-inality, use of force, the presence of weapons, and even the speed and accuracy of the decision to shoot a gun at a civilian. What would we expect to see, as a result?

One answer comes from new observations[40] by Amanda Charbonneau, Katherine Spencer, and Jack Glaser of the University of California's Goldman School of Public Policy. These researchers examined a 29-year compilation of information on fatal shootings of *off-duty* police officers mistaken for civilians in

New York State. The data, compiled by a state government task force, found 10 such fatal shootings; in this group, eight officers were black, one was Hispanic, and one was white.[41] Because roughly 75 percent of all police officers in the United States are white, the chances of this disparity occurring randomly, assuming that black and white officers face the same risks, is one in a million. Charbonneau and her colleagues note that the disparity contrasts starkly with figures for police-on-police fatal shootings in which the victims were *on duty*. In the 14 on-duty fatal shootings in which the officer was shot mistakenly, one victim was black, one was Hispanic, and 12 were white. The difference becomes striking, in spite of the small numbers of these shootings (as compared to police shootings of civilians), because "they are known errors that involve a misperception of threat ...."[42] These patterns of racial disparities "suggest that there are situational factors [that] vary systematically and contribute to the observed outcomes."[43]

The researchers point to six situational factors as explanations for these differences:

1. black officers would find themselves in higher crime areas more often when off duty than white officers would;[44]
2. the presence of implicit racial bias;[45]
3. the greater proclivity to perceive weapons with blacks;
4. a "shooter bias" which prompts officers to fire faster at armed blacks than armed whites;[46]
5. the well-established mental association between blacks and criminality, danger, and threat;[47] and
6. the differences between unplanned and planned police encounters, with the former more likely to involve off-duty officers unidentified to their peers, and latter more likely to involve identified on-duty officers, with danger randomly distributed among officers representing demographic groups.[48]

The researchers then went further and compared their analysis of mistaken police-on-police shootings, with police shootings of civilians. The small numbers of police-on-police shootings made analyses challenging, and the data on fatal police shootings of civilians were difficult for another reason. Prior to 2015, no comprehensive government data existed on officer involved shootings (OISs) resulting in civilian deaths; remarkably, as these words are written in 2019, *this has not changed*, despite virtually universal condemnation of this embarrassment, including by then Attorney General Eric Holder.[49] Two media outlets, *The Washington Post* and *The Guardian*, stepped into this gap and created their own compilations of data on OISs in the United States. Charbonneau, Spencer, and Glaser examined the data from *The Washington Post* for OISs resulting in civilian deaths in 2015 and 2016.[50] *The Washington Post* data (like the data in *The Guardian*) showed that most uses of deadly force by police involved suspects who were armed. The data also exhibited clear patterns among victims, but these patterns differed between black and white victims. According to the researchers, "while the civilians armed with lethal weapons who were fatally shot by police in 2015 and 2016 were predominantly white, unarmed civilians fatally shot by police during that period were more likely to be black."[51] Among all *unarmed* civilians shot and killed by police in those years, 39 percent were black and 38 percent were white. Among armed civilians fatally shot, 25 percent were black and 51 percent were white. All of this occurs, of course, in the context of a national population that is just 12 percent black.[52] Against this background, a finding that eight out of ten fatal shootings of off-duty police officers were black seems particularly striking.

The researchers caution that they cannot pin down the cause of these disparities without more analysis.[53] The work of others has established that the differences persist when controlling for general variables such as regional crime rates and the sizes of the police departments and cities involved.[54] Charbonneau and her colleagues recommend that police agencies create strategies and policies that "emphasize practices that reduce the potential for biases to affect officers' judgments and decisions regarding the people they encounter, whether civilians or officers."[55] Among those possibilities, they recommend practices that would reduce uncertainty and ambiguity, because those changes would "reduce racial disparities in policing decisions."[56] Improved methods for officers to identify themselves could help; so could discouraging officers from spontaneously joining the enforcement operations of others.[57] Second, police agencies should seek out and put in place practices that would reduce the use of lethal force by officers. This could include a greater emphasis on de-escalation, more scenario-based training, and an emphasis on increasing the time available to officers to make decisions.[58]

As helpful as the Charbonneau, Spencer, and Glaser study is, we need to remember that it has a significant limitation, beyond those that the authors correctly point out themselves. The data covering police-on-police shootings, as well as *Washington Post/Guardian* data on police shootings of civilians, all cover just one kind of police use of force: *shootings in which the victims died*. These data, as sparse and as difficult to gather as they are, do not represent a complete picture of all police use of force; in fact, they do not even give us a full picture of police discharging their guns at people while on duty. For every fatality, many more shootings likely take place in which a victim sustains injury but does not die, or in which police shoot but miss entirely. Surely, we must see *any* situation in which an agent of the state uses lethal force on a civilian as part of the category that covers the most serious kind of action a government can take, whether that agent (such as a police officer) hits the person or not, and whether the person dies or not.

Dr. David Klinger, a former Los Angeles Police Department officer and now an eminent criminologist whose career has spanned decades, expresses this thought better than anyone. Noting the abysmal record of the U.S. government in tracking the number of people killed by the police, Klinger says that even doing that job thoroughly would not be enough. "I think there is nothing more important for the government to track than the numbers of times that government agents try to kill people."[59] Therefore, whatever biases show up in the existing data are definitely incomplete, if what we want to measure is the total number of police shootings. In fact, the biases that show up in the Charbonneau, Spencer, and Glaser study and in the *Washington Post/Guardian* data may actually underestimate the prevalence of the use of deadly force.

THE BOTTOM LINE

With decades of research on the subject, little doubt remains on the question of whether or not race influences the use of force by police. A first wave of research, after the Second World War, established the truth long suspected but hidden: American stereotypical beliefs about black Americans associated them with crime, violence, and danger. More recently, a new generation of researchers has taken this work to a deeper and more important level. Much of the effect of stereotyping lies out of conscious view or experience. Our biases make it easier for Americans to see blacks as dangerous, to interpret their ambiguous actions as hostile and aggressive, and to see weapons and associate them with blacks. It becomes easier to justify the use of force against black citizens. Blacks in America therefore walk the land with targets on their backs, and no situation presents this more starkly than when blacks face police officers. Put simply, blacks face a greater likelihood of having police officers perceive them as criminals, of having their actions interpreted as hostile and dangerous, of having any ambiguous object—a bulging pocket, an angled stance—as an indication of the presence of a weapon and of having their very bodies seen as larger and more menacing than they are. Their very presence raises the specter of "crime" and "guns" in the minds of those who see them. All of this means it becomes more likely for officers confronting a young black man to react as if they are facing an armed criminal.

CHAPTER 7

HOW FEAR IMPACTS THE POLICE

Looking back at the encounter on January 12, 2010, between Jordan Miles and the three Pittsburgh Police officers, we can try to understand how it went so wrong. Questions we might ask include:

- Did the police officers—the trained professionals in the scenario—conduct themselves correctly?
- Did they operate according to the rules and policies of their agency?
- Did they follow their training?
- Did they abide by the laws of the Commonwealth of Pennsylvania and the Constitution of the United States?
- Did the Pittsburgh Police Department deploy the officers correctly, in accordance with best practices, and with the training and equipment they needed to do the job?
- Did the officers get the supervision and the oversight they needed in order to do their jobs safely, efficiently, and with due regard for the rights and dignity of the people of their city?
- Did Jordan Miles do everything he could as a citizen—a young person, to be sure, with minimal personal experience with the police—but as a person with the responsibility for his own conduct?

All of these are valid questions, and the following chapters will examine many of them. At this point, however, let us look deeper—not at these people as members of public agencies acting in public roles, like the three officers, or at Jordan as a high school senior and a young African American man. Rather, let us look at them as human beings and examine closely the most basic human patterns that might have played key roles in the tragic situation that unfolded on Tioga Street in Homewood on a cold January night.

The two most basic patterns we see here cut across all similar incidents in the United States involving an encounter between police officers and the black and brown citizens they serve. Those basic patterns of thinking involve (1) fear and (2) race. These patterns run in both directions, meaning that fear and race affect the thinking of police officers and of the African American and Latino people they serve, albeit in different ways. Only by understanding the deep well of fear on both sides, and the racial dynamics at play, can we truly grasp how a brief meeting like the one between Jordan Miles and Officers Saldutte, Sisak, and Ewing could go from nothing to a life-or-death struggle in less than the amount of time it takes to buy a hot drink at a coffee shop.

It will seem surprising to many people to talk about fear from the perspective of the police. Officers come into any situation armed, trained, and clothed in state authority; they have training and experience in asserting themselves to control situations. Yet it makes all kinds of sense to look at the police, not just because of their law enforcement *job*, which can include danger, but because the law enforcement *culture emphasizes* danger, which may in turn increase it.

Everyone involved in the case, and everyone reading this book, should feel tremendous gratitude that Jordan Miles did not die during the incident in January of 2010, and that fact makes this story different from far too many others. Jordan lived, and he can tell his own story; he has done so by talking with the author and allowing this book to be used to tell his story. But in so many other situations, a civilian of color encountering the police loses his or her life. Roughly 1,000 people die as a result of being shot by police officers in the United States every year,[1] and officers wound many more. A larger number endure the risk of death when police officers shoot at them (or at other people nearby) and miss.[2] Fear pervades all of these encounters; it stems not just from dangerous situations but from a culture of fear that seeps into police training and education.

When police training or policy discussions occur with fear at center stage, fear will inevitably shape the future thinking, actions, and reactions of officers. This almost certainly ensures that some events in which the police must take action will go wrong that might not otherwise, causing unnecessary injuries and deaths. Sometimes police officers will die as a result, but more often, civilians will pay that dire price, a disproportionate number of them people of color. Even when the worst does not occur—no one, civilian or police officer, dies or suffers a severe injury—another type of loss occurs: Fear and distrust of police by civilians deepens, damaging the already tenuous relationship between police and minority communities. And this, of course, will feed a vicious cycle of ever more fear. The streets become meaner and more dangerous, the jobs of police officers become harder to do, and everyone—police officers and civilians alike—becomes less safe. The cycle continues, and the fear grows.

No one can doubt that some danger comes with being a police officer. For example, officers may sometimes face people filled with anger or malice, and some of these people may carry weapons. Police officers deal with the grossly intoxicated and with some people simply bent on violence. They encounter those with mental illness in the throes of difficulty and decompensation, who may be unable to control themselves or respond in appropriately conventional ways to police instruction. Officers respond to situations in which people simply find themselves in the worst possible positions. These kinds of situations can—not always, but sometimes—pose real danger, and this can mean—again, not always, but sometimes—that police officers may have to use force, even deadly force, to protect the public and themselves. Such situations, however, make up far less of the daily activity of police officers than one might think, potentially creating a discrepancy between police officer expectations and fear, on the one hand, and actual experience and need, on the other. If the way police officers handle routine incidents comes first and foremost from training and policy designed for the most difficult and violent incidents—instead of for the great majority of nonviolent interactions—training and experience become misaligned, perhaps dangerously so. For example, if police officer training stresses that *all traffic stops can be dangerous and violent,* instead of that *some* traffic stops *may* be dangerous and violent, overreaction seems a certainty in some undetermined number of cases. When fear becomes ever-present in police training, policy, and action, we can begin to understand how things can go wrong.

CAUTION: NOTHING HERE CASTS DOUBT ON THE COURAGE OF POLICE OFFICERS

Before discussing the presence of fear in policing, it is critically important to understand what this chapter does *not* attempt to argue. This chapter does not question the courage of police officers; it does *not* say or imply in any way that police officers are not some of the bravest people we will ever meet. What follows in this discussion about fear does *not* mean that police officers fear their jobs, that they dread tasks they must do, or that they are in any way cowardly or faint-hearted. *On the contrary*, police officers show courage far more often than the rest of us. In a situation of real danger, police officers must, and do, act in a way the rest of us do not. As President Obama once said so eloquently, police officers "run toward the danger, not away from it."[3] Running toward danger not directed at oneself—an action that contradicts the basic fight-or-flight instinct wired deep into the human brain—tells us much about the beauty of courage and of a dedication to duty. This book does not dispute this at all, and this chapter does not argue anything to the contrary. It takes real guts—whether inborn, trained, or some combination of both—to do what police officers do in dangerous situations.

This chapter addresses something different than the presence or absence of courage. If the abiding reality of police culture relentlessly pushes the ideas of fear of death or grievous injury that may come at any time and in any situation in which officers interact with civilians, such narratives cannot help but distort the outlook of the bravest police officers. This framework will alter the training they receive, and it will impact the rules and policies under which they operate. This, in turn, may alter officers' perceptions of potential danger and the ways that they react to those perceptions—perhaps causing needless deaths or injuries to both civilians and police.

WE ARE THE WARRIORS, PROTECTING THE SHEEP IN A WORLD OF UNRELENTING VIOLENCE

Not long ago, in many places in the United States, police departments would articulate their approach to the job of policing in a simple two-word phrase: community policing. This expression included several core ideas: Police and members of the public they served would work together, as partners, to enhance and assure public safety. This kind of partnership would require shared responsibility and mutual trust. The people served would have a role—perhaps the lead role—in determining law enforcement priorities and approaches on the streets where they lived. For some departments, community policing was little more than a slogan or add-on, with one or two "community policing officers" per precinct or per department who went to meetings and took photos with neighborhood groups, while the rest of the officers in the area did "real" police work. But for police departments that practiced community policing as a philosophy, the rewards flowed. Connection between police and those they served grew. Information came to the police that would not have without mutual trust, allowing officers to become more effective in fighting crime and disorder, and safer while doing so. These departments addressed the problems the community cared about most (not those the police prioritized for their own reasons), increasing citizen satisfaction with the police.[4]

This type of policing, constructed on the twin pillars of long personal relationships and mutual investment in the community's security, put the police and those they served together, on the same team, to accomplish the joint goals of safety and order. People would necessarily get to know each other, and that experience of working with others built trust—the opposite of fear.

Unfortunately, this type of policing has gone out of fashion in many places.[5] As policing has changed, officers in most cities of any size no longer function as an integral part of the fabric of an existing community. Instead, the dominant narrative of policing—the story police tell themselves about themselves and the way they live that story out—has changed. The way that many officers now see themselves, and therefore conduct themselves in so many places, no longer positions police around preserving the community and assuring its safety and good order; instead, police officers now think of themselves as fighting a war, as warriors: not in the sense of participating in a generalized "war on crime" or "war on drugs" crusade or program but as people who dedicate themselves as soldiers, willing to use violence as necessary in the fight to protect the rest of us against an evil enemy.

The warrior culture in American policing allows—even encourages—officers to view themselves as a vanguard of crime fighters standing between society, on the one hand, and the ever-threatening forces of evil, danger, and violence on the other. Professor Seth Stoughton, a former police officer who now teaches law at the University of South Carolina, calls this "the Warrior ethos."[6] Stoughton says that the warrior viewpoint and rhetoric "has infused modern policing, shaping how officers perceive their role, and informing the way they approach and interact with the public."[7] By and large, police officers no longer just work to keep order and address problems in the communities that they know because they themselves constitute parts of those communities or interact often with members of it. Rather, Stoughton says, warrior officers view themselves as "soldiers on the front lines in the never-ending battle … against the forces of chaos and criminality," and they view the warrior outlook as critical to safety—the safety of both the public and themselves.[8]

Even as the warrior mind-set has increased within law enforcement, this viewpoint has begun to encounter criticism from outside of policing, most notably from President Obama's Task Force on 21st Century Policing.[9] Stoughton recognizes, however, that when officers see themselves in jeopardy in a dangerous and violent environment, they find the warrior outlook very attractive. First, warriors find honor in serving others for honorable ends, instead of acting to serve themselves, as so many of us do. Second, warriors find esteem in a long-term dedication to the duty of this honorable service, in an unending struggle. Third, warriors must resolve to serve in that struggle, to outlast the dark forces they face—even if that struggle never ends. Last, and perhaps most importantly, warriors must develop and even nurture a willingness to use violence in service of their cause.[10]

Few things capture the warrior idea better than a book called *On Combat: The Psychology and Physiology of Deadly Conflict in War and Peace*,[11] cowritten by a very popular, long-time police trainer named Dave Grossman.[12] Most people, Grossman says, do their best to avoid the evil and violence in the world. They run from danger, trying to escape it. The warrior has the opposite reaction, and he or she uses violence as a tool to fight the evil in the world that would otherwise consume it.[13] As Grossman says, "if you want to ... walk the warrior's path, then you must make a conscious and moral decision every day to dedicate, equip and prepare yourself to thrive in that toxic, corrosive moment when the wolf comes knocking at the door."[14] As others have noted,[15] the phrasing is not accidental; we must ask not *whether* evil will come, but *when*. And when it does, as it inevitably will, the warrior must be ready, and violence is necessary to fight it. In a training seminar in Pennsylvania, Grossman pulls no punches. "We. Are. At. War," he tells an audience of 250 police officers. "And you are the frontline troops in this war .... *You* are the Delta Force. *You* are the Green Beret. *You* are the British SAS. Can you accept that? Every single one of you is in the frontline of a live ammo combat patrol everyday of your life."[16] Grossman aims to get police officers to think more like soldiers, "training them to regard the communities they serve as territory occupied by potential insurgents."[17]

Grossman uses the nightmare of the vile terrorist attacks of September 11, 2001, as a powerful example. The attacks and the aftermath bring to life one of Grossman's favorite teaching metaphors, in which he divides the world into sheep and sheepdogs, and of course wolves. The vast majority of human beings want nothing to do with violence. They live as sheep, oblivious to the evil in the world and helpless against it, and they therefore need the protection of the ever-vigilant sheepdog. The sheepdog guards the flock, ready and even keen to use violence as necessary to protect against the ever-present wolves that lie in wait, ready to sink their teeth into the neck of any unsuspecting lamb:

> After the attacks of September 11, 2001, most of the sheep, that is, most citizens in America said, "Thank God I wasn't on one of those planes." The sheepdogs, the warriors, said, "Dear God, I wish I could have been on one of those planes. Maybe I could have made a difference." When you are truly transformed into a warrior and have truly invested yourself into warriorhood, you want to be there. You want to be able to make a difference.[18]

The warrior police officer (sheepdog) reacts to the fear all of us (sheep) have in the face of the "aggressive sociopath[s]" (wolves) who fill the world, who have "no empathy for [their] fellow citizens,"[19] by marshaling a willingness to use aggressive but righteous violence against human (or canid) predators.

Maybe Dave Grossman's words in his book and many presentations take this idea a little too far; perhaps we should not take him literally. The idea of police officer as warrior serves as a forceful metaphor, and perhaps we should not read it as more than that. A metaphor of this type gives the police officers/warriors a way to see themselves positively, in a world that, they may think, seems to neither appreciate what they do nor understand the officer's task—in fact, not even want to appreciate or understand it. Such a metaphor serves as a social reference point, a kind of group badge of honor. But this does not fully explain either the persistence of the warrior point of view in law enforcement or the full scope of what the warrior idea actually does for police. Examined in its full social context, the warrior ethos—both the mind-set and the behaviors that may spring from it—serves a more basic purpose. Adopting the warrior outlook gives officers the means for survival. It encourages them to believe that they, individually and as members of a particular agency, have come under unyielding, continuous, and illegitimate attack. The attacks themselves may come in verbal or written assaults from politicians, activists, academics, or other "outsiders" who know nothing about the realities of police work and should therefore have no standing to criticize. These attacks also come in actual, tangible form, in the constant, violent, physical assaults by those individuals who the police encounter every day. From the law enforcement point of view, adopting the warrior perspective gives police officers the ability to survive what they see as a war against police, and "failing to do so can be fatal."[20]

Officers feel the danger of their jobs increasing, and from this viewpoint, the roles they fill become more dangerous and more violent all the time. They feel menaced constantly by the threat of violence from every angle. From the police academy onward and throughout their careers, police officers get constant reminders of the risks to their lives, every day and everywhere. For example, police cadets hear constantly that "everyone they encounter on the street could kill them at any second, and their training reinforces this fearful outlook."[21] Therefore, every officer working a beat has one goal—to make it home alive— in a world where this is no sure thing. Recruits and officers hear again and again that every aspect of the job poses extreme danger. *American Police Beat* tells officers that "[t]here isn't really a part of a cop's job that isn't potentially dangerous."[22] In *Police Magazine*, officers learn that "[t]he dangers we expose ourselves to every time we [work] are almost immeasurable ... and the academy certainly does a good job of hammering this home."[23] The indoctrination of officers on this point begins when police enroll in academy training. For example, a report on one police training curriculum says that the instruction tells officers-to-be that suspects "are mentally prepared to react violently" and adds that officers "could die today, tomorrow, or next Friday."[24] These messages also come to officers through a constant stream of online training materials, print magazine articles, books, and—especially in privately run—training seminars like Dave Grossman's, available both in person and on well-known websites.[25] Adopting the warrior approach, officers learn, gives them a path to safety.

We see this in the police version of the old saying, "better safe than sorry." If one spends enough time talking with police officers about these subjects, one will hear their version: "I'd rather be judged by twelve than carried by six."[26] (In other words, it's better to gamble on legal jeopardy afterward, if necessary, at the hands of 12 jurors sitting in judgment, rather than risking death or serious injury in the moment.) From this point of view, the assumption is that everyone who officers come into contact with, in any situation, may pose a deadly threat. If officers then act with this thought in mind and use whatever force seems necessary, as rapidly as possible, they maximize their chances to return home safely. An officer who fails to act—who hesitates, no matter how briefly—risks death. This strict either/or world view excludes any other possibility. The warrior knows best; outsiders simply do not understand the fearsome risks under which police labor every day. Other people—the clueless outsiders and academics, the uninitiated who are not part of this police culture—may interpret this venerable police saying as, "shoot first, ask questions later."

Of course, keeping safe in this environment requires unique training, such as how to use special tactics, engage in physical combat in ways that give the warrior a tactical edge, and sometimes use special equipment (e.g., a Taser, a collapsible baton, or pepper spray). Perhaps more important, keeping safe requires a change in how one thinks. Officers must become hypervigilant, developing a heightened awareness to every aspect of their surroundings in order to detect any potential threat. According to Peter Kraska, who studies police militarization at Eastern Kentucky University, warrior training, like that offered by Dave Grossman, seeks to give police officers military instincts. "You gotta be on high alert, and you gotta look for any indices of threat, and you need to eliminate the threat, just like the military does, in a second."[27] To maintain a state of hypervigilance, the police officer uses an outsized amount of cognitive attention to closely observe the environment and everyone in it, at all times. Nothing must escape the officer's heightened awareness, because losing focus—on everything and everyone around, because threats can originate with everyone, everywhere—can result in missing a clue that makes the officer vulnerable to undetected fatal violence. This concept often surfaces in the idea that officers must avoid complacency at all costs. According to former police officer and now law professor Seth Stoughton, one finds the phrase "complacency kills" in "a truly staggering number" of police-oriented sources.[28] But the costs of constant hypervigilance add up. Hypervigilance increases the cognitive load on the brain of anyone living this way over the long term; a high degree of stress on the mental and physical systems of the body would inevitably follow, affecting health and job performance.[29]

Examining the entire warrior framework, a world in which officers perceive constant and increasing mortal danger, it would seem natural for the police to experience a level of fear that most of us can only imagine. It is also unsurprising that many police officers would adopt the warrior mind-set and its tactics in order to cope with such an evil, perilous world. This leads to a policing approach based on "compliance and control," which creates an "adversarial relationship" between the police and the public they serve. This then results in a culture of policing that justifies and expects to use threats of force on anyone not following police orders.[30] Writing in *The Washington Post* just days after the death of Michael Brown in Ferguson, Missouri, in 2014, Officer Sunil Dutta, then a 17-year veteran of the Los Angeles Police Department, described the mind-set necessary for police work:

> … Here is the bottom line: if you don't want to get shot, Tased, pepper-sprayed, struck with a baton or thrown to the ground, just do what I tell you. Don't argue with me, don't call me names, don't tell me that I can't stop you, don't say I'm a racist pig, don't threaten that you'll sue me and take away my badge. Don't scream at me that you pay my salary, and don't even *think* of aggressively walking towards me.[31]

Language like this may sound like a threat to civilian ears. For officers like Dutta, on the street fighting the war on crime, safety and success mean they need compliance, and if they do not get it, civilians should expect to encounter whatever degree of force the officer deems necessary to get compliance.

Constant messages about deadly threats coming from every possible source continue, and such messages are unaffected by the facts about violence directed at the police. *For certain*, officers do sometimes face violence—occasionally even deadly violence. But the rhetoric in police training varies significantly from the most reliable data about what police actually experience. In the decade ending in 2013, the FBI said that, on average, 51 officers died from felonious killings every year.[32] In some of those years the total exceeded that number, and in others it did not reach 51. Since 2013, the FBI reported 51 felonious officer deaths in 2014,[33] 41 in 2015,[34] and 66 in 2016,[35] which is an average of almost 53. Officers also experience assaults on duty. In 2014, officers suffered 48,315 assaults[36]; in 2015, 50,212 assaults; and in 2016, 57,180 assaults.[37] The 2016 assaults resulted in injuries to officers about 30 percent of the time; for the 10 years ending in 2013, about 25 percent of assaults resulted in injuries to officers.

At the very least, we can say that policing, while sometimes dangerous, has not become substantially more dangerous. If anything, the physical danger of the job seems to have reached a plateau. (Whether the upward spike in felonious deaths and assaults in 2016 represents a coming upward trend, or only one up year amid a run of up and down years, will only become clear sometime in the future.) *Every one of those deaths constitutes a tragedy*—for the officer and the officer's family, first and foremost, and also for the officer's agency and policing more generally, and every assault injures a real person—a police officer. But collectively, these data do not portray an ever-more-dangerous world getting worse for police, and taking note of these data does not insult officers or the policing profession.

This discussion leads to another question, vis-à-vis the danger police officers face: How often does violence of any kind against police officers happen, compared to the frequency with which police have encounters with civilians? To answer this question, we need data on how many police/public contacts occur. The Bureau of Justice Statistics, a division of the U.S. Department of Justice, generates such a database in the periodic Police Public Contact Survey (PPCS), which is a comprehensive survey in which tens of thousands of Americans disclose whether they have had encounters with police officers, describing some of the aspects of these events.[38] In the most recent PPCS, for 2011, we learn that "[a]n estimated 62.9 million U.S. residents aged 16 or older, or about 26 percent of the population, had one or more contacts with the police ...."[39] The data showed that civilians initiated half of those contacts (e.g., a call from a resident about a burglary), and police officers initiated the other half (e.g., traffic stops, or stops of pedestrians).[40] With over 62 million encounters, what should we make of the danger involved? Professor Seth Stoughton, a former police officer, puts it this way:

> [F]or all of its risks, policing is now safer than it has ever been .... [Given the 63 million police/civilian interactions each year,] officers were assaulted in about 0.09 percent of all interactions, were injured in some way in

0.02 percent of interactions, and were feloniously killed in 0.00008 percent of interactions.[41]

We can certainly agree that these numbers—*any* numbers—would give no consolation or solace to police officers victimized by violence, or to their families. But in terms of the way that policing as a profession and as a culture creates a narrative about itself and what it does, and in terms of the way it presents itself to the public, *the data do not justify a law enforcement culture based on continual fear of ever-present deadly violence.* That it exists despite the evidence may offer some explanation for why use of force and even violence persists at the levels we see: Officers learn to continuously fear the worst, and fear becomes the constant denominator. "Officers' actions are grounded in their expectations, and they are taught to expect the worst."[42]

VIDEOS: THE CINEMA OF REAL AND EVER-PRESENT DEADLY VIOLENCE

If police training and culture contain the continuing message that every encounter with civilians holds the potential for deadly violence, we should note that not all of that message comes in the form of training textbooks, lectures from fellow officers at the academy, or even senior officers conducting one-on-one apprenticeships called "field training," which is common in almost all departments after academy training. Police, as recruits and as full-fledged officers, receive a constant barrage of information in the form of videos, almost always showing violence directed at police officers in common encounters with civilians—frequently in traffic stops. In almost all of these videos, civilians attack officers, sometimes viciously; in some, officers die before the viewer's eyes. Sometimes the police officer sustains a grave injury, such as getting shot, and the viewer learns that the officer subsequently died. Police trainers show these videos to raw recruits in the police academy and to veteran officers during in-service trainings. In trainings conducted by private companies, such as the Calibre Press and others,[43] for which officers pay a fee, professional trainers use the videos as examples of the unpredictability of violence against police and of the tactical mistakes the officer in the video made that resulted in injury or death.

Video recordings of police interactions with civilians have become common internet content, with video clips taken by dashboard-mounted cameras,[44] civilian cell phone cameras, and police body-worn cameras. Thus before a police recruit begins the first day of academy training, the recruit has probably already seen some video examples of civilian violence directed at police officers. Then comes the academy with its serious classroom analysis of the video. While civilians may watch these videos, police recruits (and officers already on the street, of course) watch them with much greater seriousness. No one can fault the idea of using these real-life examples to help officers understand how to avoid serious tactical mistakes. But it quickly becomes clear that the sheer volume of these videos and their emotional impact go further than teaching tactics. They become a deeply disturbing drumbeat that underscores how civilians everywhere pose deadly danger.

Officers "have their own canon of disturbing videos: a collection of widely viewed and much-discussed field recordings in which their fellow officers are killed or gravely injured in the line of duty."[45] These videos "have been watched by police officers across the country for years, and they are talked about with raw emotion" between officers.[46] They represent "a chilling reminder to never lose sight of the unpredictability they face on the street"[47] because mortal danger lurks everywhere. The videos have an unmatched impact, telling recruits that every encounter with a civilian may carry life-or-death stakes. According to one officer, a sergeant in the Indianapolis Metropolitan Police Department, video of violence against police "leaves an imprint on most of us." Nothing leaves an impression on a recruit like those "that end with the killing of a police officer."[48] According to another sergeant, that very impression is the point: "we need [police recruits who become officers] to have it in the back of their minds that these things do happen."[49]

A video showing the 1998 killing of Deputy Kyle Dinkheller of the Laurens County Sheriff's Office in Georgia may have the widest circulation of all.[50] In less than four minutes of video footage, Deputy Dinkheller pulls over a speeding pickup truck and engages the driver in friendly conversation. The driver then gets out of his vehicle, ignoring numerous instructions from Dinkheller, and refuses to take his hands out of his pockets as ordered. The driver then taunts the deputy, dancing around in the roadway, cursing Deputy Dinkheller and saying, "shoot my ass." Deputy Dinkheller calls for help from other officers, but things rapidly get out of control. The driver rummages in the back of his truck, comes up with a .30 caliber M1 carbine. Deputy Dinkheller orders him to put the gun down five times; instead the man begins shooting. The viewer sees the driver running back to his truck, with his gun, and driving away. Deputy Dinkheller, hit by ten shots, is already dead.

Another video that trainers show many officers and recruits records the events leading to the death of Deputy Darrell Lunsford, from Texas. Deputy Lunsford had pulled over a car containing three men, and he searched the suspects' vehicle, discovering marijuana in the trunk. In the meantime, the viewer sees two of the men confer in Spanish, which Deputy Lunsford does not understand, planning how they will attack him. The men jump Lunsford, catching him unawares. They overwhelm the deputy, stabbing him multiple times, and then they shoot him with his own gun.[51] Police trainers use the Deputy Lunsford video (called by one law enforcement media source "one of the most famous, tragic videos in law enforcement"[52]) to show the many mistakes the deputy made. In the words of a training instructor with the Connecticut State police, Deputy Lunsford did not maintain "total control" over the suspects, and that gave them the opportunity to catch him unawares. "He allowed both suspects out of the vehicle at once, he never patted either one of them down, and then he allowed them to speak to each other in a language he didn't understand," the trainer said. "The deputy allowed that to happen."[53]

Numerous videos of similar incidents tell police (and anyone thinking about becoming, or in the process of becoming, a police officer) that any encounter between an officer and a civilian involves the potential for deadly violence. In another video, Officer Sam Hodge pulls over a man named Charles Reynolds in a parking lot. Reynolds, at first compliant with instructions, reaches toward his waistband and shoots Hodge, who then fires back and shoots Reynolds dead. In another video, used by the Police Officer Safety Association, an officer makes a traffic stop and walks to the passenger side of the vehicle. With no forewarning, the driver shoots the officer and drives away. Police trainers use the video to illustrate how little time and information an officer may have during a traffic stop to spot a potential threat. Another video commonly seen in training and elsewhere records the murder of Corporal Mark Coates of the South Carolina Highway Patrol in 1992; in yet another, we see a shootout between an Oregon State Trooper and a military veteran, which the trooper thankfully survived. Dave Grossi, who worked for 12 years as an instructor for Calibre Press, a leading provider of private law enforcement training, claims a collection of more than 200 video recordings of police/civilian encounters involving deadly force; he uses them in his training lectures.[54]

A large number of these videos involve traffic stops, and this is not by chance. Video recording systems first appeared in policing decades ago, with cameras mounted on squad car dashboards. The first videos taken of police action in the field often came from these "dashcam" systems: Police stops of vehicles, in which the police place themselves so that the civilian vehicle remains in front of the police car, positioned it perfectly for a forward-looking dashboard-mounted camera system. We also know that traffic stops of vehicles constitute the single most common type of encounter most civilians have with police officers. According to the federal government's comprehensive PPCS, described above, 42 percent of Americans who had any encounter with police said that the encounter occurred as a result of a traffic stop.[55] The combination of these facts conveys an important message to police, which is that any traffic stop—the most common way in which you may confront the people you will serve—can turn deadly without warning. Therefore, it would seem entirely reasonable for police to fear these routine encounters, which have resulted in the deaths of some fellow officers. Seeing all this video evidence of mayhem and murder during standard police actions—simple traffic enforcement actions—could easily influence a police officer to think that he or she should view any member of the public as a dangerous, potential killer.

GUNS ARE EVERYWHERE

Examining the police warrior culture, its emphasis on the near constant presence of violence, and the ubiquitous use of videos of killings of police in police training allows us to see the creation of fear in our police officers as coming from inside police culture and organizations. One source of fear, however, begins outside of police and their organizations and cannot disappear through changes by law enforcement agencies or individual police officers. This most important source of fear among the police derives from the presence of guns. Firearms are everywhere in the United States, and this abundance of guns changes the way police must do (and think and feel about) their jobs.

Looked at another way, given the presence of guns in every corner of American society, perhaps police officers *should* feel fear because firearms may show up in any encounter with any person, anywhere, on any given day. Put yourself in the shoes of a police officer. If your job included confronting people every day, often in circumstances that might induce anger, and you know that any of these people might have a firearm within easy reach or even in hand, fear might seem rational—indeed, perhaps *the only* rational response. According to David Kennedy, a professor of criminal justice at John Jay College of Criminal Justice and the director of the National Network for Safe Communities, the possible presence of guns means that American police officers "need to be conscious of and are trained to be conscious of the fact that literally every single person they come into contact with may be carrying a concealed firearm." This is true for any kind of civilian contact. "It's true for everything."[56] This reality changes things for American police officers; their counterparts in most other countries simply do not face this reality and therefore do not have to think this way. Kennedy, who has worked with police all over the world, has noted this difference in Europe, Canada, and Japan. "In none of these other settings do police officers feel this way," he said; they just do not have the same concern about facing the same level of instantaneous and deadly violence that the presence of guns puts on law enforcement officers in the United States.[57] We find this dynamic reflected in the Jordan Miles case: In the words of Officer Saldutte's deposition, "I presume that everyone I come in contact with is a potential threat and could be armed until I know otherwise."[58]

Let's look at the basic numbers concerning guns in the United States. According to one oft-cited statistic, the United States now has more guns than people.[59] This may not be correct, but even conservative methods of counting estimate the number of guns at approximately 265 million.[60] Of those firearms, 113 million (more than 40 percent) are handguns. Not every American owns a firearm, but the average person who does own guns has two.[61] Approximately 8 percent of gun owners own 39 percent of all guns, that is, 8 percent of all gun owners have 10 or more guns.[62]

Perhaps a more telling statistic would involve the *rate* of gun ownership. Rates of gun ownership by state vary widely, from 5.2 percent in Delaware and 5.8 percent in Rhode Island, to 61.7 percent and 59.7 percent in Alaska and Arkansas, respectively. A worldwide comparison helps. According to one estimate, every 100 American civilians own 89 guns; the next highest-ranking countries are Yemen (55), Switzerland (46), and Finland (45).[63] In addition, many American states now allow people to carry concealed handguns. This means that any person who a police officer encounters may have one of those 113 million handguns within easy reach, where the officer cannot see it. As of April 2018, states have collectively issued over 16 million concealed carry permits—an increase of more than 250 percent since 2007.[64] The State of Florida, alone, has issued almost 1.8 million permits; Pennsylvania has issued 1,275,000.[65] Advocates for gun ownership often point out that people with gun permits may pose little danger of criminal activity or violence.[66] Assuming the truth of that statement, the fact remains that with America's copious supply of guns, police officers must keep the possibility of the presence of a gun in any encounter in mind at all times.

Perhaps, one could argue, the focus on guns gets things backward. Crime, not guns, poses the most danger to police officers. In other words, with more crime, our police officers face more danger, and the presence of guns does not change the level of danger. However, the data do not support this argument. Despite some very prominent claims that the United States now suffers from an overwhelming wave of crime and violence,[67] the rate of crime in the United States *does not* stand out among comparable Western countries. According to

Jeffrey Swanson of Duke University, among 15 Western industrialized nations, the United States sits around the middle of the pack in overall rates of crime,[68] and it has a *lower than average* rate of violent crime (violent crimes include those like robbery and aggravated assault). The average rate of violent crime among all 15 countries is 6.3 percent, with the U.S. average at 5.5 percent. In other words, it is not our rate of crime that makes the environment dangerous for our police officers (and our citizens too, of course); rather, where the United States does stand out is its level of *lethal* violence: we are the leader in the rate of *homicidal, murderous* crime. In 2017, the United States had 17,284 murders; the national homicide rate in the United States was 5.31 per 100,000 population[69]— about seven times what we see in comparable wealthy industrialized countries. The toll is far worse for young African American and Latino men. For young Latino men, homicide is the second leading cause of death; for young African American men, it is the number one cause and outpaces the next nine causes of death combined.[70]

In their trailblazing 1997 book *Crime Is Not the Problem: Lethal Violence in America*,[71] Franklin Zimring and Gordon Hawkins found that America's problem with crime originates not from violence but from *the deadly nature* of our violence, which is tightly connected to our profusion of firearms. Comparing property crime and violent assault in London and New York City, for example, Zimring and Hawkins found similar numbers of and patterns concerning crime, but "enormous differences in death risks." What explained this? "A preference for crimes of personal force and the willingness and ability to use guns in robbery make similar levels of property crime *fifty-four times as deadly in New York City as in London*."[72] So, for example, in 2012, all of the 14 comparison countries in Jeffrey Swanson's list had an overall homicide rate of less than 2.0 per 100,000 people; for the United States, the homicide rate per 100,000 was 5.1.[73] Factoring the presence of guns into these numbers, the rate of homicide by firearm per 1,000,000 people in 2012 ranged from 1.7 in Australia to 7.7 in Switzerland— to *29.7 per 1,000,000* in the United States.[74] "People in every country get into arguments and fights …. But in the U.S., it's much more likely that someone will get angry … and be able to pull out a gun and kill someone. This is something that police in the U.S. have to constantly fear."[75] Note that not all of this deadly violence comes at the end of the barrel of a gun; Americans also die in higher numbers from beatings, stabbings, and other kinds of attacks than people in comparable countries. But guns account for between 65 and 70 percent of all the criminal homicides in the United States.

A new look at the data in this field in 2018 gives some indication of where the plentitude of guns in America might lead. John Roman, a senior fellow at

NORC at the University of Chicago, in association with German Lopez of Vox Media, analyzed several categories of widely available statistics, focusing on state gun control laws and rates of gun ownership in individual states. They also included available data on police violence; they used the Police Violence Report[76] and cross-referenced it with the *Washington Post*'s database[77] on police killings of civilians. The result: "There is a correlation between killings by police officers and state's gun control laws and gun ownership rates. The stronger the gun control laws, the fewer police killings. The higher the gun ownership rates, the more police killings."[78]

Roman and Lopez include several appropriate caveats concerning their data and conclusions.[79] The study is a "crude analysis," not a peer-reviewed article. Roman and Lopez did not use a control group and a treatment group, so the examination cannot boast that sort of controlled-experiment precision. The data on gun control laws come from National Rifle Association composite scores and thus may not have sufficient analytical depth. In addition, the gun ownership survey they used may not have had sufficient sample size to allow conclusions concerning some small-population states. Perhaps, most importantly, the study shows a correlation; it cannot prove causation. Nevertheless, Roman and Lopez say, the evidence does show that any rigorous analysis must include consideration of the strength of state gun control laws and state-level gun ownership rates as possible reasons for police shootings and killings of civilians.

The Roman and Lopez analysis may be preliminary, but it stands with other significant studies. For example, in "Firearm Legislation and Fatal Police Shootings in the United States,"[80] published in 2017 in the *American Journal of Public Health*, Aaron Kivisto and colleagues examined the relationship between gun control laws and officer-involved shootings that resulted in deaths. Kivisto and his fellow researchers found that, controlling for demographics, "states in the top quartile of legislative strength"—the 25 percent of states with the strongest gun control laws—"had a 51% lower incidence rate" of fatal police shootings of civilians "than did states in the lowest quartile. Laws aimed at strengthening background checks, promoting safe storage, and reducing gun trafficking were associated with fewer police shootings." According to Kivisto and his team, this means that "when police are less often in situations in which they might reasonably fear that a gun is going to be pulled, they're less likely to react with the use of lethal force."[81]

Like Roman and Lopez, Kivisto and his colleagues make no claim of a causal relationship. But both studies show that the presence of greater or lesser numbers of firearms seems related in some way to the rate of fatal police shootings. Couple these findings with others—for example, a 2015 study finding

that each 10 percent increase in firearms ownership correlates with 10 additional homicide deaths of officers over a 15-year period[82]—and the evidence
cannot be ignored.

What connects the analysis of Roman and Lopez, and Kivisto and his
colleagues, to police shootings? According to social scientist and Yale law
professor Tracey Meares, the connection makes intuitive sense and aligns neatly
with the empirical evidence. "In situations where police officers say, 'I was in
fear for my life,' and later substantiate that with, 'I thought the person had a
gun,' the reasonableness of someone's assumption that somebody could possibly
have a gun is naturally related to the prevalence of guns in the environment."[83]
In other words, more guns in the environment, due to either less strict firearms
control laws or higher rates of gun ownership, make the claim of reasonable
fear of the presence of a gun more rational and the likelihood of an officer
responding to the fear of a firearm with a gun more likely.

This certainly does not mean that we should always believe police claims of
having seen a gun in a fast-moving encounter with a civilian. But it does mean we
cannot cast aside as irrational the fear of deadly violence from guns that police
may say they feel in any encounter with a civilian. Firearms violence remains
"something that police in the U.S. have to constantly fear," because police work
often involves confrontations, and those confrontations can more easily turn
deadly in the United States than anywhere else in the world. According to
David Kennedy of John Jay, this "affects every single contact they have with
members of the public," and it "changes how everyone behaves."[84] And *everyone*
would include not just police but civilians, and particularly civilians who live in
neighborhoods with an increased risk of firearms violence. Not coincidentally,
police in those neighborhoods will also have a heightened sense of danger. This
creates a deadly combination of real danger and palpable fear, which can easily
lead to more deadly violence. Plenty of reasons for fear, or other problems, may
explain the many ways in which police encounters with civilians go wrong. The
presence of guns throughout American society does not explain everything. But
to assert that guns play no role—that the problems of violence we face have
nothing to do with guns—constitutes willful blindness.

Thus while in no way disparaging the courage and bravery of American police officers, they
have every reason to feel real fear in the context of their daily tasks. They learn
to expect violence as a matter of course; they see it occur, in video after video;
and they cannot miss the presence of guns everywhere. Along with its toxic
twin, race, the effects of fear become magnified. In terms of the interactions
police may have in minority communities, the combination of racial effects and
the baseline fear present in policing combine into an accelerant, fueling the

worst impressions whites and blacks might have of each other, making every interaction between them fraught at best, and a potential catastrophe at worst.

Tioga Street may have been the physical setting for the confrontation between Officers Saldutte, Sisak, and Ewing and Jordan Miles. However, the street and its homes, the snow and ice, and the yards of the modest houses, played host to the specter of race and the fear that all American police feel in their work. The officers, however, were not alone in their fear. Jordan, like other African Americans who the officers could have encountered that night, would have harbored the same emotion: They would have feared the police, too.

CHAPTER 8

HOW FEAR IMPACTS BLACK AMERICANS

If American police officers live with constant fear and if the deeply held stereotypes of black Americans in American society associate them with crime and danger, we must also recognize a parallel reality: Fear runs both ways. Black Americans fear the police in the United States, and not simply because they represent authority or because they can penalize civilians with traffic citations. Rather, African Americans fear the power of the police to harass, to arrest, to injure—and even to kill them. These fears simply do not compare to the feelings white Americans may have about police officers. And these fears are real. They come from history, from personal experience, and from every story every person in black communities hears repeatedly time and again. In short, African American fears of police spring from a separate reality in which they live in, and which most whites never see.

The African American writer Nikole Hannah-Jones tells white readers, "[T]his is my chance to tell you that a substantial portion of your fellow citizens in the United States of America have little expectation of being treated fairly by the law or receiving justice." She explains the difference in perspective in geographic terms. "It's possible this will come as a surprise to you. But to a very real extent, you have grown up in a different country than I have."[1] In his book *The Condemnation of Blackness*,[2] Harvard Kennedy School Professor Khalil Gibran Muhammad says that white people do not know what it means or feels like to experience the aggressive, even abusive, style of policing used in black communities. "They don't understand it because it is not the type of policing they experience. Because they are treated as individuals, they believe that if 'I am not breaking the law, I will not be abused.'" Whites believe, mistakenly, that blacks live in the same reality.

Guthrie Ramsey, born in Chicago and living in Brooklyn, told his own story to Hannah-Jones.[3] Ramsey found himself engaged in one of the most common of parental duties, driving his teenage son to a soccer game. For Ramsey, described by others as an easy-going type, his upbringing did not include hatred or distrust of police. "I was socialized to believe that the police were our friends," he said. But the usually uneventful drive to the soccer game upended this. The police pulled Ramsey over. In just minutes—too little time to understand—he found himself and his young son sprawled on the ground. The police pointed loaded guns at both of them because they "fit the description of a suspect." In this terrifying moment, Ramsey managed to get the officers to look at his ID. It identified him as a faculty member at the University of Pennsylvania. (He is a Penn professor; his Penn web page says that he is "a musicologist, pianist, composer, and the Edmund J. and Louise W. Kahn Term Professor of Music" at Penn, with numerous books, musical works, and recording to his credit.[4])

Try to imagine a person of accomplishment and great stature, a person who creates works of art and writes books, respected by his university colleagues and fellow musicians—all of that washes away, stripped from him in an instant by this police action. Imagine him lying on the street with a loaded gun pointed at him. Even worse, imagine this man as a father, next to his young son, watching as the police point a different loaded gun at the boy. Any parent would feel the deepest, coldest fear and utter helplessness in that moment. "It was so frightening. It was humiliating," Ramsey said later. "You get so humiliated that it's hard to even get to the anger." Ramsey and other black Americans simply do not have dealings with the police that resemble those that whites have—just everyday encounters like getting help after a traffic accident or reporting a crime in one's neighborhood. As a black person, "you just don't get to experience interactions with the police as a garden-variety circumstance." Instead, his contact with the police involved powerlessness, detention, and the threat of deadly violence to himself and his beloved son.

What is remarkable about Guthrie Ramsey's story is not how awful it is but how common. It is impossible to quantify precisely, of course, but one need only listen to African Americans talk about the police, and the stories come spilling forth. Thankfully, not all involve deadly weapons pulled; some involve "only" harsh and disrespectful talk from officers. But many involve the use of force, beatings, and worse—even deaths. One meets few African Americans in the United States who cannot tell a story of mistreatment at the hands of police—to themselves, to a family member, or to a close friend. More men suffer this treatment than women, but some women do also, and even those who have not had this experience can speak about a father, husband, brother, son, male relative, or friend who has gone through it. In short, these stories stand as a testament to a universal part of the African

American experience in the United States. Not all police officers mete out such treatment, of course, but it happens enough, at the hands of some of them, that a profound but simple truth emerges: most black people have had such experiences or know others who have. The stories of these experiences move down and through each generation and are then reinforced by every new frightening experience, every new injury, and every new humiliating command. The all-pervasive cell phone (and, now, body camera) videos bring this all home, again, for everyone to see.

THE HISTORY STILL LIVES

The incidents that have brought fear to black Americans in their perceptions of the police did not begin with Ferguson, Missouri, in 2014, or even with Rodney King suffering a beating at the hands of Los Angeles police officers in early 1991. They go back much further, to the first presence of African slaves on this continent.

Most historians date the start of professionalized police forces to the mid-nineteenth century in Britain, with the famous "bobbies" (so named for their creator, Sir Robert Peel; some called them "Bobby's boys"). Before that, both Britain and the emerging United States had less formal police service, such as night watchmen or town constables. Among the first organized law enforcement mechanisms, however, at least in the American South, were slave patrols.[5] These loosely assembled groups of white citizens had the power to hunt down escaped slaves, to demand identification and permission badges from black people unaccompanied by whites, and to take blacks into custody for the purpose of restoring them to their rightful owners or places. They also had powers that allowed them to search slaves and their dwellings and to seize illegal materials, such as books. In short, these patrols could use all the physical force they wanted or felt they needed and had all the powers of the state, against any unaccompanied black person they might come upon. These slave patrols come from another time, of course; one cannot imagine them apart from the institution of chattel slavery itself. Yet some of their core functions outlived slavery. These groups used the power of the state to control racial boundaries in southern society, and they had full control of the freedom and bodily integrity of almost any black man or woman they might come across.

The history of American power structures beyond the time of slavery shows that these characteristics persisted well into the twentieth century in places—and some would say even later. In many parts of the South and also in some northern U.S. states, the Ku Klux Klan of the 1920s included many leading citizens across the country.[6] When a well-known Alabama trial lawyer and political figure named Hugo Black won a seat in the U.S. Senate in 1927, the Klan could count one of its own in that august body. Black claimed to have resigned from the Klan, in 1925, but evidence exists that he remained a member secretly. When Congress confirmed Black as an Associate Justice of the U.S. Supreme Court, the *Pittsburgh Post-Gazette* ran the headline "Justice Black Revealed as Ku Klux Klansman" on September 13, 1937.[7] The paper's investigation revealed Black's resignation in 1925 as both "temporary" and nothing more than a politically expedient ruse.[8]

In the era of the Civil Rights Movement of the 1950s and 1960s, police officers and police departments formed the vanguard across the South in enforcing the laws that mandated not just racial separation but white supremacy. The many photographs of the period tell the story in ways words cannot. In one image, the police force well-dressed black men sitting at a lunch counter to leave—exercising their state-derived power to arrest and to use force. In another, several elegantly dressed black women are marched away from a public area—by police officers. In photos from March 1965, of the attempt to cross the Edmund Pettus Bridge from Selma to Montgomery, Alabama, police officers attacked marchers with clubs, tear gas, and other weapons, charging them with horses and beating many (including future Congressman John Lewis, then a 25-year-old leader of the march).[9] In many other photos we see police officers use large snarling dogs on terrified men and women, ripping their clothes and their flesh—all for having the temerity to demand the equal rights given to all by the law. These images have a horrifying, almost paralyzing, effect on any viewer who might have thought, as Guthrie Ramsey did growing up, that the police are supposed to help you. Maybe so—but not then, not there, and not when the job included serving as the tip of the country's spear in enforcing the vile statutes of segregation, Jim Crow laws, and racist customs. While the northern states and cities do not have the reputation for racism attained by the South of that period, police participation in enforcing the sometimes-more-subtle forms of racism occurred with regularity. "In the North," says Hannah-Jones, "police worked to protect white spaces by containing and controlling the rising black population. It was not unusual for Northern police to join white mobs as they attacked black homeowners attempting to move into white neighborhoods, or black workers trying to take jobs reserved for white laborers."[10]

The 1960s saw the proverbial chickens come home to roost. As black Americans, led by Martin Luther King Jr.'s Southern Christian Leadership Conference, demanded change, progress seemed to come with the passage of the Civil Rights Act and the Voting Rights Act under President Lyndon Johnson. These legislative landmarks, which would become incredibly significant, did nothing to change the realities on the ground for African Americans who encountered the police. During several successive years in the mid-1960s, American cities experienced significant riots—urban unrest that claimed many lives and destroyed untold millions of dollars of value in residential buildings, business, industrial installations, and personal property. Whole areas in cities such as Chicago, Washington D.C., Detroit, and Los Angeles went up in flames; most of these areas still have not recovered, many decades later. When President Johnson set up a commission to study these disasters (formally called the National Advisory Commission on Civil Disorders, but usually known as the "Kerner Commission," for its chairman, Illinois Governor Otto Kerner), the group created a sensation when it released its report.[11] It identified over 150 riots or major disorders in U.S. cities between 1965 and 1968. It implicated white society and its institutions in the ghettoized, ingrained poverty of American blacks, and it famously warned that "our nation is moving toward two societies, one black, one white—separate and unequal."[12] The report also zeroed in on one of the core causes of the unrest: abusive police actions. The report made clear that, while other grievances existed in black communities (such as discrimination, poverty, and unemployment), many of the incidents that served to build the tension to the point of unrest involved police.[13] In half of the riots the Commission examined closely, the final precipitating incident consisted of a killing or other abuse of blacks by police officers.[14]

The Commission's report and its voluminous recommendations did not change the dynamic of police interactions with black Americans. In almost any American city, one can trace these same dissatisfactions with policing and race from the Civil Rights era into the 1990s, up to and including the beating of Rodney King in 1991. This was captured on video for the entire country to watch on the nightly news, as were the devastating riots in Los Angeles that followed when the police officers were charged in the assault on King. In 2001, when Cincinnati police officers shot and killed a young black man named Timothy Thomas as he fled, that city erupted in three days of unrest. And among all of the images from the unrest in Ferguson, Missouri, in the fall of 2014, one stands out for the way it harkens back to an earlier time. In it, a line of demonstrators with signs, hands visible, face a police officer who stands a short distance away, perhaps 10 feet; the officer holds the chain of a large, snarling German shepherd dog, teeth bared. The officer raises his other arm, perhaps making a gesture of calm, but the dog's presence carries another message, one with a long and hateful lineage.

Pittsburgh, where Jordan Miles grew up and where he encountered Officers Saldutte, Sisak, and Ewing near his mother's house on a January night in 2010, has its own history of devastating incidents between its police officers and black residents. This history was introduced in Chapter 4, with discussion of the cases involving the deaths of Jerry Jackson and Jonny Gammage, as well as discussion of the class action lawsuit filed by the ACLU against the city of Pittsburgh.

Thus in Pittsburgh, and in the rest of America, the history of relations between police departments and the black people they interact with begins in dark injustice. The present day contains constant reminders of the past, in the procession of tragedies just in the last few years: Laquan McDonald, Eric Garner, Tamir Rice, Alton Sterling, Philando Castile, Samuel DuBose, and so many others.

THE PROBLEMS REMAIN WITH US IN THE PRESENT

If the problem of police violence directed at black people had become part of a receding past, and if improved relations between police and black communities now predominated everywhere, perhaps the fear that African Americans feel regarding the police would fade. But there remain too many indications that, however much things may have improved, incidents that feed this fear keep happening. Each time they do, each time a damning video goes viral on the internet or makes the news, the old fears are present, reinforced, and recreated.

First and foremost, police in the United States continue to kill young black men at a disproportional rate. We might have only suspected this in the past. Indeed, with the glaring lack of statistics on civilian deaths at the hands of police in the United States—a situation that then-Attorney General Eric Holder called "troubling" and "unacceptable"[15]—we could only guess. Incredibly, the federal government *still* does not perform this important function, but as discussed earlier, in 2015, *The Washington Post* and *The Guardian* began to use multiple sources to track killings by police officers in the United States. These two sources show a remarkable consistency, both with each other and year over year (so far). For 2015, *The Washington Post* recorded 995 killings of civilians by police officers. Of those, 259—over a quarter—were black, though blacks make up only about 12 percent of the U.S. population. Among all people killed by police that year, 94 had no weapon. Blacks made up 40 percent of all those unarmed people shot and killed by police in that year.[16] Patterns in 2016[17] and 2017[18] looked the same: Black people were killed in disproportionate numbers, both in the full population of those killed by the police and among those unarmed.

Death at the hands of the police, at the rate of almost 1,000 Americans per year, has impacted the culture—at least over the last several years. In this age of ubiquitous, widely viewed videos, Americans from every walk of life and ethnic or racial group have become aware that an encounter with a police officer, even an everyday occurrence like a traffic offense, can turn deadly in a heartbeat. While this message has reached every kind of person, the racial inflection of the experience remains unmistakable. For example, consider an incident in Cobb County, Georgia, in August 2017. Lt. Greg Abbott of the Cobb County Police Department made a traffic stop on Interstate 75, at approximately 3:00 a.m., on suspicion of driving under the influence. The driver, a man, was arrested; a white woman was the lone passenger. In the course of the encounter, captured by the dashboard-mounted audio and video recording system in the patrol car, Lt. Abbott stands at the passenger side door and tells the woman that she should call the person who was coming to get her—"tell them they don't need to come." (In driving under the influence stops, police sometimes order the car towed away, and a passenger would need to find a ride. Here, the officer seems to be telling the passenger (who seems to have already called someone for a ride) that she will not need a ride—she will be able to drive the car away, even though the driver has been arrested—so the passenger should call the person who she asked to pick her up and tell that person not to come.) The woman says that she cannot call, and Abbott asks why. "Because I will not put my …." He cuts her off and tells her, "Use your phone. It's in your lap right there." The woman replies, "I just don't want to put my hands down. I'm really sorry." She continues, "I've just seen way too many videos of cops …." Lt. Abbott suddenly understands that she is afraid that if she puts her hands down, he'll shoot her, and he says that she has no reason to be afraid. "But you're not black. Remember, we only kill black people. Yeah, we only kill black people, right? All the videos you've seen, have you seen any white people get killed?"[19]

For the sake of argument, assume that Lt. Abbott meant these remarks as a way to break the tension in a difficult situation with a joke—maybe the worst joke ever made. The recording of the incident still tells us some important things. First, the knowledge of police shootings of civilians has penetrated everywhere, and even this white woman, who would have a very low risk of death at police hands, seemed well aware of the danger. Second, the officer almost certainly knows that his dashboard camera is recording what he says and does because in 2017, almost all dashboard-mounted cameras and their integrated microphones activate automatically with the use of vehicle emergency lights and sirens, which the officer would have used to signal the car to pull to the side of the road. Despite this, the officer feels free to attempt to calm the woman by assuring her that shooting and killing by police only happens to black people, not to whites like her.

If Lt. Abbott presumes that the white woman (and white people in general) knows who police shoot, black people certainly know it too—all too well and all too personally. And they, of course, would not feel relief but fear. And why would they not see a threat, enough to inspire fear? As Lt. Abbott helpfully (if jokingly) explained, "we only kill black people."

CONSEQUENCES ARE RARE

What happens when police break the rules, especially when they use force on people, white or black, resulting in injuries or death? Based on the well-known cases over the last several years, not much happens to the officers. Police rarely face criminal charges, even when a civilian dies; police sometimes face termination or disciplinary sanctions, but this does not usually happen either. The public notices this. There are reasons why prosecutors do not usually bring criminal charges against police, and even in rare cases when they do, acquittals often result. Below are examples from the last few years, some of which have been discussed in earlier chapters:

- In 2012, Rekia Boyd was with three friends in a Chicago park, when a police officer approached in a car and complained about the noise the group was making. When one of the male members of the group approached the officer and a verbal altercation started, the officer fired his gun multiple times. He later claimed the man approaching him had a gun, but no gun was ever found. Boyd, shot in the head, died almost 24 hours later. The officer was charged with involuntary manslaughter and other crimes and was later acquitted of all charges in the case.[20]
- In the 2014 death of Eric Garner, in Staten Island, New York, in which an officer killed Garner using an illegal chokehold, the officer faced no criminal charges. It took four years for the New York Police Department (NYPD) to file internal disciplinary charges against Officer Daniel Pantaleo.[21]
- In the 2014 death of 12-year-old Tamir Rice in Cleveland, Ohio, in which Officer Timothy Loehmann shot the boy within three seconds of pulling up next to him in a squad car, the officer faced no criminal charges. The Cleveland Police Department fired Loehmann, and he appealed his firing to an arbitrator. When the arbitrator denied the appeal in December of 2018, refusing to give him his job back, a police union spokesman attacked the decision and said that the union would pursue further court action to have Loehmann reinstated.[22]

- Also in 2014, in Bostrop County, Texas, Yvette Smith died when police came to a home to answer a call about several men fighting. A sheriff's deputy told Smith to come out of the house. When she stepped through the doorway, the deputy shot and killed her. The statement by the Sheriff's Office claimed that Smith was armed when she came out of the house, but the statement was later retracted.[23] The deputy was tried on murder charges and found not guilty.[24]
- In 2016, in suburban Minneapolis, Minnesota, Officer Jeronimo Yanez killed Philando Castile as Castile sat in his car with his girlfriend and her daughter, telling Yanez that he had a firearm and a license to possess it. Yanez faced criminal charges but the jury acquitted him.[25]
- In the 2016 death of Alton Sterling, at the hands of two police officers in Baton Rouge, Louisiana, neither officer faced federal or state criminal charges.[26] One officer was fired, and the other received a three-day suspension.[27]
- In 2016, Terence Crutcher was shot and killed by Tulsa, Oklahoma, Police Officer Betty Shelby. Reports of a vehicle that stalled in the road brought Shelby to the scene. Crutcher was unarmed. A jury acquitted Shelby of manslaughter.[28] She resigned from the force and hired on with the sheriff's department in a nearby county, where she began teaching a class for other officers in "surviving" controversial shooting cases like the one in which she had been acquitted.[29]

A few cases do turn out differently. In Chicago, Officer Jason Van Dyke shot and killed Laquan McDonald. The killing, caught on dashcam video, shows Van Dyke entering a situation that other officers had under control and firing 16 fatal shots within seconds of arrival. Van Dyke wrote in his report, and testified in his trial, that McDonald posed a direct and immediate threat to him, lunging at him with a knife, when the video showed no such thing. The jury rejected Van Dyke's story and convicted him of second-degree murder.[30] (If the case represented a moment of accountability, it lost that sheen when, just months later, three officers who had written reports backing Van Dyke's story—refuted by the video—were acquitted by a judge in a bench trial,[31] and just a day later, a judge gave Van Dyke a sentence of less than seven years.[32]) In New York, a jury convicted the officer whose apparently accidental gunshot killed Akai Gurley in the stairwell of a city housing project (although that officer got no jail time for his manslaughter conviction).[33] We cannot, however, miss the overall picture: In cases in which police kill black victims, officers do not suffer consequences in the end. This result would tend to make officers less fearful of consequences, which, in turn, could only make black Americans fearful of police.

Matthew Horace, a veteran of three decades in law enforcement, a CNN commentator, and author of the 2018 book *The Black and the Blue: A Cop Reveals the Crimes, Racism and Injustice in America's Law Enforcement*,[34] tells a revealing story. As he did his research in preparation for writing the book, he checked in with a high-ranking NYPD officer who he'd known for some time. Horace said to the NYPD vet that he wanted to make sure his book communicated to the public, especially to African Americans, that they needed to understand that police officers have a very difficult job to do. The man told Horace that he was worrying about the wrong thing. "Black people know how hard the job is. What they don't understand is how it is that we, the police, are *never* wrong. They don't understand how, in case after case, a person is shot and killed by police, but the police never are at fault. They never do wrong."[35]

WHAT DO AFRICAN AMERICANS FEEL ABOUT THE POLICE?

All of the above influences appear to have impacted the attitudes of black Americans toward police. This emerges clearly from polling data, not just in terms of what blacks think but in how what they think compares to the attitudes of their white compatriots. Looking at these results suggests that Nikole Hannah-Jones has it right: As far as policing, black and white Americans have grown up, and live, in different countries.

The Associated Press–NORC Center for Public Affairs Research at the University of Chicago created an extensive survey to look for clear and accurate insights into how the public views law enforcement, police misconduct, and violence and to break those views down demographically, to see differences among white, black, and Hispanic Americans.[36] The survey included over 1,200 American adults, with enough black respondents to assure fully representative results. The findings help us understand what black and white Americans believe about police in the United States.

Researchers asked people whether they, or a member of their family, "ever felt treated unfairly by a police officer specifically because of (your or their) race?" Two-thirds of all blacks—almost 66 percent—said yes; only 8 percent of whites said that they had, and 51 percent of Hispanics said yes as well. This collection of bad experiences at the hands of police, the researchers said, made those people "more likely to have a negative opinion of law enforcement than those who have not had racially shaded encounters with police." One can see this clearly in answers to another question: "How serious a problem do you think police violence against the public is in the United States?" The overall picture splits evenly: a third of all Americans say the problem is extremely or very serious, a third say moderately serious, and a third say it is not serious or not too serious. But the experiences of black Americans yield something different: Nearly three-quarters (73 percent) of blacks call the problem of police violence against civilians either extremely or very serious. By contrast, only 20 percent of whites—just one in five—agree. Put another way, nearly four times as many blacks as whites believe the problem of police violence against civilians constitutes an extremely or very serious problem. (Fifty-one percent of Hispanics join blacks in their assessment.)

The point is reinforced even more when we look at the answers to other questions: 80 percent of blacks believe that police use deadly force far too quickly; only 33 percent of whites agree. About 85 percent of blacks believe the police are much more likely to use deadly force against black people in most communities; only 39 percent of whites believe this. As for how the police treat people generally, the results also show a racial gap. Asked whether police in their communities treat people of all groups equally or whether "they sometimes deal more roughly with members of minority groups," 81 percent of blacks said minorities get rougher treatment; 47 percent of whites agreed (along with almost two-thirds of Hispanics).

The researchers asked respondents about the treatment of police in the justice system when officers injure or kill civilians. Americans as a whole seem evenly divided over whether the system treats officers accused of hurting or killing civilians too leniently, fairly, or too harshly. But there is a huge divide on this question when researchers break down answers by demographic group. Approximately 70 percent of blacks think the justice system treats accused police officers too leniently; only 32 percent of whites agree. This division seems to reflect the long list of cases over the last several years in which officers accused of harming or killing civilians faced little or no consequences.

Given all of this, it comes as no surprise to learn that when the researchers asked how much of the time people felt that they "can trust the police to do what is right for you and your community," 72 percent of whites answered always or often; only 33 percent of blacks agreed. Those numbers, which are nearly the exact opposite of the answers black and white people gave on whether they believe police use of violence against the public is an extremely or very serious problem, explain a lot about the degree of fear a black person in the United States might feel toward the police. Two-thirds of blacks say either they or a family member have experienced maltreatment by the police because of their race. Such treatment leads them to feel, by even larger majorities, (1) that police violence directed at citizens constitutes an extremely or very serious problem, (2) that police have become too quick to use deadly force and are more likely to use deadly force against blacks, and (3) that police treat minorities roughly. Blacks believe that when these things happen, officers get the benefit of unduly lenient treatment.

For anyone living in the world that these views describe, fear of police might seem the only reasonable reaction.

THE CONSEQUENCES: CALL 911! OR DON'T?

Since 1968,[37] when an emergency occurs, Americans have always known what to do to summon help: call 911. Calls to 911 can summon an ambulance, firefighters, or—most commonly—police, when a citizen has witnessed a crime or becomes a victim of one. A call to 911 for police help has become an almost reflexive response to crime and disorder in the United States.

But it turns out that not everyone in American society feels this way. It has nothing to do with 911 per se; rather, it concerns the summoning of police. Some black Americans feel deep discomfort about calling 911. This does not mean they do not want help or do not feel deeply concerned about crime. In point of fact, blacks in the United States generally feel more concerned about crime than do whites.[38] Rather, African Americans may hesitate to call the police because they fear what will happen when the police arrive: they themselves— the callers—may end up in jeopardy.

Writer Nikole Hannah-Jones tells a story about a Fourth of July outing with family and friends on Long Island.[39] Walking along the beach, their small group—adults and children, including an out-of-town guest —suddenly witnessed a shooting nearby. No one sustained injuries. The shooter fled on foot and quickly disappeared, and Hannah-Jones and others had only seen the person's back and could not describe him. But when the guest who was part of the group that day called the police, Hannah-Jones realized to her surprise that *only* the guest (a high-school intern from Oregon, staying with her family for a few weeks) had called the police. Neither she nor any of the other adults in her group had even thought to do so. Speaking of her family and friends, she said none of them had even considered calling the police:

> We are also all black. And without realizing it, in that moment, each of us had made a set of calculations, an instantaneous weighing of pros and cons …. Calling the police posed considerable risks. It carried the very real

possibility of inviting disrespect, even physical harm. We had seen witnesses treated like suspects, and knew how quickly black people calling the police for help could wind up cuffed in the back of a squad car. Some of us knew black professionals who'd had guns drawn on them for no reason.

At the bottom of their thinking, she said, lay a deep, cold fear. "We feared what could happen if police came rushing into a group of people who, by virtue of our skin color, might be mistaken for suspects."

This is the truth, surprising as it is to those who do not have black or brown skin: When encountering crime and disorder, even when experiencing these things as a victim, calling the police is not automatic. Rather, one must ask whether doing so will make things worse—perhaps much worse.

The same point emerges from another story, in reverse. Shauna-Kaye Spencer, a graduate of the University of Pittsburgh School of Law, grew up in South Florida.[40] Born to parents who had emigrated from Jamaica, she describes her upbringing as typically middle class. As a teen, she recalls herself as a young black American no different from her peers, but because her parents had not grown up in the United States, they carried none of the historical baggage that other black adults in the United States usually do concerning police. For her family, she said, the attitude toward police was, "the police can help, they are good, you can rely on them for anything." Her parents never had "The Talk" with her, as so many black parents do in the United States—the conversation in which parents tell their driving-age children how to act so they survive the dangers of a police encounter when stopped by police.

Spencer vividly recalls an experience that she had at age 16. She and a group of other black kids the same age had gone to a party in a part of town that none of them really knew. The neighborhood did not seem safe. At some point, the police arrived at the party and shut it down, forcing everyone to leave, including Spencer and her friends. Spencer knew she could call her mother to come and pick the group up, but her mother did not have a good sense of direction and Spencer did not know the neighborhood either, so she needed to get to some kind of landmark on a recognizable street—a store or gas station that her mother could find. Neither she nor her friends knew where to go, not even which way to walk to get to a major street. So Spencer told her friends she would ask one of the police officers (who had just thrown them out of the party and remained at the scene) for directions. It seemed like the obvious and logical thing to do, but her friends reacted in a way she did not expect. "They were like, 'why would you ask a cop?' " She found this perplexing; none of them knew where to go, so who else would she ask, she remembers thinking. "I was the only one who walked over to [the police]—everyone was afraid to come with me." She approached the officer and politely asked how to find a major intersection and explained why she wanted to know. Spencer got another surprise. The officer seemed just as baffled as her friends. Why was she talking to him, in this situation? She could tell from the look on his face that the officer was confused. According to Spencer, the officer seemed to be thinking, "Why [are you] talking to me? What do you want?" He seemed just as puzzled that Spencer would speak with him, as her own friends were. He gave her the directions she needed, and Spencer and her friends made it home.

But the incident left a deep impression. Spencer had been oblivious to the fact that her friends would not want to talk to the police, that they might even be afraid, and also that the officer would not expect her to ask for help because of fear or distrust. Throughout the rest of her high school years, Spencer was known as the girl who was "not afraid to talk to the police." Not until a few years later did she learn how different her attitudes and experiences were. "I didn't know, actually, that black people were … afraid of police until I went to college." Spencer's story stands as a photo negative to Nikole Hannah-Jones's beach story: A black woman raised by parents who come from outside the African American experience has a totally different reaction to the idea of approaching police than her African American peers. She simply expected to interact with the police and get help, like any other citizen.

Lest anyone think that the stories of black people not calling the police are *just stories*, researchers now have solid proof of the phenomenon. Matthew Desmond, Andrew V. Papachristos, and David S. Kirk, of Harvard, Yale, and Oxford Universities, respectively, used statistical patterns of 911 calls to create an empirical picture of what happens when police assault or kill a black person and the whole community learns of it. In a study published in the *American Sociological Review*,[41] the researchers say that, of course, such an incident could lead to "legal cynicism—the deep-seated belief in the incompetence, illegitimacy, and unresponsiveness of the criminal justice system." Many believe that this cynicism "pervade(s) many poor, minority communities." But, they asked, even if that is true, does it mean that people in those communities *will not engage with the police*? Perhaps these people become deeply cynical, but in the end, who else would they call to report crime or victimization? To find out, the researchers focused on Milwaukee, Wisconsin, a city that consistently ranks as highly segregated—making it easier to distinguish black and white neighborhoods—and one that has had its share of police misconduct. They focused on one particularly egregious incident, the vicious beating of a black man named Frank Jude.

Jude incurred the ire of a group of police officers, who believed he had stolen another officer's badge at a house party. (No evidence ever emerged that Jude took the badge, and even if he had, it would in no way excuse what the police did. And after an acquittal in state court of three of the officers, prosecutors in federal court convicted seven of the eight officers involved.) The full story of the horrific incident hit the front page of the *Milwaukee Journal-Sentinel* almost four months later,[42] marking the point at which almost everyone in Milwaukee would have learned about the incident. The researchers used that date as their marker, to denote the before and after points of wide diffusion of knowledge about the Jude incident, which might or might not affect the rate of 911 calls to police to report crime and victimization. They collected all 911 calls in Milwaukee between March 1, 2004 (months before Frank Jude's beating, in late October of 2004) and December 31, 2010, years later. They screened out calls that originated outside the city and eliminated those involving fires, vehicle accidents, and the like.

The researchers could determine from these more than 880,000 calls where the calls came from and (because of the city's heavy residential segregation) whether the calls originated in black or white neighborhoods. They compared (1) the numbers of 911 calls before and after the Jude story broke widely, (2) contrasts between white and black neighborhoods, and (3) the numbers of actual calls by neighborhood after the story broke (compared with the predicted numbers of calls based on past history, had the Jude incident never happened). The upshot is that 911 calls in black neighborhoods went down significantly when the Jude story broke, and they stayed down for over a year. In white neighborhoods, a small dip in 911 calls occurred but soon disappeared, with calls returning to and even exceeding the former expected level. All in all, the researchers said, "[T]he beating of Frank Jude had a much more substantial effect on citizen crime reporting in black neighborhoods than in white neighborhoods." In that first year after the media exposed the Jude story, people in Milwaukee made 22,200 fewer 911 calls than they would have otherwise, and based on precedent, well over half of those lost calls would have come from black neighborhoods, even though blacks made up only 40 percent of Milwaukee's population. There was no drop in noncrime 911 calls (e.g., for accidents and fires), which remained the same. In other words, the drop only happened for incidents involving crime.

Reporting on the Milwaukee 911 call study, journalist Jesse Singal put the results into wider perspective. The study tells us, of course, that "[W]hen people are given a reason to be scared or distrustful of the police, they're less likely to call them for help." But the consequences spread further than that individual action and deep into our communities. "This, in turn, likely does a lot of societal damage: The absence of a functional relationship between police and a given community makes things harder for everybody, especially in areas with high levels of violent crime." Black and poor people would, in the racially and economically segregated United States, tend to live in exactly those areas, creating further cycles of crime (when criminals and predators do not get reported and thus remain free to victimize others).

Widespread fear of police among African Americans exists. It is a real phenomenon that cannot be dismissed as a figment of the black imagination. It has its basis in a real and abundant history of abuse and mistreatment by police, and in a continuing plague of black death and injury at the hands of police today, even conceding that the relationship between police and black Americans has improved significantly overall. African Americans' fear of the police is both real and logical.

A black man facing the police, having done nothing wrong, might choose to stop, answer questions patiently, and wait until the officers decide that he has done nothing to deserve detention or scrutiny. Or, facing the same situation, this man might think of his past experiences, or those of friends or family members, or the stories he has heard his entire life—of disrespect, humiliation, beatings, and injuries. And such a man might choose, if he could, to try to escape. Running would not be illogical or without reason, and no amount of repetition of the old question, "If you've done nothing wrong, why did you run?" will make that reality go away.

CHAPTER 9

IF HE DIDN'T DO ANYTHING, THEN WHY DID HE RUN?

As we think about the incident on Tioga Street, *how* the incident started remains the biggest point of contention. Did the officers jump out of an unmarked car, dressed in plain clothes, and without identifying themselves run at Jordan while yelling, "Where's the drugs? Where's the money? Where's your gun?" Or did they see Jordan next to the wall of a house, stop him and question him carefully, identifying themselves as police officers, and then pursue him only when Jordan ran away, unprompted? The Mountain Dew bottle also separates the stories. Jordan says he never had a bottle in his pocket. The officers say that they fought with him, with Jordan struggling mightily to get his right hand to his right coat pocket, and from that pocket, they pulled the Mountain Dew bottle and tossed it away.

Another question remains, however, as touched on in Chapter 8: Why did Jordan run? If he was just a short distance—less than a minute's walk—from his mother's house, why run? This question certainly seemed central to everyone on the police side. Officers Saldutte, Sisak, and Ewing always maintained that Jordan simply could not have failed to know he faced not three unidentified men but three police officers, because they clearly identified themselves verbally and displayed their badges. Having done that, they said, Jordan simply should not have run, and when he did, the responsibility for everything else that happened (the struggle, any blows that Jordan took, and any injuries he sustained) rests with him. The officers had a powerful ally in this argument. Recall that when federal prosecutors announced that they would bring no criminal charges against the three officers, the Pittsburgh's Chief of Police, Nathan Harper, announced the next day that he would reinstate the officers. At his news conference, Harper made clear that, even assuming Jordan had committed no crime, he agreed with the officers' assessment. "From this, we would hope that the young people realize that when a police officer approaches them, and they've done nothing wrong, to see what the police officer wants instead of running away from the police officer," the Chief said. "We aren't the enemy out there."[1]

So why did Jordan run? Take the question, first, from Jordan's point of view, assuming he is telling the truth. He had left his mother's house on a residential street, for the short walk to his grandmother's home, where he slept every night—something he'd done hundreds of times before. He doesn't notice any activity except for a single car, toward the end of the block, down near the bus stop. He has his friend Jamiah on the phone, undoubtedly paying at least as much attention to that conversation as he is to his very ordinary and quiet surroundings as he walks through the cold night. Then without any warning, the car speeds up, comes toward him, and closes in, causing Jordan to jump backward from the street to the sidewalk. Three large men he does not know, all in dark clothes and with no identification of any kind, jump out and begin to yell about drugs, guns, and money. If we assume the truth of these facts, we can see how almost anyone might run. Jordan is faced with a sudden, perhaps dire, threat from strangers, who seem to want to surprise and overwhelm him in an effort to get money and drugs, as well as deadly weapons. The neighborhood in which he is walking experiences considerable violent crime, and robbery would not seem out of the realm of possibility. In short, Jordan is facing a classic fight-or-flight situation.[2] Faced with three men, all larger than himself and all threatening him as they move toward him, flight seems not just instinctive but the smart choice. If Jordan can get away, he should do so as fast as possible; he would be facing long odds in a fight.

Now do the same exercise from the officers' point of view by assuming the truth of their story of the beginnings of the incident. They testified that they pull their car even with where Jordan is coming out from between the houses and walking down a driveway toward the street. They surprise him; they identify themselves, both visually (displaying badges) and by announcing themselves as officers; and they ask him to stop and take his right hand out of his pocket. Then they question him. Where does he live? If not at the house where they'd seen him, why was he sneaking around that house? After that question, knowing the men in front of him were police officers, Jordan tried to run. Why?

One possibility is that the officers see Jordan standing by the side of a house not because he has taken the first step toward committing a burglary, but because he has seen their car approach and decides to hide. Perhaps Jordan thinks that the car contains gang members or some other criminals who, even though they have not stopped or shown any sign of having seen him, might mean him harm or pick him out as a target of opportunity for a crime. He therefore does what he can to hide himself, by ducking between the two houses, until he can be sure the car had passed. (Of course, Jordan denies that he did this, but for this exercise, let us accept as true what the police said happened.) But when the young man goes back to the street, the car suddenly reappears—and police officers come out and begin to question him as if he has done something wrong: "Take your hand out of your pocket …. Do you live there?" When Jordan answers no, he lives down the block, they become more suspicious: "So why were you sneaking around that house, if you don't live there?" That is when alarm bells might start going off for Jordan. He was walking toward his grandmother's house, as he did every night, and was acting only a little differently by ducking between the houses, to make sure he arrives safely. The police now seem to accuse him, right off, of doing something wrong—maybe something criminal. Police go after criminals by stopping them and questioning them like this all the time; Jordan would have seen it in his own neighborhood, perhaps many times. And just because one has done nothing wrong—well, perhaps Jordan might think that police did not always seem to care if this is true or not. Thinking about this in the moment, maybe Jordan panics and runs, perhaps just trying to get back home.[3]

But this scenario requires a number of assumptions in order to accept it as true. Jordan has to have seen the car go by. He has to have had the thought that a lone car rolling by posed some kind of danger to him. In all of the hundreds of times he has walked, at night, to his grandmother's house down Tioga Street, it seems unlikely that only on this night he saw a car, which unnerved the young man to such an extent that he felt the need to hide. Even if Jordan had acted this way, when he saw the men and their police badges and heard their announcements of their police authority, why not simply say, "I just ducked in there because I thought you might be gangbangers"? It would have been easy and uncomplicated, and Jordan knew he had not done anything wrong, and the people in that house—they would know him, they would tell the police he would not be trying to break in to their house. Why, instead, attempt a run for his life?

Unfortunately, there are answers that explain exactly why Jordan would have run. Such reasons have much in common with understanding the fear of police, as discussed in Chapter 8. Black people, especially young black men like Jordan, may fear the police, and this fear is not without reason. Making a choice in the heat of the moment to avoid the police—and to run, if necessary, to do that—is not irrational at all, given this group's experience and worldview. In fact, for them, it makes all the sense in the world. Young African American men fear mistreatment at the hands of the police—sometimes physical, sometimes verbal, sometimes legal, and sometimes all three. This fear often suffices to provoke flight, and anyone who calls this reaction unreasonable probably has not the experienced the world in which these young people live.

THE STORIES OF POLICE ABUSE TRAVEL EVERYWHERE ACROSS BLACK COMMUNITIES

Black people, especially men, grow up hearing about mistreatment of blacks by police. According to many who have studied the phenomenon, narratives passed down through families and in black communities often touch on experiences of abuse suffered by fathers, uncles, older brothers, cousins, or friends at the hands of officers. Scholar Rod K. Brunson, who has examined the experiences of many African American men with police, says that stories of police mistreatment of black citizens are "abundant" in African American communities. Brunson says that "[T]he dissemination of these narratives increases the likelihood that neighborhood residents will come to view local policing strategies as racially biased."[4] In making appraisals of police, Brunson says, black people "not only draw from their own experiences but also from patterns of events they are exposed to in their communities and knowledge imparted by members of their racial group."[5] They consider not only their own experiences but also the experiences of "family members', friends', and neighbors' interactions" that they hear in stories told and retold.[6] In his work, Brunson found that African Americans were more likely than whites to hear negative stories about police mistreatment from family members, friends, and community members.[7] In *Living with Racism: The Black Middle-Class Experience*, Joe R. Feagin and Melvin P. Sikes explain that such narratives spread across the whole black population because "[A] black victim frequently shares the account with family and friends, often to lighten the burden, and this sharing creates a domino effect of anguish and anger rippling across an extended group."[8]

According to researchers Lois Weis and Michelle Fine, the narratives and stories that African American men tell about society often center on police harassment.[9] In these stories, police view all black men as criminals or drug dealers, which allows police to "viciously seep through poor black neighborhoods" and harass the black men there.[10] In many of these stories, "[Y]ou don't view the police as protecting you, but as your enemy. And you watch them because it's almost like they're legalized gangs."[11] One black man included in the Weis and Fine study, who had lived in a majority white neighborhood that eventually became mostly black, relates how police behavior changed from respectful to harassing when the neighborhood's demographic makeup shifted. "I know for a fact that they didn't do this in a white neighborhood. Because when our neighborhood was white, they didn't do that. As soon as it turned mostly black, everything changed."[12]

Of course, year after year, stories in traditional media and on social media become part of these stories—often accompanied by powerful videos of horrific violence. In today's world, with sophisticated cameras at the fingertips of anyone with a mobile phone and also on the uniforms of many police officers, the videos of sometimes fatal violence against young black men by police have become horrifyingly common. In a study of groups of African American boys ages 14 through 17, Raja Staggers-Hakim found that these young people had a "general knowledge and awareness around national cases of police brutality and extrajudicial killings" and the "wave of violence targeting African American boys and men."[13] Most of this information comes from the media, consumed traditionally or on students' smart phones. All of this input reinforces fear of the police and makes this fear real in a very graphic and concrete way. Any individual incident might have taken place in a faraway city or town, but all of these boys seemed to know that it could happen in their own neighborhoods. One young person, noting that it could happen in his community, told Staggers-Hakim, "[I]t could happen here … it can happen to anybody …. I've had an encounter with a cop that was just the same as the other guys. It can happen anywhere."[14]

The young African Americans who Staggers-Hakim studied also have another insight, without the benefit of studying the social science research presented earlier in Chapter 7: They understand, intuitively, that the police fear *them*—that officers see them as dangerous and threatening. Police see them, these black teens said, through social perceptions and stereotypes, with officers assuming that black men are criminals until proven otherwise. These young people said that officers presume that every young black man they encounter deals drugs or steals or robs or engages in other criminal activity.[15] Thus the highest ideal of the legal system becomes inverted for black males. The law (embodied by the police) presumes them guilty until proven innocent because of the immutable characteristic of skin color. Some of the teens studied believe that this thinking goes even further in that police officers talked and acted as if young black men were not even human. One boy recalled hearing about an infamous killing of a young black man by an officer, in which the officer described his fear of the man he shot with the words, " 'it approached me' "— talking about the victim of the shooting like an animal.[16]

All of this leaves young black men with a visceral fear of physical assault or even death at the hands of police. One young man told researchers, "I am in fear for my life. If I walk by a policeman or someone in authority, being a black man in this country in general"[17] means these people might fear him, and spurred to action by that fear, hurt or kill him. Another said, similarly, "It could be me. I feel scared when I walk by a policeman or [police] woman."[18] A third said, "t[T]hat's a fear—just the fact that I could be killed or beaten down."[19] Actual police use of force may happen rarely in an overall, statistical sense, but people in black communities see force used much more often, at higher rates, and for lesser reasons, according to those who actually live the experience.

What these young people see on the streets every day in their neighborhoods, carried further through community narratives, reinforces the sense of physical danger. In a piece for the *Chicago Defender* titled "Why Do Black Men Run from the Police?," Kai El'Zabar explains the familiarity that most of these youths would have with police activity. "[I]t is not unusual," El'Zabar says, "to find the police menacing the poorest, crime-ridden communities every day. Instead of serving to protect these communities, police have instigated and intimidated the residents with reckless and irresponsible manhandling." This leaves black men fearful of ending up dead or injured at the hands of police.[20]

Of course, the abuse suffered need not be physical; it may take a verbal form. In one of a series of articles examining the experiences of both black and white young people and comparing white, black, and mixed neighborhoods, Rod Brunson and Ronald Weitzer identified verbal abuse as among the difficulties young black males faced in ways that whites did not.[21] Officers regularly used derogatory, offensive, and condescending language in interactions with citizens, they said, but with black youths, the language went beyond discourteous. It included inflammatory words, racial slurs, and demeaning name-calling. One young white male told researchers that the police might say insulting things to him, but they reserved the worst verbal treatment for young blacks. He said that he has not had racial insults flung at him by police but has heard it directed at other young men in his presence. "I have heard white cops call my black friends nigger and 'boy' like how they say 'boy' in the South."[22] One young black youth said that police like to curse at him and his friends and "shout bitches, hoes, niggers."[23] The officers humiliate and embarrass them with this language by using the kinds of taunts and insults designed to offend, belittle, and abuse. It is an assertion of power by officers over the targets of their insults, too. Officers receive training in using a "command presence" and strong vocal commands to get compliance from those who might not want to do what they say, although one would have difficulty finding any kind of police training justifying this sort of talk toward citizens.

Such verbal abuse does not happen accidentally, and it may serve another purpose besides belittling and trying to disempower the people treated this way.

In some instances, some officers intend to provoke a reaction by the people they verbally abuse. According to the young black people studied, police "routinely provoked youths to have a reason to assault them."[24] In another of their black and white youth comparison studies, Brunson and Weitzer found that officers' "adversarial and provocative" demeanor and language aimed at the same goal. To provoke the young black men into taking action would allow officers to inflict a beating on them, along with an arrest,[25] and sometimes this works. A young man who loses his temper, either by "mouthing off" or by reacting physically, will experience a physical attack by police and a serious set of charges such as assault on a police officer (often a felony) and resisting arrest.

Apart from the fear of physical assault that may leave them hurt or killed, and the verbal abuse that aims to humiliate and even provoke a response, young black men live in fear of legal jeopardy. This goes beyond simply not wanting to get caught if engaged in criminal activity or in possession of something illegal. A deep-seated fear exists that any encounter with a police officer can result in criminal charges, whether or not one has done anything to deserve this. Behaving properly and following the law provides them no protection. "[L]aw-abiding status did not insulate them from aggressive policing strategies, (and) they likewise found that it did not protect them from physical abuse." Even if police violence did not occur every day, "[I]t happened enough to convince them that it was a real possibility during *any* encounter with police officers."[26] In short, behaving oneself guarantees nothing in terms of protection from police abuse, and the threat of encountering this treatment always remains an arbitrary possibility in any encounter with law enforcement. No amount of studiousness or learning, no social status, no especially neat clothing or perfected personal presentation can change this.

With all of this fear and the past experiences of the elders an ever-present lesson for every young man, we should ask, What would black parents do? How would a black mother or father prepare a child or an adolescent for these kinds of encounters with police—unwanted, undeserved, and deeply feared? When a black parent knows that his or her child, doing nothing out of the ordinary, could have a deadly confrontation with police, how should that parent try to prevent this from happening? Of course, all parents will tell their children to act properly, behave within the law, and not give police officers a reason to approach them. But what if, as a parent, you knew that these encounters would likely happen anyway? What would you tell your child or teen? You would do what any black parent would do: You would have "The Talk."

THE TALK

The Talk has long been an almost universal feature of black life in America. Yet few white Americans may have heard of it, or would even guess what it could be. In the simplest terms, black parents understand—from their own experiences or the experiences of loved ones or friends, or the narratives of mistreatment discussed above—that any encounter with a police officer can go badly, resulting in verbal or physical abuse, arrest, or even injury or death. For African American parents, this creates a straightforward imperative: They must do what they can to ensure the safety and survival of their children, and they do not have the option of calling the police to help with this because for them, this particular danger comes in the form of the police. The task becomes instructing their children how to behave in order to survive a police encounter. If this statement sounds dramatic or overdone, think of the parents of 12-year-old Tamir Rice, killed by a Cleveland police officer; or the parents of 15-year-old Jordan Edwards, killed by a police officer in Balch Springs, Texas; or the parents of 17-year-old Antwon Rose, killed by an officer in East Pittsburgh, Pennsylvania. Think of these parents and countless others, grieving for a young life they nurtured, now lost at the hands of the state and its police. With so many examples, across so many years, preparing one's child for police encounters this way has nothing to do with drama. Indeed, failure to do so would seem like parental malpractice.

Do white parents tell their children how to behave should they encounter a police officer? Of course, many do. Those parents might tell their children to act respectfully and not to talk back. Black parents impart another set of lessons to their children: You must act this way, do these things, and not do these other actions to assure that you live. For white parents and children, any discussion revolves around showing appropriate respect. For black parents and their children, this discussion concerns survival.

The Talk comes at driving age, certainly; it may come even earlier, but young black people must have instructions on this subject if they drive. Black parents know to a near certainty that their children will encounter the police during traffic stops, which many police departments use not just to assure traffic safety but—with black drivers—to investigate them for suspicion of other crimes for which the police have no evidence.[27] Black parents tell their children to pull over when signaled; to keep their hands visible at all times; to never move or pick up anything without telling the officer first and getting his or her okay to do so; and to never, ever argue with the officer, even if the child thinks the officer has done something wrong or said or done something abusive. *No matter how the officer treats you, no matter what he or she says*, "do what the cop says—once it's all over, go to my parents and tell them what happened instead of having [a] conflict with the police."[28] Writer Tess Martin, an African American parent, described the discussion she had with her nearly driving-age daughter this way:

> I told her that there were rules for dealing with the police. That she was to say *yes, sir* and *no, sir* instead of arguing, even if she was in the right. She was to give over her ID even if it wasn't warranted. She was to stay in her car during a traffic stop, with her hands on the steering wheel. I warned her not to go digging around in her pockets, her purse, the rest of the car. She was to tell the officer what she was planning to do before she did it—*I'm reaching for my license; I'm going to lean over for my registration*.
>
> She asked me, "What if I didn't do anything wrong?" and my heart grew almost too heavy to bear.
>
> My answer: "It doesn't matter what you did. Just do what the police officer tells you. It could mean your life."[29]

Martin has no doubt that her white counterparts do not need to do this:

> White parents don't have to have these conversations with their children. They don't have to stress that digging around in a purse or pocket for a license could literally cost that child his or her life. Smarting off could become a reason to shoot. Having a cell phone or a wallet. Approaching the officer for help could be a reason to shoot. Simply being black could be a reason to shoot.[30]

But The Talk ranges much more widely than driving and what to do when (not if) stopped by police. Black parents stress one theme over and over—*get home alive*[31]—and many strategic and tactical variations. Never do or say anything to incite an officer; instead, comply. Interact with—indeed, overemphasize— courtesy and respect. As one youth put it, "just beat them ... shock them with politeness. You know, be what they wouldn't expect you to be."[32] Black children learn that when encountering police, they must "avoid sudden movements, keep their hands in view, and ... behave in a courteous and respectful manner toward officers."[33] Kai El'Zabar says that "Black men are taught by their fathers [the] behaviors that will keep them safe when confronted by the police. Most know to keep their hands visible and ask permission to make any move with hands or body."[34] This consistent and intense instruction from parents, and from many elders, amounts to "a set of 'best practices'" that black parents must instill in their children in the event of crossing paths with police.[35]

In addition to instructions on how to interact with the police to avoid danger, parents and elders give other advice: If you can avoid police, do so. Interaction can bring trouble. As one young man said he had learned, "[I]f possible, unless in dire circumstances, [I] stay away from a man with a badge, in general."[36] Another said his father told him, "Cops are just as bad as criminals, so it is probably best just to try to avoid them."[37]

For the sake of these young people and their parents, one hopes that these talks and the grave instruction on survival in an encounter with a police officer will penetrate and take. Any person who has raised children into teenagers and then into young adults knows well that immaturity may keep younger people from absorbing every lesson. Given the seriousness of the issue and the reality of the stakes in these situations, perhaps such parental messages will sink in, save some lives, prevent injuries, and head off life-altering events such as arrests and prosecutions. But The Talk, in its seriousness, its urgency, and its infinite variety, may also do something else, something unintended. It may increase the degree of fear that young African Americans feel toward the police. When a parent—the person who most loves the child, the person most concerned and responsible for a child's physical safety and emotional security—tells a 10- or 12- or 16-year-old child that police officers may pose a mortal danger to the child, what child would not feel fear of police? Of course, the parent might say, not every police officer poses a danger, but some might, even some of the good ones because of the way they see you, my black or brown child. What child or teen would not be afraid?

WHAT NOW?

We now have a picture of the world of a young African American. He or she hears stories starting at a young age, within the family and all over the community, of fathers, uncles, brothers, and cousins, even sisters and mothers, suffering maltreatment at the hands of the police. The same kinds of stories permeate most black communities, and online reports and videos bring these same experiences from around the country, with a personal, visceral closeness. Parents and authority figures tell young people that they must exercise the most extreme care and caution in how they behave with police, because one mistake could prove fatal. Given all of this background, imagine an African American teen encountering police unexpectedly late at night in a high-crime area. Even assuming that the police tell him who they are and assuming that their questioning takes a suspicious turn, what might that young African American do? He might, of course, stand still with hands visible and answer all questions politely. But he might also feel quickly rising fear that something bad would harm him some way, no matter what he did or does now. Given that the teenage brain has an underdeveloped capacity for good judgment and consideration of long-term consequences, that young person might indeed just take off. He might run, and many, in fact, do just that.

In Baltimore, where Freddie Gray died in a police van after an arrest, and where the black community's relations with the police have long experienced deep strains, many young people flee from the police, "even when they have done nothing wrong." They run out of fear—fear of trumped-up charges or just fear that something bad will happen.[38] In Chicago, Kai El'Zabar says, young black men "run not from guilt" but because they know that they can end up dead, injured, or just in trouble. "[M]inor infractions can result [in] lifetime imprisonment that plagues their community. They witness this every day."[39]

Stories of running away from police appear frequently in the sociology and criminology literature. One young black man told researchers that while he and his friends walked home from school, the police told him to come over to their car. When the youth refused, he said that the officer said to him, "[I]f you don't get over here you know what is gonna happen." When the officer would not relent, the young man said, "I just ran." He was afraid that the officer would plant drug evidence on him or something worse, just to "get" him.[40] According to Ronald Weitzer and Rod K. Brunson, the black teens they studied practiced "systemic evasion." They avoided police encounters and conversations if at all possible, and if they could not easily avoid the situation, the method of avoidance was to run from the police. The teens "said that they fled not because of their guilt but because of their fear of mistreatment."[41] In the words of one of them,

> People I know, every time they see [the police], they just run. I be runnin' sometimes because I don't know what kinda day the police is having. They have pissed off days where they just come through [the neighborhood] … tryin' to lock everybody up …. People [are] scared to come out in the neighborhood. They think they gonna get locked up.[42]

This brings us back to the beginning of the chapter. Let's assume that the police have told the truth and have identified themselves. We can imagine Jordan Miles facing three police officers asking the young man where he lives and why he is standing between the houses on his street. We could say, as former Chief Nathan Harper did, "Do not run from the police. We're not the enemy; we're trying to help." Or we can look at Jordan, the 18-year-old black kid on his own block all by himself at night, being questioned by suspicious and hostile police officers, and we might say something else entirely: "Running might not be smart, but it sure isn't hard to understand."

Figure 6 Jordan Miles' high school photo. Courtesy of Terez Miles.

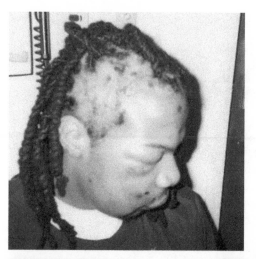

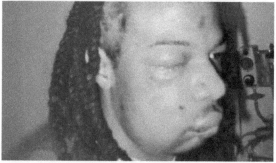

Figures 4, 5 and 7 Three photos of Jordan Miles taken by Terez Miles on January 13, 2010, at the hospital, after his release from jail, following the incident of the previous night on Tioga Street in Pittsburgh. Courtesy of Terez Miles.

Figures 1, 2 and 3 Demonstrations in Pittsburgh demanding police be held accountable for the beating of Jordan Miles, outside the Allegheny County City County Building. Photos by Ashley Woodson.

Figures 1, 2 and 3 (Cont.)

PART III

WAS JUSTICE SERVED?

In Part I, we learned what happened on Tioga Street on January 12, 2010. We learned what occurred in the aftermath, as Pittsburgh saw what had happened to Jordan Miles a few houses down the block from his own. We saw the charges dropped against Jordan. We also came to see how the case divided the city as first the federal U.S. Attorney and then the local District Attorney declined to prosecute, and the questions in the case lingered, unanswered.

In Part II, we learned about some of the reasons why the incident on Tioga Street, and so many like it, happen. We saw how race infects us at the most basic level, causing us to view our fellow African American citizens in many situations as criminal, threatening, dangerous, and violent. We saw how police culture and training, as much as they emphasize strength and courage, are also suffused by fear: fear of instantaneous violence, fear of ever-present guns, and fear of those who, sad to say, carry the weight of the American stereotypes of black skin signifying criminality. We saw how the fear runs both ways. Police officers may fear African Americans and other people of color, but those people also fear the police. Some of them— particularly young men—might well react to that fear by running.

In Part III we ask if courts, even civil courts, can arrive at a just result in a case stemming from a police/civilian confrontation. In the end, a civil lawsuit for money damages was the only avenue left for Jordan to seek justice and for the officers to get some kind of vindication, some validation of their actions that night. The case was tried not once but twice. What happened in those two civil trials, in the U.S. District Court for the Western District of Pennsylvania? Was some measure of justice achieved? And in the end, did it help?

CHAPTER 10

THE FIRST TRIAL: JORDAN'S CASE

On July 16, 2012, the civil case of *Jordan Miles, Plaintiff, vs. Michael Saldutte, David Sisak, and Richard Ewing, Defendants*, began in the U.S. District Court for the Western District of Pennsylvania. The trial started two years and seven months after the incident on January 12, 2010 that formed the core of the case, which was the encounter and violent struggle between Jordan and the three officers on Tioga Street in Homewood. The case had taken nearly two years to come to trial, dating back to the filing of the complaint in August of 2010. In the intervening time:

- Judge Oscar Petite had thrown out the criminal charges against Jordan.
- An internal investigation by the city's Office of Municipal Investigations had investigated Jordan's complaints against the officers and entered a finding of "not resolved"—effectively, "we don't know who to believe."
- Both the federal U.S. Attorney and Allegheny County's District Attorney had decided not to file criminal charges against the officers.

THE PROCEEDINGS BEGIN

Vetting the Jury

Proceedings began with the selection of the jury. First, Federal District Judge Gary L. Lancaster, an African American judge who was discussed in Chapter 5, questioned prospective jurors to ferret out the possibility of biases against either side. Attorneys for Jordan and the officers then raised challenges "for cause" based on possible biases, against several potential jurors; Judge Lancaster granted all of these challenges and excused these jurors.[1] The lawyers then got to use "peremptory challenges"—challenges for which they did not have to give any reason—to remove a few more potential jurors. Limits exist on the use of peremptory challenges; lawyers cannot use them to exclude jurors because of race[2] or gender,[3] but prosecutors need only give any plausible reason other than race for excluding the jurors, making the standard easy to meet. When the officers' lawyers excluded the only black juror on the panel, Jordan's lawyers argued that they had done this based on race.[4] The officers' lawyers responded with seemingly race-neutral reasons,[5] but Judge Lancaster did not buy the explanation, and he seated the black juror.[6] He also explicitly acknowledged the obvious, that race was, and would remain, present as an issue in the trial. "As much as I'm trying to be polite, you can't eliminate the issue of race and racial tension between the police and the black community from the case."[7]

Preliminary Instructions to the Jurors

At 1:00 p.m., on July 17, the court convened, and the clerk seated the eight jurors and swore them in. Judge Lancaster made some opening remarks.[8] He thanked the jurors for their important service, discussed trial logistics, note taking, and how he would give them instructions on the law at the end of the trial. He told them that they would decide the facts of the case, and with those facts in mind, use the law as he instructed them in it to decide the outcome of the case. The judge also stressed that the members of the jury were to discuss the case with no one—not even among themselves—until deliberations, and under no circumstances should they make use of the internet or social media regarding the case: no research, no comments—nothing. They should also give no consideration at all to whatever media reports they might have read prior to beginning jury service and should definitely not read or watch or listen to any media reports on the trial as it progressed. They must pay attention only to the evidence presented in the courtroom—nothing else.

Then Judge Lancaster outlined the specific allegations in the case, which were false arrest, excessive force, and malicious prosecution. On false arrest, Judge Lancaster said, the Fourth Amendment to the U.S. Constitution requires that, if officers make a person *stop temporarily* for purposes of asking something, the officers must have a reasonable fact-based suspicion and not just a hunch or a guess. If they *arrest* someone, the officers must have "probable cause" (which is more evidence than the reasonable fact-based suspicion required for a temporary stop) to believe that a crime has occurred and that the person arrested is involved.[9] The jurors would decide, the judge said, whether the police had sufficient objective facts to temporarily stop or arrest Jordan, in the view of "an objectively reasonable officer." This phrase was the assertion of a key legal concept that undergirds police actions in trials like Jordan's: "[I]t will not matter what ultimately happened to the criminal charges against Miles, and it will not matter what the subjective, personal or actual beliefs or motivations of the three police officers ... were." Rather, the jury would look at the facts and determine "what an objectively reasonable police officer faced with the same facts would have concluded and done based on those facts."[10] The jurors thus received their first lesson on the law of the case: The correct point of view the law requires involves the conclusions of a reasonable officer. This could not help but put the jurors in the position of viewing the case through the eyes of the police officers.

Judge Lancaster then briefly explained the *excessive force* claim.[11] The Fourth Amendment to the Constitution, which prohibits unreasonable searches and seizures, also protects citizens against excessive force during an arrest. Even with a lawful arrest, he said, the police may only use an amount of force necessary to make the arrest. Just as with the false arrest claim, Judge Lancaster let the jurors know that the legal standard of reasonableness governs this aspect of police behavior, too: "you will be applying an objectively reasonable police officer standard" to the excessive force claim, and subjective personal motivations of the police will not matter. Instead, "[Y]ou will be creating this ideal of an objectively reasonable police officer in your mind and deciding ... what that objectively reasonable police officer would have done under the same circumstances." Judge Lancaster said that as jurors, they must place themselves "at the scene of the incident on January 12, 2010, and decide what actually happened that night ... and then determine whether the amount of force used against Miles on that night was objectively reasonable based on the facts."[12]

At this point, Judge Lancaster paused before moving to the third claim, to describe the idea of the term "objectively reasonable." In general, he said, "[O]bjectively reasonable actions and beliefs are those that are taken or reached based on logic, sound judgment, and good sense." They are the opposite, he said, of "actions and beliefs founded on personal feelings prejudices, or biases, which we call subjective actions or beliefs. Objectively reasonable beliefs and actions are rational and moderate, not emotional and extreme."[13]

Finally, Judge Lancaster described Jordan's claim of *malicious prosecution*.[14] To sustain the allegation, Jordan would have to prove that the police officers charged him with crimes "not in order to bring a suspected criminal to justice but instead to act with malice or spite against him."[15] The police must have probable cause of involvement in criminal activity to bring charges against someone; they cannot bring charges for any other reason.

Opening Arguments

With those introductions to the case and a few other comments—especially urging the jurors to keep an open mind throughout[16] and the important idea that Jordan's case had to have enough evidence on any claim so that it is "more likely so than not so"[17]—Judge Lancaster turned the case over to the lawyers for opening arguments. (Note that the arguments, evidence, witness testimony, and the experts would go on for days. This chapter gives a complete picture of the case by presenting the most important events in the courtroom, leaving out the voluminous detail that, although legally important, might distract an observer from the most important events that happened in court.)

Kerry Lewis, for Jordan Miles, would give the first opening argument, because the plaintiff (the party who brings the case) always has the burden of proving the case. After the normal pleasantries of thanking the jury, Lewis plunged directly into the center of the case, holding back nothing:

> The police in this case used deadly force to the point where they beat this young man until he was unrecognizable. They beat him to the point where one of those defendant officers said to investigators, we thought he was going to die. You will hear the facts, the gruesome facts and circumstances of the defendants' savage beating of this young man. You'll see pictures of his gruesome injuries.[18]

Lewis then went back, describing Jordan prior to the event. Jordan, "a young man that any parent … would be proud of," attended the city's elite Creative and Performing Arts (CAPA) High School, where he became an honor student. He had the respect and love of his family, his peers, and his teachers. "He was a good student, he respected authority, he was never in trouble with the law or in school or his neighborhood. He wasn't a problem. He was good." Jordan played the viola in the CAPA orchestra and had played in the group that performed for the spouses of world leaders when Pittsburgh had hosted the G-20 Summit, in the fall of 2009. But the encounter with the three police officers on January 12, 2010, had changed the course of Jordan's life, Lewis said. It left the 18-year-old with a brain injury and posttraumatic stress disorder (PTSD), which "will plague him for the rest of his life."[19]

In describing the incident, as Jordan had in his deposition, Lewis emphasized that Jordan had done nothing to justify police attention. He was just walking to his grandmother's home, not standing up against a house, and had suddenly come face-to-face with three men, all much larger than himself. They did not identify themselves in any way, let alone as police officers, and were yelling at him about drugs and money. Jordan tried to run away, but he'd fallen on the ice, and the beating began.

Fear overcame Jordan, and "he thought that he was going to be killed or taken away."[20] A hard blow to the head finally stopped him from struggling. The officers found no weapon on or near Jordan, Lewis said, but they arrest him based on a made-up story about a nonexistent bottle of Mountain Dew in Jordan's pocket. Lewis called the police version of events "a clear and unmistakable fabrication." The police never produced the bottle because according to them, they threw it away because it did not constitute evidence. Lewis promised the jury he would put the lie to this tale: "You will hear testimony from Chief of Police Harper, the commander of the whole force, is [sic] that the bottle was evidence and was required to be safeguarded and logged into the evidence room."[21] Lewis ended with the same kind of gut punch with which he started. The police officers, he said, "took an oath to uphold the law, serve and protect the public but instead they ignored the law. They chose to violate it, they corrupted justice by using the law to bring charges against him, but the worst of all is that they were so mad and beat him so bad that his life has been forever changed. Nobody can give him back the mind he had before."[22]

The first opening argument for the three officers came from James Wymard, a very experienced trial attorney, who represented Officer David Sisak. Wymard told the jury that the credibility of the witnesses—who told the truth—would decide the case. The officers would testify and would swear to a very different version of what happened on January 12 on Tioga Street, and other witnesses would back up their account.[23] Wymard then explained that the three officers were on patrol in one of the highest crime areas of the city, at a very dangerous time of day, doing a very dangerous job. "I suggest to you it's the most difficult job in the City of Pittsburgh, but they ... put themselves on the line every night after night ...."[24] He summarized the officers' version of events: seeing the male figure next to the building, turning the car around, and questioning the man, identifying themselves all the way, and then how the man exhibited many signs that he had a gun in his coat pocket.[25] When the man tried to run away, the officers had cause to stop him, and when Officer Saldutte grabbed him and took a blow from the man's elbow as the man tried to escape, the officers then had probable cause to believe the man had committed the crime of aggravated assault. The man put up a hard fight, Wymard says; he may weigh only 150 pounds, but "he is 150 pounds of dynamite."[26] He minimized Jordan's injuries: "no fractures, no stitches, swelling" and a piece of a branch, maybe from the hedges in front of the house where the struggle took place, impaled in his gum.[27]

Wymard then came to the crux of the facts in the case. Jordan said he did not know the three men were police officers until the uniformed officers came to the scene, but how could he ignore the fact that the men tried to put handcuffs on him? "Well, what did you think when they tried to put handcuffs on you?" Wymard said. "Who has handcuffs?"[28] With the indications that the man seemed to have something heavy in his right coat pocket, and during the struggle tried to pull his hand away from the police and toward that pocket underneath him, Saldutte "hollers 'gun' "—and the law backs him up, Wymard said, asking the jurors to put themselves in the officers' shoes. "What would you think? What would an objectively reasonable police officer think" about why the man is trying to get away? Certainly, any reasonable officer—the legal standard, as quoted by Judge Lancaster—would believe the man had a gun and wanted to get it in his hand, to use it.[29] The bottom line, according to Wymard, was that Jordan caused the whole incident. "For some reason after the [officers] kept announcing Pittsburgh Police, stop, you're under arrest, he refused," Wymard said. "All he had to do was to stop on the sidewalk and we wouldn't be here, but he didn't, for whatever reason."[30] The whole thing did not have to happen; Jordan had only himself to blame.

After Wymard, the jury heard from attorney Bryan Campbell, representing Officer Michael Saldutte. Campbell, another experienced courtroom lawyer, also had the most experience of the three defense lawyers with police cases, since he regularly represented members of Pittsburgh's Fraternal Order of Police lodge, the department's union.[31] Campbell touched on the facts of the case, labeling the two versions as different as night and day. But he spent most of his opening argument outlining the testimony of the officers' main witness on the use of force.[32] After Campbell came Robert Leight, representing Officer Richard Ewing. Leight described Ewing as a decorated Marine who served two tours in Iraq, a father of three, and husband of a schoolteacher.[33] Leight implied that the evidence would show that the claims made about Jordan—an honor roll student, who had lost cognitive ground due to injuries sustained in the fight with the officers—might not hold up. Most of all, he stressed that blame for the whole incident fell on Jordan.[34]

JORDAN'S WITNESSES: FAMILY AND FRIENDS

Perhaps the obvious way to begin Jordan's case would be with Jordan himself, the witness who could tell the story from his point of view, thoroughly and completely. But lawyers Kerry Lewis and Tim O'Brien chose instead to present several other witnesses before Jordan, and the first was Patricia Porter, Jordan's grandmother.[35]

Ms. Porter, a composed, proper-looking, and well-spoken retired Pittsburgh Public Schools teacher, made a good impression as a witness. She explained how, since the eighth grade, Jordan had a bedroom where he slept most nights at her house, on Susquehanna Street, around the block from Jordan's home with his mother and siblings.[36] She testified about Jordan's personality, calling him a "pensive, quiet individual, very sweet-natured," an introvert; helpful around the home; and respectful of adult authority.[37] He liked school, attended the prestigious CAPA High School, which required an audition for enrollment.[38] Ms. Porter had more to say than simply attesting to Jordan's character, as almost any grandmother would have. She told the jury that when she hadn't seen or heard from Jordan by 11:00 p.m. on January 12, she'd been concerned enough to call him, but she could not reach him. She went to bed, but when he still had not shown up in the early hours of the morning, she became very worried, "hysterical," and called Jordan's mother, Terez Miles, because Jordan would not do something like this. If he had gone elsewhere—perhaps to a friend's home—he would have called.[39] When Terez had not seen Jordan either, both women, mother and grandmother, "were just beside ourselves with worry" and remained up waiting for Jordan for the rest of the night. With no word by morning, Ms. Porter called CAPA High, and when they had not seen him either, she called the police, eventually learning that the police had arrested Jordan and that anyone concerned should go downtown, to city court, for his arraignment. As Ms. Porter and Ms. Miles got ready to go, the grandmother received a call at last from Jordan: "Nana, I've gotten arrested," Jordan said, "but I don't know why." Those words from her grandson pierced her heart, she told the jury, and they stuck with her still.[40]

Hours passed, with no word, and then, as the hour got late, Jordan emerged from the county jail holding area, walking outside to meet them. Ms. Porter testified that when Jordan came outside and Terez saw him, she screamed, "Oh my God, oh my God, look what they did to my son, look what they did to him."[41] Ms. Porter did not look at Jordan; she was afraid that if she did, she might end up unable to drive. They took him immediately to the emergency room at Shadyside Hospital, the facility closest to their home, and it was there that she first took in Jordan's horribly swollen face, the wounds to his head and face, and the right front side of his head, which was bald and bloodied where Jordan's dreadlocks had been torn from his scalp. The jury saw photos of what Ms. Porter saw in the emergency room, some of which were the same pictures that appeared in the newspapers after the incident surfaced publicly.

Jordan's lawyers asked Ms. Porter to testify about Jordan's behavior and manner after the incident. She told them that her grandson had changed: He'd become darkly moody and withdrawn. Jordan, formerly upbeat and friendly, became "very sullen," unlike himself, as if embarrassed. He had trouble sleeping, even confessing to nightmares. In school, he couldn't concentrate and couldn't remember things he had studied.[42] She said that the following fall, when he started college, Jordan had withdrawn after just two weeks, when he had witnessed an incident in which the police went to the dorm room across the hall from his. In sum, Jordan had changed since the incident. Before January 12, he functioned well and seemed happy, helpful, and interested in school; after January 12, his ability to concentrate, remember, do his work, and take care of his daily tasks fell off markedly. His grades dropped, and he became withdrawn. Ms. Porter called it "a dramatic change in his personality."[43]

That ended Ms. Porter's testimony for Jordan, the plaintiff, as elicited by questions from Jordan's lawyer. But as most watchers of television courtroom dramas know, this only brings half the story to the jury. Cross-examination, by the other side, famously called "the greatest legal engine ever invented for the discovery of truth,"[44] permits the use of leading questions, such as, "you didn't hear the noise that night, did you?" or "when you walked up to the scene, you did not know what had happened, did you?" Cross-examination aims to bring out the opposing slant from a witness who may favor the side for which he or she testified. Thus cross-examination questions strongly suggest the answer, and they attempt to get agreement with the lawyer asking them.

James Wymard, the attorney for Officer Sisak, handled the cross-examination of Ms. Porter. Wymard used this examination to attack her portrayal of Jordan as a good, quiet kid. Did she know he'd been in a fight in the eighth grade, leading to a three-day suspension from school? Ms. Porter conceded that she did not know this but doubted that Jordan would have started something like that, given the type of person she knew him to be.[45] Wymard then moved on to an attempt to minimize Jordan's injuries, asking questions about the results of the hospital visits on the night of the incident and the day after. He made the point that none of the examinations or tests of Jordan showed any fractures ("no broken bones, is that correct?") or any stitches.[46] Yes, Ms. Porter said, she'd learned that Jordan had some kind of large twig or piece of a branch stuck in one of his gums. In a photo of Jordan taken two weeks after the incident, the swelling in his face had lessened.[47] Wymard then asked Ms. Porter whether Jordan might not have attempted to take a shortcut by going through the yards, from Tioga to Susquehanna, instead of walking all the way around the block on a very cold night. Ms. Porter told him no, "there is no shortcut."[48]

Wymard then focused on the claims that Jordan had been an honors student and that he'd lost some of his academic and cognitive abilities after the incident. He took Ms. Porter through Jordan's SAT scores, showing that they would have put him "down in a very low percentile"[49]; this might have struck some as a mean-spirited attack on a victim, but it constituted fair cross-examination. Jordan had taken the SAT test before the incident, so it arguably showed lower-tier ability beforehand that was not the result of any injuries. Moreover, the officers and their lawyers simply did not accept Jordan as a victim. Wymard then took Ms. Porter through Jordan's complete high school grade record, showing that he'd actually had poor grades in his first two years of high school, and even after that, Jordan had only earned high grades in music classes, not in *real* subjects like English, Biology, Geometry, or Civics. In only one semester, in Jordan's senior year, had he attained even B grades in nonmusic subjects; he may have attained honors status in that semester, but other than that, did not have a good record. While this cross-examination devalued all of the top-flight arts training at CAPA, implying it had no real worth, Wymard's argument went deeper. Jordan's portrayal as an honors student whose future had been stolen in a brutal beating on January 12, 2010, was a sham, as was his posture as an innocent—and his gullible grandmother had bought the whole package.

The next two witnesses called by Jordan's lawyers helped fill out the core facts of the night of the incident. First came Jordan's mother, Terez Miles.[50] Ms. Miles explained that she had raised all her children, including Jordan, to respect all of their elders, no matter who they were or what they did. This included police officers. "We had nothing but respect for the police. We saw them around the community a lot. We knew they were fighting crime," she said, "and we were not against them in any way."[51] Jordan's lawyer Tim O'Brien then took Ms. Miles through the events of the evening of January 12. Jordan had arrived home after spending some time at a friend's house, and he went upstairs to play video games with his brother. Sometime later, around 11:00 p.m., Jordan came downstairs, ready to leave for his grandmother's house, and Ms. Miles noticed he was wearing a new pea coat she did not recognize. The coat, a birthday gift from his grandmother, fit Jordan well. He stood in the kitchen, putting on his hat, with his cell phone glued to his ear—a pose any parent of a teen will recognize—even as he told his mother about getting the coat from his grandmother.[52] Ms. Miles testified that she took a good look at the coat, "to see how it was made."[53] She liked it. Tim O'Brien seized the moment to ask about a crucial element of the case:

Q.   Does that coat have pockets on the left and the right?
A.   Yes, it does.
Q.   Was there any bulge in either one of those pockets?
A.   No.
Q.   Did your son at approximately 11 p.m. on January 12, 2010, when you saw him in that coat, have in his possession a bottle of Mountain Dew?

A.   No.

Q.   During the time that your son was at your house on January 12, 2010, from the time that he arrived until the time you saw him leave at approximately eleven p.m., did you see him consume any Mountain Dew?

A.   No.

Q.   Did you see him consume any kind of soda drink at all?

A.   No.

With that, she said, she and Jordan exchanged "I love yous" and he went out the doors, on his way to her mother's house.

Terez Miles went on to describe the first call from her mother in the early morning hours, finding out that Jordan had not arrived at her mother's home, and how her worry built over the next few hours. Ms. Miles then discussed how she learned in the morning, from her mother, that the police had arrested Jordan and that they would need to go to arraignment court downtown, next to the county jail, to pick him up. They waited and waited there. When Jordan finally came out of the building hours later, he walked up to his mother, but his face had become so misshapen that she did not know who he was, until she heard him saying, "[M]om, I need to go to the hospital."[54] It made her "hysterical," and she became even more upset when she could not hug her son without his whole body shuddering from pain when she touched him.[55]

It was then time for cross-examination, this time by attorney Robert Leight, representing Officer Ewing. Leight started with a series of questions that seemed designed to denigrate Ms. Miles:

Q.   You said you were single. Have you ever been married?

A.   No.

Q.   How far did you go in school?

A.   I graduated from high school. I graduated from the Art Institute of Pittsburgh and I graduated from Mortuary School.

Q.   Is it [the case] that you have a GED, you didn't graduate from high school?

At this point, Jordan's lawyer, Tim O'Brien, objected, telling the judge that the questions had no relevance. In response, Judge Lancaster asked Ms. Miles, "[D]o you have a high school diploma?" Ms. Miles answered, "I have a GED, which to me is a high school diploma."[56]

One can certainly debate whether the GED (which stands for the General Equivalency Diploma, earned by millions of Americans over decades in place of graduating from a high school) is the same as a high school diploma. This clearly seems to be what it is intended to be, given the name and the stated purpose of the program. But the larger point of this first interaction between Jordan's mother and a lawyer for one of the officers seems not to be to illuminate these small points of marital status and education; Mr. Leight never asked about the details of Ms. Miles's degree from the Art Institute or what profession her education had led her to (interior design). Rather, this line of questioning seemed to be about disparaging her—to paint Terez Miles as an uneducated person of little worth (just a GED—couldn't finish high school!) and even low morals (four children and never married?) These types of questions may fall well within standard cross-examination strategies and techniques, filed under ways to show the jury they should not believe the witness. None of it came to anything other than an attack on the character of the plaintiff's mother. If a lawyer wanted to attack the credibility of a witness like Ms. Miles, it would take just one or two questions: "You're Jordan's mother, aren't you? And you love him very much, don't you?" Nothing more needs to be said; the rest—what mom wouldn't do anything for her son?—comes by unspoken implication.

Leight's final point also involved something that could have happened, although Ms. Miles could not know if it did or did not. It had been dark when Jordan left the house, and he'd gone out the front door. Had she looked outside to watch Jordan walk down the front steps of the house as he left? No, she had not. So, Leight said, "you don't know if he picked up anything that may have been on the porch prior to walking to your mother's, do you?" Ms. Miles seemed confused by the question, perhaps understandably. "On whose porch?" she asked. Leight replied, "your porch." Ms. Miles answered "no."[57] Thus it was possible, Leight implied, that Jordan (with no bulge in his coat pocket in the house) picked up a bottle of Mountain Dew from the porch while outside, even though (1) no one had testified that a bottle had sat there and (2) any bottle of soda out there would have frozen into a nondrinkable block of ice. When he had another turn to ask questions, Jordan's lawyer Tim O'Brien asked Ms. Miles whether she kept "six packs of Mountain Dew" or "any items of consumables, any kind of soda drinks" on her porch; she said she did not.[58]

Jordan's lawyer Tim O'Brien then called Jamiah Anderson as the final witness of the day. She was Jordan's close friend and CAPA schoolmate, and the telephone records brought into court showed that she and Jordan had been talking that evening, in several different conversations, as they often did. The calls went back and forth between them that evening, including one that began at 10:32 p.m. and that ended just after 11:00 p.m.[59] Jamiah was the one on the phone with Jordan when he came into his mother's kitchen with his cell phone to his ear, preparing to go to his grandmother's house around the block. Jamiah testified that she heard Jordan tell his mother goodbye and "I love you," and she heard the door open and close, too. And then, the last thing she heard came from Jordan: "I heard Jordan yell, 'stop, chill,'" and then nothing but scratchy sounds as she called out to him. Eventually, she hung up.[60] O'Brien wound up with one final detail. He used his questions to point out to Jamiah that she'd made an obvious error in her statement to the FBI agent who talked to her about the case during the federal investigation. They wrote down that she said the call between her and Jordan ended at 7:00 p.m., but the phone records made clear it had ended at 11:00 p.m. Jamiah could not explain the inconsistency but acknowledged it.[61]

On cross-examination, lawyer Wymard went after Jamiah with this discrepancy. He insisted that Jamiah was "changing [her] story from the one you told the FBI two years ago to what you're telling us today" and implied that Jordan's lawyers had coached her into a version better for Jordan.[62] Wymard pushed the young woman hard, and she became flustered.[63] Wymard then pushed even harder. Had she met with Jordan's lawyers? Had they shown her the phone records? When did she first see the FBI report? Who gave it to her? Had they pointed out the discrepancy in the time? When was that meeting? Didn't she just say something else? She said she told the agents that Jordan said goodbye and I love you to his mother, so why isn't that in the FBI report?

All of this, of course, was largely beside the point. The time of the call, who made it and who received it, and how long it lasted were all undisputed. Jamiah did not add much to that, except what she heard in the last minute of the call. Nevertheless, Wymard attacked her credibility—her believability— with great vigor. As with defense attorney Leight's attack on Terez Miles, this questioning constituted standard, allowable cross-examination but with comparatively little gain. It also paralleled the defense's use of Jordan's grandmother to attack Jordan as a sham honors student with no real injuries. While treating Jordan's grandmother relatively gently, the lawyers had gone after all of these witnesses—three black women—in ways that seemed to show a needless effort to embarrass them.

Jordan would have the chance to testify on the second day of the trial, but before he was called to the stand, his lawyers called another witness, Melissa Pearlman, the current principal of the CAPA High School. Pearlman began her stint as principal with Jordan's senior year, so she had served as principal during the year that the incident occurred on January 12. For Jordan's lawyers, Pearlman offered straightforward testimony, that Jordan had attended school on January 12, records showed[64]; he'd retaken a state proficiency test during the fall of 2009, to attain a proficient score in math, necessary for graduation[65]; and his transcript showed that while he had started high school slowly (in academic terms), he did get himself on track, earning honors grades for a semester (defined as a 3.0, B average or greater) just once in his first four semesters but in three out of four of his last four semesters. The last semester of his senior year, Jordan did not earn honors grades; the incident on Tioga Street had occurred at the beginning of that very semester.[66] Ms. Pearlman also testified that, as far as his personal manner, "Jordan was respected by all students and staff, myself included, kind, mild-mannered, always greeted adults with hello, how are you ma'am, sir, was jovial, often making funny and clever remarks."[67]

Robert Leight, the attorney for Officer Ewing, used his cross-examination of the principal to do the same thing the defense had done with Jordan's grandmother Patricia Porter. He attempted to strip away the idea of Jordan as an honors student. He pointed out that even if the school customarily recognized honors status for *each individual* semester, standing alone, Jordan's *cumulative* grade point average remained under a B at the end of his junior year despite two semesters that year of honors grades.[68] One can't fault Leight for pursuing this line of questioning, since any claim that Jordan had a strong record as a student would tend to increase potential damages awarded, and the logical move becomes tearing the record down. But it is also easy to imagine how this line of questioning might look to communities outside the courtroom: Here's a good, well-behaved kid, with, at the very least, an improving school record as he matured, doing everything right, even getting on the honor roll for most of his last two years. And people can do nothing except tear him down and deny the significance of his accomplishments.

Attorney Leight's job, of course, had nothing to do with what anyone outside the courtroom might think; his job, and the job of all the lawyers, was to win over the jury. So the real question was, would this sort of treatment of Jordan's academic record (and later of Jordan himself) seem like good lawyering work, or mean-spiritedness?

JORDAN TESTIFIES

After Principal Pearlman, it was Jordan's time to testify. His lead attorney, Kerry Lewis, first took Jordan through his normal school-day routine, from morning through return to his neighborhood, dropping his school things at his grandmother's house, then to a friend's home, and then to his mother's house, where he would spend time with his mother and siblings (including dinner), and then on to his grandmother's house again, around the block on Susquehanna, to sleep.[69] Jordan confirmed that he took no shortcuts through any yards from Tioga to Susquehanna, and that no such shortcuts existed, particularly one that bordered Monica Wooding's house at 7940 Tioga.[70] He described his warm feelings for the CAPA High School and his teachers, told of his love for playing the viola and how he had become first-chair viola as a senior, and how he'd had no disciplinary or other problems since one incident in eighth grade—the one that got him suspended, referred to in earlier testimony. (Jordan explained that he'd had an altercation with a bully.)[71]

Jordan also testified about his feelings regarding police. Before the January 12 incident, he had never experienced an arrest or an accusation of criminal activity. He had always, and still did, respect the police and what they did.[72] The night of the incident, he went downstairs at his mother's house at about 11:00 p.m., to leave for his grandmother's house and his own bed. His mother stopped him in the kitchen to admire his new coat, which she hadn't seen before. At that point, and as he left the house, he had nothing in the pockets of this coat—no bottle of Mountain Dew and certainly no gun.[73] Walking into the frigid January night, five to eight inches of snow and ice coated the neighborhood sidewalks, so Jordan walked on the street to have better footing.[74]

Just a few steps down Tioga Street, Jordan saw a car—unmarked, no light bar on top, no agency insignia—drive up the middle of the street, and as it got close, swerve in very close to him. He quickly moved toward the sidewalk, "because I believed I was going to get hit."[75] He could see that the people in the car wore "very dark clothes," and the driver's and passenger's doors flew open. He saw "three white males in the motion of exiting the vehicle, and I heard, 'where's your gun, money, and drugs.'"[76] He immediately dropped the phone and tried to run back toward his mother's house. Attorney Lewis asked:

Q.   Did [the three men] identify themselves?
A.   No, they didn't.
Q.   Did you see any badges?
A.   No, I didn't.
Q.   What did you think was happening when these men yelled those words to you?
A.   I thought I was going to be robbed ....
Q.   When these men had yelled this, can you describe were you frightened?
A.   I was terrified.
Q.   What was racing through your mind?
A.   Thoughts of being robbed.
Q.   Is your neighborhood primarily black?

A.   Yes, it is.

Q.   Did the fact that these men appeared to be white, did that cause you any fear?

A.   Not really.

Q.   Well, what did cause you fear?

A.   When they got out of the car and demanded for the gun, money, and drugs.[77]

Running away proved futile. Jordan fell on the ice, and one of the three men, then the others, jumped on him and began to beat him. The testimony unfolded as Jordan had told it before: the blows, all over his body; feeling the handcuffs and becoming terrified that he would be thrown into a car trunk and killed somewhere; praying aloud; and then, finally, hammered into submission with a stunning blow to his head.[78] *Then* the police wagon came and the realization that the men who had beaten him were police officers, not thugs or robbers.[79]

The patrol wagon officers took Jordan to West Penn Hospital, where a doctor examined him and assessed his injuries, also removing a large piece of a branch or bush from his gum. He consented to (and took) a drug test, knowing it would show no presence of drugs, and eventually he was taken to the county jail. The other people detained, with whom he shared a cell, told him that some of his hair had been pulled out; he had not seen the ugly bald place or bloody patches. When the authorities finally released him, many hours later, Jordan recalled that he saw his mother standing by the car. As he approached he said nothing, until he said, "Mom, I need to go to the hospital," which caused his mother to break down and cry, screaming about what the police had done to her son. He could not receive his mother's hug, Jordan said, because his pain remained so extreme.[80] His mother and grandmother took him to Shadyside Hospital, and he ended up missing about three weeks of school.[81]

Jordan's grotesque facial swelling went down in that time, but the other effects (migraine headaches, pain in his eyes and in other areas of his body) remained. Mentally, the impact was far worse. "I'm not the same as I used to be." He'd been diagnosed with some brain injury, depression, and PTSD. He became angry more easily and quickly, and he experienced flashbacks and nightmares of the incident. His academic work suffered, and two attempts at attending college, at Pitt and Penn State campuses, ended in failure. All of this, he said, began with the incident of January 12, 2010. "I had never had an experience like that night before in my life. At that moment, when they jumped out demanding for guns, money and drugs, I was scared. I was terrified. I knew that the environment where I lived was very dangerous .... I thought, ... hearing their demands as soon as they stopped, that I was going to be robbed."[82]

Lewis ended his questioning of Jordan with unambiguous denials of some of the major contentions of the case. No, he had never stood along Monica Wooding's house. No, he had had no Mountain Dew bottle in his pocket on the night of January 12. He'd heard no verbal identification of Pittsburgh police officers and seen no identification badges. There'd been no emergency lights or siren, and no police department logo on the vehicle. No, he hadn't reached for anything in a pocket during the struggle. And no, he had never had a gun.[83]

JORDAN IS CROSS-EXAMINED

Attorney Wymard began his cross-examination with a tried and true tactic, which is asking a witness if he had met with or talked with his lawyers, with regard to his testimony. Of course, Jordan had met with his lawyers to prepare his case, and doing this represented no wrongdoing or misconduct, as the question seemed to imply.[84] Jordan also told Wymard that there was plenty of crime in the neighborhood where he lived.[85] The parties contested neither point; Wymard seemed to want to make these points to rattle Jordan a little and to establish that police officers would know about the crime too—bolstering his client's case that the officers were both fearful and justified under the law governing law enforcement.

Wymard eventually got to the main point. The three men, he said, put first one, then a second handcuff on him. Wymard let his disbelief show right through his questions:

Q   You still believed that you were being robbed and abducted, didn't you say?

A.   Yes, I did say that.

Q   Did it ever occur to you that the only people that you ever seen or dealt with that have handcuffs are police officers, Mr. Miles? You don't know anybody else that have handcuffs that aren't police officers, do you?

A.   I saw—well, I know there's other people that can get ahold of handcuffs. They're sold in stores. I'm not sure if they are real or fake but they are sold in stores so I did not know these were police officers ....

Q   You said you thought you were being robbed? Nobody pulled a gun on you, did they?

A.   No, they didn't.

Q   Nobody pulled a knife on you, did they?

A. No, they didn't.

Q   Just the only thing they were trying to do, using any force, was to put handcuffs on you, correct? …

A. Use force—I don't understand what you're saying.

Q   What I'm saying is it was obvious they were police?

A. It was not obvious because when they stopped, they demanded for guns, money and drugs. They did not identify themselves, they were not riding in a marked police car when—

Q   Nobody took any guns, money, or drugs from you, did they?

This may have been one question too many. Jordan's response explains things in a way that Wymard probably would not have preferred.

A. When they handcuffed me, they continued to beat me. I didn't know or hear of any cops that did that. And also, I didn't do anything wrong. I didn't think that cops would act in that manner. So, no, I did not believe these were cops.[86]

But one other subject reared its head during the cross-examination, even if the questioning did not raise it head-on: race. The defense managed to state not once, but several times, that in Homewood that night, Jordan had encountered not just three men who jumped out of a car at him, none of whom wore police uniforms but three *white* men. The point comes out of nowhere, almost unnoticeable, with the jury listening in the courtroom with the young black man on one side and the three white police officers on the other. But a subtle underlining of the point does the job, whether intended or not. The first comes as Attorney Wymard takes Jordan through the beginning of the incident:

Q   Okay. Now, you indicated these three white men jumped out of the car, is that correct?

A. Yes.

Q   And they got out simultaneously, at the same time?[87]

And just like that, the narrative moves on to other subjects. The race of the three men comes out of the blue, so perhaps it just describes them. Jordan describes himself as frightened and terrified of the men. But race surfaces again, just a bit further into the cross-examination, as Attorney Wymard discusses the use of handcuffs by the men:

Q.   Well, they did get one handcuff on you to start, didn't they?
A.   Yes.
Q.   And it took them a while before they got the second handcuff on you, correct?
A.   I don't know what you mean by "a while."
Q.   Ten seconds, 30 seconds, a minute, you're struggling with them trying to keep them from putting the handcuffs on you.
A.   I didn't know what they were doing.
Q.   I understand because you thought you were being robbed, right?
A.   Yes.
Q.   Okay. Even though these three white men are putting handcuffs on you, correct, Mr. Miles?
A.   Yes.[88]

Again, nothing in the legitimate point—handcuffing—that the cross-examining attorney makes here has anything to do with race. But there it sits.

And then, race appears a third time. In the context of attorney Wymard's argument that Jordan must have known that the men he struggled with belonged to the police department because after the struggle, he heard one of them say that they thought he had a gun. In this exchange, Wymard gives Jordan the FBI report to read in order to refresh his memory of what Jordan allegedly said to the FBI agents, and then Wymard says this:

Q.   Does that serve to refresh your recollection as to what you told the FBI when they interviewed you … that you heard the police tell the—the plainclothes men, these three white men, these three white mystery men, that you didn't know who they were, you heard them telling … (the other officers that) … they believed Miles had a gun? You told the FBI that? Do you remember that?
A.   I don't specifically remember hearing that ….[89]

As the reader can plainly see, race comes up twice in that last example, within one sentence. The point here is *not* that James Wymard did anything wrong, or that he has asked a racist question, or that he made a racist statement. Perhaps neither he nor anyone else in the courtroom would have noticed him talking about the officers as white. Rather, whether intended or not, the use of this language served to subtly but plainly underline certain important assumptions. The point made, even if unintentionally, is this: Whites, especially in the black neighborhood of Homewood, could not be criminals; they could only be the police. No other plausible reason for their presence could exist. They could not be there to rob or steal; they could be there only as the embodiment of state power and authority—not to buy or sell drugs, burglarize homes, or assault people to obtain their "drugs, guns, money." All of this, of course, reinforces the dominant racial stereotypes: black people are the criminals and thugs we should fear in a community like Homewood, and whites are there to keep order and to be obeyed.

JORDAN'S MEDICAL WITNESSES TAKE THE STAND

With Jordan's testimony completed, several other witnesses testified. First the jury saw a video recording of a deposition of a doctor who had treated Jordan for his injuries,[90] followed by live testimony from Dr. Maria Twichell, a doctor who focused much of her work on concussion and brain injury. She had treated Jordan and testified about his symptoms—memory difficulties, dizziness, headaches, and balance problems, as well as flashbacks, mood swings, depression, confusion, seeing spots, loss of concentration, and decreased comprehension, among others.[91] She diagnosed Jordan with "a concussion, as well as symptoms compatible with post-concussive syndrome."[92] She prescribed a treatment plan and sent Jordan to another doctor for a comprehensive evaluation of his brain function; that evaluation ruled out any false reporting of symptoms by Jordan and found lowered scores on math skills, visual skills, and cognitive flexibility. Dr. Twichell agreed with the other doctor's findings of cognitive disorder, depressive disorder, and anxiety disorder.[93] A reevaluation of Jordan in March 2012, just months before the trial, showed some improvement but also many of the same symptoms. All in all, Dr. Twichell anticipated that "Jordan is going to have lifelong difficulty from this injury ... [including] ongoing psychological care, from a psychologist or psychiatrist, potential medication, intervention for treatment of PTSD, certainly psychological therapy."[94] On cross-examination, she not only confirmed the subjective nature of many symptoms reported to her from her patient but also said that objective testing can rule out the magnifying or exaggerating of symptoms.[95]

CHIEF NATHAN HARPER TAKES THE STAND

Jordan's lawyers then called the City of Pittsburgh's Chief of Police, Nathan Harper. They believed that Harper would help them prove their case, especially on the issue of the Mountain Dew bottle's absence at the trial. It did not work out that way.

After some preliminary introduction and side issues, Jordan's attorney Kerry Lewis took Chief Harper to a subject strongly implied by Attorney Wymard's cross-examination of Jordan, that only blacks might pose a danger of crime or robbery in Homewood but never whites:

Q.   Now, is Homewood and Tioga Avenue a high crime area?
A.   Yes, it is.
Q.   And are there whites and blacks involved in crime in Homewood, and in Tioga Street?
A.   Yes.

After an objection from the defense, Judge Lancaster intervened. "The fact of the matter is, there is in that Section of Zone 5" (the police patrol area that includes Homewood), "you can say for a fact that there have been crimes committed by whites and crimes committed by blacks." Chief Harper answered, "That's correct."

Lewis then took Chief Harper through the various aspects of the incident—first from Jordan's point of view, then from the officers'—and finally came to the issue of the Mountain Dew bottle:

Q.   Now, you were asked in your deposition whether you would consider that Mountain Dew bottle evidence; weren't you?
A.   That's correct.
Q.   And let me ask you this …. Wouldn't the police officer want to justify his use of deadly force, if he believed that there was something in Jordan Miles' pocket that resembled a weapon?
A.   The officers wanted to see if he did in fact, have a weapon in that right hand, right pocket.
Q.   All right. To the extent that the bulge is alleged to have been a weapon, and there was a basis for using any force … in accordance with the custom and practices of the City of Pittsburgh, is it your testimony that the bottle of Mountain Dew should have been retained for purposes of evidence? And you said under oath, yes? Is that correct?
A.   That is correct.

Court then recessed for the day. When the trial resumed the next day, with Chief Harper still on the witness stand and still under questioning,[96] Lewis started by asking him again about the Mountain Dew bottle. In his deposition, Chief Harper had *disagreed* with the officers' statements that they did not keep the bottle after the incident because they did not consider it to be evidence— that is, Chief Harper did believe the bottle *was* evidence and said that it *should have been* preserved.[97] Lewis brought him back to this point:

Q.   Chief, am I correct that you do not agree with the defendant officers' assertion in this case that the Mountain Dew was not evidence.

A.   The Mountain Dew, according to the charges that the officers filed, would not be evidence in a criminal case. It would be evidence in a civil court case.

Would not be evidence in a criminal case. Lewis reminded Harper of what he had said in his deposition. He'd been asked whether he agreed with the officers that the bottle did not constitute evidence. What was his answer? "At that time," Harper said, "it was, no, I don't agree with that." *At that time.* Lewis pressed further, referencing the Chief's deposition in which he had been asked, "[B]y failing to preserve evidence, is that a violation police policy?" How had he answered? "Yes."[98] Those two phrases (*would not be evidence in a criminal case; at that time*) portended a change in the direction of Harper's testimony. The first clear sign of this came just moments later. Lewis asked Harper whether the bottle could have been an important piece of evidence in the criminal case against Jordan:

Q.   Wouldn't it be evidence supporting their right to search and seize, or [the officers'] right to stop him?

A.   It wouldn't be evidence that would be inventoried in our property room, nor at the county jail, because it was a, a beverage or food.

Q.   Well, even though it was a beverage or food, it was central to the case, wasn't it?

A.   Yes. And they documented it in their report.

Q.   Yes. And the officers, when they seized it, they are required to take all the evidence to the evidence room, according to your procedures; is that right?

A.   According to our procedures, it wouldn't have been accepted in our property room.[99]

This testimony put a completely different spin on the question of why the police had not kept the bottle: The bottle wouldn't have been evidence in a criminal case against Jordan, which was the only kind of case the officers would have had in mind. In addition, the rules of the police evidence storage facility were suddenly as important as good investigative technique, since the facility would not have accepted a Mountain Dew bottle, given its status as a "beverage or food." All the officers had to do was *document* it. This apparently meant that the officers needed only to write in their report that they had found the bottle and nothing else, even though Harper had said, in his deposition, that failure to *preserve* evidence—not just document it—violated police policy.[100]

The full extent of the change in Chief Harper's testimony became clear in the cross-examination by James Wymard. With Jordan charged with two counts of aggravated assault and one count each of resisting arrest, loitering and prowling, and escape, would the Mountain Dew bottle have any relevance to those five charges? "No, it does not. Those charges does not show that the Mountain Dew bottle was necessary ...," the Chief said. No possible way? The bottle wouldn't be like a crowbar used in a break-in, if a suspect was arrested for that? "That is correct."[101] The only possible benefit to retaining the bottle, Wymard asked, was if the officers "had anticipated that Jordan Miles was going to file some civil suit. Is that correct?" "It is correct," Harper said. Are officers supposed to anticipate civil suits and act accordingly? "No, sir," said the Chief.[102]

By this point, everyone could see that Chief Harper had emerged as a very good witness *for the officers*, even though Jordan's team had called him as their witness. The scope of this problem for Jordan's lawyers became clear not just in the facts and interpretations of those facts that Chief Harper laid out but also in the *way* that the cross-examination proceeded. Wymard, as the cross-examiner, had a witness with all kinds of positive things to say for his clients, and he could use leading questions to get exactly what he wanted from the witness. As in all leading questions—the standard, accepted type of question for cross-examination—the questions themselves contain the answers the lawyer wants. The witness need only agree or disagree, as Chief Harper did. "That's correct ... Yes, sir ... Yes, sir, I have." It was a trial lawyer's dream come true—your own best witness, called by the other side.

Then came another surprise. In his deposition, Chief Harper had stated that failure to preserve the Mountain Dew bottle constituted a violation of department policy. Wymard asked:

Q. You made a determination also, Chief, did you not, that the failing to retain the Mountain Dew bottle was not a violation of the rules and regulations; is that correct?

A. After review, yes, I did.

Q. And as a result, no disciplinary charges were filed against these officers ...?

A. That is correct.[103]

Over the following moments, attorney Wymard took Chief Harper through almost every aspect of the defense case and had him affirm that the officers had done things according to policy, protocol, and the law. He put the entire police version of the facts before the jury, using Jordan's own witness, and he had that witness—the Chief of Police, no less—approve and endorse everything the officers did, telling the jury that the officers had acted properly.

When it was Attorney Lewis's turn again to ask questions, he attempted, again, to get across some argument attacking the failure to preserve the Mountain Dew bottle, and thus implying that no such bottle existed. "Will you tell me," Lewis asked Harper, "why this honor student, this kid that has never been in trouble before, would know how to [act as if he had a gun], when he had no gun?" Wymard objected, and Judge Lancaster sustained the objection; Lewis's rhetorical question asked for speculation, a violation of evidence rules.[104] Lewis tried again. "I'm going to ask you, Chief, if the evidence is, in your words, that the officer had a bottle of—found a bottle of Mountain Dew, do you have any explanation as to whether or not, or why Jordan would be ... protecting a bottle of Mountain Dew ... as if it were a gun, and then, reach for it while they were beating him up?" Wymard objected, prompting Judge Lancaster to say, "It's a rhetorical question if I ever heard one." Lewis tried again. "Chief, does it make sense to you that somebody who had a bottle of pop, somebody in this case, Jordan Miles, had a bottle of pop in his jacket, [assuming the police version is true], would [that person] protect it as a gun under these frightening circumstances as he described them?" Another objection came, and Judge Lancaster could take it no longer. He asked the question himself. "In your experience in ... 35 years as a police officer, have you ever seen a situation in which someone was being assaulted, at that moment figured, 'I sure could use a cold drink right now'?" Harper answered, deadpan: "No, sir."[105]

MONICA WOODING AND THE REST OF JORDAN'S WITNESSES

If the testimony of Chief Harper had proven a disaster for Jordan's side, the next witness helped. Monica Wooding lived at 7940 Tioga Street, and the struggle between Jordan and the three police officers took place directly in front of her house on January 12. She had testified at the preliminary hearing in the case against Jordan in March of 2010, and her testimony cast enough doubt on what the police had said about the whole encounter that Judge Oscar Petite threw the case out.[106] Now called as a witness in the civil case by Jordan's lawyers, she repeated that earlier testimony. Most importantly, the men never asked her to look at anyone, never asked if she could identify an individual they showed her, and never asked whether the person had permission to stand around her house or enter it. No other person stood with the police who must have already put whoever they had arrested in the wagon, because it was already "pulling off, going the opposite way uphill, on Tioga."[107] This directly contradicted the testimony of the officers later in the trial, just as it had at the preliminary hearing. Ms. Wooding said that she certainly would have known Jordan if the police officers had shown him to her that night; she had known Jordan "for some years" from the neighborhood as one of the kids who played basketball in the yard behind her house with her son and other neighborhood kids. She did not know that the police had arrested Jordan in front of her house until a couple of days later, when a relative of Jordan's whom she knew called and told her.[108]

Attorney Wymard's cross-examination did not cause Ms. Wooding to change any of that testimony, even when he implied, none too subtly, that she had lied under oath and changed her story in order to help Jordan. Ms. Wooding did not flinch. "No, now that part is not correct," she said.

As Jordan's lawyers moved toward the end of their case, they called an expert witness on police use of force. The expert's testimony proved largely ineffective, and cross-examination diminished its value even further, focusing on the expert's lack of actual experience on the street as a police officer and pointing out that this experience came in a small-town environment.[109] For the police officers, attorney Bryan Campbell also pointed out that for much of his testimony, the expert had simply assumed that Jordan Miles had told the truth. If, on the other hand, the police officers had told the truth regarding the crucial disputed facts (whether or not they identified themselves and the Mountain Dew bottle, in particular), his answers might differ.[110]

Campbell used the examination, as attorney Wymard had with the questioning of Chief Harper, to tell the officers' side of the story, even if sometimes the answers from the expert did not support that side of the case.

Another familiar theme also resurfaced: race. Again, perhaps without intention, one of the officers' lawyers managed to point to the race of the officers:

Q.   And of course, when you assume the facts that Jordan Miles has given … he's minding his own business, walking up the street. He sees a car. It's parked up the street. All of a sudden the car comes down the street in his direction, and then pulls over, and three white males jump out and yell, your gun, your drugs, your money, and then, run him down and basically beat him up.

A.   Yes.

Q.   And that during the course of that, he's handcuffed behind his back; isn't that his version?

A.   That's what he said, yes ....

Q.   And while he's sitting there handcuffed, after some period of time, a police vehicle comes up. And only when he sees these three white males talking to the uniform policemen does it suddenly dawn on [him], those people are police officers that came to me.

A.   Yes.[111]

Neither the identity nor the race of the three officers who encountered Jordan that night were in question. No one needed a description of them. Thus the implication of including this fact, over and over, brings us to the same conclusion: Yes, the three men were white, and they therefore would not be trying to rob Jordan or commit any other crime. Jumping out on someone in a black neighborhood, administering a beating, and putting that person in handcuffs— perhaps they could be criminals but not if they were white—all white. White men could only be there as police.

Jordan's lawyer's presented only two more witnesses, both via videotape. One was a psychiatrist who treated Jordan and the other was an economist, who discussed the impact of the incident on Jordan's projected lifetime earnings prospects.[112]

The presentation of Jordan's case had proven rocky. He had been a good, calm witness, who was not shaken on the central parts of his story. But Jordan was attacked (1) for not telling the truth, according to the officer's version of what happened, (2) because he had not consistently earned honors grades, and (3) because his injuries (to his body, to his academic abilities, and to his psyche) might not be quite as serious as attorney Lewis had portrayed in his opening argument. Chief Harper's testimony had also caused significant and unexpected damage to Jordan's case. This could not have been the way that Jordan's lawyers had hoped to put their best foot forward in front of the jury. Their own case should have ended with the evidence at a high point for their side. That had not happened, and now the three police officers—all with considerable experience as witnesses in court—would testify, along with their supporting witnesses, telling a very different story.

CHAPTER 11

THE FIRST TRIAL: THE POLICE CASE

With the end of the testimony presented by Jordan's lawyers, the defendants (Officers Saldutte, Sisak, and Ewing) had the chance to put on their case. The defense case would tell a different story as far as the altercation that night, and it would emphasize many of the points they made during cross-examination of Jordan and his witnesses. For the officers' lawyers, telling that different story—one more consistent with the average juror's view of the police as helpful, law-following public servants—would govern every question they asked and everything they did.

The officers' lawyers began with a witness named David Wright, a long-time Pittsburgh Police officer and an instructor at the police academy since 1999, who trained officers in the use of force, defensive tactics, and physical fitness.[1] The defendant police officers called Officer Wright for the purpose of explaining to the jury the correct way to understand the use of force by police. He could not, and did not, testify to whether the officers had used force correctly in the confrontation with Jordan Miles—only to the correct way to use force.

In his testimony, Wright told attorney Bryan Campbell that officers learn to use force by classifying each type of force into one of five levels. The five levels are arranged, from least to most, along the *continuum of force*.[2] Officers then learn how to classify what people they face may do. A person confronted by a police officer may comply with the officer's orders, or he or she may resist. Actions that fail to follow police orders fall into six *levels of subject resistance*.[3] The level of subject resistance that an officer faces determines what level of force the officer can use. Police in the United States almost universally use what Wright called the "Plus 1 Rule," in which the officer doesn't meet a type of resistance from a civilian with the same level of force; they go one level higher, in order to overcome the resistance that the civilian poses.[4] Wright laid this out for the jury, and Campbell would use this testimony later to tell the jury, in his closing argument, that the officers had used force properly.

OFFICER SALDUTTE TAKES THE STAND

The real substance of the defendants' case started with the next witness, Officer Michael Saldutte, whose testimony set the template for the testimony of the two other defendants. Saldutte testified first among the three officers, no doubt because he could testify about first spotting the indications of the presence of a gun; Saldutte had seen both the person and those signs first. His testimony loomed large enough that the other defendant police officers came not directly after him but after other witnesses.

Officer Saldutte's lawyer, Bryan Campbell, took Officer Saldutte through a brief personal biography and into his Pittsburgh Police service. His first permanent assignment was as a uniformed patrol officer performing routine patrol duties[5] in Zone 5, which is the area of the city that includes the Homewood neighborhood. After a little more than three years of patrol duties, in August of 2009, Saldutte got the assignment to work in plain clothes in the 99 car, along with his partners, Officers Richard Ewing and David Sisak.[6]

Saldutte then told the story of the confrontation on Tioga Street. He tracked his testimony from the preliminary hearing almost perfectly: seeing the male figure against the house; how the man, seeing their car, "put his right hand in his pocket," and "turned his body away from me."[7] This made Saldutte "highly suspicious of what he was doing ...."[8]

Saldutte testified that he got partly out of the car and began talking to the man. "I said 'Pittsburgh Police' and I held my badge [up]," Saldutte said. He told the man, "Hold up. Take your hands out of your pocket." He already thought the man might have a weapon. "[Y]ou want to be able to see their hands .... Whether it's a gun, a knife, or a fist, a punch, their hands are what's going to enable some type of weapon to happen." A hand in the pocket means "I'm suspicious of maybe he's reaching for a weapon, or has a weapon on him." Putting the hand in the pocket is called "a security pat or security feel."[9] He knew this, Saldutte said, because he had taken specialized training, given by the Bureau of Alcohol, Tobacco and Firearms (ATF, now called the Bureau of Alcohol, Tobacco, Firearms and Explosives), on "identify[ing] the characteristics of an armed individual."[10] He'd also learned there that when a police officer confronts an armed individual, the person may take a "bladed" posture—move his body so the location of the gun he carries faces away from the officer, to conceal it. The man adopted this sort of bladed posture, Saldutte saw. The man followed his instructions and pulled his hand out.

At this point, with his training on identifying armed people, his prior suspicions about lurking around the house, the high-crime neighborhood, and the late hour on a cold night, Officer Saldutte would have had enough facts to harbor a reasonable suspicion that the man was engaged in criminal activity and was perhaps armed. This would allow him, under the law, to perform a "stop and frisk," which means ordering the man to remain still and to put his hands up and onto a structure or perhaps onto the police car, so that Saldutte could frisk him by patting down his outer clothing in a search for weapons. This would have frozen the action, and Saldutte would have discovered any weapon the man had. The stop and frisk, grounded in the U.S. Supreme Court case of *Terry v. Ohio*,[11] is a standard police tactic in every department, especially when an officer suspects the presence of a weapon. The Supreme Court allows stops and frisks for the purpose of assuring the safety of officers and others present, when the facts support a reasonable suspicion that the person observed is engaged in crime and has a weapon.[12]

It's worth stopping Officer Saldutte's story at this point to ask what others think of this crucial moment of the encounter. Sheldon Williams, a retired 20-year veteran of the Pittsburgh Police force who taught at the police academy while still in service, finds the failure to perform a stop and frisk at this juncture baffling. Williams, now a pastor in Pittsburgh, says that at the moment the man stopped and put his hand in his pocket as he saw the officers, Williams would have been much more direct, taking a somewhat tougher attitude: "Put your hands where I can see them, do not move—I am going to pat you down." Then he would have gone right in for the pat down, which would have dispelled the suspicion of the officers, by discovering the pop bottle in the pocket, or confirmed their suspicions if they found a gun. Instead, the approach indicated by Saldutte was way too casual to reflect the threat: "[H]old up, do me a favor ...." In addition, the officers "commit their hands" to holding up their badges, instead of having their hands free. They had already determined, in their minds, that the man likely had a gun before the questions even started, but instead of a stop and frisk, which the law would allow, the encounter moves into a question and answer session: "Is that your house ...?" With what the officers had already seen, Williams said, "warning bells should be going off like mad." With the kind of threat the officers already perceived, Williams says, a stop and frisk is the correct and obvious next step. Instead, we see a tactical approach that makes no sense.[13] Maurita Bryant, the former Pittsburgh Assistant Chief who had commanded Zone 5 in the 1990s, does not necessarily agree.[14] She says that the approach of the officers has everything to do with their perceptions and knowledge at that moment. "Every situation is different," Bryant says; it is not a "sure thing" that the officers should have moved directly to frisk Jordan then, even if some officers would have done so before talking to him any further.

Elizabeth Pittinger, the long-serving Executive Director of Pittsburgh's independent Citizen Police Review Board, agrees with Williams. In an interaction in which the officers say they already have strong suspicions that the person they see has a gun, the whole conversation sounds way too friendly. If they believe he has a gun, they need to neutralize it, unless "they are just incompetent, and having a friendly conversation with a guy they think has a gun."[15] Of course, without saying so directly, Williams and Pittinger suggest a possible theory for the reported approach and casual conversation, instead of a stop and frisk, which is that the incident simply did not happen the way it was reported.

Returning to Officer Saldutte's testimony, he said that he and his partners did not immediately stop and frisk. Instead, Saldutte started that conversation. He asked, "Is that your house you're coming from?" The man said no, it wasn't, and he rotated his body, pointing the other way, saying, "I live down the street." The way the man turned, Saldutte said, allowed him to see him straight on, and "I was able to see he had a bulge in his right front pocket, where just a few seconds earlier he had his right hand."[16] Even with this additional information, no frisk—instead, more conversation.

"As soon as he said no, I live down the street, I said, why are you sneaking around someone's house?" The man did not answer; instead, "[H]e just turned around and started walking (down) Tioga Street."[17] And with that, the situation goes downhill and rapidly spirals into violence.

As the man walked away, Saldutte said, "[H]e kept his right arm straight down, along one side of his body," as if to protect or hold the object causing the bulge in the pocket. "I could see the bulge was actually weighting down his pocket."[18] Only then did Saldutte order the man to stop. When the man kept going, Saldutte turned back to the car and said to Sisak and Ewing, "[H]e's going to go on us ... he's going to run." And sure enough the man took off. The officers all began to yell "stop" and "Pittsburgh Police," and Saldutte began to run, too. The man went about 15 or 20 feet before he fell, face down, on the ice. Saldutte and the other three officers ran toward him, and the struggle on the ground began. Saldutte's description of the fight matched what he'd testified to at the preliminary hearing. As Saldutte worked to get the man's right arm cuffed, he "felt something hard hit my left forearm. It was on the right side of his body." At that point, all doubts left him. "I thought he had a gun on him ... he's got a gun." Saldutte said to his partners, "I think he's got a gun. I think he's got a gun."[19] This caused all three of the officers to beat the man, hard, using fists and knees, "delivering pain" to his lower body and legs, so that the man would move his hands toward that area, and away from the deadly object in his pocket. That would allow them to cuff his hands. Saldutte got a cuff on one hand, but the man pulled the hand away and out of Saldutte's control, toward his body, trying to get it underneath him, toward the pocket and the danger there. Saldutte testified that he called out, "[I]f he's got a gun, he's going for it."[20]

There may be no more dangerous moment that the one Saldutte described. Believing the man almost had the gun, deadly force was in play. Anything could happen. Life hung in the balance.

Hearing Saldutte, Officer Sisak hit the man with three hard punches to the head at the same time that Ewing kneed the man in the head. And that, at last, stopped the man. The handcuffs went on him; the fight was over.[21]

With the handcuffs on and the man at last still, Saldutte immediately searched him. Saldutte "went to that front right pocket, stuck my hand in his pocket and pulled out, he had a bottle of pop, bottle of Mountain Dew in his front right pocket." Saldutte threw it to the side immediately and kept searching, because "I thought he had a gun on him. That's the thing. He probably did have a gun on him."[22] Convinced of the presence of the gun—"Figured [he] probably dropped it, lost it in the snow, while he was arguing and fighting with us"—Saldutte searched the man thoroughly, "checked his whole body," but found no gun. Saldutte told Sisak and Ewing, "[H]e had a gun. He lost it in the snow." All three officers began to search the snow over the whole area, including the front yards of both 7938 and 7940 Tioga, the sidewalk, and along the street. They found keys, a wallet, and a phone. But no gun—not that night, or ever.[23]

Saldutte then testified about the conversation with Monica Wooding: how, leaning out her window, she told the officers she did not know the man they showed her, who they had just arrested. (Wooding had already denied the key parts of this story.) Attorney Campbell then turned to the inevitable Mountain Dew bottle. Why, Campbell asked Saldutte, had he not kept and preserved the Mountain Dew bottle that had become so central to the case? Saldutte was ready for the question. "You heard the Chief say it's not evidence; it's not evidence of a crime or part of a crime. And there's nowhere to put it. You can't—the property room won't, doesn't even take it." An officer could not put it in a personal locker or at home since department rules would forbid it.[24]

Jordan's attorney Kerry Lewis then cross-examined Officer Saldutte, largely to little effect. But he eventually brought his questioning to the effect of race. He targeted the moment when Officer Saldutte said he had asked the man if he lived in the house next to which he'd seen the man standing, and the man said no, he lived down the street. "When he said he lived down the street, did it occur to you at that time to get out and say, could you show us some identification? Or did you already assume, because he's a black kid, walking up [the street in] a high-crime neighborhood at 11:00, that he is doing something wrong?" Saldutte had no real answer and wisely stuck to the facts: "Like I stated, my next question was, why are you sneaking around someone's house." Lewis pushed the point. "That's exactly what you said, why are you sneaking around. If you [were] in Mt. Lebanon or Fox Chapel," both affluent, mostly white suburban communities outside of Pittsburgh, "you would have said, wouldn't you, can I have some identification. And he could have shown you the wallet you ultimately seized from him."[25] A good set of questions, going to the heart of the case, but in the press of the courtroom action, Lewis never got an answer.

After several other lines of questioning, Lewis ended the cross-examination with a set of questions that echoed Judge Lancaster's earlier question to Chief Harper. Would a person in a struggle in the snow with three men, whether police officers or civilians, suddenly reach for a refreshing cold drink held in his pocket? Lewis took Saldutte through the characteristics or indicators that a suspect had a gun, according to Saldutte's ATF training, to which Saldutte had already testified. Lewis then pounced: "And then, you would agree, officer, that would be unusual, perhaps, you know, irrational for somebody to act that way and do those things to protect ... and hold fast a Mountain Dew bottle, wouldn't you?" Campbell objected, and Judge Lancaster sustained the objection, ruling the question out of the jury's consideration, with no answer from the witness.[26] Judge Lancaster would not allow that question, asked in the form Lewis used because it called for the witness to speculate. Instead, Lewis could have asked, "And the object you found in that very pocket was a bottle of Mountain Dew, wasn't it Officer? You found no gun in that pocket, just a bottle of soda, correct?" Saldutte could have said nothing but "yes." Lewis could then have slammed the point home in his closing argument.

Other Witnesses for the Defense

With Officer Saldutte's testimony complete, the defense did not move directly to Officers Sisak and Ewing. Instead, they chose to call several other witnesses who had not participated in the struggle that night.

Pittsburgh Police Sergeant Charles Henderson played a key role on the night of the altercation between Jordan Miles and the three police officers. At that time, Henderson (a police officer in Pittsburgh since 1993) had served as a sergeant for three years in Zone 5. He was on duty the evening of January 12, as the second-in-command in the zone, leading to his involvement in the events.

On January 12, Sergeant Henderson had spoken with Officers Saldutte, Sisak, and Ewing, to get their version of events, and he had checked on the injury to Sisak's knee. Henderson's commanding officer, Lieutenant O'Connor, told Henderson to go to West Penn Hospital, where the police officers driving the wagon had taken the person arrested,[27] in order "to ensure that our policies and procedures had been followed correctly and to make sure that everything seemed as it appeared."[28] When he got to the hospital, Henderson talked with the two police officers who brought Jordan there in the wagon and with the doctor who treated Jordan, standing outside the room. The sergeant then spoke with Jordan Miles himself:

The Witness:	I asked Mr. Miles what happened and he said that he was in a fight with the police. I asked him why he was fighting with the police and he said he was scared and did not want to go to jail.
Q.	Did he use the term "fight?"
A.	Yes.
Q.	Did you follow-up after he told you that with any further questioning of him?
A.	I did.
Q.	What did that consist of?
A.	I asked him what it was he would be going to jail for and he told me he didn't know, he wasn't doing anything.
	He also indicated at one point [that] he was afraid he was going to be robbed. Not being consistent with the other statements that the officer had made and what I had learned so far, I questioned him further and I asked him, where he had grown up. He said he had grown up in Homewood.
	I asked him when was the last time you heard of three white males jumping out of a car identifying themselves as police officers and committing a robbery, and he sat quietly for a minute, and I said, that doesn't make sense to me. Does it make sense to you? And he said no. He ... further stated, I just didn't want to go to jail.[29]

Just like that, race surfaced again. Other issues emerged in this exchange too, and cross-examination took them on. But the same racial implication filled the story and the courtroom: White people, in Homewood? White people committing crimes like robbery, in Homewood? No, we'd only find black criminals there. Whites would only—could only—be the police, on the scene to enforce the law, not break it.

Handling the cross-examination of Sergeant Henderson, attorney Tim O'Brien focused most intensely on the sergeant's recounting of his conversation with Jordan at the hospital. O'Brien's questions showed how the way in which the sergeant went about his tasks helped to shape that conversation:

Q.   You never asked Jordan Miles for his version, did you?
A.   That was the first question I asked him.
Q.   Did you ask him specifically the question of whether the police confronted him without identifying themselves? Did you ask him that?
A.   No. I asked him what happened.
Q.   Did you ask Mr. Miles whether the police when they confronted him identified themselves?
A.   No.
Q.   The answer to that question would have been particularly relevant for you to determine whether your procedures had been complied with, correct?
A.   Had I had any doubt, absolutely.

That answer—"Had I had any doubt, absolutely"—says a lot. Going into the hospital, Sergeant Henderson had already spoken with the three officers, and he felt he knew what had happened. *He had no doubt.* Everything that followed would aim not at finding out what *actually* happened but in confirming what he already knew:

Q.   Well, how would you know if you had any doubt if you didn't ask a person who had the interaction what happened?
A.   Because I see these officers—at the time I saw them on a daily basis and I know how they dressed and I know how they presented themselves and I know how they carried their badges.
Q.   You weren't there that night, were you?
A.   I was in the station ....
Q.   So you don't know what happened first hand on Tioga Street at eleven o'clock that night, do you?
A.   First hand, no, I wasn't there.
Q.   There's only four people who know what happened, that would be the three officers and Mr. Miles, correct?
A.   That's correct.

Simple and clear. The sergeant took the word of his officers as truth, without any doubt. Attorney O'Brien then began to work on the order of the statements

Jordan made as Sergeant Henderson had recounted them as well as some things Henderson had not recounted in his earlier testimony:

Q   Okay. What did he tell you?
A.   He told me that he did not want to go to jail. He had been in a fight with the police and he did not want to go to jail.
Q   Isn't it a fact that what Mr. Miles said to you was I thought I was going to be robbed, that's what he told you, isn't it?
A.   Later on in the conversation, yes he did.
Q   Isn't that the first thing that he told you?
A.   No, it's in my police report.

Attorney O'Brien knew that that answer could not stand, given the other evidence in the case. He reminded Sergeant Henderson that in a deposition, O'Brien had asked Henderson what Jordan Miles had said to him, and Henderson had replied that, "[H]e told me he was afraid he was going to be robbed." O'Brien then asked Henderson to recall that he had gone to the FBI's offices in Pittsburgh on April 13, 2010, accompanied by a lawyer, to answer questions about the case. According to the FBI report, Henderson had told the agent that he had asked Jordan Miles, "[W]hy did you give my guys such a hard time?" Henderson then continued, "Miles thought he was getting robbed." Those two phrases appeared in quotation marks in the FBI report.

Henderson attempted to backpedal, saying that the words may not be exactly what he said. "[A] lot of things … were not verbatim" in the FBI report. But O'Brien would not have it. "Are you suggesting here that the FBI agent didn't take down correctly what the FBI agent put in quotes?" he asked. "Not everything that's in this FBI report is in quotes. This particular section is in quotes, correct?" Yes, Henderson said. And nowhere in the paragraph in the FBI report where Henderson is quoted recounting Jordan Miles's response to him does it say anything like, "I didn't want to go to jail"—the phrase Henderson used in his testimony and elsewhere.[30] Henderson claimed that the FBI agent had "paraphrased" his comments and not taken them down "word for word." Had he read the statement over, after the statement was taken, O'Brien asked? Yes. And when he did that, and noticed the lack of accuracy of the quoted material, had he called the FBI and spoken to the agent and told her that she had not quoted him accurately? No, Henderson said. He had not.[31]

O'Brien covered one more key issue. When the officers had met with Sergeant Henderson after the incident, they told him they had not found the gun. As a sergeant on duty at the time, he had the authority to "send a team out there to inspect where this happened ... to do a complete search of the area."[32] O'Brien continued, "[Y]ou would expect if there really was a belief that someone had a gun and that it somehow wasn't found and left there, that somebody would go out and look for it, wouldn't they?" But Henderson answered no, not in this case. O'Brien again forced Henderson to confront the statement he had made before the trial, this time in his deposition, where he had faced questioning under oath by lawyers from both sides. In the deposition, Henderson had been asked, "If the police officers actually believe that there was a weapon but they hadn't been able to locate it, they would have told you that, correct, so that you could follow the [Standard Operating Procedures and send out a team]?" In the deposition, Henderson had answered, definitively, "[W]ell, not only a weapon but contraband, anything certainly." Even more importantly, Henderson had also been asked, "[A] weapon ... in other words, if the police had reason to believe that somewhere in the vicinity of an arrest, there is an actual weapon lying on the ground somewhere, your priority would be to secure the weapon, right?" Henderson had answered, "certainly." O'Brien had then asked, "You would expect officers who had a belief that there was such a weapon in the vicinity to tell you that, correct?" Henderson had agreed. But, O'Brien said, "[T]he officers did not tell you that when you had your discussions with them ... that it was still their belief that a weapon had been discarded and it was in the vicinity." Henderson had answered, "I don't recall having that specific discussion." The lack of any information about a gun, Henderson said, caused him to conclude "that this was just a common, routine arrest of a person on the street suspected of engaging in illegal activities ...."[33]

The examination of Sergeant Henderson had started as the defense's attempt to use Jordan's words to undermine his version of the story. It ended with the witness having to admit that he'd told a story to the FBI with a crucially different emphasis, and that the three officers had not even mentioned to their sergeant that they believed a loose gun sat on the snow-covered ground in a yard in Homewood.

The next two witnesses were Officer David Sisak, who drove the unmarked 99 Car through Homewood that night, and Officer Richard Ewing, who sat in the back seat. Their story did not vary from Officer Saldutte's testimony in any significant respect. Both of the men testified that they had feared for their lives. Officer Sisak said that during the struggle, when his partner Officer Saldutte said the man had his hand going to his pocket for a gun, he (Sisak) was positioned at the man's head. "If he pulls his hands back out, I'm the one in front of him ... I'm the first one that he is going to point that gun at and he is going to shoot me."[34] Richard Ewing testified that "I knew there was a high probability that [he] had a gun …. I was scared for my life and I was scared for my partner's life, more importantly to me."[35]

With the testimony of all three of the police officers and two other minor witnesses (a doctor who treated Jordan the night he was injured and another use-of-force expert who accepted only the officers' version of events), the testimony had finished, and the jury had all of the evidence.

THE FINAL PHASE OF THE TRIAL

Judge Lancaster would now instruct the jury in the correct law to apply to the case. After that, the lawyers would deliver their closing arguments to the jury, and the jury would begin deliberations. The decisions that the jury would make in the case would end a difficult period for Jordan Miles and his family, for the officers, and for the city. As this last phase of the case began, no one knew what the results would look like; because the case was civil and not criminal, the jury could only decide to award money damages to Jordan, or not to do so. But the prospect of the end—of some kind of accounting for what had happened, whichever way the jury decided—could not help but bring hope of relief.

The Judge's Instructions

Judge Lancaster's instructions contained no surprises for the lawyers who had argued over the points of law in dispute at the end of testimony the day before in Judge Lancaster's conference room, after the jury left and court adjourned.[36] Judge Lancaster made decisions over these disputed points and told the lawyers what he would say. This included his decision not to instruct the jury that they should draw a negative inference about the absence of the Mountain Dew bottle that the police had not collected; Jordan's lawyers strenuously pushed for the judge to tell the jury not collecting the bottle counted against the police, but Judge Lancaster refused, calling it an "illogical" request that "defies common sense," since Jordan testified that no bottle had existed.[37] Therefore, with the usual cautions about what to consider as evidence, using common sense, how to evaluate the testimony of witnesses, and the proper amount of proof that Jordan Miles had to show on his claims (i.e., enough evidence to show that "a claim or a fact is more likely so than not so"[38]), the focus remained on Lancaster's recitation of the law on the three main points of what Jordan's lawyers had to prove to establish their claims of (1) malicious prosecution, (2) false arrest, and (3) excessive force. Jordan Miles would have to prove, under federal law, that the officers (who, as police

officers, acted "under color of state law") "deprived Miles of a federal constitutional right" by subjecting him to an unlawful seizure, excessive force, and
a malicious prosecution.[39] All of this, Judge Lancaster said, must be viewed
through an "objectively reasonable police officer standard"—a rule taken
directly from the governing Supreme Court precedent.

Judge Lancaster began with the unlawful seizure claim, then moved to the
excessive force claim, and then to the malicious prosecution claim. On each, he
told the jury what the law said and what Jordan, as the plaintiff, would have to
prove. In one important section of instructions, Judge Lancaster reemphasized
the "objectively reasonable officer" standard:

> You will assess the events from the viewpoint of an objectively reasonable
> police officer, not from any other viewpoint such as your own personal
> viewpoint, the viewpoint of these three officers, the viewpoint of a reasonable
> suspect, or the viewpoint of Miles.[40]

If the officers' actions were objectively reasonable, Judge Lancaster added,
any "personal and subjective bad motives and contentions toward Miles is
irrelevant."[41]

With just a few other instructions, Judge Lancaster turned back to the
lawyers to make their closing arguments. Apart from whatever force the closing
arguments would have, Judge Lancaster's recitation of the law made several
things clear. First, to win the case, the jury would have to believe Jordan's version
of the events. Nothing less would do for him, if he were to prove all of the
elements of these three legal claims. No view of the officers' version of what had
happened, under the reasonable officer test, would support Jordan's claims. The
jury would have to accept Jordan's version of the incident in order for him to win
the case. Second, the emphasis of the Supreme Court's "reasonably objective
officer" standard was a correct statement of the law, but it was more than that
too, whether intended or not. The repeated highlighting of what a reasonable
officer would do—in the judge's instructions and in the closing arguments of the
officers' lawyers—told the jurors that they should take a law enforcement point
of view of the evidence. Most jurors would likely start off thinking that officers
would do the right things for the right reasons; for most Americans, this would
be the logical assumption. Thus the command to view the facts as a reasonable
officer would have could not help but bolster the officers' position in the case,
unless the jurors saw something unreasonable in what had happened. And in
order for them to see that, they would have to believe one young black teenager
over three experienced white police officers.

Closing Arguments

Closing arguments give the lawyers for each side in a case the opportunity to bring all of the evidence together, in a complete and coherent picture. While lawyers giving opening statements in a case can only tell the jury what they expect the evidence to show and nothing more, closing arguments give the advocates considerably more leeway. They can not only tell the jury about the evidence, of course, but also argue about the inferences that the jury should draw from the evidence—something not allowed in the openings. Lawyers may also argue about which witnesses the jury should and should not believe and what conclusions the jury should reach. They may also discuss the instructions in the law that the judge has given the jurors, as well as the legal and constitutional rights and burdens of proof involved. In short, closing argument allows the lawyers to paint the full picture of the case and the client they represent, and it represents the last chance the lawyers will get to persuade the jury to decide the case in their favor.

The order of closing arguments generally follows the burden of proof, meaning that the party who must prove the case gets to have the last word. This order supposedly gives an advantage to that party because that last closing argument will be the last thing the jury hears before deliberations begin. The order in this case would follow that common trajectory: James Wymard would argue for Officer Sisak, Bryan Campbell would speak for Officer Saldutte, and Robert Leight would argue for Officer Ewing. The jury would then hear from Jordan's lead attorney, Kerry Lewis.

James Wymard took the lead and made it clear quickly that he would take on the central role: telling the officers' version of the story and laying out their theory of the case while discrediting the case of the other side. He began by reemphasizing the legal standard: "[W]hat would an objectively reasonable police officer do under the circumstances …?" He paired this standard of reasonableness, which would move jurors toward the perspective of police officers, with the issue of credibility. "You remember in my opening statement I told you that the central issue of this case was going to be credibility, pure and simple credibility." To judge credibility, Wymard said, members of the jury should use common sense and should pay close attention to the credibility of "independent witnesses"—neither Jordan nor the officers but those who had nothing at stake in the case.[42] He made clear that only one of the versions of the story—either Jordan's or the officers'—could actually make sense. Jordan, he said, had simply testified that he was walking in his own neighborhood when the police drove up, jumped out of their car, and beat him for no reason without identifying themselves—a "preposterous" picture—while the officers' story made all the sense in the world. They had simply done their duty upon seeing a suspicious character lurking in the shadows next to a house.[43] Wymard minimized Jordan's injuries. According to the doctor who saw Jordan in the emergency room the night of the incident, Jordan suffered "no fracture to the skull, no broken nose, no fracture to the occipital orbital bones surrounding the right eye," no gouges, no cuts, no need for surgery. In fact, he looked much better after just a few weeks.[44]

Attorney Wymard acknowledged that the testimony of Monica Wooding cast doubt on the officers' story. She flatly contradicted their assertion that they showed Jordan to her on January 12, that she said she did not know the person who they showed her, or that the person certainly had no business next to her house. Wymard attacked Wooding's credibility, saying that she had "changed her testimony" to favor Jordan. (In fact, this had not happened. Every time Wooding testified—at the preliminary hearing, in a deposition, and then during the trial, each time under oath—she had testified to the same facts, always stating that the officers had not shown her anyone, and that if they had, she would surely have recognized Jordan, who lived down the block and played ball in the yard with her own son. The only different version of the encounter came from the officers' own report.[45]) Despite all but calling Wooding a perjurer, Wymard insisted that she'd said some things in her testimony that supported the officers' testimony— and that the jurors should believe these statements. "She knew [the men on her lawn outside] were police," Wymard said, "yet Jordan Miles is still telling us he didn't know they were police," ignoring every difference in context.[46]

In the core of Wymard's closing, he explained what happened—why a young man who had just emerged from his mother's house, just up the block, would end up hiding between two other houses, where the officers claimed they saw him. It brought the role of fear—on both sides of the struggle—to center stage. And it laid the blame squarely on Jordan.

According to Wymard, Jordan, walking down his street, a little later than usual, "senses a car coming behind him." This is an area with high crime, Wymard said; Jordan felt fear—of violence, of gunshots, of robberies—and, most of all, gangs. He's even talked about gangs afterward, in a remark to the police. That fear caused him to try to hide himself. Seeing the car, Wynard said, Jordan quickly decides, "I'm going to duck into the nearest house, let that car go by, I'll just stand up against the side of the house, hope they don't see me, I'll let it go by and then I'll come back out and continue going to grandma's." When Jordan comes back out and walks toward the street, he's surprised by the car, which has "come back and confront[ed] him." Now Jordan's fear jumps: "[H]e is concerned. He is scared. How is [he] going to explain this to mom and grandma …?" Wymard continued, "He is scared. They ask him do you live there" and when he says he lives down the street, the men ask, "[T]hen what are you doing sneaking around that house?" He could of course explain himself, but he does not. "Now, he is scared. Now he is really in a jam." Without another word, he begins to run, back toward his mother's house, and he falls. "The police are now out and on him. He panicked, he is in a total state of panic. Fear has enveloped him, fear from what he thinks were gang bangers, fear now it's the police. 'I got to go home to mom and explain what I did.'"

The officers were now in fear as well. Wymard explained that they knew they were "in the highest crime zone of Western Pennsylvania,"[47] and when Officer Saldutte loses the grip on one of Jordan's arms and calls out that the person is going for a gun, things escalate in seconds. "If you're Officer Sisak and you think he has a gun and if he gets to that gun, you are the first one he is going to shoot."[48] Sudden, violent death is in the air, and Wymard made sure that the members of the jury understood that officers stood for them—in their place. They were in "the highest crime zone at the highest crime rate time of the day. They served without complaining in areas of the city that you and I wouldn't drive through because of fear of harm and danger."[49] And yet, they'd done everything correctly—violating no law, no departmental regulation, and using no more force than necessary, according to Chief Harper—who'd been called as a witness by Jordan.

And why had all of this happened? Why did the city and these officers have to go through all of this? The fault lay with Jordan and no one else. He had made a mistake: "He ran, and he never should have run. He should have just [stayed] there and we wouldn't be here today …. But he chose to run and we know the consequences when you run from the police." If Jordan had just shown the police some identification, to show that he lived down the street, and had explained why he was hiding, the whole thing would never have happened. But, "[H]is response is to book, run, which he does." And the officers give chase, and the struggle on the ground begins. Jordan had the power to change the outcome, but he chose not to, so the fault lies with him.[50]

Of course, Wymard's argument does not take account of the fear black Americans might feel about the police, and all of the reasons that blacks, especially young black men, might run from officers. But assume, for the moment, that the officers had the legal right to bring Jordan down after he ran and to engage with him physically in order to subdue him. Wymard's version, while plausible, fails to explain what happened. Assuming that Jordan hid from a passing car full of gang members, nothing explains why he thought he had done something wrong in doing so—certainly nothing so wrong that he'd have any trouble explaining to his mother what he had done. Jordan's mother, Terez Miles, certainly appreciated the dangers of living in Homewood; she knew the risks that lurked on the neighborhood streets. How would telling his mother that he had ducked between houses to avoid what looked like a car of full of dangerous gang members or criminals mean that Jordan is "really in a jam"? If the officers had approached the way they said they had (not bursting from the car, in plain clothes, yelling, "[W]here's your gun? Where are the drugs? Where's the money?" but "[W]ould you mind taking your hand out of your pocket?" and "[D]o you live in that house?" or even "[S]o why were you sneaking around that other house?") what would make Jordan fear giving an explanation that his mother would surely accept or that would likely convince police officers patrolling this high-crime area? Both sides agree on this much: Jordan ran. But the idea of shielding himself from some kind of blame just does not wash. And if not that, then—as has been asked repeatedly in this book—why did he run?

Bryan Campbell, the lawyer for Officer Saldutte, gave his argument next, in which he reemphasized the law: The jury must view the evidence through the eyes of an objectively reasonable police officer and look at the amount of force used through that lens.[51] Campbell then walked the jurors through a "mini seminar" on officers' training on the use of force given by the witness David Wright, giving it to them again, step by step.[52] According to Campbell, these standards mapped perfectly onto what the officers had done. They reacted appropriately at every step, and they did only what their training had indicated they should.[53] Jordan's version, in contrast, made no sense, and for good reason: His story had only one purpose, and it had nothing to do with what had actually happened. Attorney Campbell then turned to why Jordan had done this. "This case is about one thing, money. He wants money. He wants you to bring verdicts against these police officers for money."[54]

Attorney Robert Leight made the third defense closing, on behalf of Officer Ewing. Leight laid the blame, again, directly on Jordan. "What [the case] is about is a young man, who for whatever reason, on January 12, 2010, when he was lawfully stopped by police, made a conscious decision to run from the police."[55] Leight argued that the defense did not wish to attack Jordan, who he called a "fine young man," but only "these false allegations he has made ..." and his "ridiculous claims."[56] Yet he went on to assert that Jordan could not call himself "quote ... an honor student"[57] and had lied to the jury in numerous ways. Among the defense attorneys, only Leight addressed the missing Mountain Dew bottle, and really only to say that the jury should not think of it as missing. "... [I]t wasn't evidence of any crime .... An objectively reasonable police officer would not have retained that Mountain Dew bottle that night because they couldn't take it to the jail with them, they couldn't log it into evidence .... [I]f they would have photographed it, [Jordan's lawyers] would be saying [the photo was] fabricated."[58] That constituted the sum total of all the comment in all of the defense closing arguments about the item in the pocket that the officers thought contained a gun—the only object that would have demonstrated that the officers had, in fact, seen something weighing down the pocket.

Jordan's attorney Kerry Lewis then had his final chance to make Jordan's case. He called the police actions "bad enough," but said the "cover-up and the attempt to avoid responsibility"[59] embodied by the "phony"[60] narrative of the police report made it all worse. What had actually happened, Lewis said, was what the police call a "jump out": officers coming up suddenly on a person and jumping out of a vehicle, shouting orders and accusations and questions about drugs and guns. For Jordan, the high school viola player with no prior police involvement, this tactic put the worst kind of fear into his heart in an instant: "[H]e was confronted in the dark of night by three men who jumped out of a car, dressed in dark clothing," yelling about drugs and guns and money. Fear caused Jordan to run, and that fear explained why the defense assertion (that three white men in Homewood could only be police officers) missed the mark, even as it appealed to racial stereotypes. "Why did he run? He ran because he saw three white men ... in a car jump out with dark clothing yelling guns, drugs, and money. What are the odds that Jordan Miles would know those were words that these police were using?"[61] To suggest that the three fearsome, intimidating white men could only be police, because the only criminals in that neighborhood had to be black, smacked of the worst kinds of stereotypes. "Jordan was running because he was afraid, he was terrified," Lewis said. "Think about that street, think about the darkness, think about that car coming at you and those three guys coming out of that car and you ask yourself, was that kid terrified?" He then answered his own question, "Of course he was."

Lewis also addressed the missing Mountain Dew bottle. Jordan, of course, had sworn he never had a bottle of the soda in his pocket, but "[E]ven if he had it, these officers have been telling you for three weeks that he is treating that [bottle] like a weapon"—shielding that side of his body turning that side away—"blading"—and touching or clutching that pocket to make sure the weapon remains secure. Then channeling Judge Lancaster's questions to a witness, Lewis continued, did it seem likely that, during a life-and-death hand-to-hand struggle with three larger, stronger men, Jordan would be reaching for—a cold, refreshing drink of soda?[62] In the end, Lewis contended, the event came down to a simple but grave mistake, one rooted in injustice and race. "They thought he was some black drug dealing punk and they wanted to take him down; and they took him down, and they have taken him down for the rest of his life, and that's the way it is."[63]

DELIBERATIONS AND VERDICT

With the closing arguments finished, Judge Lancaster handed the case to the jurors, who would have the final say. They began their deliberations on Thursday, August 2, 2012, in the afternoon. They deliberated the next day, Friday, August 3, and then resumed deliberations on the following Monday, August 6, sending a note containing several questions to Judge Lancaster. The jurors' note was a perfect example of the difficulties that the law, as spelled out by the U.S. Supreme Court, had created. "What does it mean," they asked, "to be assessing events from the officers' point of view or Miles point of view, which we are not to do? How do we discuss the events unless we talk about their respective versions? When considering what an objectively reasonable police officer would do, doesn't this fictional character have to be inserted into the events as detailed by the officers?"[64]

The questions captured perfectly one of the central problems with the law as it stood then and still stands now: The "objectively reasonable police officer" seems to direct jurors to consider the facts through the eyes of a reasonable police officer, in order to decide what happened. No one can fault the jurors' reaction, which reflects a perfectly reasonable understanding of the legal standard. One cannot help but wonder how many juries use that very reasoning—view the facts as a reasonable officer would—and come to a verdict, never asking the judge whether this represents the correct way to proceed. After much back-and-forth with the lawyers, Judge Lancaster set the jurors straight. The correct path remains the way he had told the jurors to proceed in his instructions. He explained:

Jurors, you are being asked to do two things in this case.

First, you are being asked to make decisions about the facts by determining what happened on the night of January 12, 2010.

For example, you have to decide whether Miles was lurking between two houses when the officers saw him that night, or simply walking down the street talking to his girlfriend on the phone.

By way of further example, you will have to decide whether the officers identified themselves as police officers or not, and whether the officers struck Miles after he was handcuffed or not.

In doing this, you are going to have to discuss Miles' side of the story and these three police officers' side of the story and consider the testimony of all of the other witnesses, as well as the documents.

There is obviously disagreement about what happened that night, and as the judges of the facts, you will be the ones to decide what actually happened.

To do this, you will have to consider each witness's version of the facts and decide who to believe and who to disbelieve.

Then you must decide from the facts as you have found them to be whether these officers violated Miles' Fourth Amendment rights. To do that, *once you have decided factually what happened that night,* you will look at each of Miles' legal claims and apply the law as I have given it to you.

This is where you will apply the objectively reasonable police officer standard that I have referred to many times in the final jury instructions. You will have to decide, based on the facts as you have found them to be, whether an objectively reasonable police officer would have [acted as they did.].[65]

In this instruction, Judge Lancaster delivered a crucial lesson in how the law actually works: *First,* decide what happened and *then* ask whether what the police did met the standard of an objectively reasonable officer. The jury should not decide what happened by asking what an objectively reasonable police officer would think of the testimony.

Deliberations continued though the day and into the next. On August 7, at 1:30 p.m., the jurors sent out a note indicating that they had reached a verdict on one of the claims but could not reach a unanimous decision on the other two.[66] Judge Lancaster brought the jury into court and gave them an "Allen charge," instructing them to resume deliberations and to try hard to reach a full verdict if they could do so without violating their consciences.

On August 8, the jurors sent out another note: They could deliberate no further.[67] They were brought into the courtroom to deliver the verdict, and Jordan and his family, the three police officers, the lawyers, members of the media, and others assembled to hear it. Judge Lancaster called the court to order, and the time for the verdict had at last arrived.

On the count of malicious prosecution (in which to be successful, Jordan would have to prove that the police officers had charged him with crimes "not in order to bring a suspected criminal to justice but instead to act with malice or spite against him"), the jury found in favor of all three police officers. Jordan had not proved that the officers had violated his Fourth Amendment rights by subjecting him to malicious prosecution. But on the other two counts—unlawful seizure (sometimes called false arrest) and use of excessive force, both of which would violate the Fourth Amendment—the jury could not reach a verdict. Judge Lancaster declared a mistrial on those two counts and dismissed the jury.[68] The remaining two claims could still be decided, but it would not happen that day or in that trial.

Directly after the trial, the lawyers spoke to the media. James Wymard, attorney for Officer David Sisak, said, "We feel this is a win, obviously, a major win."[69] According to Robert Leight, who represented Officer Ewing, "We said all along once this case was exposed to the light of daylight these allegations would not stand."[70] Wymard also told the media that the case was nothing but a money grab by Miles and his family. "[T]hey have tried to trade [on] that picture" of Jordan's horribly swollen face and "parlay it into a winning lottery ticket."[71] Bryan Campbell, the lawyer for Officer Saldutte (and also for the Pittsburgh Fraternal Order of Police), said that the verdict showed that the jury believed the officers. "The jury had to decide which story they wanted to believe," and they believed the police.[72] Leight added that the officers wanted more. "They want to be vindicated on the other two counts."[73] Timothy O'Brien, one of the attorneys who represented Jordan Miles, took a different view, emphasizing that the case had not come to a full conclusion. "There will be a new trial on the most important issue: Was there excessive force?"[74] O'Brien added that he hoped a new jury in a second trial would see the case differently, especially if the judge would allow some evidence that had been barred from the first trial—specifically "testimony that Saldutte and Ewing had made up claims to support similar arrests in the past."[75]

Neither the officers nor Jordan Miles commented on the verdict immediately after it came from the jury, and the jurors themselves would not comment as they left. But the next day, the Miles family released a statement, through Jordan's mother Terez Miles:

> Jordan Miles was a victim of racial profiling and was badly injured in a vicious, unprovoked attack. His attackers then spun a web of lies in order to protect themselves. Everything that they did was with callous disregard for Jordan's life, health and future. The fact that his attackers happened to be three white police officers does not absolve them of guilt. In fact, we believe that they are even guiltier, because police should be out to protect and serve, not to act as a gang of self-aggrandizing thugs, drunk on their own sense of power and impunity.
>
> Several people have asked members of our family how we stay so calm given all that we're going through. It's no secret that we're Christians and

much prayer and Bible reading has kept us comforted, assured and peaceful. Although the first trial ended in a mistrial, Psalm 37:1–2 says, "Do not fret because of evildoers, nor be envious of the workers of iniquity. For they shall soon be cut down like the grass and wither as the green herb." And while they are too long to include in their entirety, Proverbs 6:12–19 brings to mind the defendants in this case and Proverbs 26:24–26 seems to speak directly of racists.

We do not consider the mistrial a setback but rather a bump on the road to justice. We will continue to trust in the Lord, and will gladly proceed to the next step. We continue to covet the prayers and support of the many people who have been with us from the beginning. Please be encouraged and don't give up because we never will.[76]

Mike LaPorte, then president of Pittsburgh's Fraternal Order of Police lodge, could not let the family's statement go unanswered. The family highlighted the proverb about "God hating troublemakers," he said, just to "keep people stirred" despite a jury verdict that "vindicated" the officers. "That's exactly what they're doing … they're distorting the facts."[77]

A week later, one of the jurors spoke. Gerald Bowman, the foreman of the eight-person jury and its only African American member, said that six of the eight jurors simply could not find fault with the police. While some or all agreed that the police had made mistakes, they would spin scenarios to justify those same errors. "They were very adept at explaining things away," Bowman said.[78] He felt particularly troubled by the testimony of independent witnesses who said that Miles always respected authority in general, and the police in particular. That meant, he said, that "his natural tendency would have been to stand there" as police questioned him, "so something scared him so badly he went against his own tendency." At least four of the jurors, Bowman said, believed that it did not matter whether Jordan Miles had been walking down the street, as he had said, or lurking next to a house; the police had the absolute right to stop him just for walking at night in a high-crime neighborhood. "It was the police officers who had the rights, and Jordan Miles based upon the fact that he lived in a high-crime neighborhood and didn't go home earlier—he didn't have any rights," Bowman said.[79]

Calling the malicious prosecution verdict in favor of the police a "major win" certainly went beyond the facts; the reality was a partial victory, at best, and a real disappointment all around. The only thing certain was that there would be another trial, in an attempt to resolve the questions surrounding use of force and false arrest.

CHAPTER 12

THE SECOND TRIAL

In March of 2014, Jordan Miles, the three Pittsburgh Police officers, and their lawyers reconvened in federal court for another trial. With abuse of process no longer part of the case, the parties would focus on the remaining two claims—that the police had falsely seized Jordan, without probable cause, and that they had used excessive force against him when subduing him.

The great bulk of the evidence and the facts in the case would remain the same. Several important changes took place between the first trial and the second, however, and those changes seemed likely to matter.

CHANGES THAT OCCURRED BETWEEN THE FIRST AND SECOND TRIALS

The Judge

Judge Gary Lancaster, who presided over the first trial and would have presided over the second one, died on April 24, 2013.[1] Judge Lancaster, the first African American chief judge of the U.S. District Court for the Western District of Pennsylvania, was 63 years old. Judge David Cercone, of the same U.S. District Court for the Western District of Pennsylvania, would preside over the second trial. In the months prior to the second trial, Judge Cercone made rulings on the admissibility of evidence. Some of these rulings differed from those that Judge Lancaster had made, while others did not. For example, Judge Lancaster had ruled that the officers could not bring into evidence a gun magazine and several bullets found near the scene of the altercation between Jordan and the officers because nothing linked the items to Jordan. Judge Cercone reversed that ruling; the magazine and bullets could become part of the evidence in the second trial.[2] Lawyers for Jordan asked that Judge Cercone allow them to use prior complaints against the three police officers in the second trial, which Judge Lancaster had not allowed, and Judge Cercone also refused.[3] He ruled that while evidence of those past acts of the officers would perhaps prove motive, that motive had no relevance to the two legal questions in the case: whether the officers had probable cause to arrest and whether the officers had "used force that was objectively reasonable under the circumstances ...."[4]

Some of this evidence of prior conduct could have mattered to the jury confronted with questions of the policing practices of these officers, with the ultimate question of their credibility, that is, whether or not to believe them. According to reporting in the *Pittsburgh City Paper* by journalist Alex Zimmerman, just 19 days before the incident with Jordan Miles, Officers Saldutte, Ewing, and Sisak, riding in an unmarked 99 car and in plain clothes, had a similar confrontation with a man named Lamar Johnson.[5] The officers reported that, while driving, they smelled burning marijuana and turned around to investigate. Johnson, one of a pair of men walking together in the Lincoln-Lemington area (an African American neighborhood very near Homewood, where Jordan lived), found himself confronted with the three officers and almost immediately under assault. According to the *City Paper* report, the officers "wrestled him to the snow-covered ground, suspecting he might have a gun in his coat, and that he might be trying to swallow narcotics."[6] As in Jordan's case, the officers suspected Johnson had a gun because of the way his right coat pocket sagged and bounced off his body as he walked, because he had his hand in his pocket, and because of his stance, but they found no gun; they also recovered no drugs.[7] Johnson filed a complaint against the three officers, but no disciplinary action resulted.[8] The similarity of the incidents, Jordan's lawyers argued, just a short time before Jordan's own confrontation with the same officers, with a similar rationale regarding the suspected presence of a gun, made the Johnson incident relevant and important. But the jurors never learned about it, because of Judge Cercone's ruling: he found the danger that the evidence would prejudice the jury against the officers outweighed any benefit to hearing about it.

The Lawyers

Two new lawyers, Pittsburgh trial attorney Joel Sansone and Michigan attorney Robert Giroux, would handle Jordan's case.[9] Giroux, who had considerable experience with lawsuits against police officers, practiced with the firm of attorney Jeffrey Fieger, well known at that time for defending Dr. Jack Kevorkian, the doctor convicted in Michigan for assisting in several suicides.[10] All three of the police officers had the same attorneys.

The Officers

One of the three officers, Richard Ewing, had left the Pittsburgh Police Department and joined the department in McCandless, a small municipality outside of Pittsburgh. Officers Saldutte and Sisak remained with the Pittsburgh Police.[11]

The Witnesses

Several significant witnesses had the potential to make the second trial different than the first—one by her presence and the other by his absence. First, Commander RaShall Brackney (discussed earlier in Chapter 5), who had once had two of the officers under her command, had handled disciplinary matters involving both of those officers. According to media reports, in portions of a deposition taken earlier in the case, Commander Brackney had testified about the officers' conduct. "I recommended repeatedly that they were to be closely monitored, that they had a history of lying ...."[12] This kind of evidence, particularly about the truthfulness of the officers, could have an enormous impact on how the jury viewed the officers and their testimony in the current case. At every turn in the first trial, the officers' lawyers had asserted that the whole case came down to credibility—who the jury would believe. Commander Brackney had not testified in the first trial. She would testify in the second trial, but Judge Cercone ruled before the trial started that she could *not* testify about these crucial matters of lying and telling the truth. He limited her testimony to proper police procedures and use of force.[13] While testimony from Brackney on other subjects would help Jordan, not having the chance to ask about the officers' past truthfulness constituted a substantial missed opportunity.

The second significant change in which witnesses would testify involved Chief of Police Nathan Harper. Called as a witness for Jordan Miles in the first trial, no doubt because his testimony in a pretrial deposition had favored Jordan in some significant ways, Chief Harper gave important, perhaps decisive testimony in favor of the officers. As discussed in Chapter 10 of this book, he testified regarding a crucial piece of evidence, the Mountain Dew bottle, which the officers testified they found in Jordan's coat pocket.[14] They had not saved the bottle as evidence, and Jordan's lawyers made this a central part of their case. In his deposition, Chief Harper had said that the officers should have saved the bottle and that their failure to do so violated police policy. But when he testified at the trial, Chief Harper told the jury that the bottle did not constitute evidence. The officers arrested Jordan that night for assaulting two of the officers and for lurking near a house; the bottle had no relevance to those charges. Additionally, the Chief said that neither the police property room nor the jail would have accepted the bottle if the police had brought it in, because it was a food or beverage item.[15] Harper's testimony came as a surprise, and Jordan's attorney Kerry Lewis was unable to counter it effectively. Harper was an experienced witness with a certain gravitas as Chief, and his testimony was a major setback.

In the second trial, Harper would not testify as anyone's witness. He had become ensnared in the criminal law himself—as a defendant. A federal investigation of the Pittsburgh Police Department's system of paying officers eventually revealed that Harper took about $30,000 meant for "secondary employment" of officers for his own use.[16] (Such secondary employment is for outside jobs in which bars, concert venues, sports arenas, and other places hired off-duty police officers to keep the peace; the employers paid into a department account instead of paying the officers directly.) Harper pled guilty in February of 2014 and received a sentence of 18 months in prison.[17] Given these events, neither party in Jordan's case would call him as a witness.[18]

A third witness who had not testified at the first trial, Officer Robert Horak, would take the stand in the second trial. His testimony might help the jury see some important facts from Jordan's point of view. His role is discussed later in this chapter.

The Jury

A different jury presided, of course; this one consisted of four white men and four white women. It had no black members.[19] The court removed the only potential black juror because she "expressed strong feelings about the case."[20]

THE TRIAL

In his opening statement to the jury for Jordan Miles, attorney Robert Giroux boiled the case down to simple facts. The officers, he said, while patrolling in plain clothes in an unmarked car in Homewood, looking proactively for signs of crime in a high-crime area, saw "a young black male in a big black coat, with dreadlocks ... there is a prevalence of drugs in the area and other crimes. They jump to the conclusion that he was up to no good"—that Jordan, in this criminal neighborhood, was himself a criminal. The three officers "jumped to a horribly wrong conclusion" and then brutally beat him. They saw him, did not identify themselves in any way, and "they assumed the worst of him."[21]

Giroux told the jurors to expect the officers to perform well on the witness stand and that he did not contend that the officers were bad people. Rather, he said, "I'm asking you to judge what they did that night."[22]

The opening statements of the defense lawyers for the three officers tracked closely what they had said in the first trial: The three officers had come upon Jordan at the side of a house; he appeared to have a weapon in his coat pocket when they stopped him, which became noticeable when he began to run; and they eventually subdued him, using fist and knee strikes, in a furious fight in which he hit two of the officers—one hard enough to cause injury. While they'd been sure that he had a gun in his pocket—that Jordan had struggled to pull his right hand to his pocket so he could use the gun on them—they had found a Mountain Dew bottle in his pocket instead. They had shown him to the owner of the yard in which they had struggled, and she had said she did not know him. In that same yard, sometime later, after they had searched thoroughly and found no gun anywhere, an ammunition clip and some bullets had been recovered (a piece of information that the jury in the first trial had never heard). Jordan had made up his version of the story. The officers had identified themselves as police. There was no way that Jordan could not have known they were police officers, and he had run from them and seemed to have a gun.

Most of the witness testimony in the case hardly differed from the testimony in the first trial, though the order in which the witnesses appeared had changed. (For example, Jordan's lawyers called the police officers as their own witnesses in their own case—for Jordan—for tactical reasons.) Jordan Miles recounted what had happened to him that night in response to questions from Joel Sansone, one of his new attorneys.[23] This time, Sansone had Jordan make strong and direct denials of police assertions about what he had supposedly done. In particular, Jordan said he had not known that the three men were police. They never announced that they were police; he saw no badges; they yelled about drugs, guns, and money and ran at him.[24] He thought the men were going to rob him, and he tried to run.[25] Sansone confronted one of the statements attorney Wymard' made to the jury in his opening argument, centering on race:

Q.   Now, Mr. Wymard told this jury that three white guys are coming at you and trying to stop you, that they had to be police. What did you think?

A.   They were regular people. I've seen white people in Homewood. I've seen white people walking dogs in Homewood. I've seen white people riding bikes in Homewood. I saw white people buying drugs in Homewood.[26]

In other words, the men certainly did not have to be police officers; they could have been anyone, and the fact that they were white did not mean they were police. They could just as easily have been people out to rob him. Jordan also denied that he had stood next to one of the neighboring houses, where Officer Saldutte said he'd spotted someone,[27] or that he had had a weapon.[28] And he strongly denied that he had had a bottle of Mountain Dew in his coat pocket. He had not left the house with a bottle; did not drink the stuff; never had.[29]

Cross-examination followed, led again by attorney James Wymard. Just as in the first trial, the centerpiece of the cross-examination remained the same: Wymard insisted that Jordan's assertion that he did not know the men confronting him that night were police simply did not wash. He *had* to have known. "They were trying to put handcuffs on you, Jordan,"[30] Wymard said. Jordan said that the men had tried to get his hands behind his back; he was unaware at that point that they were trying to use handcuffs.[31] Again, Wymard asserted, the race of the people involved mattered: Since the three men, not wearing uniforms and not in a police car, were white and not black, they could *not* be criminals. According to Wymard, "[Y]ou have three white guys in Homewood," therefore "it could only be police officers."[32] "Didn't it dawn on you that it had to be police officers that were trying to do this?"[33] Of course, the "three white guys in Homewood" caused Jordan to run *well before* any attempt to pull his arms back and put handcuffs on him, but this inconvenient fact never came up in Wymard's attack. Nobody had pulled a gun on him, or a knife, or a club; yet, Jordan expected the jury to believe that he didn't know they were police? That he was being robbed? Yes, Jordan answered—they were not in uniform, and he'd never seen anything like this happen.[34] Wymard also repeatedly implied that Jordan had indeed possessed a bottle of Mountain Dew soda that night.

Examining Officer Saldutte, Jordan's attorney Joel Sansone echoed the late Judge Lancaster in the first trial, asking Saldutte why, during the heat of the struggle, Jordan would have reached toward his pocket for a bottle of soda. After all, according to Saldutte and his fellow officers, they found the bottle in that very pocket after they handcuffed him. Saldutte said that he thought Jordan had reached not for the bottle but for a gun. "In my mind," Saldutte said, "I believed he had a gun."[35] Officer Sisak said the same thing. "I've said all along, I believe he had a gun …. I thought he was going to pull out a gun and shoot me," even thought he could not explain how Jordan could have disposed of a gun during the incident. "I'm telling you that night that I believe[d] he had a gun on him."[36] Officer Ewing agreed with Saldutte and Sisak; he told the jury that he still believed that Jordan had had a gun that night, even if he never saw one.

Commander RaShall Brackney's testimony[37] marked the biggest departure from the first trial. Commander Brackney (refer back to Chapter 5) brought the experience and credibility of a 30-year career, with numerous command postings throughout the city and the Police Department—everything from commanding several police zones, including Zone 5, to running the Department's Training Academy, its Dignitary Protection Unit, and Special Operations (SWAT operations, bomb squad, etc.).[38] She had deep familiarity with use of force training and had served as a defensive tactics training instructor.[39] She had also been consulted on the case by the FBI and by former Chief Harper because she regularly reviewed use of force reports and had reviewed them in the incident involving Jordan.[40] Even though Judge Cercone had limited her testimony, she offered a considerable amount of important information for the jury.

Lawyer Robert Giroux first took Brackney to one of the important points made in the officers' case, which was that Homewood had considerable dangerous and violent crime. Having served two stints as the Commander of Zone 5, which includes Homewood, Brackney knew this intimately. She had a deep familiarity with the statistics of the Zone's Uniform Crime Reports (UCR) to the FBI, which is the data that the FBI uses to put together crime rates and trends in every city and town across the country.[41] The UCR compiles data on crimes in different categories. Part I data includes violent crimes, such as murder, rape, aggravated assault, robbery, and burglary.

Commander Brackney's understanding of the data, especially for Zone 5, allowed her to make nuanced observations about crime in Homewood, which, Brackney said, "is a high crime area," in fact "rated as the most violent neighborhood in the State of Pennsylvania." But she made clear that this danger applied to the residents and inhabitants of Homewood. "If you live there, and you meet certain criteria, you're more likely to be a victim of a homicide, or a victim of being shot in Homewood."[42] These statistics enabled her to draw a distinction between the danger of violence toward civilians and the danger faced by officers. For police, Homewood did not even rank in the top three of all neighborhoods in Pittsburgh (let alone in Pennsylvania) for the danger of assault against an officer. Police officers experienced assaults most often in the Hill District in Pittsburgh. Officers working the South Side (an area with a high concentration of bars and other night spots serving alcohol and popular with young people), the North Side (with the city's two major sports stadiums and clusters of bars and restaurants around them and the city's casino), and the Oakland neighborhood (with its two major universities) all faced greater danger of police assault than officers working in Homewood.[43]

Giroux next moved to counter attorney Wymard's assertion that three white men in Homewood would be so unusual that they could only be police officers. Commander Brackney could speak directly to this point because she knew Homewood intimately. She told the jury that she had grown up there from birth, went to school there, still owned property in the area, went to church in the neighborhood every week, and still served on community boards and committees. She still spent time with her extended family who lived in Homewood.[44] Giroux approached the question gingerly but directly:

Q: Okay. I'm not being facetious, or cute, or smart-alecky, I just need to
        ask this to dispel something that's been thrown about [in this case]. Are
        there any white people living in Homewood?
A: Yes.
Q: Okay. Are there any white people committing crimes in Homewood?
A: Um, yes, there's white people that commit crimes in Homewood.[45]

In other words, assertions by the defense team that the only white people in Homewood would be police, and that they could not be criminals, was wrong.

Based on her considerable experience at the Training Academy as a defensive tactics instructor and her regular reviews of use of force reports, Brackney testified about two critical use of force issues in the case. First, she testified that the department did not train officers to use fist strikes to the head; if nothing else, this could cause injury to the officer's hand, in addition to injuring the suspect.[46] Using a knee to strike a subject in the head would constitute a use of deadly force, and the department did not teach officers to use knee strikes in that fashion.[47]

Attorney Giroux then asked Commander Brackney about two central pieces of evidence: (1) the Mountain Dew bottle that the officers said they had found in Jordan's pocket and (2) the gun for which the officers pursued Jordan. Police officers seize items of evidence all the time, she said. Police would record and document all types of items and then keep them as evidence (in the police property room), return them to their owners (say, a piece of stolen personal jewelry that the owner wants back), or dispose of them properly. If the item is perishable, "you would take a picture of it,"[48] in addition to recording its existence in the police report. Officers also have the ability to have an object fingerprinted or tested for the presence of DNA by making a request to crime scene forensic teams, available 24 hours a day.[49] (Of course, the officers had taken no photographs of the bottle, much less asked for the taking of fingerprints or DNA processing.)

The officers never found a gun at the scene, although they searched for one and remained convinced that Jordan had had a gun that night. Brackney's testimony raised another issue regarding the gun. At the time of the incident in 2010, the Pittsburgh Police had specially trained dogs available to search for guns or bombs. These dogs, the commander testified, get trained "specifically to look for, or detect, or to help you discover where there may be guns … so, those are available."[50] Department policy *did not require* that the officers call a gun dog in a situation like the altercation on Tioga Street, but the officers *could have requested* that gun dog. Apparently, they did not do this at any point, although they testified that they believed Jordan had a gun they had not found.

On cross-examination, one of the officers' attorneys asked Brackney about the gun dog. It was correct, wasn't it, that department policy did not require officers to summon the gun dog whenever officers believed someone had a gun but they could not find it? Yes, Brackney said—no policy required it. The attorney continued, "one would consider maybe calling the gun dog out, only if you felt there might be a gun somewhere in the area, isn't that correct?" Yes, Brackney answered. "I would call a gun dog for thinking there was a gun, yes"[51]—exactly the point that Jordan's lawyers had made. If the officers thought Jordan had a gun, and they could not find it, they could call for the dog—but they did not.

Jordan's lawyers also called another witness, Officer David Horak,[52] who had had no role in the first trial. Officer Horak, formerly of the Pittsburgh Police (by the time of the second trial, he worked for another police department in Pittsburgh's suburbs), was one of two officers summoned to the scene of the altercation on Tioga Street. He arrived with the police wagon to transport a handcuffed Jordan Miles first to the hospital and then to the county jail. Attorney Robert Giroux asked Officer Horak what he'd seen and heard from the officers when he arrived. Horak testified that the events had apparently just ended; the three officers were huddled around Jordan, who sat handcuffed in the snow. Officer Saldutte had a red face, as if from exerting himself. Horak testified that when he walked up, the officers said, "[W]e jumped out on him, and then he ran."[53] This statement from the officers to one of their own, at the scene of the action and directly following it, supported a key contention in Jordan's case. Instead of pulling up to Jordan as he walked away from the house where he seemed to hide himself, identifying themselves as police officers, and then asking him what he was doing, the three had just "jumped out" on the young man—a well-known tactic designed to startle and overwhelm suspects, taking them by surprise. Horak's testimony dovetailed neatly with Jordan's, in which Jordan said the car came up on him suddenly and the men jumped out without any effort to identify themselves, yelling about drugs and guns. Speaking to the media, Jordan's lawyer made the connection clear. Jump-outs, a troubling tactic, had caused Jordan to run. "They jumped out, said, 'Give me your drugs, guns, and money.' "[54]

Attorney Giroux also questioned Officer Horak about the presence of a gun, which according to the three officers was the possibility that caused them to fear for their lives and resulted in the struggle to subdue Jordan. As Horak walked up to the officers surrounding Jordan, the officers never mentioned the presence of a weapon. Giroux asked, "[D]id any of the officers tell you that they thought [Jordan] had a gun, or had had a gun?" Horak answered, "no."[55] Of course, the absence of any conversation did not prove that the three officers who struggled with Jordan had *not* thought that, but since they *had* told Horak about what had happened in some respect—"we jumped out on him, and then he ran"—mentioning that they thought he'd had a gun seems both likely and logical.[56]

With the witness testimony completed, the lawyers gave their closing arguments. James Wymard, for Officer Sisak, articulated the defense theory: Jordan went outside to walk to his grandmother's house and, seeing the officers' car, believed it contained gang members. He ducked between houses to hide himself from them, and when the officers saw the figure hiding between the houses, they understandably doubled back to check out the situation. When the officers confront him, asking why they had seen him sneaking around a house, Jordan "panics and thinks that if he can get home to his mother, she'll explain everything."[57] Wymard said the jury simply should not believe Jordan. "Everybody is wrong but Jordan," he said. "Everybody lied but Jordan."[58] Then he went back to the racial message that white men in Homewood could only be police officers. "Three white guys in Homewood trying to put handcuffs on him. Who, other than police officers, would do that?" he said, ignoring again that Jordan had fled, and most of the struggle took place well before any handcuffs came out.[59] Defense attorney Robert Leight, who represented Officer Ewing, portrayed the officers as the real victims. "Jordan made a mistake that caused this issue to snowball. Jordan's wounds healed, but these officers continue to bear the scars of the allegations against them."[60]

For Jordan, attorney Joel Sansone said that the officers had made the mistake by jumping out on a young black man in dreadlocks, assuming that criminal activity constituted the only reason to walk through Homewood at night. Once they discovered their mistake—Jordan "had no burglary tools, he had no gun"—they had to cover it up, which they did with lies about the phantom Mountain Dew bottle. Sansone ended emotionally. "This will be hard," he told the jury, "but you must believe the word of an 18-year-old boy rather than three sworn police officers. For the love of God, do what's right."[61] Judge Cercone then gave instructions to the jury, this time only on false arrest and excessive force, and sent them to deliberate.

THE VERDICT

The jurors worked for a day and a half, at one point asking for readings of some pieces of testimony.[62] Then, on March 31, 2014, they announced that they had a verdict in the case. On Jordan's claim of an illegal seizure, the jury found in favor of Jordan, awarding a total of $119,016.75 in damages ($101,016.75 in compensatory damages, paying for injuries of all kinds, and $6,000.00 in punitive damages against each of the three officers). On the claim of excessive force, the jury found in favor of the three officers.[63] The arrest, the jury's verdict said, lacked probable cause and violated the Constitution. But the amount of force used to effectuate the arrest did not exceed legal standards. None of the jurors made any public statements or gave any interviews explaining the seeming contradiction: If the officers falsely arrested Jordan, how could the law justify *any* amount of force? But if the use of force did not violate the law, how could the officers have conducted an illegal arrest?

The contradictory findings clearly disappointed the lawyers for the police officers. "There's no logic behind it whatsoever, it makes no sense. It's an inconsistent verdict," said Robert Leight, attorney for Officer Ewing.[64] "These are three fine police officers, and you have got to wonder what message this sends to the police department ... they'd do it all over again. They did nothing wrong." Perhaps, he said, the jury had acted out of sympathy for Jordan Miles.[65] For his part, Jordan's attorney Joel Sansone had no easier time understanding the verdict. "I cannot explain the jury's failure to find excessive force," he said, and it will remain "a mystery" unless and until the jurors explain it (which they never did).[66] Pittsburgh's mayor, Bill Peduto, said that the events in Homewood four years earlier "have echoed through our city, our neighborhoods, and our police force ever since." The case "hurt us all in some way. Our community must start healing and must start rebuilding the trust we must have for safe communities and a better police force. I am ready to start that now."[67]

Alone among those affected, Jordan took a different perspective. He chose to treat the mixed verdict as a victory and as a bridge to something better. "The jurors found the police officers to be guilty, at least in one aspect, and that's all I really needed," he said. "We may not agree with everything [about the verdict], but it's good to know, so now I can put this behind myself and try to go back to school."[68] He had just wanted some accountability, a statement that the officers had done wrong, "and that's what this court brought out. I'm very satisfied that these jurors were able to come to that conclusion and see that these police officers were wrong."[69]

But the verdict did not end the case. More legal maneuvering lay ahead—much more than anyone anticipated, even on the disappointing day of the verdict that told no coherent story.

EVEN WITH THE SECOND VERDICT, IT'S NOT OVER

With the verdict announced, and no one satisfied except perhaps Jordan himself, further maneuvering began almost immediately. Jordan's attorney Joel Sansone called for the federal government to reopen the investigation of whether the officers had committed a criminal violation of Jordan's civil rights. "We have brought to light in that courtroom facts that should cause the authorities to look into whether or not these individuals should be allowed to carry a gun and protect and serve our citizens," Sansone said.[70] U.S. Attorney David Hickton, who had supervised the federal investigation when he began his tenure and eventually decided not to bring charges because he could not prove the case with the available evidence, said he would not do so. He said that while he respected the jury's decision in the second trial, nothing about the split civil verdict would change his mind about closing the investigation.[71] Hickton's reference to the verdict in the civil case—which used a lower burden of proof on the plaintiff than prosecutors would face under the federal criminal law—highlighted the fact that the case had proven tough for the plaintiff even under that lower standard. If Hickton had found the case unprovable beyond a reasonable doubt before, the mixed civil verdict could not encourage him to pick up the prosecution again.

The lawyers who had defended the three police officers immediately began to focus on the damages. In April, the month after the trial and the verdict, they filed a motion arguing that Judge Cercone should considerably reduce the damages the jury awarded. As noted in Chapter 5 of this book, the *City* of Pittsburgh (not the officers) had already settled with Jordan for $75,000; the officers' lawyers argued that that amount should therefore be deducted from the $119, 016.75 the jury had awarded. In addition, they argued, Judge Cercone should reduce the jury's verdict even further, to reflect the actual out-of-pocket costs that Jordan and his family had paid for his medical bills. All told, they said, the damage award should be reduced to $8,415.05.[72] In addition, they argued that Jordan's lawyers could only ask for court-awarded attorney fees up to the day that the plaintiffs rejected a settlement offer of $180,000 back in June of 2011.

Recall the discussion in Chapter 5 about rejected settlement offers in civil rights litigation. The U.S. Supreme Court decided that once defendants make an offer to settle the case, and the plaintiffs reject the offer, that amount sets a benchmark for any verdict that eventually results. If the eventual jury award does not exceed the settlement offer, the plaintiff's attorneys cannot collect any fees for their work from the date of the rejection of the settlement onward. This makes rejecting any offer of settlement risky for plaintiff's lawyers. They can end up with no payment for a case in which they had invested a considerable amount of work and expense necessary to take a worthy case to trial, *even if they win the case*, if the eventual award does not exceed what the plaintiff rejected. This puts plaintiffs and plaintiffs' lawyers in a potential conflict because plaintiffs may not want the settlement offered and may wish to go on to trial, but this increases the risk for their lawyers. Jordan's lawyers, it seems, got caught in this very trap. Jordan, their client, rejected the settlement offer, won the case in part but did not receive sufficient damages to avoid putting a great deal of the lawyers' expenses in jeopardy. To rub more salt in the wound, the Supreme Court's rule allowed the city to charge its trial preparation costs following the June 2011 rejection of the settlement against the damages awarded to Jordan Miles.[73] The defense lawyers ask Judge Cercone to follow this rule to the letter.

One can only imagine how these arguments—*fully legal though they were*—must have appeared to Jordan, his family, and those in the city who saw the case his way. Jordan had insisted on some measure of justice, had the charges against him dismissed, had then gone through not one but two civil trials and come up with half a loaf in what seemed like a compromise verdict, with a sum that seemed modest by comparison to many civil cases finding against police. At the end, Jordan himself seemed to have salvaged some meaning from the opposing findings of the jury, pronouncing himself satisfied that they found the police at fault in at least some respect. The mayor of the city followed the verdict with words expressing the hope that the city could move past the event and toward healing. But now, that same city—through the lawyers employed to defend the city's police officers—was moving aggressively to take away all but the smallest slice of the money awarded. Of course, the lawyers were only following the legal opportunities the law gave them to minimize the damages for those they represented. But most people would not distinguish between the city and its mayoral words of healing and reconciliation, and what seemed like an attempt to subvert the verdict by lawyers hired by that city, in any way possible, through "legal technicalities." The lawyers' actions would speak louder than the mayoral words—indeed, the legal actions would cause the words to ring hollow.

For their part, Jordan's lawyers did not remain silent after the verdict, either. Joel Sansone contended, in his own posttrial motions, that because the jury had concluded that the officers falsely arrested Jordan, without probable cause, any amount of force used exceeded legal limits. Therefore, the court should reverse the jury's verdict for the officers on excessive force and hold a hearing to assess damages on that count for Jordan.[74] Alternatively, the court should grant Jordan a new trial on the excessive force claim; Judge Cercone had erred when he allowed the jury to see the gun magazine and the bullets, and the judge had excluded evidence favorable to Jordan from a witness (discussed later in this chapter) who had come forward during the trial, offering evidence that would have "negatively impacted the credibility of one or more" of the police officers.[75]

In June of 2014, two months after the second trial, Judge Cercone ruled. Jordan Miles would not get a new verdict in his favor or a new trial on the claim of excessive force. Cercone simply did not accept the premise that the verdicts on false arrest (that the police arrested Jordan without probable cause, finding in his favor) and excessive force (that the police did not use excessive force, finding for the officers) were inconsistent.[76] "Though the jury found that the defendants lacked probable cause to arrest the plaintiff, the fact remains that an arrest occurred," Cercone said. "The jury obviously found that during such arrest, plaintiff was not subjected to excessive force."[77] As far as the evidence, he wrote, the arguments made by Jordan's lawyers fall "woefully shy of convincing this Court that the great weight of the evidence cuts against the verdict."[78] As far as the defendant's arguments that the jury's verdict should be reduced by the $75,000 settlement already paid, and further to reflect actual out-of-pocket costs, Judge Cercone ruled against the defendants. The $75,000 settlement was for attorneys' fees, he said, and the fees-after-the-settlement-offer argument might affect that amount, but it had nothing to do with the jury's award. Since the jury had not specified what the amount awarded compensated for, we could not know how much of the award covered medical costs and how much covered discomfort, pain, fear, humiliation, or mental anguish.[79]

Two months later, Judge Cercone ruled on the defendants' motion to deduct their preparation costs incurred after the settlement rejection date from the damage award. On August 19, 2014, Cercone reduced Jordan's damage award by $20,692.79.[80] This left Jordan just under $100,000 in damages.

THE APPEAL

As the months went by, it became clear that Judge Cercone's rulings on the various posttrial motions had not ended the case either. In August of 2015, Jordan's lawyers filed an appeal of the case, to the U.S. Court of Appeals for the Third Circuit. Among the grounds for the appeal, Joel Sansone included a claim not publicly aired before. Sansone revealed that during the second trial, Jordan's lawyers received a message from a woman who worked as a bartender on Pittsburgh's South Side, an area filled with rowdy bars and restaurants popular among young people. She reported to them that Officer David Sisak had come into the bar where she worked, and during the course of the conversation they had, he showed her a picture of Jordan's injured and swollen face on the screen of his phone. "That's who I am," he told her. The woman asked Sisak whether he had any regrets; she said that he told her he regretted that he had not "killed that fucking nigger"—referring to Jordan. The woman told Jordan's lawyers that this had happened shortly before the second trial began.

The attorneys brought the information to Judge Cercone during the second trial, outside the hearing of the jury, as soon as they had made face-to-face contact with the woman, and they asked the judge to allow her to testify. The officers' lawyers protested, and Judge Cercone eventually refused to allow the testimony, calling it inflammatory and highly prejudicial to the officers' case. (This was apparently the witness referred to in the plaintiff's posttrial motions, whose testimony would have "negatively impacted the credibility of one or more witnesses.") The judge also prohibited the lawyers from discussing the potential evidence. The refusal to allow this testimony formed the centerpiece of the appeal, and at a news conference in August of 2015 announcing the appeal, Sansone described the evidence in detail, saying that it showed that racism explained the beating Jordan Miles took at the hands of the officers.[81] (He also said that with the trial concluded, the court's gag order that had been put in place long before no longer applied.) Officer Sisak denied the allegations, and Mayor Bill Peduto stated that an investigator for the city had looked at the allegations at the time and did not find them credible.[82] Making specific reference to the fact that the national climate around police violence had changed beginning in the summer of 2014, with deaths at the hands of police in Ferguson, Missouri, Staten Island, New York, Cleveland, Ohio, and so many other places, Sansone again argued that with this new evidence, the U.S. Department of Justice should reopen its civil rights investigation against the officers. Again, U.S. Attorney Hickton refused, saying that the case had been "exhaustively investigated" and did not merit yet another look.[83]

IT FINALLY ENDS

It was not until ten more months went by, after the filing of the appeal in August of 2015, that the final stage of the case was reached.

In late May of 2016, reports surfaced that the city of Pittsburgh had offered to settle the litigation with Jordan Miles, for $125,000. Jordan had decided to accept the settlement, forgoing any appeal and the possibility of yet a third trial. "We have accepted the city's proposal to settle," Sansone announced. "Jordan Miles is not defined by what three rogue police officers did to him when he was 18." He said Jordan wants to "move on with the next phase of his life."[84] According to a spokesman for Mayor Peduto, the settlement was reached during federal mediation. "The city offered $125,000, and Miles' attorneys accepted it."[85] The final step required approval of the settlement by the Pittsburgh City Council. That came with a vote of the Council on June 7, 2016.[86] With Mayor Peduto's agreement, the settlement went into effect. Sansone said that Jordan and his lawyers felt "gratified" by the settlement. "This will close a long and very difficult chapter for Jordan and his family, but Jordan looks to the future, which for him is very bright," said Sansone. "The lawless conduct of these police officers has not deterred Jordan from his life's mission, and he remains as good a man as I have ever met."[87]

On June 7, 2016, almost six-and-a half years after the incident on that frigid night on Tioga Street in Homewood, the case was—finally and fully—over. Yet it lives on in the minds and memories of Jordan, his family members, the police officers, and numerous citizens of Pittsburgh. For many in the African American community in Pittsburgh, from that time until now (and into the future), they mention Jordan Miles's name when they speak of others, some not fortunate enough to have survived, such as Jerry Jackson and Jonny Gammage.

But the end of the case does not mean the end of the questions it raises and the issues it exposes. Looking forward, what can be done to address these problems? How can we keep something like the terrible incident on Tioga Street on January 12, 2010 (or something even worse) from happening again?

PART IV

WHAT'S NEXT?

As we look back over Part I of this book, we know what happened on Tioga Street, on January 12, 2010, from Jordan's point of view and from the perspective of the officers. We also know what happened in the aftermath, from the initial criminal charges against Jordan, to the investigations, to the beginnings of the federal civil rights lawsuit brought by Jordan. In Part II, we learned why these things happened and why they keep happening—the influence of race and fear on both sides of these interactions. In Part III, we saw what happened in the civil litigation: how, even with two full trials, justice remained elusive.

In Part IV, the time has come to ask our remaining question: **How can we prevent these incidents from occurring again?** *What can we—as a society, as a government, as a country—do to try to prevent these unfortunate incidents from happening, or at least from happening as frequently and with such devastating consequences? We must ask this question not just from the point of view of changing the law; that will form part of the solution, but only part. We must ask how law enforcement can do things differently from its own internal points of reference, such as policy, training, supervision, accountability, and relationship. No one should believe that police confrontations with civilians will ever disappear entirely; that simply is not realistic. But how can we minimize their number, their danger, and their consequences?*

Finally, in the Epilogue to this book, we will leave with a sense of what has happened to those people and entities with whom and with which we have become familiar: Jordan, the three officers, the main witnesses, the Homewood neighborhood, the city of Pittsburgh, and its police department.

CHAPTER 13

WHAT CAN WE DO?

With the full, multifaceted story of the incident on Tioga Street on January 12, 2010, and the case of *Jordan Miles v. Michael Saldutte, David Sisak, and Richard Ewing* in hand, we can see the case as an example of how modern policing in urban America works and how the law and the legal system in our country respond. What we see, of course, are ways in which our institutions, customs, rules, and laws can make mistakes, respond inadequately, and fail to find justice for anyone.

This conclusion remains true even if we assume, for purposes of argument, that the police officers told the truth and did everything by the book. Surely they would wish that there had been some better way to resolve the situation on the scene that might have avoided everything that happened on that winter night. Can we imagine some ways in which some such moments could have turned out differently?

There is much to be done to reform and change American policing. If the focus of police reform should be on how police can create public safety,[1] one of the ways this must happen is to minimize the causes of incidents like the violent encounter between Jordan and the three officers. This chapter will offer ten suggestions:

1. Moving police from a warrior to a guardian police outlook;
2. Separating fear from threat;
3. Returning to community policing;
4. Racial reconciliation as a necessary precursor to any reform effort;
5. Recalibrating the law on the use of force by police;
6. Action on guns;
7. Training on implicit bias and procedural justice;
8. Reducing urban violence;
9. Transparency; and
10. Accountability.

Many of the suggestions overlap or could be listed in a different category. The point is that we can, in fact, do things, set goals, and create changes that will allow us to see fewer situations like the one that developed that night on Tioga Street.

1. CHANGING POLICE CULTURE: FROM WARRIOR TO GUARDIAN

Police work—being a police officer—is, of course, a job, an occupation; others may call it a craft, or a profession. Thus it may seem odd to refer to police culture or to think of policing as having its own culture. Yet, by any reasonable definition, police culture is real; it pervades policing in the United States; and it makes a difference in how police officers see themselves, their job, and everyone else who does not wear the badge and the uniform. Police culture pervades officers' thinking and has become a big part of their training.

Sir Robert Peel, who served twice as British prime minister and twice as home secretary in the first half of the nineteenth century, created the first organized police force in London in 1829. He famously espoused[2] nine "Peelian Principles"[3] of modern policing, and one of the most well-known was the seventh, which said that officers must

> maintain at all times a relationship with the public that gives reality to the historic tradition that *the police are the public and that the public are the police*, the police being only members of the public who are paid to give full-time attention to duties which are incumbent on every citizen in the interests of community welfare and existence.[4]

Looking at many aspects of police culture today, law enforcement in the United States has drifted far from this idea. Police conceive of themselves as specialists, with skills and authority setting themselves apart from members of the public. They see themselves as warriors, fighting the ever-present, violent forces of evil, not as fellow citizens. They conceive of themselves as the vigilant sheepdogs, guarding the rest of us—the sheep—willing to use righteous violence to do this. No doubt a willingness to use force occasionally becomes part of the police officer's job. But when that aspect of the job becomes a pervasive part of the culture of the people in that job, we get Tioga Street–type incidents, and some end much worse than that one did. Therefore, things must change. There is an old saying: "Organizational culture eats policy for lunch." That is why the recommendations in this book begin not with policy or even law but with police culture. If we want real change, it is the culture of policing in general and each police department in particular that must evolve. Change in police culture demands, first and foremost, moving from a warrior to a guardian mind-set.

Recall from Chapter 7, the extensive trainings and commentary on "police as warriors." The focus there and here is not on police participation in programs or initiatives that form part of metaphorical wars, like the "war on drugs." Rather, think of Lt. Col. Dave Grossman's evocation of the warrior as the sheepdog, who will use righteous violence to defend the sheep. Professor Seth Stoughton's wide cataloguing and critique of the warrior mind-set (also discussed in Chapter 7) also gives us an idea of just how pervasive this kind of thinking has become. This warrior culture puts fear of violence and violent response front and center in police culture. But, in domestic policing, officers should not act as warriors. Our various "domestic wars"—such as wars on crime and on drugs—in which we've turned our police into soldiers must end. We must understand that domestic policing is a means of assuring public safety and order. According to the Peelian Principles, the job of the police is to "prevent crime and disorder, as an alternative to the repression of crime and disorder by military force and severity of legal punishment."[5] Such prevention must occur with public support, not in spite of public opposition. "The ability of the police to perform their duties is dependent upon public approval of police existence, actions, behavior and the ability of the police to secure and maintain public respect."[6]

According to Susan Rahr, the former Sheriff of King County, Washington, and currently the Executive Director of the Washington Criminal Justice Training Commission and a member of the President's Task Force on 21st Century Policing, acting as a soldier or a warrior on the one hand and as a police officer on the other are two fundamentally different things.

> In 2012, we began asking the question, "Why are we training police officers like soldiers?" Although police officers wear uniforms and carry weapons, the similarity ends there .... The soldier's mission is that of a warrior: to conquer .... The police officer's mission is that of a guardian: to protect .... Soldiers come into communities as an outside, occupying force. Guardians are members of the community, protecting from within.[7]

That explains why the President's Task Force made turning toward the guardian role their first recommendation: "Law enforcement culture should embrace a guardian mindset to build public trust and legitimacy. Toward that end, police and sheriffs' departments should adopt procedural justice as the guiding principle for internal and external policies to guide their interactions with the citizens they serve."[8] Police officers who aim to guard the safety and order of the community, instead of constantly looking for immediate threats of violence in every interaction, especially with African American men, would lead the way to a different vision of policing that would be more cooperative, based to a greater extent on communication and relationships and less on fear.

The emphasis on procedural justice in the Task Force recommendation is no accident. *Procedural justice* comes from decades of thoroughly vetted research, much of it conducted by Professor Tom Tyler,[9] showing that people will more likely obey the law, and consider the authority of police legitimate, when people see that police act in procedurally legitimate ways.[10] Procedural justice includes four central principles: (1) treating people with dignity and respect; (2) giving individuals voice, that is, an opportunity to speak and be heard during encounters with police; (3) neutral and transparent decision-making; and (4) expressing trustworthy motives.[11] (Procedural justice will be discussed in greater depth later in this chapter.) These ideas, folded into the guardian point of view, will give the public greater confidence in police and greater satisfaction with police outcomes. The guardian mind-set would look and feel less like a military occupation and more like a police presence designed to serve and protect. "The goal of the guardian officer is to avoid causing unnecessary indignity," said Professor Stoughton. "Officers who treat people humanely, who show them respect, who explain their actions, can improve the perceptions of officers, or their department, even when they are arresting someone."[12]

What would guardian policing look like? To start with, training would change, shifting from the military boot camp style to an approach emphasizing other aspects of the job. According to Rahr, "[Y]ou may have a conflict where it is necessary for an officer to puff up and quickly take control. But in most situations, it's better if officers know how to de-escalate, calm things down, slow down the action." After the terrorist attacks of September 11, 2001, police in the United States began to use what some call the "Ask, Tell, Make," or ATM, protocol. "Ask a citizen to do something, such as providing identification. Upgrade the request to a command if they don't immediately comply. And use force if the command is not quickly followed." To replace this idea, Rahr created LEED, which stands for "Listen and Explain with Equity and Dignity." At Rahr's Washington State academy, "[R]ecruits practice LEED during mock training drills in which they are expected to handle antagonistic suspects without losing their cool."[13] Recruits still have considerable training on fighting skill and firearms use; in fact, Rahr has increased that training. But the emphasis is different.

According to "From Warriors to Guardians: Recommitting American Police Culture to Democratic Ideals," a document from the National Institute of Justice (an agency of the U.S. Department of Justice) and Harvard's Kennedy School of Government, the shift will not leave officers defenseless. It will, instead, expand the available tools for greater public and officer safety. "Officer safety is critical, and we must maintain vigorous instruction on physical control tactics and weapons. Those skills will always be necessary for dealing with individuals who refuse to comply and present an immediate threat. But we need to significantly increase the level of training and importance placed on communication skills and human behavioral science if we truly care about the safety of our officers."[14] As Lt. Jim Glennon, the author of training materials for Calibre Press tactical training programs, explains, "Mastering the skill of communication provides an officer with deep insight into what the public wants, who they are, and what their intentions might be."[15]

2. SEPARATING FEAR AND THREAT

This idea comes from the eminent criminologist Professor Geoff Alpert (University of South Carolina) and his collaborators Kyle McLean (Florida State University), Carol Naoroz (the body-worn camera management analyst for the Richmond Police Department), and Arif Alikhan (Director of Constitutional Policing and Policy for the Los Angeles Police Department). For Alpert and his colleagues, a central problem exists in policing as we teach new recruits how to do the police officer's job in the United States and as we reinforce it through training, policy, and practice: Policing does not distinguish between fear and threat. According to Alpert, we must separate fear and threat.[16] They are not the same thing, and when we merge the ideas instead of recognizing the difference and treating them differently, we disserve both the public and police officers.

The governing constitutional standard on the use of force, the case of *Graham v. Connor*,[17] is the source of the "reasonable objective officer" test for measuring police use of force, as discussed in earlier chapters. That standard calls for jurors or judges to look at the totality of the circumstances and to view the actions of the officer not in terms of the juror's own reactions, or even from the point of view of the actual officer on the scene, but in terms of the abstract idea of the reasonable objective officer. Jurors must not second guess officers' actions with the benefit of hindsight; the question is what the reasonable officer would have done in the moment, keeping in mind the danger posed and the frequent necessity for split-second judgments in "circumstances that are tense, uncertain and rapidly evolving." And the underlying intentions of the officers—whether good or bad—do not matter at all.[18]

According to Alpert and his colleagues,[19] the *Graham* standard has evolved to focus only on the threat posed by resistance of the suspect to the police officer and the amount of force necessary to overcome that resistance. This became the basis for *the use of force continuum*, a way of analyzing and making use of force decisions. Levels of police uses of force and levels of subject resistance were matched. For each level of resistance a suspect would put up—passive resistance, active resistance, and so on—officers could use a level of force one level greater, in order to overcome that resistance. A similar approach, called the force factor model, and other variations exist, but most of them come down to a similar analysis, "where levels of force are directly related to the amount of resistance a subject presents ...."[20] This standard presents potentially serious problems for police officers. First, as discussed below, the public has begun to demand that police deescalate confrontations when possible, in order to avoid using force. Second, it ignores an important piece of the *Graham v. Connor* analysis mandated by the U.S. Supreme Court. While the Court pointed to particular circumstances to attend to—the severity of the crime, whether the suspect poses an immediate threat, and whether the suspect is actively resisting or trying to get away—the Court said that one must look at *all* the facts and circumstances of each case. The use of force continuum and other ways of viewing force in decades past has led to a nearly complete focus on resistance by the subject as the justifying factor for use of force, with virtually no attention paid to all the rest of the circumstances. "A force model that suggests levels of force based solely, or even primarily, on resistance is not an approach that considers all the facts and circumstances."[21]

This approach has another impact as well: It tends to focus officers on what they might fear from the suspect's resistance. This viewpoint, coupled with the aspects of policing that already focus fear in the minds of officers during encounters with civilians, can lead to an unhealthy and potentially lethal combination in which fear leads to action; possibilities other than force, like deescalation and using time and distance to create safety, have little place in the conversation.

Alpert and his colleagues point out that there are other approaches. The key, they say, is to focus police officers not on suspect resistance and accompanying fear but instead on threat. By separating fear and threat (i.e., by not assuming that fear and threat are the same and by looking at the presence of threat as the important fact), police will (1) have better outcomes, (2) use force less often, and (3) be safer themselves. The researchers point to two modern police forces that have developed successful models based on threat assessment. Officers in the Queensland (Australia) Police Service use the Situational Use of Force Model, which "moves beyond the traditional models by outlining the use of tactical repositioning and situational containment as force options"[22]—that is, they are integrated into use of force analysis and training. In New Zealand, police use the Threat Exposure Necessity Response (TENR) model. This model has particular advantages in a climate in which the public wants the police to consider alternatives like deescalation, which requires officers to consider "the necessity to intervene and the risk exposure to the officers and bystanders."[23] According to the researchers, "both models encourage officers to consider the totality of the circumstances and integrate alternative tactics," enabling the use of approaches that the public now demands, such as deescalation, delaying the encounter, greater use of communication, and "most important, discouraging using force before it is necessary." Such approaches also decrease the impact of what Alpert and his colleagues call "state-created danger" and "the split-second syndrome," both of which, they say, "are arguably the result of officers rushing into tactical situations when there is time to consider other options."[24] Such changes in U.S. police training will bring the use of force into full compliance with the *Graham* standard, which requires the consideration of all the facts and circumstances, not just the degree of subject resistance and any fear it may cause.

3. REINVIGORATING THE COMMITMENT TO COMMUNITY POLICING

One can go to almost any police department, anywhere in the United States, and in each one, those running the operation will claim the mantle of community policing. When asked to define it, they will articulate an almost infinite variety of definitions and examples. "We have two" (or three, or 20) "community policing officers, totally dedicated to going to each community event, and interacting with the public." "We use community policing in the way we explain everything to our citizens." "We have had a community policing policy in this department for ten years, and it's fundamental to our mission." "We are a community policing department, top to bottom, in everything we do."

In truth, many police departments' community policing efforts range along a continuum from sloganeering and public relations, to a few dedicated officers who go to community meetings. A relatively few think of community policing as what it actually is, which is a philosophy that must permeate every aspect of police operation, training, policy, and decision-making. The core ideas that make up community policing include:

- Deep, ongoing connections and relationships between police and the people they serve, with the goal of establishing community partnerships based on mutual trust;
- A commitment to shared responsibility, decision-making, and priority setting in order to fight crime and disorder;
- A view of fighting crime and maintaining order through problem-solving, and not just reactions such as response to reports of crime and arrest; and
- Openness, transparency, and frequent honest communication that undergirds the relationship.

Community policing is not a separate program, a one-off experiment, or a public relations or feel-good approach to dealing with constituents. It must be a philosophy of how policing is done that permeates everything the department does and includes every member of the agency, from top to bottom.[25] One definition might emphasize some of these ideas over others, or add some not represented here, but even this brief definition provides a fair idea of what real community policing is and must be. The implications of this definition, and others like it, would sweep broadly across any agency, and incorporated correctly, they would have a reach that might prevent more scenarios like the one that played out on Tioga Street in January of 2010.

Community policing requires building relationships, in order for officers to know those in each community who the police serve. Relationships require continual occasions for nonemergency, nonconfrontational contact. This kind of contact, and trust-based relationships generally, put a premium on communications skills, which include the ability to talk with all kinds of people, sometimes about difficult subjects in stressful circumstances, and also just generally in social situations. All of this is especially important—in fact, could not be more important—than when police officers deal with young people.

So what would a reinvigorated approach to community policing look like? To start, police agencies must begin to prioritize, train, and reward communication skills. This has to start at the very beginning of the process of becoming a police officer: agencies must begin to hire for communication, not just confrontation. Training must emphasize the skills and ability to communicate successfully and to use communication as a tool for deescalation, organization of community effort, and obtaining cooperation. As much as is humanly possible, compliance with police demands should come through communication rather than through the always implicit threat of force or actual use of force. Hiring for communication would mean testing and screening for communication skills and ability on the front end of the process; nurturing it through training; enshrining it in policy; and enforcing the priority of communication through retraining, accountability, and (when necessary) disciplinary action. Of course, this has not been the hiring priority of police agencies in the past. Advertising used to recruit police officers tended to paint a different picture: officers in action, carrying weapons, repelling down buildings, and dressed in the military-style uniforms of SWAT teams.

We would also see a high priority put on building connections and relationships between police and communities, from the first day of the police academy onward:

1. Community members, especially people from communities with long troubled relationships with police, such as African American or Latino communities, should have a presence in academy training drafting the curriculum; speaking to police recruits about past experiences they, their family members, or their friends have had; and helping new police officers learn to deal with regular members of their communities from the very first day of training. In many cities in the United States, police officer recruits may not come from those cities. They may have grown up in a suburb or even in rural areas far from any city. This may mean that such recruits seldom—perhaps never—had any contact with a person of color, except in passing. These recruits may make fine police officers in the sense of understanding their duties and how to perform them properly, within the rules of the department and the law. But with little or no interpersonal experience with people who do not look or speak like them, and with plenty of stereotypes stuffed into their heads by the culture, such recruits seem ill prepared at best to work in communities of color. Thus the presence of civilians of color at prominent points in the academy curriculum would at least be a starting place for recruits to learn how the relationship between police and communities of color have arrived at where we now find them and what the expectations and hopes of members of those communities are of the police.

2. Beyond this, all police recruits should be required to build a working relationship with a community group in the city. The recruits would each be assigned a placement in a community nonprofit, such as a food bank, an after-school mentoring program, or a community youth center.

The assignment would be made on the basis of *nonfamiliarity*: The idea would be to get recruits out of their comfort zones and dealing with people as different from them as possible. During the course of academy training, the recruit would have to work with the group to which he or she has been assigned to create a mutually agreed upon project for the group and then carry it through to conclusion. This activity would have the same importance and stature as any other subject; academy faculty would evaluate the recruit's participation in the community group, and passing the subject would count every bit as much as training in report writing, defensive tactics, or firearms.

3. The required connection with community must not stop when the recruit leaves the academy and takes up full-time work. The requirement of working with community resource groups must continue into the job itself and become an ongoing obligation as long as an officer stays in the department. When given his or her permanent police assignment, officers would need to find a community group or post with which to serve, perhaps from a department-approved list or community-need bank. Such a group would be in the community in which the officer works or patrols, to increase the chances for face-to-face interactions and relationship building with people who live and work where the officer works. When an officer transfers to a new zone or precinct, he or she would need another assignment in the new zone of the city. The objectives of this participation would be to experience the lives and the geographic homes of those served first hand; to forge relationships with community leaders and with those utilizing the community service; and to be seen and known as more than just a head, neck, and upper torso driving by in a police car. Such community participation must count inside the police department, as real police work. That is, it must not be regarded or treated as an add-on, as "mandatory volunteer" work, or as something that takes away from "real" policing. Rather, such community involvement must be understood and rewarded as an integral part of the job and crucial to the success of the officer as an individual and as a member of the police department. Just as in the academy, the community work must be evaluated for effectiveness, connection, and community satisfaction, and it must count as part of an officer's job evaluation, just as the number of arrests that officer might make.

4. Finally, police agencies and officers must make special efforts to connect with young people in the communities in which they serve. Young people, particularly young people of color, need to have interaction with

police that stems not from fear or enforcement but from a desire for connection. For so many people in the majority population, the young black teen in a hooded sweatshirt or dressed in hip-hop garb sends off mental danger signals; the old American stereotypes die hard. One of the most effective ways to overcome these prejudgments, research tells us, is increased intergroup interaction. This has double importance for police officers. If they must keep the streets safe and orderly, they must know which one of the 20 young people wearing the ubiquitous uniform of hoodie, jeans, and sneakers is an actual threat and which are the other nineteen who dress the same but pose no danger. The best way to know *that* is to know *them*. When an officer who patrols in the community has actually met some of the kids who live there, through her work at the community center or the athletic league or the tutoring program in the neighborhood, she'll know who she's talking to and observing. Moreover, the youth—or at least some of them—will know the officer and may tell the friends they are with that this officer is okay. Any kind of program that creates sustained and positive interaction between police officers and youth, who often bear the brunt of police contact, is a net good. Any officer who participates in youth programs should receive extra credit on job evaluations and promotion applications, over and above required work in required community positions.

Such a program has begun right in Pittsburgh, in Police Zone 5, the very area covering Homewood and Tioga Street. Led by Zone 5 Commander Jason Lando, the program pairs a number (sometimes a few, other times as many as 10) of young people of color from Zone 5 schools, with an equal number of volunteer police officers.[26] Lando picks the officers for the program from a growing group of volunteers, focusing on the officers who he knows are the best communicators. The police and young people get together to get to know each other as people, not as cops and kids on corners, and to understand each other as people, in order to break through the tensions and mistrust that have historically cast a pall over these relationships. Commander Lando began the program informally in the fall of 2017, and he now runs it regularly in partnership with two community organizations: the Student Achievement Center in Homewood, which assists students with academic issues, and the Garfield Jubilee Association, a community development agency aimed at creating programs to strengthen low- to moderate-income families. The time that the officers and the young people spend together includes a 30-minute one-on-one conversation for each police/youth pair to get to know one another and to discuss frankly their opinions about police/community tensions. They also do a role reversal exercise, in which police and young people each take the others' part in a simulated street encounter. Both activities are designed to draw out the issues and difficulties in an era when police shootings and misconduct have wide video circulation on social media and in mainstream news. There is much conversation, both serious and not serious, and as people get to know each other and eat the lunch and snacks the officers have brought, you can hear laughter as well.

One 17-year-old African American, Michael, said, "I've had bad encounters with police that would either lead to me getting arrested, or I would just walk away." But talking with the officers and getting to know them as people, even a little, changed his outlook. "At first it's like, I know they're cops, so I need to make sure I'm not looking suspicious and everything like that. But now, I'm like, oh, they just an ordinary person, but with authority."[27] Officers often feel that the encounters open their eyes as well and help them understand who the kids are and the kinds of significant challenges they face in their lives. All of this, according to Commander Lando, serves the core purposes of knowing each other, creating relationships, and above all breaking down long-term barriers. "I didn't like what I was seeing all over the country with the constant tension between young people and the police, and we just thought this was a good thing to do. We know that most cops are good and we know that most kids are good, but it's not until you get to know each other on a personal level that you get like, 'oh, you are really cool,'" he said. "[T]he point is we'll never get past the problems until we get to know each other."[28]

Just imagine if this program had been in place in 2010, in Homewood. And just imagine if Jordan Miles, and one or two of the officers he encountered that night, had gotten to know each other this way beforehand.

4. THE NECESSITY OF RACIAL RECONCILIATION

In the past—even the recent past—the way to think about police reform would have involved changing practices in the field, perhaps, or upping the commitment to community policing, or even reducing arrests to create an impact on mass incarceration. One would see town halls, community meetings, and changes in departmental policies. All of these, if well thought out and needed, could help create better policing and perhaps even improve police/community relations. But one group of police practitioners and their allies have arrived at another conclusion: For any of these kinds of efforts to succeed, they must be preceded by something else that is both more difficult to do and strikes deeper into our policing problems and our collective history. Real police reform, they say, must start with *racial reconciliation*, which is an earnest attempt to address the historical wrongs perpetrated by police on communities of color—particularly, though not only, African American communities.

The reason that police reform must start with racial reconciliation requires that we view policing not as it exists today but as it was 25, 50, even 100 years ago. In the American South of 1920, the Jim Crow system prevailed, in which African Americans experienced systematic exclusion from civil life, constant discrimination enforced by law, economic oppression, and even state-sanctioned violence. These forces kept black people not only from important aspects of citizenship such as voting (keeping them politically powerless) and jury service (keeping them voiceless in the criminal justice system) but also poor, poorly educated, and permanently subservient to whites. While states in the north did not have the same kinds of laws on the books, the social customs and economic discrimination kept the black community ghettoized, in separate inferior schools, and generally kept down. All of this we know, but we forget how these vile laws and unjust economic arrangements stood for so long, with the police serving as the tip of the spear for society as it enforced its discriminatory laws and practices. The internet allows us to revisit the days of the Civil Rights Movement, both in the South and the North.[29] When we view those images, we see not only the young heroes of Bloody Sunday crossing the Edmund Pettis Bridge in Selma, we also see the police turning their weapons on the marchers. When we see black people marching for their right to vote, for equal treatment under the law, and for equal pay for equal work, we also see them arrested by police, beaten by police, with their clothing and their flesh torn by snarling, terrifying police dogs. The lynchings that took place all over the South constituted extrajudicial killings, which the police sometimes resisted but not always; the police sometimes stood by passively, and other times participated themselves. If police in Northern states did not always take such overt roles, they still served to enforce the written and unwritten rules of segregation, discrimination, and staying in one's designated place.

Even in the modern era, for the last 20 or so years, African Americans and other people of color have learned to expect disparate treatment at the hands of police. For example:

- While in vehicles, they have to tolerate stops for "driving while black" in neighborhoods where they seem "out of place" in the eyes of police.
- While on city sidewalks and in public areas, they must endure repeated stops and frisks, in cities such as New York, Philadelphia, and countless

others, in numbers far disproportionate to any measure of their population or criminal behavior.

The incidental aspects of these experiences—the rude, sometimes racially infected talk, the disrespect, the humiliation—seem designed to denigrate, not protect. We hear from the defenders of these tactics and strategies focusing on African Americans and Latinos that these measures are essential to control crime, to keep guns off the streets, and to lower the grim toll of violence and murder. But any fair analysis of traffic-stop or stop-and-frisk numbers disproves this. Statistics show that African Americans and Latinos stopped in their cars or halted for frisks while they walk, in disproportionate numbers, are not more likely to have been engaging in crime. In fact, they are less likely to be arrested or to have contraband or guns on them than are whites who police stop.[30]

The experience of many African Americans with the police, both in the past and in the present, is racialized enforcement sometimes accompanied by violence, and—at least in the past—deliberate oppression and racism. It is this set of experiences and this legacy against which African Americans and others view every current experience with police officers. This may not seem fair to current police officers in good police departments, officers who are well trained, treat people with respect, and do their jobs correctly and according to the rules. Why, they might ask, must they admit wrongdoing or apologize? The answer is simple, perhaps deceptively so, but it captures the hard truth of the matter. As an African American might say,

> This police department stood by while my great grandfather was lynched; it sicced dogs on my uncle when he protested in order to have his right to vote; it didn't investigate when terrorists put a bomb in a church that killed four little girls attending Sunday school. This police department never acknowledged those facts, never apologized for any of that—it just moved on. You, officer, in 2019, did not do those things. But you wear the same patch on your shoulder, the same badge on your chest, the same crest on your hat, so for better or for worse, you are that organization today. If we can't talk about what your organization did and why I still feel a horrible fear and a deep distrust when I see those emblems, those uniforms, or those cars, we won't have much to talk about, because I'm living that history now, every day, every time I see someone from your organization.

What must happen, therefore, is racial reconciliation. This includes an admission of past wrongs; an apology for those wrongs; a willingness to listen to,

hear, and understand the toll of those wrongs from the point of view of those
who suffered or whose ancestors suffered; and a pledge to do better. According
to David Kennedy of John Jay College of Criminal Justice, one of the leading
exponents of the need for racial reconciliation in the context of police reform,
simply coming to the table to propose reform, from a position of power, cannot
do the job. That approach "does not respect the historic experience of damaged
peoples, [does not] honor the unspeakable harm that [it] represents, or recognize
what [those experiences] mean for the way that they look at [police] on the
job today." Instead, "There has to be an opportunity for those who have been
harmed to speak to their experiences and be heard."[31]

What does racial reconciliation look like? Start with a big picture view.
Can we imagine a profession-wide attempt to start reconciliation across the
thousands of American police departments? The leader of the International
Association of Chiefs of Police (IACP), which describes itself as "the world's
largest and most influential professional association for police leaders" with
"more than 30,000 members in 150 countries ... committed to advancing
safer communities through thoughtful, progressive police leadership," decided
to try and take that kind of step. Terrence Cunningham, who became the
president of the IACP in 2015, came to the president's office with over
15 years of service as Chief of Police in Wellesley, Massachusetts. The year
of his IACP presidency (2015–16) followed multiple events in which police
around the United States killed unarmed black men, sparking protests and
grand jury investigations. The subject of racial reconciliation and apology
would always be a touchy one, but in 2015 and 2016, it would perhaps be more
delicate than usual. Nevertheless, Chief Cunningham went ahead. At one of
his organization's conventions, he began a statement with an acknowledgment
that 2015 had brought difficult and fraught times to policing in the United
States. But he praised policing as a "noble profession" and police officers as
courageous and self-sacrificing in the pursuit of the greater good. Then he
came to the topic at hand:

> At the same time, it is also clear that the history of policing has also had darker
> periods. There have been times when law enforcement officers, because of
> the laws enacted by federal, state, and local governments, have been the
> face of oppression for far too many of our fellow citizens. In the past, the
> laws adopted by our society have required police officers to perform many
> unpalatable tasks, such as ensuring legalized discrimination or even denying
> the basic rights of citizenship to many of our fellow Americans. While
> this is no longer the case, this dark side of our shared history has created

a multigenerational—almost inherited—mistrust between communities of color and their law enforcement agencies.[32]

Chief Cunningham acknowledged that officers who "do not share this common heritage" may not understand the reasons for this "historic mistrust" and therefore find themselves unable to connect with people of color in their communities:

> While we obviously cannot change the past, it is clear that we must change the future. We must move forward together to build a shared understanding …. For our part, the first step in this process is for law enforcement and the IACP to acknowledge and apologize for the actions of the past and the role that our profession has played in society's historical mistreatment of communities of color.[33]

Cunningham's statement had a major impact. Media outlets of all types—traditional print, television, internet news sources and platforms, mainstream magazines—carried the news. It received mostly positive reactions. David Alexander, then the police chief in Pensacola, Florida, welcomed the apology. "When you don't know the history and you say, 'Well, there is no problem,' then you pretty much present yourself as insensitive to the issues," adding that "racial tension has been part of American history since [the country's] settlement."[34] Delrish Moss, then chief in Ferguson, Missouri, said, "There are communities that have long perceived us as oppressors, there are communities that have long perceived us as the jackbooted arm of government designed to keep people under control, and that's one of the things we have to work hard to get past." Moss added that he was "glad it's being addressed … because the only way to get past it is to first acknowledge the existence of it."[35] But others, both individuals and particularly mainstream law enforcement organizations, reacted negatively. Lt. Bob Kroll, head of the Police Officers Federation of Minneapolis, thought Cunningham's statement went too far. "Our profession is under attack right now and what we don't need is chiefs like him perpetuating that we are all bad guys in law enforcement." Kroll said Cunningham had made "an asinine statement …. We've got officers dying on almost a daily basis now because of this environment, and statements like that don't help."[36]

But even with some strongly hostile reactions, a movement toward racial reconciliation has taken root, moving forward the relationships between police and those they serve. For example, during a 2019 conference, Stockton, California Chief of Police Eric Jones discussed how his department's racial reconciliation efforts have been difficult, but said that they have paid huge dividends in how the department has been able to make progress in connecting with its communities of color. Reform efforts in the past, such as town halls, meetings, working on issues, or changing policies, had never gotten the department what it needed, which was strong relationships with its residents based on trust. The department's reconciliation effort—acknowledging the harms of the past, apologizing for them, and then committing to listen to those communities articulate the accumulated harms so that he and his officers could understand them—changed things. Simply put, there was a need to acknowledge "the systematic racial harms experienced by African Americans, at the hands of the Stockton Police Department, though the injuries came many years ago." According to Chief Jones, "[W]e in law enforcement have to at least acknowledge those facts, because then, I've found, it breaks open actual real, true dialogue. We're able to now develop this new space where we can have these conversations, and talk about race relations head on." Though neither he nor any of his current officers had a role in the past injustices, Chief Jones wants his officers to know that the "police badge, whatever shape it is, still holds that history that needs to at least be acknowledged." By doing this, and by learning to truly listen to what his communities have to say, "[W]e've learned the connection between gun violence intervention, reducing violent crime, and trust."[37] And Jones's constituents felt the change this made too. Tashante McCoy-Ham, a member of the Stockton Community Policy Review Committee, said that Chief Jones "literally sat there and listened," recalling this as "totally different from what the perception of policing and police experiences are supposed to look like." The change, she said, was palpable. "Those who were brave enough to put their best foot forward, to be part of the change, were literally able to see the results …. It allows many to develop a relationship that was ongoing and see one another as part of one community."[38]

5. LAW ON THE USE OF FORCE MUST CHANGE

Throughout the investigations of the actions of the three Pittsburgh officers and the two civil trials, one legal standard surfaced over and over: The "reasonable objective officer" standard, from the Supreme Court's *Graham v. Connor*[39] case. The problem with the *Graham* "objective reasonableness" standard, and its focus on police-oriented details of the threat faced (see Section 2, above), is that it has devolved into a standard that "gives enormous discretion to use whatever force they [police officers] think is necessary under the circumstances," according to Professor Cynthia Lee.[40] Lee, the Edward F. Howrey Professor of Law at The

George Washington University Law Center, has produced some of the most influential legal scholarship of the past two decades on issues of the use of force by police and other topics central to American criminal law, and she has looked carefully at the *Graham* standard and what it has produced. The statistics on the subject that we have (imperfect though they are—see Chapter 6) show that most killings by officers involve armed people; they also show a steady stream of officer-involved killings of unarmed people, including a disproportionate number of unarmed black men, and yet very few if any criminal prosecutions in these cases. Lee says that even in 2019, while the numbers show a "slight increase" in the number of officer-involved homicide prosecutions, convictions in these cases remain relatively rare.[41] This happens, she says, because the law ends up prizing officers' beliefs as reasonable above all else, and this comes down to the reasonableness of an officer's fear of the suspect. Because *Graham* and state use of force laws "focus solely on the reasonableness of the officers' beliefs," Lee says, the judge or jury may find an officer's use of force justified as reasonable, even if such force was not *necessary*, given all of the circumstances:

> This is because focusing on the reasonableness of the officer's beliefs often ends up being an inquiry into the reasonableness of the officer's fear of the suspect. Judges and jurors know that police officers put their lives on the line to protect us all. Because of this they are willing to give a police officer the benefit of the doubt when that officer claims he pulled the trigger because he feared for his life.[42]

This leads to a great number of cases that Chuck Wexler, the Executive Director of the Police Executives Research Forum and himself a former officer, calls "lawful but awful" killings by police[43]: deaths which the law calls reasonable but which everyone—police and the public alike—would see as terrible, perhaps avoidable, tragedies.

No one wants to see police officers facing criminal charges for homicides or for lesser crimes. No one wants police officers to face greater danger than they must, when faced with a deadly threat to themselves or members of the public. No one wants people who would make good police officers to hesitate to become officers because they do not wish to find themselves facing a jury someday. And no one wants police officers' lives put in greater danger than they must be, given the difficult, and sometimes violent, people they sometimes encounter.

Nevertheless, it is also true that no one wants our nation's police to shoot their fellow citizens unless it is absolutely necessary. As things stand, opinion in both the general public and in police leadership seems to have shifted, with further movement to come: We want officers to use methods that can minimize civilian deaths and danger to officers. Video recordings from civilian smartphones, from police cameras, and from other sources have shown that some of the deaths of civilians seem clearly unnecessary:

- Walter Scott dies as he runs as fast as he can from Officer Michael Slager in North Charleston, South Carolina, without a weapon, when Slager takes a shooter's stance and shoots Scott in the back. A jury could not agree unanimously that Slager violated the "reasonable objective officer" standard. (Slager later pled guilty to one federal charge; all state charges were dropped.)
- When two Cleveland police officers pull their car within a few feet of Tamir Rice, instead of positioning themselves some distance away to take advantage of the cover their vehicle could provide while investigating the situation, Officer Timothy Loehmann kills Rice in seconds—before the officer has a chance to learn that the 12-year-old has a toy gun, not a real one. Loehmann faces no charges.
- Philando Castile, a gun owner with a license to carry his weapon and who discloses the license and the presence of the weapon when stopped by the police, dies when a police officer who asks for Castile's identification fears Castile is pulling out the weapon to attack him. A jury acquits the officer.

The chorus on cases such as these has become loud and clear, consistently saying, as one: These people, and others, should not have died. The use-of-force legal standard, as it stands and as put in practice, must change. We want other methods tried when possible, to avoid bloodshed. No more lawful but awful killings—or at least, many fewer.

Contrary to what critics of such a move may imagine, changing the standard from the "reasonably objective officer" to something that would require more restraint does not mean that more officers will inevitably die or experience serious injury. On the contrary, it may mean fewer officer and civilian deaths and injuries, if law enforcement adjusts its tactics, training, and approaches to come into line with what the public wants. In these tense, difficult, and dangerous situations, such changes may include approaches that emphasize deescalation of the tension and threat; strengthening the concepts of using physical distance, time, and cover to give officers the advantages and safety they need to keep a situation from going from bad to worse; and obligating police to not take actions that increase risks to the officer, to bystanders, and to the suspect. These ideas do not originate only in fringe elements of the public or with police critics.

On the contrary, many of these changes in approach, tactics, and training find their deepest and most thorough discussion and endorsement by police leaders from around the country in *Guiding Principles on Use of Force*, the landmark 2016 publication by the Police Executives Research Forum.[44] Any of America's 18,000 police departments can choose to adopt some or all of these ideas; some departments may, and others will not. Thus change, if we want to see it, must come with the force of law.

Several such efforts began in 2019. A bill introduced in California by Assembly Members Shirley Weber and Kevin McCarty, A.B. 392, would have required that any killing by a police officer be not reasonable but necessary. The bill defined "necessary" to mean that "given the totality of the circumstances, a reasonable peace officer in the same situation would conclude that there was no reasonable alternative to the use of deadly force that would prevent death or serious bodily injury to the peace officer or another person."[45] The bill met with immediate law enforcement opposition.[46] (A modified version of the bill passed both houses of California's legislature in July of 2019 and is now law.[47]) Another approach comes from Maryland. Delegate Alonzo Washington and a cosponsor have introduced H.B. 1121, which would change the standard for use of force with two requirements.[48] To be justified in using deadly force, an officer would have to (1) reasonably believe he or she needed to use deadly force to protect the officer or another person from serious bodily injury or death and (2) the officer's actions were reasonable, given all of the circumstances.[49] The bill does not require that the officer be correct in the assessment of the danger; it requires only that the officer's beliefs and actions be reasonable. As far as actions, the bill supplies a noninclusive list of factors for the judge or jury in any later legal case to consider: (1) whether the dead or injured person had or appeared to have a deadly weapon and refused a command to drop it; (2) whether the officer attempted feasible deescalation measures, such as taking cover, calling for backup, and attempting to calm the suspect; and (3) whether the officer did anything that increased the risk in the situation.[50]

This bill is based on a proposal contained in Professor Lee's 2018 article in the University of Illinois Law Review,[51] and her approach appealed to Delegate Washington. Many of the officer actions the bill says should be considered already have a place in the internal rules of the Maryland Police Training and Standards Commission, a state-level standards-setting body. The measures that H.B. 1121 would have a judge or jurors consider in any actual case thus represent actions that the state's law enforcement authorities have already supported. The difference is that putting these into a state statute, instead of just in internal rules, gives them the force of law, which "could have far more potential to shape police culture than internal police regulations," Washington said.[52] The requirement that officers' conduct also qualify as reasonable gives the measure extra specificity, so officers and their departments know what the law expects, and each department can shift their policy, training, tactics, and supervision to become consistent with what the state's law would require. Critics of the measure, including Sergeant Michael Young, president of one of the state's Fraternal Order of Police union lodges, say that any such "check box" system would distract officers from the danger at hand, perhaps to deadly effect. "What's going to run through my head ... is did I do these things right, and in the meantime a citizen can be harmed, or I could be harmed."[53] This view excludes the possibility that policing approaches adjusted to a standard requiring more actions short of using deadly force may prove safer for all involved.

Change to use-of-force law must also include an important change on the federal level. As discussed in Chapter 4, recall how U.S. Attorney David Hickton, handling the federal investigation into the conduct of the officers, ultimately concluded that he did not have the evidence to prove that the officers used excessive force in "willfully" depriving Jordan Miles of his constitutional rights. Hickton concluded that with that very high standard, he could not prove the case beyond a reasonable doubt, and therefore he elected not to prosecute. As also discussed in Chapter 4, that high standard comes from one of our country's oldest civil rights laws, Section 242 of Title 18 of the U.S. Code.[54] Hickton's understanding of the level of proof needed to meet the statute's requirement dovetails with that of other federal prosecutors, leading to merely a handful of cases pursued each year, even though the Department of Justice receives thousands of complaints of criminal civil rights violation every year.

This situation indicates the existence of two problems. First, the U.S. Supreme Court's interpretation of the statute in the *Screws* case,[55] which created the "willful" standard for violation of Section 242, may simply be set too high. The point is certainly arguable and unlikely to change, given the current conservative makeup of the Court. The other problem comes from the structure of Section 242 itself, which makes available only one possible theory for convicting officers: They must willfully deprive the victim of constitutional rights. Nothing less will do. Contrast this with the usual state laws of homicide. Most states have at least four types of homicide available to prosecutors who must decide upon the charges for a case, with different theories requiring greater or lesser mental states for each type, in a descending order of seriousness. These are first-degree murder, requiring an intentional killing with premeditation and deliberation; second-degree murder, requiring an intention but no premeditation; voluntary manslaughter, for intentional killings that happen as a result of a provocation by the victim that throws the killer into a rage, losing his or her usual control; and negligent killing, in which a person kills without knowing the risk of danger of the action he or she takes, but which a reasonable person would know.[56] This kind of system accounts for killings with different levels of moral blameworthiness and malice, and can hold a variety of killers accountable at appropriately varying levels of condemnation and punishment. Section 242, with its single "willfulness" standard, is different, and many varieties of police conduct simply would not fit under it. It is as if a state had a law for punishing criminal homicide that only included one type of action: intentional killing with premeditation and deliberation. All other types of killings—those that looked like manslaughter or even second-degree murder—would go unpunished. Section 242 needs an amendment; alternatively, Congress could pass a separate statute. Either way, the law should at least include police actions violating the Constitution that, while not willful, are reckless, defined as conscious disregard of the risk of violating the Constitution.

6. ACTION ON GUNS

"We offer our thoughts and prayers to the victims of this senseless and tragic violence." This phrase, more than any other, has become the typical reaction of many political and public figures to a horrifying event in the United States in which multiple people die at the hands of a person with a gun. Think about the mass shootings at Sandy Hook in Connecticut, which killed 20 first graders; the Pulse nightclub in Orlando, Florida, in which 49 lost their lives; the Emmanuel A.M.E. Church in Charleston, South Carolina, in which 9 died in a Bible study group; and the Tree of Life Synagogue in Pittsburgh, in which 11 worshippers gathered for Sabbath prayers lost their lives. One hears this "thoughts and prayers" sentiment over and over after each of these events, to the point that these words symbolize something very different than their literal meaning. They have come to stand for the idea that in America, the only thing constant in the arena of guns, gun control, and gun violence is chronic inaction by political leaders and institutions.[57] Thus any discussion of guns might seem a waste of space in this book, or even a fool's errand entirely. After all, in the wake of the killing of 20 children at Sandy Hook, despite months of intense effort by the president, Congress failed to pass universal background checks for all gun sales, an effort supported by the vast majority of Americans.[58] And, in the intervening years, gun laws across the United States have actually become looser. They are *more permissive* and friendly to gun ownership and possession, even as the number of mass killings carried out by people with guns has continued to mount.

Guns are clearly not the cause of all of our criminal justice ills in the United States. But in the context of the story of what happened to Jordan Miles, *not* discussing guns would constitute a great omission. We cannot understand what happened to Jordan, and why the police officers reacted the way they did, without discussing guns. The reason that Pittsburgh Police's Zone 5 commander had a unit of plain clothes officers in an unmarked vehicle prowling the streets of Homewood centered on the presence and the danger of guns, and the imperative of getting them off the street. The presence of guns helps to account for why Officers Saldutte, Ewing, and Sisak may have been inclined to think, and to believe well after no gun was ever recovered, that there was a gun in Jordan's coat pocket that night. Thinking more broadly, the ubiquity of guns helps us to understand why American police officers fear that every interaction with a citizen has the potential for deadly violence. We simply cannot have any real conversation about how to keep events like the one on Tioga Street from happening again unless we talk about guns and how to reduce their danger *for police officers*, as well as for citizens.

There are many other reasons to discuss what our society should do to live safely with guns. For example:

- How do we keep young people from killing each other with guns?
- How do we keep guns away from those most likely to use them to kill, rob, rape, or commit other crimes with them?
- How do we make children and adults safe from gun accidents in their own homes?
- How do we reduce the risk of suicide, which in the United States is often carried out with guns?

It is the first two of these points that count in the context of any discussion of how to prevent the next Tioga Street incident. Guns are everywhere in American society and can impact all facets of our lives. The focus on police officers in this chapter should not be seen as minimizing these other aspects of gun violence or gun crime; on the contrary, the scale of those other problems looms large. But, our focus here is on trying to prevent the next Tioga Street incident, so we must ask how to minimize the presence of guns in police encounters and in the pockets of people who the police will seek out.

In presenting ideas for approaching the gun problem as police face it, we must stay within the existing constitutional lines; those lines seem unlikely to change in the direction that gun control advocates would want any time in the near future. As many readers know, in *District of Columbia v. Heller*,[59] the U.S.

Supreme Court decided that the Second Amendment to the U.S. Constitution conferred on Americans a personal right to bear arms. A Washington, D.C. law that created an almost complete ban on handgun possession, and required residents to keep lawfully owned firearms unloaded and dissembled or bound by a trigger lock or similar device, could not stand.[60] But even with that personal right to own firearms for self-defense, the Court said that the Second Amendment right is "not unlimited." Governments could still enact legal limits on gun possession, use, and even presence. "[N]othing in our opinion should be taken to cast doubt on longstanding prohibitions on the possession of firearms by felons and the mentally ill, or laws forbidding the carrying of firearms in sensitive places such as schools and government buildings, or laws imposing conditions and qualifications on the commercial sale of arms."[61] *McDonald v. City of Chicago*,[62] decided just two years after *Heller*, assured that the Second Amendment protected the right to possess guns for self-defense as against state and local laws, not just against the laws of a federal enclave like the District of Columbia. Those are the constitutional boundaries as they stand today. As Justice Scalia, the author of the *Heller* opinion, said, no one should understand the *Heller* case to cast constitutional doubt on the authority of government to enact myriad kinds of gun control legislation, short of the nearly complete bans on guns in question in both *Heller* and *McDonald*. This is a vital point. We should not confuse our unwillingness to enact universal background checks in the wake of Sandy Hook or to ban high-capacity magazines in the wake of other mass-casualty gun events, with a constitutional ban on gun ownership. On the contrary, we have lacked not constitutional authority but the *political will and power* to enact such laws.

While we will not ignore the constitutional limits, for purposes of this discussion we must look past our current political limits. Those limits change and shift with time, and such movement can happen with regard to firearms, too. And if it does, we must answer the question: What kinds of firearms regulations will keep our police officers, as well as our neighborhoods, safer, while also making interactions between police officers and civilians safer and less dangerous? Below are some answers to these questions.

Enforcement of "Felon in Possession" Laws

Federal law dictates that felons have no right to possess guns. Federal law can result in significant prison sentences for "felon in possession" offenses, and the targets of these laws (those with felony convictions) are certainly a high-risk group for violence and crime, relative to the rest of the population.[63] Thus prioritizing gun possession cases in routine police matters, and sending those with guns and felony convictions into the federal system for long sentences could be prioritized. Police can stop and fully search any person on probation or parole under existing Supreme Court law, without any probable cause or reasonable suspicion.[64] This should be a regular practice for police, and every probationer and parolee should be told, upon release, that he or she can and will be searched frequently for weapons, while walking in the neighborhood, driving down the street, or just sitting at home. (One important caveat: This practice must apply to every person on parole or probation, and to felons in every neighborhood; it cannot be done only in black and Latino neighborhoods, or only with people of color. This kind of personal antigun enforcement must be an equal opportunity for everyone to share the burden. If it is not and becomes just another occasion for race-based enforcement, grim consequences for other police efforts to build relationships will follow, not to mention long and costly lawsuits like *Floyd v. New York Police Department.*) To the list of those not allowed to possess weapons, add other groups at high risk for violence, such as those convicted of violent misdemeanors and chronic alcohol abusers. The former could be identified via their criminal convictions; the latter would "qualify" after a certain number of driving while intoxicated or drunk and disorderly convictions. Efforts to add violent misdemeanants proved effective when tried in California.[65]

Stop State Preemption of Local Gun Laws

An increasing number of states have passed state laws that preempt any gun laws passed by a local government in the state. This means that state lawmakers take the power to make local safety and crime regulations involving guns away from their counties, cities, towns, and other municipalities.

States certainly have the right to pass preemption laws. They do this in other areas as well, such as antidiscrimination laws. (For example, with the so-called bathroom bill, North Carolina took away the right of cities in that state to pass laws that allow transgender people to use the bathroom of the gender with which the person identifies.[66]) These state laws typically pass when a city that is more politically liberal than the state legislature passes a law that the legislature does not like. Even if cities and towns in a state typically have some kind of "home rule," in which they have jurisdiction over their own local affairs, they are also creatures of the state government. Cities and towns exist as legal entities by permission of the state government; the state government remains sovereign over and superior to them on whatever matters the state chooses.

No one can contest this legal arrangement's legitimacy; it is reality. But to paraphrase a well-worn phrase parents use with children: Just because you *can* do something does not mean that you *should* do it. States would do well to recognize that when it comes to gun regulation, one size does not fit all. Urban and more densely populated areas generally will have a different take on the presence of guns than more rural areas or smaller towns might. Urban areas might wish to create tighter restrictions on carrying handguns or perhaps on concealed carrying of handguns. The needs of different areas will vary, and those needs should count, particularly if they will make police officers' jobs easier and their lives safer, along with those of the people who live there. Will this sometimes inconvenience those who come from another area, carrying a firearm, into a place with more narrow laws? Of course. And that type of situation should not call for an arrest and a criminal charge. But compared to the deadly threat of guns that crowded cities may wish to address in particular ways that may not suit a small town, these inconveniences sit at the margins, where we can craft accommodations.

Ed Flynn, former police chief in Milwaukee, Wisconsin, a state that preempted any local effort to regulate firearms, had to cope with this situation on the ground, in an American city with a real gun violence problem. "Right now in Milwaukee, we don't have any rights to govern ourselves when it comes to firearms. We're totally at the mercy of the state legislature, and they decided there can't possibly be enough guns in Milwaukee," he said. The law as it is now, Flynn said, "casually and legally arm[s] criminals. It is written in a way as to flood the streets of our cities with high-quality firearms." Flynn said in each year since Wisconsin relaxed firearms regulation everywhere in the state, including Milwaukee, the police have seized more guns from criminals, and both gun homicides and nonfatal shootings have increased. "This is the price Milwaukee is paying," he said, "for a law passed by a legislature whose interests are certainly not urban. I'm being as diplomatic as I can be."[67]

There are many other possibilities for addressing the presence of guns in ways that would make police officers safer and therefore less fearful. Universal background checks for all gun sales including those at gun shows and in private nonfamilial transfers will help keep guns from felons, from some people with mental illnesses, from some domestic abusers, and from others who might pose a danger. Seizing guns from anyone reported to have threatened themselves or others, and from anyone who is the subject of a protective order, will keep guns out of dangerous situations. But if there is to be any hope for any of these efforts, which would make police officers and community members safer, one thing is necessary above all else: Police officers must step up and lead the effort.

The police can be a potent political force. They are usually organized, often in unions or other professional organizations. For most Americans, they stand not just as upright individuals but as symbols of right and rectitude—literal embodiments of the law and public order. They have the expertise to speak authoritatively about both the positives and the dangers of firearms in our society. Above all, they are the ones with skin in the game—literally, their own—who can tell our fellow citizens that some reasonable gun regulation could make them, and all the people they serve, safer. They may be gun owners themselves; they may enjoy shooting sports or hunting and may want no part in banning particular kinds of guns. But surely, they can speak for themselves and the people they serve in the highest crime areas. It is time that we make reasonable efforts against guns where they take lives every day and where police officers feel they themselves have the most to fear. Police officers must help all citizens understand the need to do something to keep everyone safe.

The effort for greater gun safety must not rest only on police, of course. And they aren't the only ones put in harm's way by our sea of guns in the United States. But to pretend that they aren't in danger, and that they should have nothing to say about this, is fantasy.

7. IMPLICIT BIAS AND PROCEDURAL JUSTICE

The concepts of implicit bias (see Chapter 6) and procedural justice (discussed earlier in this chapter) can play a key role in helping to avoid or minimize the chances of confrontations like the one between Jordan and the three officers on Tioga Street. *Implicit* means unconscious feelings, of which we have no awareness; *bias* means favoring or disfavoring a particular group of people. Having an implicit bias makes no statement on a person's character; both good and bad people will harbor implicit biases. Eighty-eight percent of white Americans and over 40 percent of black Americans harbor implicit bias in favor of white people, and such implicit bias is seen in those who express strong (conscious) beliefs in equality. *Procedural justice*, you may remember, means that people treated with dignity and respect in a police encounter will more likely feel that police authority has legitimacy and will more likely obey the law.

In the last few years, training in both implicit bias and procedural justice has become available to law enforcement. At least one commercial business, Fair and Impartial Policing, teaches about implicit bias in police departments all over the country, and in 2018, they began training the New York Police Department.[68] Another organization, the Center for Policing Equity, headed by Dr. Phillip Atiba Goff of John Jay College of Criminal Justice, has designed and implemented training in both implicit bias and procedural justice for the National Initiative to Build Community Trust and Justice, a three-year pilot program discussed in the Epilogue to this book.

The theory behind implicit bias training is that one can become aware of the phenomenon, how it works, and how it can blunt one's effectiveness as a police officer. In addition, learning to counteract, or interrupt, the operation of one's implicit biases can make one a better, more effective, and safer police officer. The training itself encourages—indeed, requires—a certain degree of candor on sensitive subjects, such as race and gender stereotypes, and it must be, by necessity, interactive and not simply listening to lecture material. Training in procedural justice requires learning how to deal with the public in ways that differ significantly from the "give commands–obtain compliance" model taught in times past.

The payoff, however, is potentially large. With a police force trained top to bottom in implicit bias and procedural justice, the hope and expectation is that officers will draw closer to the public, and the public will begin to respond to them differently. By dealing with people in ways that allow the public to (1) feel respected and (2) give voice to their concerns—two key ideas in procedural justice training—routine operations will go more smoothly, and the public will feel more satisfaction (or at least more understanding) with policing service. With implicit bias training, in that moment of low information when action is required, police officers may have the impulse or the time to check themselves and avoid behavior that might make things worse. As this book is written, a comprehensive independent evaluation of the effectiveness of implicit bias and procedural justice training in the six U.S. police departments (including Pittsburgh) that form the National Initiative to Build Community Trust and Justice is pending.

8. REDUCE URBAN VIOLENCE

If fear figures as a major motivator for what goes wrong in police confrontations, anything that can reduce the level of fear can improve things. And one thing that fuels fear overall for everyone in American cities, police officers or civilians, is the pervasiveness of urban violence. We have the tools, now, to make a significant dent in urban violence and the toll it takes; adopting them, in a big way, would make our cities safer from lethal violence and lower the level of fear everyone feels. This approach—a full-court press against urban violence, prioritized over any other criminal justice or social problem—has the potential to save thousands of lives and billions of dollars, all the while creating the necessary basis for the solutions to other urban ills. In his 2019 book, "Bleeding Out: The Devastating Consequences of Urban Violence—and a Bold New Plan for Peace in the Streets,"[69] Thomas Abt, a senior fellow at the Harvard Kennedy School of Government, makes the case. He uses available data and deep analysis to focus on one central question: what works to reduce lethal urban violence? The existing evidence, Abt says, supports the contention that we can, in fact, come to grips with urban violence and greatly reduce it, using existing effective methods, proven in multiple cities.

Abt emphasizes that no two cities and their problems of urban violence are the same; attacking the problem will use one combination of tactics in one place and another combination in another. In most cities, a central tactic, making up part of the overall plan, will involve a version of a "group violence reduction strategy" (GVRS), known in some places as "focused deterrence" or "Cease Fire." GVRS plans have made a number of cities safer already; when deployed fully, according to a well-thought-out protocol, it has reduced murders by half and saved many millions of dollars over its costs.

GVRS is most often identified with the work of David Kennedy and his many colleagues and collaborators in Boston, in the early 1990s. (I wrote about the work of Kennedy and others in Boston in my 2005 book, *Good Cops: The Case for Preventive Policing.*[70]) In those years, Boston experienced a growing plague of gun homicides, mostly committed by juveniles; the work of police, in various forms of crackdowns, seemed to have no appreciable impact. Kennedy and his collaborators—police, prosecutors, community leaders, educators, social service providers, and faith leaders—pioneered a series of steps. First, they studied the problem: how extensive was the group of young people involved? Were they truly warring gangs, as some thought, or something different, looser, much less organized? What sparked the violence that eventually took lives? Once they had a real picture, based on facts and data, of who the perpetrators and victims were—and once they saw that any one of them could end up on either side of the gun—they devised a strategy. The young people at risk of participating in gun violence would be "called in." They'd be brought to meetings in small groups and given a dual message by all of the stakeholders involved—not just police and prosecutors, but by community workers, pastors, even former gang members working to reduce violence: there will be no more gun violence. No more—it ends today. We will be watching you like hawks. For those of you who want help, who want out of the street life, we are here to offer you what you need: social services, education, job training, treatment for addiction or other difficulties, or employment. For those who choose not to take these opportunities, so be it; for those who persist in using guns in crimes of violence, we will come down on you and your whole crew or set or gang like the proverbial ton of bricks. If you have a felony conviction and we find you with a gun, you'll be doing mandatory federal time, far from home. If you're on probation or parole, you're going back to prison. Abandon gun violence, and you'll have no problem from us, and if you want help of any kind, we'll get it to you. And we have the resources to do it. But continue with the gun violence, and we'll descend on you fast and with the overwhelming force of the criminal justice system.

The reaction to these call-ins and the dual proposition of carrot (stop, get help) and stick (back to prison, for as much serious time as we can get for you) had an immediate effect. Gun homicides by juveniles stopped for a month. Then for another month and another one after that. In all, Boston went two and a half years without a gun homicide by a juvenile, and even when they happened after that, they happened far less frequently.

In the years since, the GVRS approach has been adopted in a number of cities in many places in the United States and has produced strong positive results when undertaken in full, including the provision of adequate money and other resources to offer a full slate of services and help as the carrot in the program. Abt argues that putting GVRS and other elements in place nationally would reduce the number of murders of America in half in approximately eight years, saving about 12,000 lives and over $120 billion in social costs.

The success of Abt's plan, including GVRS, would depend on following a series of well-developed steps. A full description of the process lies beyond the scope of this chapter, and Abt's book should be required reading for anyone interested in reducing fear and creating public safety. But a brief snapshot of the major concepts and steps would include these.

- First and foremost, the goal of any initiative must be to reduce urban violence, defined as actions by people that can or do cause death or serious physical injuries, in cities (places with populations over 25,000). It would not be reducing crime or even violent crime; not addressing domestic violence, or terrorist attacks, or violence that takes place inside homes or schools or institutions, or violence at the hands of a state actor like a police officer. Rather, the focus is on what Abt calls street violence.[71]
- Stopping this violence must come first, before any other initiatives aimed at crime or the root causes of crime, or at poverty or lack of education or other social ills. Urban violence makes progress on any other problem impossible; cutting it will allow and even create progress on these other issues.[72]

- The various actors involved must correctly diagnose the problem. This involves understanding that crime and violence are "sticky," tending to cluster around the same dangerous people, places, and behaviors. Punishment and prevention that come in a proper balance works much better than the emphasis on draconian punishment we have had in the United States for the last several decades. And law enforcement must begin to act in ways that allow civilians to view the use of police authority as legitimate, via an emphasis on procedural justice (see above in this chapter).[73]
- Then comes the treatment: measures designed to reduce the violence. Some strategies are designed to deter potentially dangerous offenders or to keep people from becoming dangerous. The call-ins, with the dual carrot-and-stick message backed by social resources and credible police and prosecution threat, are one example. Other strategies would focus on dangerous places, and some would concentrate on dangerous behaviors: for example, using police presence and intervention to prevent potentially dangerous people from illegally carrying guns in public.[74]
- Abt then provides two concrete plans in his book—one local and one national—that promise to reduce homicide by 50 percent over eight years. And he also gives many examples—of cities (e.g., Oakland, California) where the GVRS approach has made a real difference, and of many individuals whose lives have changed as a result.[75]

Far from seeing the methods of reducing urban violence, including GVRS, as some magic set-it-and-forget-it formula, Abt approaches the work of David Kennedy and so many others from an evidence-based, experience-informed point of view. What becomes clear in prioritizing the reduction of urban violence is a way to fundamentally and dramatically change our urban environments, too often plagued by violent crime that can result in death or injury. And with that kind of reduction in violence, we would have a reduction in fear and a greater ability for community members and the police to work together, instead of in fear of each other. It would not solve every problem catalogued in this book, but it would almost certainly help.

9. TRANSPARENCY

To do what we can to head off incidents like the one on Tioga Street requires that transparency must become a core operating principle in policing and in police oversight. As applied to government and its agencies generally, *transparency* means that the operations, data, and results should become open and available to the public, media, and academics—really, everyone—absent a strongly compelling reason to keep these things out of the public sphere. The data, materials, and policies that make up what public agencies do belong to the public, and the public should therefore have access to this information. When a citizen or organization wants to know how a public agency does its job, requests access to its records, asks to see the results of its programs, or inquires how the agency makes its decisions, the response from the agency and its personnel should be, "Once we extract any information regarding citizens' privacy or other sensitive data, of course we'll get that to you." The response should not be, "Why? What do you want it for, and why should we give it to you? What makes you think you have a right to it? Unless you have some proof that you're entitled to it, no."

Yet, at many public agencies, the latter response represents reality far too often, and this happens nowhere more often than in law enforcement agencies. Many state and local governments have no rules or policies that allow the public to routinely access records from these agencies.

The idea of transparency in law enforcement is *not* to allow the public to access records on ongoing investigations of crimes or to assess wrongdoing of public officials or of regular people who have been investigated without charges resulting. But transparency must become the norm for law enforcement and police officer compliance with the law as much as is compatible with sound operations, especially on crucial issues such as the use of force, and also with routine operations such as traffic stops and stops and frisks that have become flash points in discussions in how some communities receive police services. Without routine public access to these kinds of data and records, the public has no way to understand and make judgments about how well the police department does in policing itself, and whether the work it does changes in crucial ways depending on the communities it serves.

For this kind of transparency to become a reality, the public must have the right to receive, and should routinely receive, the following kinds of data:

- Citizen complaints against police officers, including what the complaints charge, the resolution of the complaints after investigation, whether the department imposed discipline, and, if so, what disciplinary measures;
- Legal claims filed against officers related to police conduct, what resulted (case dismissed, settlement, jury or court verdict), and the amount of any settlement or verdict;

- Criminal charges filed against officers, results of these cases, and if a guilty finding resulted, what penalties the court imposed;
- Uses of force that exceed the force necessary to put a person in custody during a routine arrest without resistance by the subject;
- Traffic stops, including the reason for the initial stop, race, ethnicity, and gender of the driver (as reported and perceived by the officer), whether a search of the driver or passengers followed, and the legal basis for such a search; whether a search of the vehicle followed, and the legal basis for the search; whether the police based any search of a person or vehicle upon consent of the person or the driver/owner; whether a search led to the discovery of any contraband, and if so what, and (if illegal drugs) in what quantity; whether the search led to the discovery of a gun or other weapon; whether the driver received warnings or citations, and for what offense(s); and whether the officer made an arrest, and if so, for what offense;
- Stops and frisks, including the basis for the initial stop; the race, ethnicity, and gender of the person stopped (as reported and perceived by the officer); whether a frisk of the person followed, and the legal basis for the frisk; whether the frisk led to the discovery of a gun or other weapon; whether the frisk led to the discovery of any contraband, if so what, and (if illegal drugs) in what quantity; whether the person received any citations, and for what offense(s); and whether the officer made an arrest, and if so, for what offense.

One can imagine other categories of data that should be disclosed to the public routinely. And one can even more easily imagine that police officers, their departments, and their unions would resist this kind of transparency, especially with regard to the data on citizen complaints, legal claims filed against officers, and records of uses of force. Knowing this, one might ask whether any city in the country actually has such data transparency, and the answer might surprise people. This kind of transparency has begun to emerge in Chicago, a city that for decades covered up the "Area 2 torture scandal," under the now notorious Lt. Jon Burge and his "Midnight Crew."[76] This is also the same city that hid from the public the dashboard camera recording of Officer Jason Van Dyke shooting Laquan McDonald while McDonald moved away from the officer without threatening him, until a court forced the city to release the recording.[77] But it turns out that by 2018, Chicago had become one of the most transparent cities in the country vis-à-vis its police department.

However, this did not happen by virtue of the city government or its police department suddenly seeing the upsides of openness. It happened, instead, with the city and the police department ultimately losing a long legal battle. Journalist and human rights activist Jamie Kalven first intervened in an existing federal civil rights case,[78] sparking a long-running legal battle for access to the disciplinary records of Chicago Police Department officers. Kalven won the case in trial court, but the U.S. Court of Appeals reversed the verdict.[79] Kalven then began the effort again, this time in Illinois state courts under the state's freedom of information law, and ultimately, he won. Police disciplinary records, the Illinois courts ruled, were public records and had to be released. The first data were made public in 2015. Further legal struggles followed, especially with the police union in Chicago, but ultimately, Kalven and his allies won.[80] This has led to a process of disclosure of years of complaints and disciplinary files. Kalven and his organization, the Invisible Institute, ultimately used the data, and more records they have obtained since, to create the Chicago Police Data Project, a first-of-its-kind public data repository on police. Upon the launch of phase 2.0 of the Data Project, Kalven described the scale of the Project and its available data as "without parallel: It includes more than 240,000 allegations of misconduct involving more than 22,000 Chicago police officers over a 50-year period. The data set is complete for the period 2000 to 2016; substantially complete back to 1988, and includes some data going back to the 1960s." The idea of the Data Project, according to Kalven, was to "operationalize transparency," so that the public could use the data for any purpose, with the goal of "disable[ing] the rhetorical use of official secrecy ('f you know what we know …') and creat[ing] the conditions for the ongoing debate about police reform in Chicago to be conducted with reference to a common body of evidence."[81]

That "common body of evidence" has given those seeking to change police practices and rein in police misconduct plenty to discuss. Among other things:

- The data show "a system pervaded by racial bias." To cite just one example, those filing complaints against officers are predominantly black, but black people are "dramatically underrepresented" in cases in which abuse is found to be proven. For another, racial disparities in the use of force have significantly increased in the last 10 years, while during the same time period, Chicago's black population has fallen.[82]
- Complaints about excessive force "rarely result in discipline." Only 1.5 percent of excessive-force claims filed—more than 8,700 in all, between January 2007 and June of 2016—resulted in a finding of "sustained" (i.e., investigation finds the complaint is true).[83]

- Among all officers serving in the police department for at least one year between 2000 and 2016, 57 percent of them have less than five complaints, and almost 80 percent have less than ten. But "the 22 percent of officers who have ten or more complaints account for 64 percent of all complaints" during the years from 2000 to 2016. Yet those "with the most complaints are less likely to be disciplined."[84]
- More than 95 percent of all Chicago police officers never fired their guns from 2004 through 2016. Just 130 officers (out of approximately 12,500) have done it more than once, and they account for 29 percent of all shootings. Twenty-four officers have been involved in three or more shootings.[85]
- Between 2005 and 2015, Chicago Police used force against young black men at a rate 14 times higher than against whites. Of all people against whom force was used, nearly 90 percent were people of color. Blacks were 32 percent of the population, but 72 percent of the targets of uses of force; whites were also 32 percent of the population, but only 10 percent of the targets of use of force.[86]

This kind of transparency is still rare, but it is not difficult to envision its utility. With these kinds of data available to measure and understand the conduct and misconduct of their police, the public's ability to demand the kind of policing it wants and does not want, with specificity, will increase. Members of the public who see that a tiny percentage of officers cause a large share of problem use of force and shootings could begin to ask, "Why is the department not doing something about these (now obvious) problems? Why are these officers still on the force?" In the world of plentiful data, publicly available, vague assurances of "we have good officers" and "we do a good job policing our own" become untenable. The agency can be seen for what it actually is. If it allows officers with histories of disciplinary problems and issues with the use of force to continue to serve, without correction or discipline, there will be no hiding the fact. Arguably, the issues that became public after the disclosure of the recording of Laquan McDonald's murder by a Chicago Police officer had much to do with ending any consideration of a third term for then-Mayor Rahm Emanuel. With the picture of the police department having become clear to many, and with it Emanuel's failure to clean up the mess before it became public, continuation in office became untenable. Political accountability won out. No one can say for certain that this data proving the long history of failure to reign in misconduct had an effect on that decision, and no one can say that it did not. Change of a kind the public wants becomes easier in a world of greater police transparency.

10. ACCOUNTABILITY

Recall the story told by former police officer and federal law enforcement official Matthew Horace, author of *The Black and the Blue*, recounted in Chapter 8. As he researched the book, he spoke to a high-ranking official in the NYPD and said he was concerned that his book get across to the public that the police have a very difficult, sometimes dangerous job. Horace wanted the public to understand that reality. The NYPD official responded that, in his opinion, the public already knew that; what they could not understand, he said, was that the police are never wrong. In other words, even when something clearly goes wrong, perhaps leading to a tragic outcome, the police simply do not find themselves to be at fault.

This interaction captures one of the fundamental pieces of policing that, while improved over the past, must improve more: accountability. No one should expect police officers or law enforcement organizations to be perfect. But we have every right to expect that, when a mistake does happen, whether the mistake is individual or institutional, there will be accountability. The individual officer will be held responsible, if he or she makes a mistake. And institutional mistakes, especially patterns of mistakes, will be admitted and corrected. Accountability should, of course, come in proportion to the mistake; not every mistake must result in termination or criminal charges. In fact, most would probably not. Steps taken could range from counseling to retraining to reprimand to more harsh forms of discipline, with termination or worse reserved for the most serious cases. But far too often, it seems, police, their agencies, and their unions circle the wagons, protecting even the worst in their ranks, and attempt to defeat any efforts toward accountability. Their agencies suffer no penalty, even for egregious mistakes that better policy, training, or tactics could have avoided. Thus both individual officers and organizations fail to learn to do better. Systems do not improve. And the public is left wondering why police never admit to mistakes, when everyone knows that human beings, even the best of them, all make them.

Very often, the mantras in police reform call for more and better training, and improvement in police policy and procedure. And surely, these can make a difference. But unless police officers are held accountable when they violate policy, policy means nothing. Unless the agency insists on officers following their training and takes action to enforce that insistence when they do not, the training will not govern officers' actions. According to Professors Jeffrey Fagan and Bernard Harcourt of Columbia University, "training does not take root unless officers are held accountable for obeying the rules and practicing the

skills they are taught."[87] Most studies, they say, suggest that both departmental
discipline and criminal prosecution remain exceedingly rare, while the culture
of police—which may have little investment in unenforced rules—retains a solid
grip on police behavior. "Stronger and visible accountability would weaken the
hold of old habits and contribute to the perceived legitimacy of the police" in
the eyes of the public, generating citizen respect, cooperation, and compliance
with laws.

There is no magic formula for holding police officers accountable; in most
police departments, internal rules, departmental policy, and training are already
minimally adequate. Departmental leadership simply must show that it takes
violations of each seriously, and there will be consequences for violations in
proportion to their seriousness. This commitment must come from the top and
follow all the way down the chain of command, from the chief to the precinct
commanders, to the sergeants. As for departments themselves, one might believe
that they would feel some need to be accountable—admit mistakes, learn from
them, and change—when the actions of their officers or poor training or the
lack of a proper policy result in a judgment for money damages. The public
reads about multimillion dollar settlements in police abuse cases almost every
week, it seems. Surely, they might reason, these big budget hits have an impact.
But in point of fact, they do not. This is because most police departments do not
pay either the judgments or the legal costs to defend themselves. Rather, in the
overwhelming number of cities and towns, those costs come from the municipal
general fund—in other words, the city's budget. The police department need not
worry that its funding would suffer; any damages come from the general coffers
of the city. And, as economists would tell us, any cost that is externalized—that
is, not paid by those incurring that cost—does not matter. Thus, having money
judgments that actually bite into the police department's funding would surely
get the department's attention. At the very least, the department would need to
come to the budgeting authorities—presumably, the elected city leadership—
to ask for money to make up the damages. This could create a moment of
accountability for the department—and those political actors to whom the
request comes could then insist on improvement.

What we see when we look back to January 2010—the incident itself, the two
stories, the investigations, the polarization of Pittsburgh over the case, and then
the two civil trials—is a picture of a city struggling with many of the same
urban ills and difficulties one sees in the relationships between other police
departments and black communities. Racial bias plays a role—sometimes in the
background but occasionally clearly showing itself for the poison that it is. Fear

of each other remains an unfortunate part of the picture as well. The law and the courts emerge as deeply imperfect tools for addressing these issues. The only way to address these problems is before they happen—to bring people together, to know each other, to see past our differences, and see one another as people before things go wrong. It is in that spirit that the suggestions in this chapter, the telling of the story at the heart of this case, and this book itself are offered.

EPILOGUE

As these words are written, almost three years have passed since the final settlement in the civil case that Jordan Miles brought against the City of Pittsburgh; the Pittsburgh Police Department; and Officers Michael Saldutte, David Sisak, and Richard Ewing. The settlement ended the legal reckoning with the Tioga Street incident, and the last chapter surveyed what we might do to keep these types of confrontations from happening. But a reader of any story wants to know more: What do we know now about Jordan, the officers, and some of the other major players in the story?

THE THREE OFFICERS AND THEIR LEGAL TEAM

About the officers, we know very little.[1] Officer Richard Ewing left the Pittsburgh Police in 2012, after the first trial but before the second. He continues in law enforcement as an officer in the McCandless (Pennsylvania) Police Department.[2] According to his attorney Robert Leight, Ewing's departure from the Pittsburgh Police had nothing to do with the case or the incident on Tioga Street in January of 2010. Leight characterized this move as "a lifestyle decision"[3]—which could mean anything from a different work environment, to better pay, to a shorter commute. McCandless, a suburb north of Pittsburgh but still within Allegheny County, is almost 95 percent white, with a median family income of over $73,000.[4] McCandless reports rates of both property and violent crime vastly lower than the national average;[5] by contrast, Pittsburgh ranks higher than the national average in both categories.[6] The McCandless Police Department describes itself as "a community police organization" that "provides a wide variety of services to the residents of McCandless." It includes "20 patrol officers, two detectives, four patrol sergeants, two lieutenants, a two-person civilian support staff, and six school crossing guards ...."[7] In short, it differs considerably in size, environment, and mission from the Pittsburgh

Police. A December 2018 news article on McCandless police matters said that "[P]olice union president Richard Ewing" had no comment on a matter of public concern then under discussion in that community.[8] Of Michael Saldutte and David Sisak, we know even less. As of March 2019, both still served in the Pittsburgh Police Department: Michael Saldutte was assigned to the training academy and David Sisak worked as a motorcycle officer, in the Traffic Division.[9] All three of the officers' lawyers still have active law practices as of early 2019, and attorney Bryan Campbell continued to represent Pittsburgh Police officers as one of the main attorneys for Pittsburgh's Fraternal Order of Police lodge.

CHIEF OF POLICE NATHAN HARPER

Recall that Chief Harper, whose testimony in the first trial had an unexpected negative impact on Jordan's case, later faced an unrelated investigation into his own conduct. After the first trial, and totally independent of the case, federal investigators uncovered Harper's improper use of funds and he played no role in the second trial. In October of 2013, he pled guilty to conspiracy to commit theft and failure to file tax returns. A federal judge sentenced him to 18 months in prison.[10] He was released in May of 2015,[11] and he still lives in Pittsburgh. He now works in the home security industry.[12]

COMMANDER RASHALL BRACKNEY

Commander Brackney, who gave limited but impactful testimony in the second trial, continued to serve in Pittsburgh until retiring after 30 years. She then became Chief of the University Police Department at George Washington University in May 2015, taking over a department troubled by "complaints of a hostile work environment after several former officers filed discrimination lawsuits against the department."[13] After serving two-and-a-half years, during which she completed her PhD, Brackney resigned in January 2018. In May of 2018, she accepted the position of Chief of Police in Charlottesville, Virginia— less than one year after the 2017 "Unite the Right" event in which Nazis clashed with anti-racist protesters and one of the racist participants drove a car into a crowd, killing Heather Heyer and wounding many others. The actions of the Charlottesville police at the event generated great criticism and controversy, resulting in the resignation of Brackney's predecessor. Upon the announcement of her appointment, Brackney spoke to a crowd: "I know that Charlottesville has undergone a lot of trauma and turmoil, particularly in the last year …. I'm here to see if there's a way to move the conversation forward, particularly around policing, policing equity and narrowing the gap between the communities we serve and represent."[14] Her first 10 months on the job presented enormous challenges, including a "mass exodus" of Charlottesville police officers leaving the department, reports of low morale, and continuing public dissatisfaction and anger at police that preceded her arrival.[15]

DISTRICT ATTORNEY STEPHEN ZAPPALA

Recall that Stephen Zappala, the District Attorney for Allegheny County (which includes Pittsburgh), did not refile charges against Jordan Miles when a judge ordered those charges dismissed in March of 2010. He also chose not to file state criminal charges against the three officers, announcing his decision in May of 2012, approximately one year after the federal prosecutor, David Hickton, announced that he would not file federal criminal charges.

District Attorney Zappala ran unopposed for reelection to a fifth term in 2015 and retained his office. He then ran for Pennsylvania Attorney General in 2016, losing in the primary election to Montgomery County Executive Joshua Shapiro, who eventually won the general election.[16] In 2019, Zappala ran for reelection to the District Attorney's office; for the first time in 20 years, he had an opponent in the Democratic primary.[17] Zappala won that primary, besting his opponent 59 to 41 percent; in June of 2019, a veteran public defender announced she would challenge Zappala in the November 2019 general election, running as an independent.[18]

U.S. ATTORNEY DAVID HICKTON

David Hickton became the U.S. Attorney for the Western District of Pennsylvania in 2010, after appointment by President Obama. Recall that he presided over two rounds of the investigation of the three officers. In the end, Hickton decided he did not have the evidence to sustain and prove federal criminal charges against them.

In the aftermath of the announcement that he would not pursue federal charges, Hickton began efforts to address the damaged state of relations between law enforcement and those in the African American community. He had formed a dedicated civil rights unit in his office, but he wanted to find a way not just to take on and prove cases but also to address the almost total disconnect that followed the events on Tioga Street and the ensuing disappointment felt by the African American community witnessing what they saw as a complete lack of police accountability for the incident. Hickton eventually brought together leaders from the African American community and civil rights groups, with leadership of many of the law enforcement agencies in the county—from the Pittsburgh Police to federal agencies such as the FBI. This newly formed Community Police Relations Group began to convene regularly, in Hickton's office, to begin the difficult conversations necessary to rebuild some degree of trust among the leaders.[19] The Group became a primary source of contact and relationships, some of which had deteriorated or fallen apart, and it resulted in community meetings, the creation of a Crisis Team, and the distribution of surveys in underserved communities to enable citizens to voice their opinions and priorities. The Group continued to meet throughout Hickton's term, which ended in late 2016, and beyond.[20] Hickton resigned as U.S. Attorney after the 2016 election, and he then became the founding Director of the University of Pittsburgh Institute for Cyber Law, Policy and Security.[21]

JORDAN MILES[22]

Before January 2010, Jordan had earned a spot and a scholarship at Penn State University, and he felt prepared and eager at that point to go. After the confrontation with the police officers, however, things changed. He changed. Jordan felt less confident, depressed, not eager to socialize—as his mother had said at the first trial, not his old self. He recovered from the immediate injuries and returned to school after a few weeks, but he found he had difficulty focusing and resuming his regular activities and rhythm. Nevertheless, Jordan graduated from CAPA High School that spring, and when the following fall came he enrolled at the university. Jordan took a placement test in math and again had trouble focusing; he found himself surprised when the test results showed he had only eleventh grade skills. And he no longer played his beloved viola.

Jordan found himself unable to stay at school, however, after a police officer appeared in the dorm—for something having nothing to do with Jordan himself. He withdrew from school. He tried starting again, at another university, but that did not work out either. He still found himself unable to focus, and—unaccountably—stuck with eleventh grade math skills, no matter how hard he worked or studied. Jordan took a fulltime position as a manager with his employer, a CVS drug store.

With the end of the civil trials, Jordan determined that he would move ahead with his life. Still maintaining his full-time job, he enrolled at the Community College of Allegheny County, eventually getting into a program that would train him for work as a plumber. He did well in the program, despite having little background in the area, and he graduated in the top 5 percent of his class. But when he began to search for a job, he had no luck. First, Jordan said, potential employers would see he had dreadlocks—he'd grown them back after the second trial—and several said that he would have to cut his hair in order to be hired, which he would not do. But with others, there was something else. Jordan began to get the feeling—though he could never prove it—that the people interviewing him recognized his name or his face or both, from the years of heavy news coverage of his case. And that, along with the fact that he had an arrest record—from the night of January 12, 2010, on the charges thrown out two months later—seemed to seal his fate with these potential employers. He got nowhere in his search for an entry-level job in plumbing.

Again, as with his forays in college, Jordan faced obstacles he could not seem to overcome. "I was really low on myself. I didn't know what would happen with me," he said of that time. But again, he decided not to allow these difficulties to define him or limit what kind of life he would have. He decided to start his own business. In January of 2018, he set up Jordan T. Miles Cleaning Services, offering to deep clean whole houses, business premises, carpets, upholstery, tile, and grout—even mattresses.[23] In true millennial fashion, Jordan put his company on Facebook and put a video on the page. He explained why he started the business, detailing his own struggles, and said that he hoped he would build his business enough that he could give others the second chance that he hoped to have by opening the business for himself. Almost immediately Jordan received many responses, both from those who wanted to work for him and from people offering cleaning jobs. He began the work, and it kept him very busy. Business was good, and he had an excellent first year.

Several things made 2018 an even sweeter year for Jordan. In May, he got married, and he and his wife moved out of Pittsburgh, to the suburb of Penn Hills. Not long after his own marriage, his mother, Terez Miles, also got married. With the growth of his company and the amount of business that he had, Jordan found himself able to do something he'd always wanted to do: help his mother. Ms. Miles had spent almost all of her time raising Jordan and his siblings; his grandmother, Patricia Porter, who lived around the block, had always helped them. But with all the business he had, Jordan could now offer his mother good paying work, under a good boss: himself. Ms. Miles went to work for Jordan, which enabled her to build some savings. With that money, Ms. Miles and her husband did something they could not have done otherwise: They moved out of Pittsburgh. They now live in Louisville, Kentucky, happy to be out of Pittsburgh's harsh climate. "I am glad," Jordan says, "every day, that I was able to help her. She always did so much for me, for us. And I was able to do something for her."

PITTSBURGH

As much as any person in this story, Pittsburgh—its history, its institutions, its people, and its Homewood neighborhood—also emerges as a critical character. We cannot move on from the story without knowing how the city has changed, or not changed, in the years since the incident on Tioga Street. And for this story, we need to consider three important elements: Homewood, the Police Department, and the Department's relationship with the African American community.

In the second decade of the twenty-first century, gentrification became the word that dominated discussion of Pittsburgh's East End neighborhoods, which comprise the areas between the Monongahela and Allegheny Rivers. The East End is close to downtown, the major universities, and the health care institutions that drive the city's economy. The East Liberty neighborhood, impoverished and lacking strong commercial activity since the 1960s, has virtually been made over, with sleek new apartment buildings, cutting-edge restaurants, coffee shops, national chain stores (such as Target, Bonobos, and Warby Parker), and hotels. Long-time African American residents have faced displacement. New housing and rehabbed buildings also have sprouted all over the Larimer neighborhood, and, as 2019 comes, developers and builders seem to have Homewood, the next adjoining neighborhood, in their sights. A drive through Homewood today reveals construction sites and building projects beginning at a slow pace. Dilapidated homes and abandoned commercial structures still predominate, but with the wave of gentrification having thoroughly enveloped nearby areas, change could come. The question is whether the persistent poverty and crime that still exists will prevent the kind of change that the neighborhood needs—investment, jobs, and local ownership of neighborhood assets—without pushing current residents out. In 2015, Reverend Ricky Burgess, who has represented Homewood and the surrounding areas in Pittsburgh's City Council since 2007, wrote:

> For the past 40 years, Homewood has been ignored by economic and public policy. The results have been devastating. Homewood has the highest number of shootings and gun-related deaths in Pittsburgh. Homewood also has the city's largest number of vacant, abandoned and tax-delinquent properties. There are no grocery stores, no drugstores, no clothing stores and no name-brand store of any kind. Homewood is filled with fixed-income senior-citizen homeowners who have no equity in their homes ... and with low-income single mothers trying to raise their children in a community

with failing schools .... The terror of drugs, crime and gun violence causes fear and despair, poisoning every resident's quality of life. Homewood is the city's poorest, least-diverse, most dangerous neighborhood, with the highest amount of violence and economic distress. It is a community in crisis.[24]

Reverend Burgess goes on to note that he sees some signs of progress, but he cannot help but observe that the city has a long way to go to make Homewood the safe, livable place it could be. This will take, he says, not gentrification but "an historic infusion of financial resources that systematically address the myriad ills afflicting this community" from multiple stakeholders.[25] Gentrification often pushes existing residents out; fancy condominiums and big-name stores would not help to make Homewood a livable and safe place for existing residents. What Homewood will become in 10 years remains an open question: Will it be another gentrified enclave in which upwardly mobile people live and long-time residents lose their footholds, or a place in which those living there now can enjoy a better life?

What has happened to the Pittsburgh Police Department and its relations with the city's African American communities in the years since the incident on Tioga Street and its aftermath makes for a complicated narrative. Some of this story is positive; some is not.

In the wake of the incident involving Jordan Miles and the three police officers, the Pittsburgh Police made efforts to absorb what had happened and to make appropriate changes. Maurita Bryant, then an Assistant Chief in Pittsburgh's department and now Assistant Superintendent with the Allegheny County Police Department, calls it a "lessons learned" effort.[26] According to Bryant, the department worked to understand what had gone wrong and how they could do better. Lesson number one, she said, was the overwhelming importance of and need for direct and close supervision of specialty units such as the 99 cars. (Recall that Officers Saldutte, Sisak, and Ewing served as the crew of Zone 5's 99 car, assigned to roam through the high-crime areas in search of guns and drug activity.) The department considered whether 99 cars should be abandoned, but decided that their role was too important; without some more proactive units seeking out potential criminal activity instead of just responding to 911 calls, it would be "open season" for the bad guys. However, some change was needed. These units could not function as a "loose team"; rather, they needed someone in a supervisory role watching their work closely, if not part of the actual team. And to fight the tendency in such units for the officers to become jaded—and to gradually fail to see the difference between law-abiding civilians (who make up the great majority of any community) and the small but active and even dangerous criminal element—officers in 99 cars or other specialty units needed to serve in other roles. They should be rotated out of the 99 cars and similar duties and given other assignments. This would put the officers in more consistent contact with regular people instead of just criminals, so they could avoid the trap of thinking that everyone they encountered was "in the game" of criminal activity, which is easy to do when one only encounters criminals.

Bryant said the incident also got the department thinking about how officers perform in fights. Officers in Pittsburgh's Police Academy have always received substantial training in how to defend themselves and each other in physical combat—training referred to as "defensive tactics." Police departments, including Pittsburgh's, are quite particular about this training and about what it wants officers to do when faced with the necessity for hand-to-hand fighting. They want their officers doing what is effective and safe enough to end the civilian's fighting and resistance, with the best chance to minimize injury to either the civilian or the officer. The Jordan Miles incident, Bryant said, caused the department to think about something that had not been considered in the past: officers who trained in other types of self-defense or physical combat. Recall from Chapter 2 that Officer Saldutte had training in other forms of self-defense: "grappling" (a set of wrestling holds and techniques) and Krav Maga, a form of self-defense associated with the Israeli military, as well as Jiu-Jitsu. Assistant Superintendent Bryant said that the Pittsburgh Police wanted to make sure, going forward, that any other kinds of self-defense training officers studied and practiced did not contradict or interfere with the principles and methods of defensive tactics as the department itself taught those tactics; they wanted all of their officers working from the same instructions that the department had refined and approved. With other systems, the dangers of something going wrong were unknown at best and potentially catastrophic at worst. For that reason, the department would henceforth require advance approval of any outside self-defense training and practice an officer wished to engage in, to assure that that training would not interfere with the tactics the department itself taught.

The department also made efforts to reemphasize an important aspect of how plainclothes officers interact with any member of the public, including people suspected of criminal activity. To avoid any misunderstanding, Bryant said, the department restated a core obligation: officers interacting with citizens, especially in any proactive assertion of their authority, *must* identify themselves as officers by displaying their badges, usually hung around their necks inside their clothes when undercover, and also verbally. Looking back at the Jordan Miles case, and the contentions about whether Jordan knew the men were police officers, one could see why the department chose to send this message.

With former Mayor Luke Ravenstahl departing the political scene in Pittsburgh in the wake of the scandal that brought down former Chief of Police Nathan Harper, the city elected Mayor Bill Peduto in 2014. Throughout his campaign, Peduto made the relationship between the city's police force and its African American communities a core consideration, often saying that the relationship had reached a critically negative point in the wake of the Jordan Miles case and the trials that followed. He came to office vowing to do something to improve the situation, and in his first term he appointed the first-ever outsider to head the Police Department: Cameron McLay, a retired captain from the Madison, Wisconsin police department with a reputation as a progressive thinker and a reformer. McLay made changes to the department, bringing in a new generation of top leaders, and revamping a considerable number of policies, procedures, and practices. He met opposition, of course; the police union led an effort that culminated in a vote of no confidence two years into McLay's tenure. Nevertheless, he initiated a significant effort that outlasted his brief two-and-a-half-year tenure. With the support and cooperation of then-U.S. Attorney David Hickton and others, McLay influenced the U.S. Department of Justice to select the Pittsburgh Police Department as one of six pilot cities for the National Initiative to Build Community Trust and Justice.

McLay's successor, Chief Scott Schubert, announced at the beginning of his term that he planned to "double down" on McLay's community-building efforts. The National Initiative (as it came to be called) picked the six cities (besides Pittsburgh, they selected Minneapolis, MN; Fort Worth, TX; Gary, IN; Stockton, CA; and Birmingham, AL) to serve as models for building and maintaining better police/community relationships through training and work in three areas: implicit bias, procedural justice, and racial reconciliation. After an independent survey-based assessment in each city of the state of police/community relations, Pittsburgh and the other cities embarked on a deep and thorough effort to train all officers and the command staff of the department on implicit bias and to train the entire department in procedural justice. The training for each of these runs three full days. It was created by the best minds in the field of social psychology and race in the United States and delivered by people—both from within and outside the department—who themselves had the training as well as special training on how to deliver it to others. In Pittsburgh, police trainers also delivered the training to citizens, who wanted to know just what the department was doing under the National Initiative; these citizen trainings were so successful that police trainers and the citizens formed training groups to take the training across the city to multiple civilian audiences.

Then at the end of 2018, the department began work on the last of the three pillars of the National Initiative: racial reconciliation. As of this writing, that phase of the Initiative remains a work in progress. Many leaders in the African American community in Pittsburgh sense that these efforts, begun under former Chief McLay and carried forward by current Chief Schubert, have made a difference. Tim Stevens, the head of the Black Political Empowerment Project and one of the most visible African American leaders in Pittsburgh, has said he can tell. In 2017, he told the media that "[T]here has been significant improvement in community-police relations in Pittsburgh, particularly when compared to the many stories we see involving police encounters across the nation."[27] It was a common sentiment, shared by others.[28]

FIVE STORIES

If some progress seemed to come to Pittsburgh's police/community relations after the terrible incident on Tioga Street on January 12, 2010, there were other, less positive signals as well—signs that substantive change in police conduct would be slower.

Leon Ford

On November 11, 2012, almost three years after Jordan Miles encountered the three police officers on his street, two Pittsburgh Police officers stopped a young African American man named Leon Ford as he drove through the Highland Park neighborhood of Pittsburgh, just a mile or so from Jordan's home on Tioga Street.[29] The officers said that Ford had committed a minor traffic violation; Ford presented the officers with his driver's license, car registration, and proof of insurance. All of Ford's documents checked out, but the officers had an objective other than traffic enforcement because at some point, they began to suspect that the young man in the car was not Leon Ford but gang member Lamont Ford. Instead of proceeding as they would with a normal traffic stop after checking a person's relevant documents, they detained Ford and called a third officer to the scene, because this officer knew Lamont Ford.

By the time the third officer arrived, the original two officers had decided to get Leon Ford out of his vehicle. Ford refused, fearing what would happen, and the officers began to pull him out. As this struggle occurred, the third officer jumped into Ford's car from the passenger side door, and the car began to move forward. In seconds, the officer in the car fired his gun multiple times. Leon Ford, grievously wounded, was rushed to a hospital. He emerged from the encounter paralyzed for the rest of his life—and charged with two counts of felony assault, three counts of recklessly endangering the three officers, charges of resisting arrest and escape, and three driving offenses.[30] The Police Department's Critical Incident Review Board found that the officer who jumped into the car had violated multiple police department policies and procedures. The entire incident, the Board said, "could have been avoided had the officers followed training and protocol."[31] The case against Leon Ford went to trial almost two years later; a jury acquitted him of both charges of felony assault and could not come to a decision on the charges of reckless endangerment, resisting arrest, or escape. Ford was convicted of two traffic infractions. The District Attorney's office dropped the rest of the charges four months later. A civil suit filed by Leon Ford against the city and the officers went to trial in federal court in late 2017; the jury, using the same "reasonable objective officer" standard in play in Jordan Miles's federal case,[32] exonerated one officer and could not reach a decision against the officer who jumped into the car, despite the Critical Incident Board's findings. Eventually, Pittsburgh settled the lawsuit with Ford for $5.5 million[33]— more than five years after Leon Ford stopped for the police and—minutes later—became paralyzed because of police gunfire.

Dennis Henderson

On June 26, 2013, Dennis Henderson attended a meeting about police/ community relations. The meeting took place in Homewood. Henderson, a well-regarded African American high school teacher, walked outside the building where the meeting took place to talk to a media photographer and exchange business cards. As the two men stood on Kelly Street, next to one of their vehicles, a Pittsburgh Police car not using emergency lights or a siren passed very close to them at a high speed. One or both of them called out their annoyance, and the officer stopped, turned around, and drove back. He got out of the patrol car and confronted Henderson and the other man, asking if they had a problem. Henderson responded by asking for the officer's name and badge number. The officer responded by threatening both men, placing them under arrest, and putting them in handcuffs. The other man was identified by other officers who came to the scene as "media" (he worked as a photographer for a local publication) and was released, but Henderson was taken into custody and jailed, charged with disorderly conduct and resisting arrest.

For Henderson—a veteran of community involvement efforts with police and others, and a leader and teacher at one of the city's academic charter schools for ten years—the incident was beyond disturbing. Two weeks later, District Attorney Stephen Zappala announced that his office would drop all charges against Henderson. "I have reviewed the circumstances surrounding the matter to this point. It's clear that the encounter with police resulted in part from two individuals exercising their constitutional rights."[34] Charges would be withdrawn, he said, and the officer's conduct would be reviewed by the city's Office of Municipal Investigations.[35] Henderson filed a federal lawsuit against the police department about the incident in November of 2013. "I want to show my students that, regardless of your neighborhood, ethnicity, attire, age, or socioeconomic status, no one should be harassed, arrested, and placed into the criminal justice system by a police officer who operates under a code of profiling, provoking, and arresting individuals without just cause."[36] A settlement of $52,000.00 was reached before trial, and the settlement included a pledge by the city to meet with an expert to explore adopting rules requiring Pittsburgh officers to record data on all pedestrian stops and frisks.[37] The Pittsburgh Citizens Police Review Board recommended that the officer be fired, but the Office of Municipal Investigations recommended only a written reprimand. Sergeant Michael LaPorte, president of Pittsburgh's Fraternal Order of Police lodge, said even a reprimand was too harsh and the union would appeal. "Everything he did on the scene was appropriate," Sergeant LaPorte said.[38]

Bruce Kelley, Jr.

On January 31, 2016, Bruce Kelley, Jr. and his father were drinking alcohol from open containers in a public area in Wilkinsburg, a municipality of over 15,000 just east of Pittsburgh; it borders on Homewood. The area in which Kelley and his father drank formed part of the Pittsburgh region's busway, a dedicated roadway restricted to public buses and other public vehicles, putting it under the jurisdiction of the county's Port Authority. Thus Port Authority police officers patrolling the area were among the first to confront the two men.[39] Kelley and his father resisted the officers and their commands; Kelley pulled out a pocket knife and ran away, through neighboring back yards. Officers ordered Kelley to drop the knife and surrender; they used pepper spray, a baton, and a Taser to get Kelley to comply, but he refused. A Port Authority sergeant arrived with a police dog and ordered Kelley to drop the knife and lay on the ground or he would unleash the dog on Kelley. Kelley replied that if the dog attacked him, he would kill it. Police released the dog, it attacked Kelley, and he stabbed the animal.[40]

Port Authority officers then shot Kelley, killing him.[41] They also arrested Kelley's father, who was then held on $300,000 bail.[42]

District Attorney Stephen Zappala found the killing of Kelley justified and filed no charges.[43] The police dog died from its wounds; it received a hero's funeral, attended by hundreds, which received wide media coverage.[44]

Willie West

Willie West grew up in Homewood.[45] He now lives outside Pittsburgh, in suburban Penn Hills, but still returns to the neighborhood to see his mother. She still lives in the area where she raised Willie. As a young boy and a teen, he had run-ins with the police; he says many of them ended in various kinds of harassment and intimidation. But he feels well past that now. He works at a nonprofit organization in Pittsburgh, helping young at-risk African American youth—people very much like himself at that age.

In late May or early June of 2017, Willie, then 26, went to Homewood to visit his mother. He parked his car, and after he talked to his mother, needed to go back to his car. As he walked down the street, "a [police] task force car comes up" and passed him. Willie had come from work, so he still wore his work clothes: nice pants and a button down shirt. The police went up the block and made a U-turn, coming back toward him. The car rolled up until it came even with Willie. The officer in the front passenger seat, one of several in the car, had the window half-way down. The officer asked Willie, "where you going?" Willie told him he was going to his car. The man then asked, "where you coming from?" Willie said he had come from his mom's house. "He says, 'why don't you do me a favor and lift your shirt up and turn around?'" Willie didn't like this; he felt, "come on, I'm not even doing nothing," but decided to comply.

The officer had decided he wanted to check Willie for a gun, and Willie knew this could get bad in a hurry. He lifted his shirt and turned around, to show the officer his entire torso and waist. Willie then said to the officer, "is there anything else?" The officer got out of the car and went up to Willie, saying "gimme your ID." Again, Willie complied. The police officer went back to the police car with the ID to run it through the car's computer system. Willie was left just standing there. After some minutes, the police officer who had stopped him said to the other officers, "he doesn't have anything" on his record, and one of the other officers in the car said, "[R]un it again. There's not too many times we get a guy from Homewood that don't have a record." Willie, now aggravated, said, "[G]o ahead and run it again, you ain't gonna get nothing." This got the first officer's attention. "He said to me, 'Oh, you're a smartass, huh?'" Willie immediately understood the danger of the moment. If he said something in return, he'd be "in a situation I don't need to be in." So he settled himself as best he could. He remembers thinking to himself, "I'm just gonna wait until you run my ID, you give me back my ID, and I'm going to go on about my day."

The comment about guys from Homewood with records really stung—it's a pernicious stereotype, Willie knew. He is a black man with tattoos who comes from Homewood, but "I go to work every day." This kind of thing is a regular occurrence in Homewood if you're a black man, even now. "They want you to run, because if they catch you, they break your jaw. If you make them run and they catch you, you are going to get a beating." Instead the young man endured the humiliation of treatment as if he does not work, as if he is not a good citizen, as if he commits crimes and carries a gun. Better to do that and survive.

Antwon Rose

In June of 2018, a police officer in the borough of East Pittsburgh (a municipality of approximately 1,800 residents,[46] just southeast of the city of Pittsburgh) stopped a car containing a driver and two passengers, all African American males. The car matched the description of a vehicle involved in a drive-by shooting a short distance away, 10 minutes earlier.[47] As the officer ordered the driver out, the two passengers ran from the front and rear doors on the other side of the car. The officer immediately fired at the fleeing men, killing 17-year-old high school student Antwon Rose.[48] Rose's death sparked days of angry demonstrations, most of them in Pittsburgh proper. District Attorney Stephen Zappala charged the officer with criminal homicide. At trial, the officer testified that he feared for his life because he thought Antwon had a gun, although the teen did not. The case, tried in March of 2019 before a jury brought in from Dauphin County, Pennsylvania (because of the intense publicity in Allegheny County), resulted in a not guilty verdict.[49]

The rage and the protests over the Rose shooting and the not guilty verdict, aimed deliberately not just at the East Pittsburgh police but at the city of Pittsburgh and its separate police force, seemed to puzzle many people. But for those who felt that the death of 17-year-old African American Rose was just the latest event in a long history of police violence, taking that outrage to Pittsburgh and the entire county made perfect sense. According to journalist Brentin Mock, writing in CityLab,

> Ever since Rose was killed last summer, demonstrators have shut down shopping areas, highways and downtown [Pittsburgh] traffic centers well

outside of East Pittsburgh to make the point that black people are vulnerable to police violence no matter the setting .... The message of the Rose case is that you can be unarmed in flight, your back to the police, and a cop will be justified for killing you .... What, to the victim of police violence, does it matter what the jurisdiction's name is on the clothes of the officer who shot him?[50]

The problem, Mock says, transcends municipal boundaries. The death of Rose, just like the case of Jordan Miles, transcends Pittsburgh's municipal boundaries. The problem afflicts every city and county in Pennsylvania, and every state in the United States. Jordan's case, in 2010, and Rose's death and the officer's acquittal, in 2019, show this state of affairs is, was, and will remain a national problem. Only a willingness to look for solutions on a national level can help us keep these cases from happening over and over.

Whether Pittsburgh can emerge as a better city for all of its citizens, with a civic life that includes and encourages everyone who lives there, will depend in large part on how its police treat people like Willie West, Dennis Henderson, and Leon Ford. This does not refer to whether the city ultimately dropped charges against Leon Ford or Dennis Henderson, or how much it paid them in settlements. It will depend on the police not treating them the way they did in the first place. That better future will only arrive when a person like Willie West can walk down the street in Homewood, to or from his mother's house, without having to lift his shirt to prove he's unarmed and to stew while the police check his ID, twice, because, well, you know those guys in Homewood.

The city may be making progress. But for now, there is still a very long way to go.

NOTES

CHAPTER 2 THE PEOPLE AND THE PLACES

1 A note about how the main people involved in this incident are identified: The author often calls the young man, Jordan Miles, by his first name, Jordan. The incident took place the day after Jordan turned 18, and as a teenager, this is how people knew him and referred to him. The three officers, Michael Saldutte, David Sisak, and Richard Ewing, are referred to either as Officer plus last name or by last name only. This is how the officers referred to themselves and how the public referred to them.

2 Information concerning Officer Saldutte's life comes directly from his sworn testimony at various stages in the case. I sought to interview each officer personally as well; I made oral, in-person requests to their attorneys and also made requests through letters sent to the officers in care of their attorneys. I received no responses to these requests. Copies of the letters are on file with the author.

3 Throughout the book, there are many references to the Pittsburgh Bureau of Police. That is the agency's official name. But many people in Pittsburgh, both inside and outside of the organization itself, refer to the agency by "Pittsburgh Police" or "Pittsburgh Police Department," and I will therefore use all three names interchangeably. This style also mirrors the way most people talk about police agencies in the United States, thus allowing for greater ease of expression.

4 The same requests for an in-person interview were made to Officer Sisak as to Officer Saldutte, with the same results. See note 1, supra.

5 The same requests for an in-person interview were made to Officer Ewing as to Officers Saldutte and Sisak, with the same results. See note 1, supra.

6 The facts about Jordan Miles come from sworn testimony given at various stages of the case and in an interview with Jordan Miles on March 29, 2017. Copy/recording/notes on file with the author. Jordan Miles attended the Pittsburgh Creative and Performing Arts (CAPA) High School, in which both he and the author's son were then enrolled. Both were members of the school's orchestra; they knew each other. The author did not meet Jordan Miles until sometime after the events of January 12, 2010.

7 Interview with Terez Miles on March 29, 2017. Materials on file with the author.

8 Darlene Superville, "G-20 Spouses Tour Art School, Warhol Museum in Pittsburgh," ArtDaily.org, September 25, 2009, at http://artdaily.com/news/33536/G-20-Spouses-Tour-Arts-School--Warhol-Museum-in-Pittsburgh#.XFNfv1VKi70; Bobby Kerlik, "CAPA Students Prepare for World Stage as Leaders' Spouses Set to Visit," Trib Live, September 23, 2009, at https://triblive.com/x/pittsburghtrib/news/specialreports/g20/s_644540.html.

9 For a historical survey, see Steven Sapolsky and Bartholomew Roselli, "Homewood-Brushton: A Century of Community-Making," Historical Society of Western Pennsylvania, 1987.

10 See, e.g., David Nasaw, Andrew Carnegie (Penguin Publishing Group, 2007).

11 Steven Sapolsky and Bartholomew Roselli, supra note 9.

12 Id. at 8–9.

13 The ten plays, known as "the Pittsburgh Cycle" or "the Century Cycle," are all set in The Hill in Pittsburgh except for "Ma Rainey's Black Bottom," which is set in Chicago. "August Wilson," accessed at http://www.august-wilson-theatre.com/plays.php.

14 Interview with John Brewer, Jr., director of the Trolley Station Oral History Center, Pittsburgh, PA, April 18, 2017. Notes on file with the author.

15 Memo to the author, Pittsburgh Bureau of Police Criminal Intelligence Unit, "Crime Analysis Memo," April 21, 2017. Copy on file with the author.

16 For a graphic of all six of the city's existing zones, as of April of 2016 and unchanged since 2009, see http: pittsburghpa.gov/police/zones.htm.

17 Interview with Assistant Superintendent Maurita Bryant, July 24, 2019 (notes on file with the author).

CHAPTER 3 THE IMMEDIATE AFTERMATH

1 Interview with Terez Miles, March 29, 2017 (notes and materials on file with the author).

2 City of Pittsburgh Bureau of Police, Investigative Report, Offs. Saldutte and Ewing, Date of Offense 1/12/2010; copy on file with the author.

3 Id.

4 Western Pennsylvania Hospital Emergency Department Record for Jordan Miles, dated January 12, 2010, 2346 hrs, copy on file with the author.

5 City of Pittsburgh Bureau of Police Supplemental Report, by Officer Darren Fedorski, dated January 12 or 13, 2010; copy on file with the author.

6 City of Pittsburgh Bureau of Police Supplemental Report, by Sergeant Charles Henderson, dated January 12, 2010; copy on file with the author.

7 Timothy McNulty, "CAPA Student Claims Pittsburgh Cops Beat Him," Pittsburgh Post-Gazette, January 22, 2010, accessed at https://www.post-gazette.com/local/city/2010/01/22/CAPA-student-claims-city-police-beat-him/stories/201001220175.

8 Id.

9 Id.

10 Id.

11 Timothy McNulty, "Mayor 'Troubled' by Police Brutality Claim in Homewood," January 22, 2010.

12 "Brutality Charged as Pittsburgh Police Defend 'Fist Strikes' on Teen," January 22, 2010, CNN, accessed at http://www.cnn.com/2010/CRIME/01/22/pennsylvania.arrest.dispute/index.html.

13 Ramit Plushnick-Masti, "Pittsburgh Police Accused of Brutality in Jordan Miles Beating," January 25, 2010.

14 Id.

15 Id.

16 Rich Lord, Sadie Gurman and Dan Majors, "FBI Looking Into CAPA Student's Police Beating Claim," January 26, 2010, accessed at https://www.post-gazette.com/breaking/2010/01/26/FBI-looking-into-CAPA-student-s-police-beating-claim/stories/201001260272.

17 Id.

18 WTAE, "Police Brutality Allegations," January 21, 2010, accessed at https://www.youtube.com/watch?v=B_j_AVsTXZc.

19 KDKA, "Police Brutality?" uploaded January 29, 2010, accessed at https://www.youtube.com/watch?v=BC2I-6UP2EU.

20 Sadie Gurman and Rich Lord, "Police Incident Provokes Ire," Pittsburgh Post-Gazette, January 27, 2010, accessed at https://www.post-gazette.com/local/city/2010/01/27/Police-incident-provokes-ire/stories/201001270265. Thanks to Angelika Kane, Post-Gazette staff, for help finding this article.

21 Ramit Plushnick-Masti, "Pittsburgh Police Accused of Brutality in Jordan Miles Beating," January 25, 2010.

22 Rich Lord, Sadie Gurman and Dan Majors, "FBI Looking Into CAPA Student's Police Beating Claim," Post-Gazette, January 26, 2010.

23 "B-PEP, CAPA Youths Rally for Jordan Miles," New Pittsburgh Courier, January 27, 2010, accessed at https://newpittsburghcourieronline.com/2010/01/27/b-pep-capa-youths-rally-for-jordan-miles/.

24 Sadie Gurman and Rich Lord, "Police Incident Provokes Ire," Pittsburgh Post-Gazette, January 27, 2010, at A1.

25 Poster, "Justice for Jordan Miles Emergency Protest Rally, May 6, 2011," accessed at http://www.brothaashproductions.com/JusticeForJordanMilesPhotos.html.

26 Rich Lord, Sadie Gurman and Dan Majors, "FBI Looking Into CAPA Student's Police Beating Claim," Post-Gazette, January 26, 2010.

27 Id.

28 Associated Press, "Pennsylvania: 3 Officers Suspended," *New York Times*, February 2, 2010.

29 Pennsylvania Code, Rule 542.

30 Interview with Paul Boas, via telephone, May 22, 2017 (notes on file with the author).

31 Id.

32 Id.

33 Interview with Terez Miles, May 22, 2017 (notes on file with the author).

34 DOJ regs on this in the 1990s?? Rulings?

35 Website, The Committee to Re-Elect Judge Oscar Petite Jr., accessed at http://www.oscarpetite.com/index.html.

36 Transcript, Comm. v. Jordan Miles, OTN No. G 487345-5, Preliminary Hearing, March 4, 2010, at 8.

37 Id. at 4–6.

38 Id. at 13–20.

39 Id. at 24–27.

40 Id. at 67–68.

41 Id. at 51

42 This is exactly what Saldutte said in response to an assertion by defense attorney Lewis, when Lewis implied, unwisely, that Saldutte had no reason to suspect any crime: "due to the high crime area that we were in, a male standing up against a house, it could have been a burglary." Id. at 50.

43 Id. at 74.

44 Id. at 74, 75.

45 Id. at 76.

46 Id. at 77.

47 Id. at 77–78.

48 Id. at 93.

49 Id. at 98

50 Home page, Fraternal Order of Police Lodge No. 1, accessed at http://www. pittsburghpolicefop.com/index.cfm, (to form the union (two officers leading the effort "and 21 others 'who were willing to take a chance' met on May 14, 1915, and held the first meeting of the Fraternal Order of Police. They formed Fort Pitt Lodge #1 …. From that small beginning the Fraternal Order of Police began growing steadily. In 1917, the idea of a National Organization of Police Officers came about. Today, the tradition that was first envisioned over 90 years ago lives on with more than 2,100 local lodges and more than 325,000 members in the United States."))

51 FOP News, "Officials Address Talk of 'Blue Flu,'" March 15, 2010, accessed at https://fop.net/NewsArticle.aspx?news_article_id=2280.

52 Id.

53 Id.

54 Id.

55 Id.

56 Id.

57 Christian Morrow, "Miles Charges Dropped, Police Protest May Follow," New Pittsburgh Courier, March 10, 2010, accessed at https://newpittsburghcourieronline. com/2010/03/10/miles-charges-dropped-police-protest-may-follow/.

58 Sadie Gurman, "Pittsburgh Police Warned Against Blue Flu," Pittsburgh Post-Gazette, March 10, 2010, accessed at http://www.post-gazette.com/local/city/ 2010/03/10/Pittsburgh-police-warned-against-blue-flu/stories/201003100277.

59 Id.

60 Id.

61 Margaret Harding, "Pittsburgh Police Plan Show of Support for Accused Officers," Pittsburgh Tribune-Review, March 12, 2010, accessed at https://triblive.com/x/ pittsburghtrib/news/tribpm/s_671354.html.

62 Jill King Greenwood, "Pittsburgh Police to March for Accused Officers," Pittsburgh Tribune-Review, March 13, 2010, accessed at http://triblive.com/x/pittsburghtrib/ news/s_671466.html.

63 Id.

64 Dennis B. Roddy, "Thousands Throng Downtown for Parade," Pittsburgh Post-Gazette, March 13, 2010.

65 Paradise Gray, "Pittsburgh Police Protest Charges Dropped against Jordan Miles," video images of report from KDKA Television, Pittsburgh, PA, March 13, 2010, uploaded to YouTube March 15, 2010, accessed at https://www.youtube.com/watch?v=Fjw0508g3XE.

66 Id.

67 Erin Perry, "Speak Out: What Is Your View of Police Wearing T-shirts Supporting Officers in the Miles Case?" New Pittsburgh Courier, March 31, 2010, accessed at https://newpittsburghcourieronline.com/2010/03/31/speak-outwhat-is-your-view-of-police-wearing-t-shirts-supporting-the-officers-in-miles-case/.

68 Id.

CHAPTER 4 INVESTIGATIONS AND DECISIONS

1 Adam Brandolph, "Activists Demand Arrests in Beating of Jordan Miles," Pittsburgh Tribune Review, August 13, 2010 (according to D. A. Zappala's spokesperson, office policy forbids conducting "simultaneous investigations" and D. A. would therefore wait for "the findings of the federal investigation" before proceeding); Margaret Harding, "Officers in Teen's Beating Reinstated," Pittsburgh Tribune Review, May 6, 2011 ("Allegheny County District Attorney Stephen A. Zappala Jr. has said he would wait until federal authorities were finished before deciding what he would do.").

2 18 Pa. Code Sec. 2702 (a) (2).

3 Paula Reed Ward, "Judge Dismisses Charges against CAPA Student," March 5, 2010, accessed at http://www.post-gazette.com/local/city/2010/03/05/Judge-dismisses-charges-against-CAPA-student/stories/201003050291.

4 Bobby Kerlik, "Honors Student Jordan Miles Cleared by Judge," Pittsburgh Tribune-Review, March 5, 2010.

5 Criminal Injustice podcast, Episode 21, August 21, 2016, interview with Stephen Zappala, accessed at http://www.criminalinjusticepodcast.com/season-2/, at 39:40.

6 Chris Young, "Pay Daze," Pittsburgh City Paper, August 12, 2010, accessed at https://www.pghcitypaper.com/pittsburgh/pay-daze/Content?oid=1344118.

7 Interview with Jordan Miles, March 29, 2017 (on file with the author).

8 Office of Municipal Investigations, "OMI," accessed at http://pittsburghpa.gov/omi/.

9 Id.

10 Office of Municipal Investigations, "Functions, Services, & Goals," accessed at http://pittsburghpa.gov/omi/function.

11 Id.

12 Office of Municipal Investigations, "OMI FAQs," accessed at http://pittsburghpa.gov/omi/faq.

13 Office of Municipal Investigations, "Employee Rights," accessed at http://pittsburghpa.gov/omi/employeerights/.

14 Chris Young, supra note 6.

15 Sadie Gurman, "Dowd Demands City to Release Report on Jordan Miles Arrest," Pittsburgh Post-Gazette, accessed at http://www.post-gazette.com/neighborhoods-city/2010/04/20/Dowd-demands-city-to-release-report-on-Jordan-Miles-arrest/stories/201004200184.

16 Chris Potter, "More on Hlavac, Miles Cases, Pittsburgh City Paper," Slag Heap blog, April 23, 2010, accessed at https://www.pghcitypaper.com/SlagHeap/archives/2010/04/23/more-on-hlavac-miles-cases.

17 Id.

18 Office of Municipal Investigations, supra note 8.

19 Id.

20 Torsten Ove, "Ex-Officer Charged in Tunnel Killing," Pittsburgh Post-Gazette, February 4, 1999, accessed at http://old.post-gazette.com/regionstate/19990204charmo4.asp; Mark Warnick, "Police Homicide Charges Shake Pittsburgh," Chicago Tribune, March 23, 1999, accessed at http://articles.chicagotribune.com/1999-03-23/news/9903230107_1_jeffrey-cooperstein-black-driver-civil-rights-charges; Citizens Police Review Board, "1994–1996: Local Tragedies and Legal Milestones," accessed at http://cprbpgh.org/about/history-of-the-cprb/significant-milestones.

21 Id.; Black Talon bullets are described as an especially deadly type of hollow-point bullets. Citizens Police Review Board, "1994–1996: Local Tragedies and Legal Milestones," accessed at http://cprbpgh.org/about/history-of-the-cprb/significant-milestones. Enthusiasts describe Black Talon ammunition as having exceptional power to stop a targeted human being by opening an extra-wide "wound channel" in soft tissue when a person is hit. It was taken off the market and then discontinued after two deadly mass shootings in the 1990s. See, for example, Suzanne Wiley, "Black Talon and Today's Best Self-defense Ammo," Shooter's Log, October 12, 2014, accessed at http://blog.cheaperthandirt.com/black-talon-todays-self-defense-ammo/.

22 Torsten Ove, "Ex-Officer Charged in Tunnel Killing," Pittsburgh Post-Gazette, February 4, 1999, accessed at http://old.post-gazette.com/regionstate/19990204charmo4.asp.

23 Id.

24 Citizens Police Review Board, "1994–1996: Local Tragedies and Legal Milestones," accessed at http://cprbpgh.org/about/history-of-the-cprb/significant-milestones.

25 "Timeline: Events in the Jonny Gammage Case," Pittsburgh Post-Gazette, October 12, 2005, accessed at http://www.post-gazette.com/frontpage/2005/10/12/Timeline-Events-in-the-Jonny-Gammage-case/stories/200510120331.

26 Robyn Meredith, "Jury Acquits White Officer in Death of Black Driver," New York Times, November 14, 1996, accessed at http://www.nytimes.com/1996/11/14/us/jurors-acquit-white-officer-in-the-death-of-black-driver.html.

27 Mark Warnick, "Police Homicide Charges Shake Pittsburgh," Chicago Tribune, March 23, 1999, accessed at http://articles.chicagotribune.com/1999-03-23/news/9903230107_1_jeffrey-cooperstein-black-driver-civil-rights-charges; Citizens Police Review Board, "1994–1996: Local Tragedies and Legal Milestones," accessed at http://cprbpgh.org/about/history-of-the-cprb/significant-milestones.

28 The new statute was 42 U.S.C. Sec. 14141, part of the 1994 crime bill, the Violent Crime Control and Law Enforcement Act of 1994 (PL 103-322), which gave the Department of Justice jurisdiction and authority to investigate any police department for evidence that its officers engaged in a "pattern or practice" of deprivations of civil rights. Should the investigation yield evidence of such a pattern or practice, the statute empowered the Department to bring a civil action in federal court to stop the practices and to ask the court to order changes to the department.

29 David A. Harris, Good Cops: The Case for Preventive Policing 124 (The New Press, 2005) (discussing Pittsburgh's consent decree).

30 Citizens Complaint Review Board, "A Year of City Council Activism," accessed at http://cprbpgh.org/about/history-of-the-cprb/city-council-activism.

31 Citizens Complaint Review Board, "Citizen Police Review Board Rules and Operating Procedures," accessed at http://cprbpgh.org/about/key-documents/cprb-board-rules.

32 Transcript of Proceedings, City of Pittsburgh Independent Citizen Police Review Board, "Public Hearing: 99 Cars," December 12, 2012 (copy on file with the author). It is not clear whether the CPRB ever fully investigated Jordan's complaint and, if it did, what that investigation showed. Despite multiple requests and searches, the author was not able to obtain any record of the investigation's outcome.

33 Note that there are specific laws that apply that allow for use of force when the property is the victim's home, and the purpose of the use of force is to prevent entry for the purpose of committing certain crimes.

34 See 18 Pa. Code Sec. 2701 (a) (1), under which "a person is guilty of assault if he: (1) attempts to cause or intentionally, knowingly or recklessly causes bodily injury to another."

35 18 Pa. Code Sec. 505 (a).

36 For example, 18 Pa. Code Sec. 506 (a), which allows for the defense of others when necessary to protect the other and when the person using force believes that both he and the person seemingly under attack could use self-defense.

37 18 Pa. Code Sec. 508 (a).

38 Chris Young, "Activists Keep Pressure on Zappala in Miles Case," Pittsburgh City Paper, June 3, 2011, accessed at https://www.pghcitypaper.com/Blogh/archives/2011/06/03/activists-keep-pressure-on-zappala-in-miles-case (in August 2010, faced with petitions the district attorney's spokesperson explained that the office would not move forward because the federal investigation was ongoing).

39 18 U.S. Code Sec. 242.

40 It is important to note here that assuming that the police are the good guys is appropriate in the great number of cases, for most people most of the time. The greatest number of officers do their jobs as they are supposed to, and most citizens are better off for that. The phrasing here refers to the fact that jurors tend to assume that this is true of all officers, in all situations—even in cases in which the conduct of officers, or the situation in general, has gone terribly wrong. Those are the cases that may wind up in a courtroom, and that is when the baseline assumption that officers are the good guys can be an impediment to a conviction.

41 Screws v. U.S., 325 U.S. 91 (1945).

42 Id. at 101.

43 U.S. Department of Justice, Resource Manual, Title 8-290, p. 135, accessed at https://books.google.com/books?id=1_uGCwAAQBAJ&pg=RA3-PA98&lpg=RA3-PA98&dq=Screws+v.+United+States+specific+intent&source=bl&ots=LlFG5dzTno&sig=Tjp4QejChqdJXPE-vOdbyJVQUmA&hl=en&sa=X&ved=0ahUKEwirx9nB3ZDVAhUDND4KHWDSDNM4ChDoAQhCMAY#v=onepage&q=Screws%20v.%20United%20States%20specific%20intent&f=false.

44 Human Rights Watch, "Shielded from Justice: Police Brutality and Accountability in the United States," chapter entitled "Federal Passivity, 1998, accessed at https://www.hrw.org/legacy/reports98/police/uspo33.htm.

45 "Shielded from Justice," supra note 44, chapter entitled "Lower Rate of Federal Prosecutions," accessed at https://www.hrw.org/legacy/reports98/police/uspo34.htm.

46 This was a statement made to me when I served as a public defender, early in my career, by a prosecutor who had tried a case against a client of mine and had lost. The evidence clearly did not support the charges, and the judge dismissed the case after the state rested its case, when I moved for a not guilty verdict. The full statement was, "I knew I didn't really have enough. But I thought I'd just throw it up against the wall, see what sticks. Maybe the judge would buy it."

47 U.S. Department of Justice, United States Attorneys' Manual, Purpose, Section 1-1.100, accessed at https://www.justice.gov/usam/usam-1-1000-introduction ("The United States Attorneys' Manual is designed as a quick and ready reference for United States Attorneys, Assistant United States Attorneys, and Department attorneys responsible for the prosecution of violations of federal law. It contains general policies and some procedures relevant to the work of the United States Attorneys' offices."). In 2018, the Manual underwent a full revision and retitling. The Department of Justice renamed it the Justice Manual, or the JM. According to the Department, "The JM was previously known as the United States Attorneys' Manual (USAM). It was comprehensively revised and renamed in 2018." It is now available online, at https://www.justice.gov/jm/justice-manual. Because this revision happened after the investigation against the police officers in Pittsburgh and because the revision is still new as of this writing, I will refer to it by its former names, the U.S. Attorney's Manual (USAM) or the Manual.

48 U.S. Department of Justice, United States Attorneys' Manual, 9-27.220, Grounds for Commencing or Declining Prosecution, accessed at https://www.justice.gov/usam/usam-9-27000-principles-federal-prosecution#9–27.220.

49 Id. (emphasis supplied).

50 Interview with David J. Hickton, June 21, 2017. All of the recollections, quotes, etc., in this chapter are taken from the interview.

51 University of Pittsburgh Institute for Cyber Law, Policy and Security, Bio of David J. Hickton, accessed at http://cyber.pitt.edu/david-j-hickton.

52 The author made several attempts to speak with the attorneys involved in the decision-making other than Mr. Hickton, in both the Pittsburgh office and at the Department of Justice, a number of whom were still on staff. No permission for anyone to speak ever came, and in some instances there was no response.

53 U.S. Attorney's Office, Western District of Pennsylvania, "Federal Officials Close the Investigation Involving Pittsburgh Bureau of Police Officers," May 4, 2011, accessed at https://www.justice.gov/archive/usao/paw/news/2011/2011_may/2011_05_04_01.html. The U.S. Department of Justice released its own parallel statement.

54 Department of Justice Office of Public Affairs, "Federal Officials Close the Investigation Involving Pittsburgh Bureau of Police Officers," May 4, 2011, accessed at https://www.justice.gov/opa/pr/federal-officials-close-investigation-involving-pittsburgh-bureau-police-officers.

55 Sadie Gurman, "Feds Will Not Prosecute Police in Jordan Miles Case," May 4, 2011, accessed at http://www.post-gazette.com/local/city/2011/05/05/Feds-will-not-prosecute-police-in-Jordan-Miles-case-1/stories/201105050334.

56 Id.

57 Bobby Kerlik, Jill King Greenwood, "No Fed Charges in Jordan Miles' Beating," Pittsburgh Tribune Review, May 5, 2011, accessed at https://archive.triblive.com/news/no-fed-charges-in-jordan-miles-beating/.

58 Interview with Brandi Fisher, September 8, 2017 (copy on file with the author).

59 Interview with Sala Udin, September, 13, 2017 (copy on file with the author).

60 Timothy Williams, "Under Fire, The Mayor of Pittsburgh Quits Race," New York Times, March 1, 2013, accessed at https://www.nytimes.com/2013/03/02/us/politics/luke-ravenstahl-pittsburgh-mayor-drops-re-election-bid.html ("Ravenstahl … had been regarded as a rising star in Pennsylvania politics when as the baby-faced City Council president he succeeded Mayor Bob O'Connor in 2006").

61 "Officers in Jordan Miles Case to Be Reinstated," KDKA Television, May 5, 2011, accessed at https://pittsburgh.cbslocal.com/2011/05/05/officers-in-jordan-miles-case-to-be-reinstated/.

62 Sadie Gurman, "Three Officers in Jordan Miles Case Reinstated," Pittsburgh Post-Gazette, May 5, 2011, accessed at https://www.post-gazette.com/local/city/2011/05/05/3-officers-in-Jordan-Miles-case-reinstated/stories/201105050373.

63 Fix PA, "Ravenstahl Promotes Police Chief, Nate Harper," October 18, 2006, accessed at http://fixpa.wikia.com/wiki/Ravenstahl_promotes_police_chief%2C_Nate_Harper.

64 Joe Mendak, "Pittsburgh to Reinstate 3 Officers in Beating Case," Associated Press, May 5, 2011.

65 Sadie Gurman, supra note 62.

66 City of Pittsburgh Office of Municipal Investigations, Final Report, OMI-10-21, May 5, 2011.

67 Sadie Gurman, supra note 55.

68 Mark Nootbar, "Jordan Miles Officers Reinstated," May 5, 2011, WDUQ FM, accessed at http://wduqnews.blogspot.com/2011/05/jordan-miles-officers-reinstated.html.

69 Sadie Gurman, supra note 58.

70 KDKA Television, supra note 61.

71 Id.

72 Joe Mendak, supra note 64.

73 Christian Morrow, "Leaders React to Miles Decisions," New Pittsburgh Courier, May 11, 2011.

74 Id.

75 Sadie Gurman, supra note 55.

76 Mark Nootbar, supra note 68.

77 Christian Morrow, " 'Charge Officers in Miles Case,' Citizens Challenge Zappala," New Pittsburgh Courier, June 8, 2011, accessed at https://newpittsburghcourieronline. com/2011/06/08/charge-officers-in-miles-case-citizens-challenge-zappala/.

78 Id:

79 Len Barcousky and Sadie Gurman, "Officers Won't Be Charged in Jordan Miles Incident," Pittsburgh Post-Gazette, May 17, 2012, accessed at http://www.post-gazette.com/local/city/2012/05/17/Officers-won-t-be-charged-in-Jordan-Miles-incident/stories/201205170358.

80 Id.

81 Cliff Jobe Consulting, LLC, Report to Chris Connors, Esquire, Senior Deputy District Attorney, Office of the District Attorney of Allegheny County, August 16, 2011 (copy on file with the author).

82 Len Barcousky and Sadie Gurman, supra note 79.

83 Id.

84 Len Barcousky and Sadie Gurman, supra note 79 (quoting Jordan Miles speaking on KDKA Television)..

85 Bobby Kerlik and Margaret Harding, "No Charges in Arrest of Black Teen, DA Reveals," Pittsburgh Tribune Review, May 16, 2012, accessed at http://triblive.com/home/1810332-74/zappala-officers-attorney-civil-decision-federal-police-sisak-statements-arrest.

86 Len Barcousky and Sadie Gurman, supra note 79.

CHAPTER 5 THE REMAINING ARENA: CIVIL LITIGATION

1 42 U.S.C.A. sec. 1983 (1871).

2 The Federal Civil Rights Acts, 42 U.S.C.A. secs. 1981 to 1988 (1871).

3 42 U.S.C.A. sec. 1983 (1871).

4 Michael Avery, David Rudovsky, Karen Blum, and Jennifer Laurin, Police Misconduct: Law and Litigation S 1.1 p. 1 (updated 2017).

5 Id.

6 Id.

7 U.S. Constitution, Fourth Amendment, which reads in full, "The right of the people to be secure in their persons, houses, papers, and effects, against unreasonable searches and seizures, shall not be violated, and no Warrants shall issue, but upon probable cause, supported by Oath or affirmation, and particularly describing the place to be searched, and the persons or things to be seized."

8 Anderson v. Creighton, 483 U.S. 635, 640 (1987).

9 Hudson v. Michigan, 547 U.S. 586, 597–98 (2006).

10 The Civil Rights Attorneys' Fees Award Act of 1976, 42 U.S.C. sec. 1988.

11 Hudson, 547 U.S. at 597–98.

12 The Act carries the following opening phrase: "Proceedings in vindication of civil rights."

13 Jeffrey S. Brand, "The Second Front in the Fight of Civil Rights: The Supreme Court, the Congress, and Statutory Fees," 69 Tex L. Rev. 291, 309–10 (1990).

14 Federal R. Civ. Pro. 68 (d), accessed at https://www.law.cornell.edu/rules/frcp/rule_68.

15 David A. Harris, "How Accountability-Based Policing Can Reinforce—or Replace—The Fourth Amendment Exclusionary Rule," 7 Ohio St. J. Crim. Law 149, 184 (2009).

16 Deposition of Michael Saldutte, *Miles v. City of Pittsburgh*, Saldutte, et al., Civ. No. 2:10-cv-01135, August 26, 2011, at 53–57.

17 Deposition of David Sisak, *Miles v. City of Pittsburgh*, Saldutte et al., Civ. No. 2:10-cv-01135, August 8, 2011, at 83–87.

18 Id. at 212.

19 Id. at 222.

20 Id. at 221.

21 Deposition of Jordan Miles, *Miles v. City of Pittsburgh*, Saldutte, et al., Civ. No. 2:10-cv-01135, August 30, 2011, at 125–28.

22 Deposition of RaShall Brackney, *Miles v. City of Pittsburgh*, Saldutte, et al., Civ. No. 2:10-cv-01135, August 30, 2011; biographical details in this paragraph are at pp. 6–8.

23 Id. at 60.

24 Deposition of Nathan Harper, *Miles v. City of Pittsburgh*, Saldutte, et al., Civ. No. 2:10-cv-01135, June 16, 2011.

25 Interview with RaShall Brackney, September 9, 2016, on file with the author.

26 Deposition of Nathan Harper, supra note 24, at pp. 74–78.

27 Id. at 91.

28 Id. at 52.

29 See Chapter 4.

30 Deposition of Nathan Harper, supra note 24, at 97.

31 Id. at 129.

32 Offer of Judgment, per Fed. R. Civ. P. 68, Dkt. No. 24 (Notice of Service), June 13, 2011, Miles v. City of Pittsburgh, Saldutte, et al., Civ. No. 2:10-cv-01135.

33 Brenda Waters, "Report: City Makes Settlement Offer in Jordan Miles Lawsuit," KDKA Television, June 14, 2012, accessed at https://pittsburgh.cbslocal.com/2011/06/14/report-city-makes-settlement-offer-in-jordan-miles-lawsuit/; Bob Bauder, "Pittsburgh Poised to Settle with Jordan Miles over Police Beating for $125k," May 23, 2016, accessed at https://triblive.com/news/adminpage/10516905-74/arrest-officers-federal ("Pittsburgh in 2011 offered $180,000 to settle the suit.)." The offer to settle the case was actually amended, and it is that Amended Offer of Judgment that actually governed anything vis-à-vis settlement and attorneys' fees and costs later in the case. Amended Offer of Judgment, per Fed. R. Civ. P. 68, Dkt. No. 29, June 20, 2011, Miles v. City of Pittsburgh, Saldutte, et al., Civ. No. 2:10-cv-01135. The terms of the original and amended offers are not materially different for our purposes.

34 "Attorney: Miles Family Rejects City's Settlement Offer," KDKA Television, June 14, 2011, accessed at https://pittsburgh.cbslocal.com/2011/06/14/attorney-miles-family-rejects-citys-settlement-offer/.

35 Id.

36 Motion for Approval of Stipulation of Voluntary Dismissal of Defendant City of Pittsburgh Pursuant to Fed. R. Civ. P. 41 (1) (a) (2), Dkt. No. 65, Miles v. City of Pittsburgh, Saldutte, et al., Civ. No. 2:10-cv-01135. The court granted the motion by order the next day.

37 Brian Bowling, "Miles Incident 'Has Touched a Big Nerve' in Pittsburgh," Pittsburgh Tribune-Review, July 16, 2012, accessed at https://triblive.com/news/2181706-74/officers-police-community-case-jordan-david-homewood-michael-richard-2010.

38 Rumors circulated during the pretrial period and beyond that settlement discussions continued and that the city had made an informal—that is, not on the court record, but verbal—offer of approximately half a million dollars to settle the case, which Jordan and his family also rejected. In any event, the case did not settle and went to trial.

39 Torsten Ove, "Gary L. Lancaster: First Black Chief Judge in U.S. Court Here," Pittsburgh Post Gazette, April 26, 2013, accessed at https://www.post-gazette.com/news/obituaries/2013/04/26/Obituary-Gary-L-Lancaster-First-black-chief-judge-in-U-S-court-here/stories/201304260143.

40 Michael Hasch and Bobby Kerlik, "Gary L. Lancaster, Chief U.S. Judge for Western Pa., Dead at 63," Pittsburgh Tribune-Review, April 23, 2013, accessed at https://triblive.com/news/adminpage/3906347-74/district-chief-died.

41 Torsten Ove, "Obituary: Gary L. Lancaster/First Black Chief Judge in U.S. Court Here," April 26, 2013, accessed at http://www.post-gazette.com/news/obituaries/2013/04/26/Obituary-Gary-L-Lancaster-First-black-chief-judge-in-U-S-court-here/stories/201304260143 (describing Lancaster as "bright" and "fair").

42 Transcript of Pretrial Motions Held on July 9, 2012, U.S. District Court, Pittsburgh, Pennsylvania, before Honorable Gary L. Lancaster, District Judge, Dkt. No. 198, Miles v. City of Pittsburgh, Saldutte, et al., Civ. No. 2:10-cv-01135.

43 Id. at 3.

44 Fed. R. Evid. 404 (b), "Crimes, Wrongs, or Other Acts."

45 Fed. R. Evid. 404 (a), "Character Evidence."

46 Id. at 7–8.

47 Judge Lancaster also ruled that Commander Brackney's own disciplinary history, which the defense wanted to use should she testify, could only be used for impeachment purposes. Id. at 13–14.

48 Matthew J. Brouillette and Jake Haulk, "Miles Incident 'Has Touched a Big Nerve' in Pittsburgh," Pittsburgh Tribune Review, July 16, 2012, accessed at https://archive.triblive.com/news/pittsburgh-allegheny/miles-incident-has-touched-a-big-nerve-in-pittsburgh/.

CHAPTER 6 THE POISON OF RACE

1 See Chapter 4.

2 "All in the Family: American Television Show," Encyclopaedia Britannica, accessed at https://www.britannica.com/topic/All-in-the-Family.

3 To use just one example—but one that set the tone going forward—when then-candidate for president Donald Trump announced his candidacy, he described Mexican immigrants this way: "They're bringing drugs. They're bringing crime.

They're rapists. And some, I assume, are good people." Katie Reilly, Time, August 31, 2016, accessed at http://time.com/4473972/donald-trump-mexico-meeting-insult/.

4 For a full discussion, see Mahzarin Bajani and Anthony Greenwald, *Blind Spot: Hidden Biases of Good People* (Bantam, 2016).

5 Jesse Singal, "Psychology's Favorite Racism Measuring Tool Isn't Up to the Job," New York Magazine, January 11, 2017, accessed at https://www.thecut.com/2017/01/psychologys-racism-measuring-tool-isnt-up-to-the-job.html; see also Project Implicit, Frequently Asked Questions, "Is the IAT Related to Behavior?" accessed at https://implicit.harvard.edu/implicit/faqs.html ("While a single IAT is unlikely to be a good predictor of a single person's behavior at a single time point, across many people the IAT does predict behavior in areas such as discrimination in hiring and promotion, medical treatment, and decisions related to criminal justice.")

6 Marianne Bertrand and Sendhil Mullainathan, "Are Emily and Greg More Employable than Lekisha and Jamal? A Field Experiment on Labor Market Discrimination," National Bureau of Economic Research, Working Paper no. 9873, accessed at https://www.nber.org/papers/w9873.

7 Jennifer L. Eberhardt, Philip Atiba Goff, Valerie J. Purdie, and Paul G. Davies, "Seeing Black: Race, Crime, and Visual Processing," v. 87, *Journal of Personality and Social Psychology* 876–93 (2004).

8 B. Keith Payne, "Prejudice and Perception: The Role of Automatic and Controlled Processes in Misperceiving a Weapon," v. 81, *Journal of Personality and Social Psychology* 181–92 (2001).

9 H. Andrew Sagar and Janet Ward Schofield, "Racial and Behavioral Cues in Black and White Children's Perceptions of Ambiguously Aggressive Acts," v. 39, *Journal of Personality and Social Psychology* 590–98 (1980).

10 Birt L. Duncan, "Differential Social Perception and Attribution of Intergroup Violence: Testing the Lower Limits of Stereotyping of Blacks," v. 34, *Journal of Personality and Social Psychology* 590–98 (1976).

11 John DiIulio, "My Black Crime Problem, and Ours," *City Journal* 14 (Spring 1996).

12 Jennifer L. Eberhardt, Philip Atiba Goff, Valerie J. Purdie, and Paul G. Davies, "Seeing Black: Race, Crime, and Visual Processing," v. 87, *Journal of Personality and Social Psychology* 876–893 (2004).

13 Id. at 877.

14 Id.

15 Id. at 890.

16 B. Keith Payne, "Prejudice and Perception: The Role of Automatic and Controlled Processes in Misperceiving a Weapon," v. 81, *Journal of Personality and Social Psychology* 181–92 (2001).

17 Id. at 181.

18 Id. at 187.

19 Izadi, Elahe Izadi, Peter Holley, "Video Shows Cleveland Officer Shooting 12-year-Tamir Rice within Seconds," Washington Post, November 26, 2014.

20 Adam Ferisse, "Timothy Loehmann, ex-Cleveland Cop Who Fatally Shot Tamir Rice, Remains Fired," Cleveland.com, December 5, 2018, accessed at https://www.cleveland.com/metro/2018/12/timothy-loehmann-ex-cleveland-cop-who-fatally-shot-tamir-rice-remains-fired.html.

21 Connie Schultz, "A City of Two Tales," Politico Magazine, February 23, 2015, accessed at https://www.politico.com/magazine/story/2015/02/tamir-rice-cleveland-police-115401.

22 Mike Hayes, "Dontre Hamilton's Autopsy Shows Officer Shot Him from Behind," Buzzfeed, December 1, 2014, accessed at https://www.buzzfeednews.com/article/mikehayes/dontre-hamilton-autopsy.

23 John Paul Wilson, Kurt Hugenberg, and Nicholas O. Rule, "Racial Bias in Judgments of Size and Formidability: From Size to Threat," v. 113, *Journal of Personality and Social Psychology* 59–80 (2017).

24 Id. at 60.

25 Id. at 65.

26 Id. at 66.

27 Id. at 71.

28 Id. at 73.

29 B. Keith Payne, "Prejudice and Perception: The Role of Automatic and Controlled Processes in Misperceiving a Weapon," v. 81, *Journal of Personality and Social Psychology* 181–92 (2001).

30 Joshua Correll, Bernadette Park, Charles Judd, and Bernd Wittenbrink, "The Police Officer's Dilemma: Using Ethnicity to Disambiguate Potentially Threatening Individuals," v. 83, *Journal of Personality and Social Psychology* 1314–29 (2002).

31 Joshua Correll and Tracie Keesee, "Racial Bias in the Decision to Shoot?" The Police Chief, May 2009.

32 Joshua Correll, Bernadette Park, Charles Judd, Bernd Wittenbrink, and Melody Sadler, "Across the Thin Blue Line: Police Officers and Racial Bias in the Decisions to Shoot," v. 92, *Journal of Personality and Social Psychology* 1006–23 (2007).

33 This was done using signal detection theory, a way of measuring decision-making in the presence of uncertainty. Joshua Correll and Tracie Keesee, supra note 31, at n. 6.

34 Id. at 57.

35 Joshua Correll, Bernadette Park, Charles Judd, Bernd Wittenbrink, and Melody Sadler, supra note 32, at 1015.

36 Joshua Correll and Tracie Keesee, supra note 31, at 58.

37 Jessica J. Sim, Joshua Correll, and Melody S. Sadler, "Understanding Police and Expert Performance: When Training Attenuates (vs. Exacerbates) Stereotypic Bias in the Decision to Shoot," v. 39, *Personality and Social Psychology Bulletin* 291–304 (2011).

38 Id.

39 Id.

40 Amanda Charbonneau, Katherine Spencer, and Jack Glaser, "Understanding Racial Disparities in Police Use of Lethal Force: Lessons from Police-on-Police Shootings," v. 73, *Journal of Social Issues* 744–67 (2017).

41 Id. at 744.

42 Id.

43 Id.

44 Id. at 755–56.

45 Id. at 756–57.

46 Id. at 757–58.

47 Id. at 758–59.

48 Id. at 760–61.
49 Ryan J. Reilly, "Eric Holder: Lack of Police Shooting Data 'Unacceptable,'" Huffington Post, January 15, 2015, accessed at https://www.huffpost.com/entry/eric-holder-police-shootings_n_6479114.
50 Charbonneau et al., supra note 41, at 746.
51 Id.
52 Id.
53 Id. at 747.
54 J. Nix, B. A. Campbell, E. H. Byers, and G. L. Alpert, "A Bird's Eye View of Civilians Killed by Police in 2015: Further Evidence of Implicit Bias," v. 16 *Criminology & Public Policy* 309–40 (2017).
55 Id. at 762.
56 Id.
57 Id.
58 Id. at 763.
59 Criminal Injustice Podcast, Episode 32, "Trying to Track Police Shootings and Reform the Use of Deadly Force," guest Dr. David Klinger, November 15, 2016, accessed at http://www.criminalinjusticepodcast.com/season-2/.

CHAPTER 7 HOW FEAR IMPACTS THE POLICE

1 Fatal Force: 987 People Have Been Shot and Killed by the Police in 2017, Washington Post, accessed at https://www.washingtonpost.com/graphics/national/police-shootings-2017/; The Counted: People Killed by Police in the U.S., The Guardian, accessed at https://www.theguardian.com/us-news/ng-interactive/2015/jun/01/the-counted-police-killings-us-database.
2 Just as important as the number of people killed by police every year, we should also know how many people are injured by police use of deadly force, whether by gunshots or other methods, and how many times police attempt to use gunshots and other types of deadly force on citizens, but they miss. This information seems every bit as important as information on when a bullet strikes its intended target, but if anything, it is even less likely to be recorded. See, for example, Episode 32, interview with David Klinger, Criminal Injustice podcast, posted November 15, 2016.
3 For example, David Jackson, Obama: Police Officers Run toward the Danger, USA Today, May 12, 2014, accessed at https://www.usatoday.com/story/news/politics/2014/05/12/obama-biden-top-cops-the-national-association-of-police-organizations/9013313/ ("They run toward the danger, not away from it.").
4 These ideas are frequently expressed in the voluminous literature describing community policing. For example, U.S. Department of Justice, Office of Community Oriented Policing Services, "Community Policing Defined," accessed at https://ric-zai-inc.com/Publications/cops-p157-pub.pdf; Robert Trojanowicz and Bonnie Bucqueroux, COMMUNITY POLICING: A CONTEMPORARY PERSPECTIVE (1990); Community Policing Consortium, "About Community Policing," accessed, at http://www.communitypolicing.org/about2html; "Understanding Community Policing: A Framework for Action," August 1994, NCJ 148457, accessed at http://www.communitypolicing.org/chap3fw.html.

5 For example, Bonnie Bucqueroux, 11 Reasons Community Policing Died, Mediem, May 9, 2015, accessed at https://medium.com/@bonniebucqueroux/11-reasons-community-policing-died-fdb1b14367de; Sudhir Venkatesh, How the Federal Government is Killing Community Policing, The New Republic, September 25, 2012, accessed at https://newrepublic.com/article/107675/how-big-brother-killing-community-policing ("Increasingly, across the country, the town cop who walks a beat and relies on trust with locals may be a thing of the past …; we may be seeing the end of 'community policing' as we've known it.")

6 Seth W. Stoughton, Principled Policing: Warrior Cops and Guardian Officers, 51 Wake Forest L. Rev. 611, 612 (2016).

7 Id. at 612.

8 Id.

9 Final Report, President's Task Force on 21st Century Policing, May 2015, accessed at http://elearning-courses.net/iacp/html/webinarResources/170926/FinalReport21stCenturyPolicing.pdf.

10 Seth W. Stoughton, supra note 6, at 632–35.

11 Dave Grossman and Loren W. Christensen, On Combat: The Psychology and Physiology of Deadly Conflict in War and in Peace (3rd ed. 2008).

12 Mr. Grossman gives well-received private training to police officers in groups around the country; his recorded lectures, available on YouTube and elsewhere, are also immensely popular. For example, U.S. Military Videos, "Lt. Col. (Ret.) Dave Grossman speaks on being a Warrior!" posted March 29, 2011 (over 217,000 views by April 25, 2019).

   Warrior Poet Society, "Dave Grossman Discusses Combat and Killing," posted May 2, 2017 (over 98,000 views by April 25, 2019), accessed at https://www.youtube.com/watch?v=7vP-NnmYE8c.

13 Dave Grossman and Loren W. Christensen, supra note 12, at 181 ("And Warriors have been given the gift of aggression ….(T)hey yearn for the opportunity to use their gift to help others.").

14 Id. at 185.

15 Seth W. Stoughton, supra note 6, at 634.

16 Steve Featherstone, "Professor Carnage," The New Republic, April 17, 2017, accessed at https://newrepublic.com/article/141675/professor-carnage-dave-grossman-police-warrior-philosophy.

17 Id.

18 Dave Grossman, and Loren W. Christensen, supra note 13, at 183.

19 Id. at 181.

20 Seth W. Stoughton, supra note 6, at 638–39.

21 Steve Featherstone, supra 16.

22 "Training Day," Am. Police Beat, September 25, 2015.

23 A. J. George, "Winning a Knife Fight," Police Magazine, February 11, 2015, accessed at http://www.policemag.com/channel/weapons/articles/2015/02/winning-a-knife-fight.aspx.

24 Uriel Garcia, "Experts Say Strongly Worded Police Curriculum Is Risky with Cadets," Santa Fe New Mexican, March 22, 2014), accessed at

http://www.santafenewmexican.com/news/local_news/experts-say-strongly-worded-police-curriculum-is-risky-with-cadets/article_6fcb7d45-436c-5e48-aa06-2fc6fdcc35a1.html.

25 Seth W. Stoughton, supra note 6, at 639–40. I am indebted to Professor Stoughton for pointing me (and everyone else who has read his terrific Wake Forest Law review piece) toward the material in the previous three notes.

26 One can hear this phrase almost any time police gather and discuss the use of force, and it is not hard to find in print. For example, Seth Stoughton, "How Police Training Contributes to Avoidable Deaths," The Atlantic, December 12, 2014, accessed at https://www.theatlantic.com/national/archive/2014/12/police-gun-shooting-training-ferguson/383681/ ("A common phrase among cops pretty much sums it up: 'Better to be judged by twelve than carried by six.'").

27 Steve Featherstone, supra note 16.

28 Seth W. Stoughton, supra note 6, at 640 n.158.

29 Dr. Kevin Gilmartin has become the leading authority on this topic. For example, Kevin M. Gilmartin, Emotional Survival for Law Enforcement: A Guide for Law Enforcement Officers and Their Families (E-S Press, [YEAR]); Kevin M. Gilmartin, Hypervigilance: A Learned Perceptual Set and Its Consequences on Police Stress, published in Psychological Services to Law Enforcement, U.S. Dept. of Justice, Federal Bureau of Investigation, Reese and Goldstein, eds., Washington, DC, 1986.

30 Steve Featherstone, supra note 16.

31 Sunil Dutta, "I'm a Cop. If You Don't Want to Get Hurt, Don't Challenge Me," Washington Post, August 19, 2014, accessed at https://www.washingtonpost.com/posteverything/wp/2014/08/19/im-a-cop-if-you-dont-want-to-get-hurt-dont-challenge-me/?utm_term=.628d90c8df10.

32 Seth Stoughton, supra note 26.

33 FBI, "Law Enforcement Officers Killed and Assaulted, 2014 Report Released," October 19, 2015, accessed at https://www.fbi.gov/news/stories/2014-law-enforcement-officers-killed-and-assaulted-report-released.

34 FBI, "Law Enforcement Officers Killed and Assaulted, 66 Officers Feloniously Killed in 2016," accessed at https://www.fbi.gov/news/pressrel/press-releases/fbi-releases-2016-statistics-for-law-enforcement-officers-killed-and-assaulted-in-the-line-of-duty (also noting 2015 statistics).

35 Id. In statistics released while this book neared the end of the final editing process, the FBI stated that 55 police officers were feloniously killed in 2018 and 46 had been feloniously killed in 2017—one of these years totaling above, and the other totaling below, the average of 51 stated in the text. FBI Press Release, "FBI Releases 2018 Statistics on Law Enforcement Officers Killed in the Line of Duty," accessed at https://www.fbi.gov/news/pressrel/press-releases/fbi-releases-2018-statistics-on-law-enforcement-officers-killed-in-the-line-of-duty.

36 FBI, supra note 34.

37 FBI, supra note 35 (containing assault statistics for both 2015 and 2016). Statistics obtained during the final editing stages of this book showed just over 60,000 assaults on police officers in 2017, an increase of approximately 5 percent; assaults resulting in injuries to officers decreased by 1 percent. FBI, "2017 Law Enforcement Officers

Killed and Assaulted," accessed at https://ucr.fbi.gov/leoka/2017/topic-pages/assaults_topic_page_-2017.

38 Police Public Contact Survey, 2011 (PPCS), Bureau of Justice Statistics (2013), accessed at https://www.bjs.gov/index.cfm?ty=dcdetail&iid=251. The PPCS is a supplement to the National Crime Victimization Survey.

39 Bureau of Justice Statistics, "Study Finds Some Racial Differences in Perception of Police Behavior During Contact with the Public," September 24, 2013, accessed at https://ojp.gov/newsroom/pressreleases/2013/ojppr092413.pdf.

40 Id.

41 Seth Stoughton, supra note 27.

42 Id.

43 Calibre Press, which has been providing privately run police training seminars and materials for over three decades, continues to offer its two-day "Street Survival" seminar, which features "classic training points while also addressing current events issues impacting the profession through the use of lecture and up-to-date videos of police/citizen interactions," as well as preparing "officers for making sound, legal and reasonable decisions under stress." Calibre Press, "Street Survival Seminar," accessed at https://secure.calibrepress.com/courses/street-survival-seminar/.

44 Even the U.S. Supreme Court has used videos of police civilian encounters in its cases and posted the video on the internet. See, for example, *Scott v. Harris*, 550 U.S. 372 (2007), video accessed at https://www.supremecourt.gov/media/media.aspx (see download link), in which the video from a dashboard camera records a high-speed chase of a civilian vehicle that has refused to stop and shows how the police vehicle pushed the civilian vehicle off the road and into a ditch, resulting in injuries that made the driver of the civilian vehicle a quadriplegic.

45 Leon Neyfakh, "How Police Learn When to Shoot," Slate, May 21, 2015, accessed at http://www.slate.com/articles/news_and_politics/crime/2015/05/police_shootings_the_grim_videos_cops_watch_of_their_colleagues_being_killed.html.

46 Id.

47 Id.

48 Id.

49 Id.

50 Deputy Kyle Dinkheller Traffic Stop, accessed at https://www.youtube.com/watch?v=OlzPcUM-MQ0.

51 Police Shooting—Constable Darrell Lunsford, Nagadoches County, Texas, accessed at https://www.youtube.com/watch?v=mVDRo7-kwGc.

52 Reality Training: Lunsford Incident, Police One, September 22, 2008, accessed at https://www.policeone.com/officer-down/videos/5954598-Reality-Training-Lunsford-Incident/.

53 Leon Neyfakh, supra note 45.

54 Id.

55 Lynn Langton and Matthew DuBose, Police Behavior During Traffic and Street Stops, 2011, U.S. Department of Justice, Bureau of Justice Statistics, September 2013, NCJ 242937, accessed at https://www.bjs.gov/content/pub/pdf/pbtss11.pdf.

56 German Lopez, Police Shootings Are also Part of America's Gun Problem, Vox, April 9, 2018, accessed at https://www.vox.com/2018/4/9/17205256/gun-violence-us-police-shootings.

57 Id.

58 Deposition of Michael Saldutte, *Miles v. City of Pittsburgh*, Saldutte, et al., Civ. No. 2:10-cv-01135, August 26, 2011, at 57–58.

59 Christopher Ingraham, There Are Now More Guns Than People in the United States, Washington Post, October 5, 2015, accessed at https://www.washingtonpost.com/news/wonk/wp/2015/10/05/guns-in-the-united-states-one-for-every-man-woman-and-child-and-then-some/?noredirect=on&utm_term=.50439632db07; Sarah Frostenson, There Are Now More Guns Than People in America, Vox, July 27, 2016, accessed at https://www.vox.com/2016/7/27/12123202/more-guns-than-people-america-charts; William J. Krouse, Gun Control Legislation, Congressional Research Service, November 14, 2012, accessed at https://fas.org/sgp/crs/misc/RL32842.pdf.

60 Deborah Azrael, Lisa Hepburn, David Hemenway, and Matthew Miller, The Stock and Flow of Firearms in the U.S.: Results from the 2015 National Firearms Survey, 3 (5) Journal of the Social Sciences 38–52 (2017), accessed at https://www.rsfjournal.org/doi/full/10.7758/RSF.2017.3.5.02.

61 Id.

62 Id.

63 Kara Fox, How U.S. Gun Culture Compares with the World in Five Charts, CNN, March 9, 2018, at https://www.cnn.com/2017/10/03/americas/us-gun-statistics/index.html.

64 Concealed Carry Statistics, accessed at https://www.gunstocarry.com/concealed-carry-statistics/.

65 Id.

66 John R. Lott Jr., The New York Times Bogus Crime Data about Concealed-Handgun Permit Holders, National Review, January 19, 2017, accessed at https://www.nationalreview.com/2017/01/new-york-times-concealed-handgun-crime-numbers-are-bogus/ ("Concealed-handgun permit holders are also much more law-abiding than the rest of the population."); but see also Daniel W. Webster, Cassandra K. Crifasi, Jon S. Vernick, and Alexander McCourt, Concealed Carry of Firearms: Fact vs. Fiction, Johns Hopkins Bloomberg School of Public Health, November 16, 2017, accessed at https://www.jhsph.edu/research/centers-and-institutes/johns-hopkins-center-for-gun-policy-and-research/publications/concealed-carry-of-firearms.pdf ("Carrying a concealed handgun in public has the potential to enable would-be victims of violent crime to thwart attempted acts of violence, but also poses potential threats to public safety.")

67 Mark Berman, Violent Crimes and Murders Increased in 2016 for a Second Consecutive Year, Washington Post, September 25, 2017, accessed at https://www.washingtonpost.com/news/post-nation/wp/2017/09/25/violent-crime-increased-in-2016-for-a-second-consecutive-year-fbi-says/?utm_term=.e825a53e308e (quoting President Trump's reference to "American carnage" in his inaugural address and Attorney General Jeff Sessions's statement that increases in crime in 2016 were "the beginning of a trend"); U.S. Department of Justice, Attorney General Sessions Appoints 17 Current and Former Federal Prosecutors as Interim United States

Attorneys, January 3, 2018, accessed at https://www.justice.gov/opa/pr/attorney-general-sessions-appoints-17-current-and-former-federal-prosecutors-interim-united (describing early 2018 as a time of "rising violent crime, a staggering increase in homicides, and an unprecedented drug crisis"); Jeff Sessions Says There's "a Staggering Increase in Homicides," The Data Disagree, Washington Post, January 5, 2018, accessed at https://www.washingtonpost.com/opinions/jeff-sessions-says-theres-a-staggering-increase-in-homicides-the-data-dont-agree/2018/01/05/b0ae52fa-f169-11e7-b390-a36dc3fa2842_story.html?utm_term=.78e9b139691b.

68 Dylan Matthews, Stop Blaming Mental Illness for Mass Shootings, Vox, March 14, 2018, accessed at https://www.vox.com/policy-and-politics/2017/11/9/16618472/mental-illness-gun-homicide-mass-shootings citing Jeffrey Swanson, International Crime Victims Survey (2000). The countries are Japan, Portugal, Switzerland, Spain, Finland, the United States, Belgium, France, Poland, Denmark, Canada, Sweden, Netherlands, the United Kingdom, and Australia.

69 Federal Bureau of Investigation, "Crime in the United States, 2017," Uniform Crime Reports, Table 1, accessed at https://ucr.fbi.gov/crime-in-the-u.s/2017/crime-in-the-u.s.-2017/tables/table-1.

70 Thomas Abt, BLEEDING OUT: THE DEVASTATING CONSEQUENCES OF URBAN VIOLENCE—AND A BOLD NEW PLAN FOR PEACE IN THE STREETS 2 (Basic Books, 2019).

71 Franklin Zimring and Gordon Hawkins, *Crime Is Not the Problem: Lethal Violence in America* (1997).

72 Id. at 1–2 (emphasis added).

73 Dylan Matthews, supra note 68.

74 Zach Beauchamp, American Doesn't Have More Crime Than Other Rich Countries. It Just Has More Guns, Vox, February 15, 2018, accessed at https://www.vox.com/2015/8/27/9217163/america-guns-europe.

75 German Lopez, supra note 56.

76 2017 Police Violence Report, accessed at https://policeviolencereport.org/.

77 Fatal Force, Washington Post, https://www.washingtonpost.com/graphics/national/police-shootings-2017/ (showing 987 incidents in which people were shot and killed by police in 2017).

78 German Lopez, supra note 56.

79 Id.

80 Aaron J. Kivisto, Bradly Ray, and Peter L. Phalen, "Firearm Legislation and Fatal Police Shootings in the United States," *American Journal of Public Health* (2017), accessed at https://ajph.aphapublications.org/doi/10.2105/AJPH.2017.303770.

81 German Lopez, supra note 57.

82 David I. Swedler, Molly M. Simmons, Francesca Dominici, and David Hemenway, "Firearms Prevalence and Homicides of Law Enforcement Officers in the United States," *American Journal of Public Health* (2015), accessed at https://ajph.aphapublications.org/doi/abs/10.2105/AJPH.2015.302749 ("High public gun ownership is a risk for occupational mortality for LEOs in the United States.")

83 German Lopez, supra note 56.

84 Id.

CHAPTER 8 HOW FEAR IMPACTS BLACK AMERICANS

1 Nikole Hannah-Jones, "Yes, Black America Fears the Police. Here's Why," Pacific Standard, April 10, 2018, accessed at https://psmag.com/social-justice/why-black-america-fears-the-police. A shorter version of the article appeared as "A Letter from Black America: Yes, We Fear Police. Here's Why," Politico Magazine, March/April 2015, accessed at https://www.politico.com/magazine/story/2015/03/letter-from-black-america-police-115545.

2 Khalil Gibran Muhammad, THE CONDEMNATION OF BLACKNESS: RACE, CRIME, AND THE MAKING OF MODERN URBAN AMERICA (Harvard, 2011).

3 Nikole Hannah-Jones, supra note 1.

4 University of Pennsylvania School of Arts and Sciences, Department of Music, Guthrie Ramsay, accessed at https://www.sas.upenn.edu/music/people/standing-faculty/guthrie-ramsey.

5 See, for example, Bellesiles, Michael, Lethal Imagination: Violence and Brutality in American History. NYU Press; Edition Unstated edition (March 1, 1999).

6 For a sense of how deeply the Klan and other white supremacist group had penetrated America in the 1920s, see, for example, Jon Meacham, The Soul of America: The Battle for Our Better Angels (Random House, 2016).

7 Ray Sprigle, Justice Black Revealed as Ku Klux Klansman," Pittsburgh Post-Gazette, September 13, 1937, accessed at http://pgdigs.tumblr.com/image/30869087306.

8 Id.

9 For example, Christopher Klein, "Remembering History's Bloody Sunday," March 6, 2015, accessed at https://www.history.com/news/selmas-bloody-sunday-50-years-ago.

10 Nikole Hannah-Jones, supra note 1.

11 Report of the National Advisory Commission on Civil Disorders, 1968, accessed at https://www.ncjrs.gov/pdffiles1/Digitization/8073NCJRS.pdf.

12 Id. at 1.

13 Id. at 68–69.

14 Id. at 70.

15 Jon Swaine, "Eric Holder Calls Failure to Collect Reliable Data on Police Killings Unacceptable," The Guardian, January 15, 2015, accessed at https://www.theguardian.com/us-news/2015/jan/15/eric-holder-no-reliable-fbi-data-police-related-killings.

16 "995 People Shot Dead by Police in 2015," The Washington Post, accessed at https://www.washingtonpost.com/graphics/national/police-shootings/.

17 "Fatal Force: 963 People Shot and Killed by Police in 2016," The Washington Post, accessed at https://www.washingtonpost.com/graphics/national/police-shootings-2016/?noredirect=on.

18 "Fatal Force: 987 People Shot and Killed by Police in 201," The Washington Post, accessed at https://www.washingtonpost.com/graphics/national/police-shootings-2017/?noredirect=on (Blacks were 22.5 percent of all those shot and killed, and 29 percent of all of those killed who were unarmed).

19 Lindsey Bever and Andre deGrandpre, " 'We Only Kill Black People,' A Cop Told a Woman—On Camera. Now He'll Lose His Job," The Washington Post, Aug.

31, 2017, https://www.washingtonpost.com/news/post-nation/wp/2017/08/31/remember-we-only-shoot-black-people-georgia-police-officer-told-a-woman-on-camera/?utm_term=.82b4bce3b4ee (video embedded).

20 " 'We Just Want to Know What Happened?' Distraught Family Sue after Their Daughter Is Shot in Head by Off-duty Cop," Daily Mail, April 7, 2012, accessed at https://www.dailymail.co.uk/news/article-2126697/Distraught-family-sue-daughter-shot-dead-duty-cop-charged.html.

21 Mark Morales, "Four Years after Eric Garner's Death, Officer Faces NYPD Trial to See If He Will Keep His Job," CNN, December 6, 2018, accessed at https://www.cnn.com/2018/12/06/us/eric-garner-nypd-daniel-pantaleo/index.html. In August of 2019, the officer was fired, spurring the head of one of New York's police unions to assert that the firing showed that the commissioner of the New York Police Department was "cringing in fear." John Bacon, "NYPD Union Chief: Commissioner 'Cringing in Fear' by Firing Officer in Eric Garner Death," USA Today, August 19, 2019, accessed at https://www.usatoday.com/story/news/nation/2019/08/19/eric-garners-death-officer-daniel-pantaleo-fired/2051861001/.

22 Adam Ferrise, "Timothy Loehmann, Ex-Cleveland Cop Who Shot Tamir Rice, Remains Fired," Cleveland.com, December 5, 2018, accessed at https://www.cleveland.com/metro/2018/12/timothy-loehmann-ex-cleveland-cop-who-fatally-shot-tamir-rice-remains-fired.html.

23 Katey Abbey-Lambertz, "These 15 Black Women Were Killed during Police Encounters. Their Lives Matter, Too," Huffington Post, accessed at https://www.huffpost.com/entry/black-womens-lives-matter-police-shootings_n_6644276.

24 Chris Sadeghi, "Fired Deputy Daniel Willis Found Not Guilty of Murder," KXAN, accessed at https://www.kxan.com/news/closing-arguments-today-for-former-bastrop-deputy-charged-with-murder/1049688204.

25 Ralph Ellis and Bill Kirkos, "Officer Who Shot Philando Castile Found Not Guilty on All Counts," CNN, June 16, 2017, accessed at https://www.cnn.com/2017/06/16/us/philando-castile-trial-verdict/index.html.

26 M. L. Nestel, "Police Won't Face Charges in Alton Sterling Shooting Case," ABC News, March 27, 2018, accessed at https://abcnews.go.com/US/police-face-charges-alton-sterling-shooting-case/story?id=54039904.

27 Richard Fausset, "Baton Rouge Officer Is Fired in Alton Sterling Case as Police Release New Videos," New York Times, March 30, 2018, accessed at https://www.nytimes.com/2018/03/30/us/baton-rouge-alton-sterling.html.

28 Erik Ortiz and Phil Helsel, "Jury Acquits Tulsa Officer Betty Shelby in Shooting Death of Terence Crutcher," NBC News, May 17, 2017, accessed at https://www.nbcnews.com/news/us-news/jury-acquits-tulsa-officer-shooting-death-terence-crutcher-n761206.

29 Doug Criss, " The Police Officer Who Fatally Shot an Unarmed Black Man in Tulsa Now Teaches a Course on How Other Cops Can 'Survive' Controversial Shootings," CNN, August 28, 2018, accessed at https://www.cnn.com/2018/08/28/us/betty-shelby-class-trnd/index.html.

30 Megan Crepeau, Christy Gutowsky, Jason Meisner, Stacy St. Clair, "Van Dyke Taken Into Custody after Jury Convicts Him of 2nd-degree Murder, Aggravated Battery for Each of 16 Shots," Chicago Tribune, October 5, 2018, accessed at

https://www.chicagotribune.com/news/local/breaking/ct-met-laquan-mcdonald-jason-van-dyke-verdict-20181005-story.html.

31 Julie Bosman and Monica Davey, "3 Officers Acquitted for Covering Up for Colleague in Laquan McDonald Killing," New York Times, January 17, 2019, accessed at https://www.nytimes.com/2019/01/17/us/laquan-mcdonald-officers-acquitted.html.

32 Mitch Smith and Julie Bosman, "Jason Van Dyke Sentenced to Nearly 7 Years for Murdering Laquan McDonald," New York Times, January 18, 2019, accessed at https://www.nytimes.com/2019/01/18/us/jason-van-dyke-sentencing.html.

33 Matt Pearce and Matt Hansen, "No Prison Time for Ex-NYPD Officer Peter Liang in Fatal Shooting of Akai Gurley," L.A. Times, April 19, 2016, accessed at https://www.latimes.com/nation/la-na-liang-sentencing-20160419-story.html.

34 Matthew Horace, The Black and the Blue: A Cop Reveals the Crimes, Racism and Injustice in America's Law Enforcement (Hachette Books, 2018).

35 Id. at xv.

36 The Associated Press—NORC Center for Public Affairs Research, Issue Brief, "Law Enforcement and Violence: The Divide Between Black and White Americans (2015), accessed at http://www.apnorc.org/projects/Pages/HTML%20Reports/law-enforcement-and-violence-the-divide-between-black-and-white-americans0803-9759.aspx.

37 Carolyn Abate, History of 911: American's Emergency Service, before and after Kitty Genovese, January 19, 2017, accessed at http://www.pbs.org/independentlens/blog/history-of-911-americas-emergency-service-before-and-after-kitty-genovese/.

38 The Associate Press—NORC Center for Public Affairs Research, supra note 36 (Blacks are three-and-a-half times more likely to be extremely or very worried about violent crime than Whites are).

39 Nikole Hannah-Jones, supra note 1.

40 Interview with Shauna-Kaye Spencer, February 27, 2019 (recording on file with the author). Ms. Spencer is a former student of the author.

41 Matthew Desmond, Andrew V. Papachristos, and David S. Kirk, Police Violence and Citizen Crime Reporting in the Black Community, 81 American Sociological Review 857–76 (2016), accessed at http://journals.sagepub.com/doi/10.1177/0003122416663494 (abstract).

42 John Diedrich, "Police Suspected in Frank Jude's Beating, Milwaukee Journal-Sentinel, February 6, 2005, accessed at https://www.jsonline.com/story/news/investigations/2016/09/29/archive-police-suspected-frank-judes-beating/91253086/.

CHAPTER 9   IF HE DIDN'T DO ANYTHING, THEN WHY DID HE RUN?

1 "Officers in Jordan Miles Case to Be Reinstated," KDKA Television, May 5, 2011, at https://pittsburgh.cbslocal.com/2011/05/05/officers-in-jordan-miles-case-to-be-reinstated/.

2 For example, "Understanding the Stress Response: Chronic Activation of This Survival Mechanism Impairs Health," Harvard Health Publishing, Harvard Medical

School, May 1, 2018, accessed at https://www.health.harvard.edu/staying-healthy/ understanding-the-stress-response ("A stressful incident can make the heart pound and breathing quicken. Muscles tense and beads of sweat appear. This combination of reactions to stress is also known as the 'fight-or-flight' response because it evolved as a survival mechanism, enabling people and other mammals to react quickly to life-threatening situations. The carefully orchestrated yet near-instantaneous sequence of hormonal changes and physiological responses helps someone to fight the threat off or flee to safety.")

3 In fact, this is the very argument made by one of the lawyers, James Wymard, in his defense of one of the three officers. See Chapter 10, infra.

4 Rod K. Brunson, " 'Police Don't Like Black People': African-American Young Men's Accumulated Police Experiences," 6 Criminology & Public Policy 71, 71–102 (2007), accessed at https://www.ncjrs.gov/App/Publications/abstract.aspx?ID=239773.

5 Id. at 72.

6 Id.

7 Id. at 74. According to Brunson, Hispanics were also more likely to hear these kinds of stories than were whites.

8 Joe R. Feagin and Melvin P. Sikes, *Living with Racism: The Black Middle-Class Experience* 16 (Beacon Press, 1994).

9 Lois Weis and Michelle Fine, "Narrating the 1980s and 1990s: Voices of Poor and Working-Class White and African American Men," 27 Anthropology & Education Quarterly 505 (1996).

10 Id. at 510.

11 Id.

12 Id. at 511.

13 Raja Staggers-Hakim, "The Nation's Unprotected Children and the Ghost of Mike Brown, or the Impact of National Police Killings on the Health and Social Development of African American Boys," 26 Journal of Human Behavior in the Social Environment 390–99, 393, accessed at https://www.tandfonline.com/doi/abs/10.1080/10911359.2015.1132864?journalCode=whum20.

14 Id. at 396.

15 Id. at 394.

16 Id.

17 Id.

18 Id.

19 Id.

20 Kai El'Zabar, "Why Do Black Men Run from Police?" Chicago Defender, May 20, 2015.

21 Rod K. Brunson and Ronald Weitzer, "Police Relations with Black and White Youth in Different Urban Neighborhoods," 44 Urban Affairs Review 858–85, 869–70 (2009), accessed at https://www.researchgate.net/publication/249734933_Police_Relations_With_Black_and_White_Youths_in_Different_Urban_Neighborhoods.

22 Id. at 869.

23 Id.

24 Id. at 870.

25 Ronald Weitzer and Rod K. Brunson, "Strategic Responses to the Police Among Inner-City Youth," 50 Sociological Quarterly 235–56, 244 (2009), accessed at file:///C:/Users/Harris/Downloads/SSRN-id2049917.pdf.

26 Rod K. Brunson, supra note 4, at 88.

27 See, for example, David A. Harris, PROFILES IN INJUSTICE: WHY RACIAL PROFILING CANNOT Work (The New Press, 2002); Frank Baumgartner, Derek A. Epp, and Kelsey Shoub, SUSPECT CITIZENS: WHAT 20 MILLION TRAFFIC STOPS TELL US ABOUT POLICING AND RACE (2018).

28 Raja Staggers-Hakim, supra note 13, at 395.

29 Tess Martin, "'The Talk' Is Different for Parents of Black Kids," Medium, April 3, 2018, at https://medium.com/@tessintrovert/the-talk-is-different-for-parents-of-black-kids-77d5e8238c64.

30 Id.

31 Raja Staggers-Hakim, supra note 13, at 395.

32 Id.

33 Ronald Weitzer and Rod K. Brunson, supra note 25, at 250.

34 Kai El'Zabar, supra note 20.

35 Id.

36 Raja Staggers-Hakim, supra note 13, at 395.

37 Ronald Weitzer and Rod K. Brunson, supra note 25, at 250.

38 John Eligon, "For Some, Running from Police Is the Norm," N.Y. Times, May 11, 2015.

39 Kai El'Zabar, supra note 20.

40 Rod K. Brunson and Ronald Weitzer, supra note 21, at 874.

41 Ronald Weitzer and Rod K. Brunson, supra note 25, at 241.

42 Id.

CHAPTER 10 THE FIRST TRIAL: JORDAN'S CASE

1 Id. at 8.

2 *Batson v. Kentucky*, 476 U.S. 79 (1986).

3 *J.E.B. v. Alabama ex rel. T.B.*, 511 U.S. 127 (1994).

4 Jordan Miles v. Michael Saldutte et al., Civ. No. 10–1135, Transcript of Proceedings held on July 17, 2012, U.S. District Court, Pittsburgh, PA, at 14.

5 Id. at 15–18.

6 Id. at 19.

7 Id. at 5.

8 Id. at 23–28.

9 Id. at 28–31.

10 Id. at 30.

11 Id. at 33–34.

12 Id.

13 Id. at 35–36.

14 Id. at 36–37.

15 Id. at 37.

16 Id. at 41.
17 Id. at 47.
18 Id. at 52.
19 Id. at 52–54.
20 Id. at 57–58.
21 Id. at 61–62.
22 Id. at 62.
23 Id. at 65.
24 Id. at 66–67.
25 Id. at 68–71.
26 Id. at 75.
27 Id. at 79–80.
28 Id. at 76.
29 Id. at 77.
30 Id. at 75.
31 Interview with Bryan Campbell, September 8, 2016, Pittsburgh, Pennsylvania (Campbell states that he has been the attorney for Pittsburgh's FOP unit for 45 years) (copy on file with the author).
32 Id. at 83–92.
33 *Jordan Miles v. Michael Saldutte et al.*, Civ. No. 10-1135, Transcript of Proceedings held on July 18, 2012, U.S. District Court, Pittsburgh, PA at 21–22.
34 Id. at 22–23.
35 Id. at 27.
36 Id. at 28–29.
37 Id. at 31, 35.
38 Id. at 32.
39 Id. at 42.
40 Id. at 44–45.
41 Id. at 49.
42 Id. at 56, 66.
43 Id. at 68–69.
44 John Henry Wigmore, 5 EVIDENCE Sec. 1367 p. 32 (Chadbourn revision, 1974).
45 Transcript of Proceedings held on July 18, 2012, supra note 33, at 77–78.
46 Id. at 80–81.
47 Id. at 93.
48 Id. at 76.
49 Id. at 101.
50 Id. at 134–35.
51 Id. at 136.
52 Id. at 141–42.
53 Id. at 143.
54 Id. at 151.
55 Id.
56 Id. at 157.
57 Id. at 161.
58 Id. at 164.

59 Id. at 175.
60 Id. at 176.
61 Id. at 187–88.
62 Id. at 195.
63 Id. at 198.
64 *Jordan Miles v. Michael Saldutte et al.*, Civ. No. 10-1135, Transcript of Proceedings held on July 19, 2012, U.S. District Court, Pittsburgh, at 17–19.
65 Id. at 19–21.
66 Id. at 21–24.
67 Id. at 27.
68 Id. at 33.
69 Id. at 40–41.
70 Id. at 41–42.
71 Id. at 43–45.
72 Id. at 46.
73 Id. at 49–51.
74 Id. at 51–52.
75 Id. at 54.
76 Id.
77 Id. at 55–57.
78 Id. at 58.
79 Id. at 63–64.
80 Id. at 66–67.
81 Id. at 67–68.
82 Id. at 71.
83 Id. at 77–82.
84 Id. 83–84.
85 Id. at 84–86.
86 Id. at 117–19.
87 Id. at 101–2 (italics added).
88 Id. at 117 (italics added).
89 Id. at 120–21 (italics added).
90 Id. at 177; *Jordan Miles v. Michael Saldutte et al.*, Civ. No. 10-1135, Transcript of Proceedings held on July 23, 2012, U.S. District Court, Pittsburgh, at 21.
91 Id. at 24–27.
92 Id. at 32.
93 Id. at 38–39.
94 Id. at 45.
95 Id. at 54.
96 *Jordan Miles v. Michael Saldutte et al.*, Civ. No. 10-1135, Transcript of Proceedings held on July 24, 2012, U.S. District Court, Pittsburgh.
97 *Jordan Miles v. Michael Saldutte et al.*, Civ. No. 10-1135, Deposition of Nathan Harper, June 16, 2011, at 128–29.
98 *Jordan Miles v. Michael Saldutte et al.*, Civ. No. 10-1135, Transcript of Proceedings held on July 24, 2012, U.S. District Court, Pittsburgh, at 29–30.
99 Id. at 33.

100 Id. at 30.
101 Id. at 38–39.
102 Id. at 42–43.
103 Id. at 44–45.
104 Id. at 93.
105 Id. at 93–94.
106 See Chapter 3.
107 Id. at 124–26.
108 Id. at 126–27.
109 Id. at 207.
110 Id. at 211.
111 Id. at 210–11 (italics added).
112 *Jordan Miles v. Michael Saldutte et al.*, Civ. No. 10-1135, Transcript of Proceedings held on July 25, 2012, U.S. District Court, Pittsburgh. The contents of the video recordings of Leathers and Kenkel were not transcribed, and therefore the testimony in the recordings does not appear in the record of the trial itself. In-camera proceedings for the day, prior to the beginning of the day's court session, reveal that the deposition of Dr. Kenkel exposed a mistake he had made in a prior case. Because of a record-keeping foul-up, Kenkel had been asked for a report on the damages in one case by both of the parties—the plaintiff and the defendant. The requests had come in separately, and Kenkel had not realized or known that they involved the same case. The two sides submitted different information and assumptions to Dr. Kenkel, and therefore it was not surprising that he came to very different conclusions. But the outcome—the same expert, in the same case, coming to wildly different conclusions, depending on who hired him—created an appearance that could only have damaged Kenkel's credibility, even though the reasons for it (the initial mistake of accepting two sides as clients in the same case, and receiving two very different sets of facts and assumptions to go on) could be, and were, explained during the deposition. Id. at 6–9. Jordan's lawyers argued that the matter was "completely collateral" to the case, id. at 7, but Judge Lancaster allowed the jury to hear it as part of cross-examination attacking credibility. Id. at 17–18.

CHAPTER 11 THE FIRST TRIAL: THE POLICE CASE

1 *Jordan Miles v. Michael Saldutte et al.*, Civ. No. 10-1135, Transcript of Proceedings held on July 26, 2012, U.S. District Court, Pittsburgh, at 26–27.
2 Id. at 29.
3 Id. at 42.
4 Id. at 46–48.
5 Id. at 102–5.
6 Id. at 105–7.
7 Id. at 116–17.
8 Id at 117–18.
9 Id. at 119.

10 Id. at 119–20.

11 Terry v. Ohio, 392 U.S. 1 (1968).

12 Id. at 30.

13 Interview with Sheldon Williams, former Pittsburgh Police office and currently Administrative Pastor at Allegheny Center Alliance Church (notes on file with the author).

14 Interview with Assistant Superintendent Maurita Bryant, July 24, 2019 (notes on file with the author).

15 Interview with Elizabeth Pittenger, Executive Director, Citizens Police Review Board (notes on file with the author).

16 Transcript of Proceedings held on July 26, 2012, supra note 1, at 120–21.

17 Id. at 121–22.

18 Id. at 122.

19 Id. at 134.

20 Id. at 137.

21 Id. at 138–39.

22 Id. at 139–40.

23 Id. at 140–41.

24 Id. at 150.

25 Id. at 165.

26 Id. at 183–84.

27 *Jordan Miles v. Michael Saldutte et al.*, Civ. No. 10-1135, Transcript of Proceedings held on July 30, 2012, U.S. District Court, Pittsburgh, at 102.

28 Id. at 102–3.

29 Id. at 104–5.

30 Id. at 118–19.

31 Id. at 120–21.

32 Id. at 125–26.

33 Id. at 126–28.

34 *Jordan Miles v. Michael Saldutte et al.*, Civ. No. 10-1135, Transcript of Proceedings held on July 31, 2012, U.S. District Court, Pittsburgh, at 27–31.

35 Id. at 117–18.

36 *Jordan Miles v. Michael Saldutte et al.*, Civ. No. 10-1135, Transcript of Proceedings held on August 1, 2012, U.S. District Court, Pittsburgh, at 150–78.

37 Id. at 167–69.

38 *Jordan Miles v. Michael Saldutte et al.*, Civ. No. 10-1135, Transcript of Proceedings held on August 2–3, 2012, U.S. District Court, Pittsburgh, at 3–16.

39 Id. at 18.

40 Id. at 21.

41 Id. at 22.

42 Id. at 48–49.

43 Id. at 48–50.

44 Id. at 53, 67, 68.

45 Id. at 65–66.

46 Id. at 55.

47 Id. at 69.

48 Id. at 71.
49 Id. at 73.
50 Id. at 62–64.
51 Id. at 75.
52 Id. at 75.
53 Id. at 84–90.
54 Id. at 93.
55 Id. at 98–99.
56 Id. at 100, 103.
57 Id. at 104.
58 Id. at 112–13.
59 Id. at 118.
60 Id. at 123.
61 Id. at 120.
62 Id. at 134–135.
63 Id. at 138.
64 *Jordan Miles v. Michael Saldutte et al.*, Civ. No. 10-1135, Transcript of Proceedings held on August 6–7, 2012, U.S. District Court, Pittsburgh, at 2.
65 Id. at 10–11 (italics added).
66 Id. at 15.
67 *Jordan Miles v. Michael Saldutte et al.*, Civ. No. 10-1135, Transcript of Proceedings held on August 8, 2012, U.S. District Court, Pittsburgh, at 2.
68 Id. at 6.
69 Rich Lord, and Sadie Gurman, "Jordan Miles Jury Finds for Pittsburgh Police in Partial Verdict," August 9, 2012, accessed at https://www.post-gazette.com/local/city/2012/08/08/Jordan-Miles-jury-finds-for-Pittsburgh-police-in-partial-verdict/stories/201208080180.
70 Joe Mandak, "Cops Accused of Beating Jordan Miles, Pittsburgh Teen, Cleared of Malicious Prosecution Charge," Associated Press, August 8, 2012.
71 Brian Bowling, "Family of Jordan Miles Releases Statement, Calls Police Officers 'Thugs,'" Pittsburgh Tribune Review, August 9, 2012, accessed at https://archive.triblive.com/local/pittsburgh-allegheny/family-of-jordan-miles-releases-statement-calls-police-officers-thugs/.
72 Joe Mandak, supra note 70.
73 Rich Lord and Sadie Gurman, supra note 68.
74 Joe Mandak, supra note 69.
75 Id.
76 Sadie Gurman, "Jordan Miles' Mother 'Shocked and Disappointed' at Split Verdict," Pittsburgh Post-Gazette, August 10, 2012, at http://www.post-gazette.com/local/city/2012/08/09/Jordan-Miles-mother-shocked-and-disappointed-at-split-verdict/stories/201208090337.
77 Brian Bowling, supra note 71.
78 Brian Bowling, "Miles Juror Agreed Police Officers Made 'Mistakes,' Foreman Says," Pittsburgh Tribune-Review, August 16, 2012.
79 Id.

CHAPTER 12 THE SECOND TRIAL

1 Michael Hasch and Bobby Kerlik, "Gary Lancaster, Chief U.S. Judge for Western Pa., Dead at 63," Pittsburgh Tribune Review, April 24, 2013, accessed at https://triblive.com/news/adminpage/3906347-74/district-chief-died.

2 Brian Bowling, "Context Key to 2d Trial of Pittsburgh Police Offices in Homewood Man's Arrest," Pittsburgh Tribune Review, March 3, 2014, accessed at https://triblive.com/news/allegheny/5717541-74/officers-trial-police.

3 Rich Lord, "Judge Won't Allow Past Complaints Against Officers as Evidence in Jordan Miles Civil Trial," Pittsburgh Post-Gazette, March 7, 2014, accessed at http://www.post-gazette.com/local/city/2014/03/07/Judge-wont-allow-past-complaints-against-officers-as-evidence-in-Jordan-Miles-civil-trial/stories/201403070181.

4 Id. (quoting judge's order).

5 Alex Zimmerman, "99 Problems: Run-in With Jordan Miles Wasn't First Controversial Incident for Three 99-car Cops," Pittsburgh City Paper, December 17, 2014, accessed at https://www.pghcitypaper.com/pittsburgh/99-problems-run-in-with-jordan-miles-wasnt-first-controversial-incident-for-three-99-car-cops/Content?oid=1797137&storyPage=2.

6 Id.

7 Id.

8 Id.

9 Id.

10 See, for example, Feiger Law, "Famous Cases," accessed at https://www.fiegerlaw.com/case-results/famous-cases/.

11 Brian Bowling, supra note 2.

12 Rebecca Nuttall, "Commander RaShall Brackney Testifies Regarding Police Procedures in Jordan Miles Civil Trial," Pittsburgh City Paper, March 18, 2018, accessed at https://www.pghcitypaper.com/Blogh/archives/2014/03/18/commander-rashall-brackney-testifies-regarding-police-procedures-in-jordan-miles-civil-trial.

13 Rich Lord, supra note 3.

14 See Chapter 10.

15 Id.

16 "'I'm a Broken Man': Ex-Pittsburgh Police Chief Sentenced to Prison," WPXI, February 25, 2014, accessed at https://www.wpxi.com/news/local/ex-pittsburgh-chief-facing-fed-prison-or-probation/140348696.

17 Id.

18 Harper was released from prison in May of 2015. Luke Nozicka, "Former Pittsburgh Police Chief Nate Harper Released from Prison," Pittsburgh, Post-Gazette, May 30, 2015, accessed at http://www.post-gazette.com/local/city/2015/05/30/Former-Pittsburgh-police-chief-Nate-Harper-released-from-prison/stories/201505300157.

19 Joe Mandak, "Opening Statements Set in Jordan Miles Police Beating Trial," Associated Press, March 11, 2014, accessed at https://newpittsburghcourier.com/2014/03/11/opening-statements-set-in-jordan-miles-police-beating-trial/.

20 Rich Lord, "Jury Selection Completed in Jordan Miles' Civil Case Against Police Officers," Pittsburgh Post-Gazette, March 10, 2014, accessed at

https://www.post-gazette.com/local/region/2014/03/10/Jury-selection-underway-in-Jordan-Miles-civil-case-against-police-officers/stories/201403100129.

21 *Jordan Miles v. Michael Saldutte, David Sisak, and Richard Ewing*, Civ. Action No. 10-1135, U.S. District Court, W. Dist. Pa., transcript excerpt, Opening Statement of Robert Giroux, March 11, 2014, at 2–4.

22 Id. at 10.

23 *Jordan Miles v. Michael Saldutte, David Sisak, and Richard Ewing*, Civil Action No. 10-1135, U.S. Dist. Ct., W. D. Pa., transcript excerpt, Trial Testimony of Jordan Miles, March 20, 2014, excerpted pages 276–534.

24 Id. at 320–23.

25 Id. at 325.

26 Id. at 323.

27 Id. at 333.

28 Id. at 322.

29 Id. at 334–35.

30 Id. at 446.

31 Id.

32 Id. at 447.

33 Rich Lord, "Jordan Miles 'Had No Idea Those Were Police Officers,'" Pittsburgh Post-Gazette, March 20, 2014, accessed at https://www.post-gazette.com/local/city/2014/03/20/Miles-testifies-about-his-encounter-with-police-at-trial-seeking-damages-for-abuse/stories/201403200269.

34 Id. at 448.

35 Rich Lord and Liz Navratil, "Last of Three Officers Testifies in Jordan Miles Civil Case," Pittsburgh Post-Gazette, March 18, 2014, accessed at https://www.post-gazette.com/local/city/2014/03/18/Last-of-three-officers-testifies-in-Jordan-Miles-civil-case/stories/201403180148.

36 Liz Navratil, "Police Say They Were Suspicious of Jordan Miles, Believe He Had a Gun," Pittsburgh Post-Gazette, March 13, 2014, accessed at https://www.post-gazette.com/local/city/2014/03/13/Officer-in-Jordan-Miles-case-said-he-grew-suspicious-talking-to-suspect/stories/201403130296.

37 *Jordan Miles v. Michael Saldutte, David Sisak, and Richard Ewing*, Civil Action No. 10-1135, U.S. Dist. Ct., W. D. Pa., transcript excerpt, Trial Testimony of RaShall Brackney, March 18, 2014, excerpted pages 173–274.

38 Id. at 176–78.

39 Id. at 178.

40 Id. at 174–75.

41 Id. at 179–180.

42 Id. at 180.

43 Id. at 181. Brackney was asked on cross-examination about a deadly attack on three Pittsburgh Police officers in Zone 5: the 2009 ambush assault in which three officers were killed. Id. at 271. She said that this had happened, of course; the point seemed to be that there could in fact be grave danger to officers in Zone 5. Perhaps this would make all Pittsburgh officers feel danger, but the idea seemed both inaccurate and overplayed. Brackney had testified not that Zone 5 was not dangerous for officers, but that Homewood—one of many neighborhoods in Zone 5—was far from the

most dangerous. And in point of fact, the horrific 2009 killings of the three officers happened in another Zone 5 neighborhood, Stanton Heights—a place known as a relatively safe area, in which many Pittsburgh police officers live.

44 Id. at 187–89.

45 Id. at 188–89.

46 Id. at 225–26.

47 Id. at 228.

48 Id. at 228–30.

49 Id. at 230–34.

50 Id. at 235.

51 Id. at 256.

52 Rich Lord, "No Talk of Gun at Jordan Miles Scene, Officer Says," Pittsburgh Post-Gazette, March 12, 2014, accessed at http://www.post-gazette.com/local/city/2014/03/12/Testimony-in-Jordan-Miles-trial-focuses-on-the-night-of-his-arrest/stories/201403120158.

53 Id.

54 Id.

55 Id.

56 Horak also testified that he had turned Jordan Miles around toward the house in front of which he was arrested for a woman looking out the second floor window, so she could see the person (Jordan) and identify him as someone who had, or had not, permission to be near her house; she said she did not know the man. The woman, Monica Wooding, testified in both the first and the second trial that that did not happen and that she would have known Jordan by sight.

57 Brian Bowling, "Lawyers Question Miles' Believability in Closing Arguments," Pittsburgh Tribune-Review, March 27, 2014, accessed at https://www.wpxi.com/news/local/closing-arguments-set-pittsburgh-police-retrial/139764201.

58 Id.

59 Harold Hayes, "Closing Arguments Conclude in Civil Re-trial of 3 City Officers," KDKA Television, March 27, 2014, accessed at https://pittsburgh.cbslocal.com/2014/03/27/closing-arguments-underway-in-civil-re-trial-of-3-city-officers/.

60 Id.

61 Id.

62 Rich Lord, "Jury Asks Questions during Deliberations in Jordan Miles Civil Trial," Pittsburgh Post-Gazette, March 28, 2014, accessed at https://pittsburgh.cbslocal.com/2014/03/28/jury-in-jordan-miles-civil-case-asks-to-hear-portions-of-testimony-again/. Among the read-back snippets of testimony was a section in which defense attorney Wymard appeared to get Jordan to admit that one of the officers had asked him, "where do you live?" This seemed to contradict Jordan's testimony that there was no such exchange. The defense believed that this put the lie to Jordan's entire defense and therefor it foretold a verdict in their favor. Id. But the eventual verdict did not reflect that.

63 Deanna Garcia, "Jury Reaches Mixed Decision in Jordan Miles Suit," WESA FM, March 31, 2014, accessed at https://www.wesa.fm/post/jury-reaches-mixed-decision-jordan-miles-suit/.

64 Id.

65 Rich Lord and Liz Navratil, "Jordan Miles Jury Reaches Split Verdict," Pittsburgh Post-Gazette, March 31, 2014, accessed at https://www.post-gazette.com/local/city/2014/03/31/Jury-reaches-verdict-in-Jordan-Miles-civil-trial/stories/201403310142.

66 Id.

67 Deanna Garcia, supra note 63.

68 Rich Lord and Liz Navratil, supra note 65.

69 Deanna Garcia, supra note 63.

70 Rebecca Nuttall, "After Split Verdict, Attorneys in Jordan Miles Trial Look Ahead," Pittsburgh City Paper, March 31, 2014, accessed at https://www.pghcitypaper.com/Blogh/archives/2014/03/31/after-split-verdict-attorneys-in-jordan-miles-trial-look-ahead.

71 "Feds Won't Reopen Pittsburgh Police Rights Probe," Associated Press, April 1, 2014, accessed at https://newpittsburghcourier.com/2014/04/01/feds-wont-reopen-pittsburgh-police-rights-probe/.

72 Rebecca Nuttall, "Fight over Miles Verdict Continues," Pittsburgh City Paper, April 30, 2014, accessed at https://www.pghcitypaper.com/Blogh/archives/2014/04/30/fight-over-miles-verdict-continues.

73 Brian Bowling, "Lawyers on Both Sides of Miles Case Ask Judge to Reconsider Jury's Verdict," Pittsburgh Tribune-Review, April 26, 2014.

74 Id.

75 Rebecca Nuttall, supra note 72.

76 Brian Bowling, "Judge Upholds Jury Verdict, Damage Award in Miles Case," Pittsburgh Tribune-Review, June 18, 2014.

77 Id.

78 Rich Lord, "Judge Says Jury's Decisions in Jordan Miles Case Will Stand," Pittsburgh Post-Gazette, June 18, 2014.

79 Brian Bowling, supra at 76.

80 Brian Bowling, "Federal Judge Cuts into Damage Award in Jordan Miles Case," Pittsburgh Tribune-Review, August 20, 2014.

81 Andy Sheehan, "Racism Allegations Could Prompt New Trial in Jordan Miles Case," KDKA Television, August 25, 2015, accessed at https://pittsburgh.cbslocal.com/2015/08/25/racism-allegations-could-prompt-new-trial-in-jordan-miles-case/; Bob Mayo, "Jordan Miles Seeks New Trial in Civil Rights Lawsuit v. City Police," WTAE Television, August 25, 2015, accessed at https://www.wtae.com/article/jordan-miles-seeks-new-trial-in-civil-rights-lawsuit-vs-city-police/7164830.

82 Id.

83 Andy Sheehan, supra note 81.

84 Lexi Belculfine, "Pittsburgh Council Could Settle With Jordan Miles for $125,000," Pittsburgh Post-Gazette, May 24, 2016, accessed at https://www.post-gazette.com/local/city/2016/05/24/City-could-settle-with-Jordan-Miles-for-125-000/stories/201605240075.

85 Bob Bauder, "Pittsburgh Poised to Settle with Jordan Miles Over Police Beating for $125K," Pittsburgh Tribune-Review, May 23, 2016, accessed at https://archive.triblive.com/news/pittsburgh-poised-to-settle-with-jordan-miles-over-police-beating-for-125k/?printerfriendly=true.

86 Lexi Belculfine, "Pittsburgh Council Approves $125,000 Settlement with Jordan Miles," Pittsburgh Post-Gazette, June 8, 2016, accessed at http://www.post-gazette.com/local/city/2016/06/08/Pittsburgh-council-approves-125-000-settlement-with-Jordan-Miles/stories/201606070209.

87 Id.

CHAPTER 13 WHAT CAN WE DO?

1 The focus on public safety (as opposed to simply limiting the harm done by policing) should perhaps be obvious, but it has received new attention from the policing scholar Barry Friedman. See Barry Friedman, "Reimagining Public Safety," 2019, unpublished manuscript, at p. 2 (copy on file with the author).

2 Commentators on the Principles have long suspected that Peel himself did not write them, though he is said to have discussed them often. Susan A. Lentz and Robert H. Chaires, "The Invention of Peel's Principles: A Study of Policing 'Textbook' History," 35 Journal of Criminal Justice 69–79 (2007), accessed at 10.1016/j.jcrimjus.2006.11.016.

3 For one web-based version of these nine principles, see "Sir Robert Peel's Principles of Law Enforcement, 1829," accessed at https://www.durham.police.uk/About-Us/Documents/Peels_Principles_Of_Law_Enforcement.pdf (italics in original of this document).

4 Id.

5 Id. at Number 1.

6 Id. at Number 2.

7 Final Report, The President's Task Force on 21st Century Policing 11 (May, 2015).

8 Id.

9 The foundational text in the field is Tom R. Tyler, WHY PEOPLE OBEY THE LAW (Yale University Press, 1990).

10 Final Report, The President's Task Force, supra note 7, at 9–11.

11 Lorraine Mazerolle, Sarah Bennett, Jacqueline Davis, Elise Sargeant, and Matthew Manning, "Legitimacy in Policing: A Systemic Review," The Campbell Collection Library of Systemic Reviews 9 (The Campbell Collaboration 2013).

12 Kimberly Kindy, "Creating Guardians, Calming Warriors," Washington Post, December 10, 2015, accessed at https://www.washingtonpost.com/sf/investigative/2015/12/10/new-style-of-police-training-aims-to-produce-guardians-not-warriors/?utm_term=.2180b01e6466.

13 Id.

14 Sue Rahr and Stephen K. Rice, "From Warriors to Guardians: Recommitting American Police Culture to Democratic Ideals," U.S. Department's National Institute of Justice and Harvard's Kennedy School of Government Program in Criminal Justice and Policy Management, New Perspectives in Policing Series, April 2015, accessed at https://www.ncjrs.gov/pdffiles1/nij/248654.pdf.

15 Jim Glennon, ARRESTING COMMUNICATION: ESSENTIAL INTERACTION SKILLS FOR LAW ENFORCEMENT 35, LifeLine Training (2010).

16 The author heard Professor Alpert discuss this concept at a conference at the University of South Carolina School of Law on March 1, 2019 called "The Law of the Police." Notes on file with the author.

17 Graham v. Connor, 490 U.S. 386 (1989).

18 Id. at 396–97.

19 Geoff Alpert, Kyle McLean, Carol Naoroz, and Arif Alikhan, "Research in Brief: Toward a Threat Analysis Model (TAM) of Force," Police Chief Magazine, accessed at http://www.policechiefmagazine.org/rib-toward-a-tam-of-force/.

20 Id. at 2.

21 Id. at 3.

22 Id.

23 Id.

24 Id. at 3–4.

25 These five points represent my views on what the basics of community policing are; I have articulated some of this elsewhere. For example, David A. Harris, GOOD COPS: THE CASE FOR PREVENTIVE POLICING 23–26 (2005). One can find many other views, though most have some or all of these elements in common. For example, Community Policing Consortium, "Understanding Community Policing: A Framework for Action," August, 1994, NCJ 148457, accessed at https://www.ncjrs.gov/pdffiles/commp.pdf; Robert Trojanowicz and Bonnie Bucqueroux, COMMUNITY POLICING: A CONTEMPORARY PERSPECTIVE (1990).

26 Lacretia Wimbley, "Hands Down, Let's Talk: City Police Seek to Ease Tensions Between Youth, Officers," Pittsburgh Post-Gazette, March 15, 2019, accessed at https://www.post-gazette.com/local/city/2019/03/15/Hands-down-lets-talk-Pittsburgh-police-Homewood-tensions-engagement-sessions/stories/201903150096.

27 Id.

28 Id. Since this description of the program was written, Commander Lando has been transferred within the Pittsburgh Police department to another assignment.

29 See, for example, Black History Album, "Birmingham Dog Attacks," https://i.pinimg.com/originals/95/ef/b5/95efb52754136f4715590f6016d51f14.jpg; Smithsonian Institute Learning Lab, "The Civil Rights Movement in Pittsburgh," https://learninglab.si.edu/collections/civil-rights-movement-in-pittsburgh/6aJKMy8N2YYBXkFW#r/29975; PBS, "The Rage and Rebellion of Detroit," https://d3i6fh83elv35t.cloudfront.net/newshour/app/uploads/2015/05/460590080-1024x821.jpg; All That's Interesting, "The Civil Rights Movement in 55 Powerful Images," https://allthatsinteresting.com/wordpress/wp-content/uploads/2017/05/cop-and-young-protester.jpg.

30 Two books—one more than a decade and a half old, the other much more recent—make this very point. David A. Harris, PROFILES IN INJUSTICE: WHY RACIAL PROFILING CANNOT WORK (2002); Frank R. Baumgartner, Kelsey Shoub, and Derek A. Epp, SUSPECT CITIZENS: WHAT 20 MILLION TRAFFIC STOPS TELL US ABOUT POLICING AND RACE (2018).

31 Roman Gessier, "Face Up to Racist Legacy, Police-Community Relations Experts Say," The Crime Report, March 13, 2019, accessed at https://thecrimereport.org/2019/03/13/can-acknowledging-u-s-racism-transform-police-community-relations/

32 STATEMENT of CH. CUNNINGHAM IACP; Hannah Koslowska, "A Major Police Organization Has Issued a Formal Apology to Minorities for 'Historical Mistreatment,'" Quartz, October 17, 2016, accessed at https://qz.com/811672/the-iacp-a-major-police-organization-has-issued-a-formal-apology-to-minorities-for-historical-mistreatment/.

33 Id.

34 Elliot Spagat, "IACP President Apologizes for 'Historical Mistreatment' of Minorities," PoliceOne, October 18, 2016, accessed at https://www.policeone.com/officer-shootings/articles/232664006-IACP-President-apologizes-for-historical-mistreatment-of-minorities/.

35 Id.

36 Id.

37 Roman Gessier, supra note 31, at 3.

38 Id. at 4.

39 Graham v. Connor, 490 U.S. 386 (1989).

40 Tatyana Hopkins, "GW Law Professor Crafts Police Use of Force Legislation," GW Today, March 20, 2019, accessed at https://gwtoday.gwu.edu/gw-law-professor-crafts-police-use-force-legislation.

41 Cynthia Lee, "Testimony to the House Judiciary Committee, Maryland Legislature, Re: H.B. 1121," March 12, 2019 (copy on file with the author).

42 Id. at 2.

43 J.B. Wogan, "How Police Chiefs Plan to Avoid 'Lawful But Awful' Shootings," Governing Magazine, February 2, 2016, accessed at https://www.governing.com/topics/public-justice-safety/gov-police-chiefs-shootings.html (quoting Wexler as describing such justified but tragically avoidable shootings as "lawful but awful").

44 Police Executives Research Forum, Guiding Principles on Use of Force, Critical Issues in Policing Series, March 2016, accessed at https://www.policeforum.org/assets/30%20guiding%20principles.pdf.

45 Assembly Bill No. 392, California Legislature—2019–2020 Regular Session, February 6, 2019, accessed at https://leginfo.legislature.ca.gov/faces/billNavClient.xhtml?bill_id=201920200AB392.

46 Robert Salonga, "New Police Alliance Emerges in Opposition to California Use of Force Bill," Enterprise Record, March 4, 2019, accessed at https://www.chicoer.com/2019/03/04/new-police-alliance-emerges-in-opposition-to-california-use-of-force-bill/; Peace Officers Research Association of California, "Comprehensive Use-of-Force Legislation," February 5, 2019, accessed at https://porac.org/wp-content/uploads/PORAC-UOF-press-release-Final-public-2.11.19.pdf (announcing support, along with California Police Chiefs Association, for a competing bill that would support other measures but would not mandate any change in use of force standard).

47 Hannah Wiley, "All That's Left to Overhaul California's Police Use-of-Force Law Is Gavin Newsome's Signature," Sacramento Bee, July 8, 2019, accessed at https://www.sacbee.com/news/politics-government/capitol-alert/article232424862.html.

48 House Bill 1121, A Bill Entitled an Act Concerning Criminal Procedure—Law Enforcement Procedures—Use of Force, February 8, 2019, accessed at https://legiscan.com/MD/text/HB1121/id/1901640/Maryland-2019-HB1121-Introduced.pdf.

49 Id.
50 Id. When the Maryland legislature adjourned in the spring of 2019, H.B. 1121 (and all other pending bills) expired and will have to be reintroduced again in order to have a chance at becoming law.
51 Cynthia Lee, "Reforming the Law on Police Use of Deadly Force: De-Escalation, Preseizure Conduct, and Imperfect Self Defense," 2018 UNIVERSITY OF ILLINOIS LAW REVIEW 629.
52 Tatyana Hopkins, supra note 40, at 2.
53 Id.
54 18 U.S. Code Section 242, "Deprivation of Rights Under Color of Law," accessed at https://www.law.cornell.edu/uscode/text/18/242.
55 Screws v. U.S., 325 U.S. 91 (1945).
56 See, for example, Michigan Penal Code Section 750.316 (1) (a) (first-degree murder); New York Penal Law Section 125.25 (A) (1) (second-degree murder); California Penal Code Section 192 (a) (voluntary manslaughter, in killings "upon sudden quarrel or heat of passion"); California Penal Law Section 192 (b) (involuntary manslaughter, in killings "without due caution and circumspection").
57 Rick Noack and Shibani Mahtani, "New Zealand Just Banned Military-Style Firearms. Here's Why the U.S. Can't," Washington Post, March 21, 2019, accessed at https://www.washingtonpost.com/world/2019/03/21/why-new-zealand-could-do-what-us-cant-change-gun-laws-face-tragedy/
58 Grace Wyler, "Why Congress Was Too Wimpy to Pass a Gun Control Bill That Almost Everyone in American Wants," Business Insider, April 18, 2013, accessed at https://www.businessinsider.com/why-background-check-bill-failed-2013-4.
59 District of Columbia v. Heller, 554 U.S. 570 (2008).
60 Id at 1–54.
61 Id. at 54–55.
62 McDonald v. City of Chicago, 561 U.S. 742 (2010).
63 Philip J. Cook and Kristin A. Goss, THE GUN DEBATE: WHAT EVERYONE NEEDS TO KNOW 141–42 (2014).
64 Pennsylvania Bd. of Probation and Parole v. Scott, 524 U.S. 357 (1998).
65 Philip J. Cook and Kristin Goss, supra note 63, at 146–48.
66 Tal Kopan and Eugene Scott, "North Carolina Governor Signs Controversial Transgender Bill," March 24, 2016, accessed at https://www.cnn.com/2016/03/23/politics/north-carolina-gender-bathrooms-bill/index.html. The bill was later modified, but the modification did not change the state's power to overrule its municipalities.
67 Simone Weichselbaum, "Milwaukee's Police Chief on Open-Carry Gun Laws," The Marshall Project, August 16, 2016, accessed at https://www.themarshallproject.org/2016/08/16/milwaukee-s-police-chief-on-open-carry-gun-laws.
68 Fair and Impartial Policing, accessed at https://fipolicing.com/.
69 Thomas Abt, BLEEDING OUT: THE DEVASTATING CONSEQUENCES OF URBAN VIOLENCE—AND A BOLD NEW PLAN FOR PEACE IN THE STREETS (BASIC BOOKS, 2019).
70 David A. Harris, GOOD COPS: THE CASE FOR PREVENTIVE POLICING 63–71 (The New Press, 2005).
71 Thomas Abt, supra note 69, at 6–9.

72 Id. at 24–27.

73 Id. at Chapter 3, 4, and 5.

74 Id. at Chapters 6, 7, and 8.

75 Id. at Chapters 10 and 11.

76 Kira Lerner, "What Happened the Last Time Chicago Tried to Cover Up a Major Police Scandal," Think Progress, December 7, 2015, accessed at https://thinkprogress.org/what-happened-the-last-time-chicago-tried-to-cover-up-a-major-police-scandal-4cc6b50293e4/.

77 Id.

78 Jamie Kalven, "Invisible Institute Relaunches the Citizens Police Data Project," The Intercept, August 16, 2018, accessed at https://theintercept.com/2018/08/16/invisible-institute-chicago-police-data/.

79 Id.

80 Id.

81 Id.

82 Id.

83 Id.

84 Id.

85 Rob Arthur, "130 Chicago Police Officers Account for 29 Percent of Police Shootings," The Intercept, August 16, 2018, accessed at https://theintercept.com/2018/08/16/chicago-police-department-officer-involved-shooting/.

86 Andrew Fan, "Chicago Police Are 14 Times More Likely to Use Force against Young Black Men Than against Whites," The Intercept, August 16, 2018, accessed at https://theintercept.com/2018/08/16/chicago-police-misconduct-racial-disparity/.

87 Jeffrey Fagan and Bernard Harcourt, "The New 'New Policing,'" The Marshall Project, December 19, 2014, accessed at https://www.themarshallproject.org/2014/12/19/the-new-new-policing.

EPILOGUE

1 As said at the beginning of the book, the author made attempts to contact the police officers through their attorneys, including written request to each officer sent to them in care of the attorney for each one. No reply ever came.

2 "1 of 3 Cops in Jordan Miles Beating Case Quits Force," WTAE Television, October 23, 2012, accessed at https://www.wtae.com/article/1-of-3-cops-in-jordan-miles-beating-case-quits-force/7458660.

3 Cindy Cusic Micco, "McCandless Police Hire Officer Involved in Jordan Miles Case, Post-Gazette Reports," Patch, October 24, 2012, accessed at https://patch.com/pennsylvania/northallegheny/mccandless-police-hire-officer-involved-in-jordan-mil9fcfff0c6f.

4 2010 Census, U.S. Census Bureau, American FactFinder, accessed at https://factfinder.census.gov/faces/nav/jsf/pages/index.xhtml.

5 "McCandless Crime Rate Report (Pennsylvania)," CityRating.com, accessed at https://www.cityrating.com/crime-statistics/pennsylvania/mccandless.html (the "violent crime rate for McCandless in 2016 was lower than the national violent crime

rate average [sic] by 88.67% and the city property crime rate in McCandless was lower than the national property crime rate average [sic] by 67.95%").

6 Pittsburgh Crime Rate Report (Pennsylvania), accessed at https://www.cityrating. com/crime-statistics/pennsylvania/pittsburgh.html ("The city violent crime rate for Pittsburgh in 2016 was higher than the national violent crime rate average [sic] by 97.01% and the city property crime rate in Pittsburgh was higher than the national property crime rate average [sic] by 33.13%.").

7 McCandless, Pennsylvania Police Department, accessed at https://www. townofmccandless.org/police-department.

8 Shelly Bradbury, "McCandless Police Officers Vote 'No Confidence' in Chief under Investigation," Pittsburgh Post-Gazette, December 5, 2018, accessed at https://www. post-gazette.com/local/north/2018/12/05/McCandless-police-officers-vote-no-confidence-in-chief/stories/201812050181.

9 Telephone inquiry with Pittsburgh Bureau of Police Administration, March 26, 2019 (notes on file with the author).

10 Rich Lord, "Former Pittsburgh Police Chief Harper Gets 18-month Prison Sentence," Pittsburgh Post-Gazette, February 25, 2014, accessed at https://www. post-gazette.com/local/city/2014/02/25/Former-Pittsburgh-police-chief-Nathan-Harper-sentenced/stories/201402250123.

11 Luke Nozicka, "Former Pittsburgh Police Chief Nate Harper Released from Prison," Pittsburgh Post-Gazette, May 30, 2015, accessed at https://www.post-gazette.com/ local/city/2015/05/30/Former-Pittsburgh-police-chief-Nate-Harper-released-from-prison/stories/201505300157.

12 This information came from a source known to former Chief Harper on April 17, 2019. Confidential notes on file with the author.

13 Dani Grace, "UPD Chief, Assistant Chief, to Resign Next Week," GW Hatchet, January 8, 2018, accessed at https://www.gwhatchet.com/2018/01/08/upd-chief-assistant-chief-to-resign-next-week/.

14 "Charlottesville Hires First Black Female Police Chief and There's Already Controversy," NewsOne, May 22, 2018, accessed at https://newsone.com/3801510/ charlottesvilles-rashall-brackney/.

15 Nolan Stout, "Charlottesville Police Department Seeing a 'Mass Exodus'," The Daily Progress, December 30, 2018, accessed at https://www.dailyprogress.com/ news/local/city/charlottesville-police-department-seeing-a-mass-exodus/article_7b6621a0-0c9c-11e9-b094-6b73c596a053.html.

16 Jamie Martines, "Turhan Jenkins to Challenge District Attorney Stephen Zappala in 2019," Pittsburgh Tribune, July 2, 2018, accessed at https://archive.triblive. com/local/allegheny/13825131-74/turahn-jenkins-to-challenge-district-attorney-stephen-zappala-in-2019.

17 Jamie Martines, supra note 16.

18 An-Li Herring, "Public Defender Lisa Middleman Announces Bid for District Attorney," WESA, June 24, 2019, accessed at https://www.wesa.fm/post/public-defender-lisa-middleman-announces-bid-district-attorney#stream/0.

19 Rich Lord, "U.S. Attorney Hickton Wins Praise for "Listening Sessions," Pittsburgh Post-Gazette, October 30, 2011, accessed at https://www.post-gazette.com/news/ nation/2011/10/30/U-S-Attorney-Hickton-wins-praise-for-listening-sessions/ stories/201110300197.

20 The author of this book was involved in the organization, formation, and activities of the Group from the beginning and remains involved at the time of this writing; the Group continues under the leadership of a new U.S. Attorney.

21 University of Pittsburgh Cyber Institute, David J. Hickton, J.D., accessed at https:// www.cyber.pitt.edu/about-institute#our_team.

22 Interview with Jordan Miles, March 25, 2019 (notes on file with the author).

23 Jordan T. Miles Cleaning Services, LLC, accessed at https://jordanmilescleaning service.com/.

24 Reverend Ricky Burgess, "What Homewood Could Be," *Pittsburgh Post-Gazette*, September 23, 2015, accessed at https://www.post-gazette.com/opinion/2015/09/23/What-Homewood-could-be/stories/201509230017.

25 Id.

26 Interview with Assistant Superintendent Maurita Bryant, July 24, 2019 (notes on file with the author).

27 Rob Taylor, "Fisher Disagrees with Comments Made by Stevens during the News Conference on Ford," *New Pittsburgh Courier*, October 18, 2017, accessed at https://newpittsburghcourieronline.com/2017/10/18/get-this-case-behind-us-new-settlement-offer-proposed/.

28 Id.

29 Christian Morrow, "Ford Acquitted of Assault Charges," *New Pittsburgh Courier*, September 17, 2014, accessed at https://newpittsburghcourieronline.com/2014/09/16/ford-acquitted-of-assault-charges-da-may-re-file-on-lessor-charges/

30 Ashley Johnson, "Ford Files Civil Suits against City Police," *New Pittsburgh Courier*, September 25, 2013, accessed at https://newpittsburghcourieronline.com/2013/09/25/ford-files-civil-suits-against-city-police/.

31 Christian Morrow, supra note 29.

32 Joe Mandak, "Lawyer: White Officer Terrorized, Paralyzed Black Man," *Philadelphia Tribune*, October 6, 2017.

33 "Settlement Reached in Pittsburgh Police Shooting," *Philadelphia Tribune*, January 23, 2018.

34 Charlie Deitch, "D.A. Zappala Dismisses Charges against Teacher Dennis Henderson," *Pittsburgh City Paper*, July 9, 2013, accessed at https://www.pghcitypaper.com/Blogh/archives/2013/07/09/da-zappala-dismisses-charges-against-teacher-dennis-henderson.

35 Id.

36 Christian Morrow, "Henderson and ACLU File Lawsuit against City and Police Officer Gromek," *New Pittsburgh Courier*, November 20, 2013.

37 Robert Zullo, "Pittsburgh to Settle Lawsuit for $52,000 with Teacher Accosted and Arrested by Police," *Pittsburgh Post-Gazette*, December 9, 2014, accessed at https://www.post-gazette.com/local/city/2014/12/09/Pittsburgh-to-settle-lawsuit-with-teacher-accosted-by-police-for-52-000/stories/201412090203. The author served as the designated expert in these talks.

38 Liz Navratil and Rich Lord, "Officer Gets Reprimand after Teacher's Arrest," *Pittsburgh Post-Gazette*, November 26, 2013, accessed at https://www.post-gazette.com/local/2013/11/26/Written-reprimand-recommended-for-Pittsburgh-police-officer-after-teacher-s-arrest/stories/201311260142.

39 Torsten Ove, "Family of Man Killed by Port Authority Police in Wilkinsburg Sues over Excessive Force Claim," *Pittsburgh Post-Gazette*, December 11, 2017, accessed

at https://www.post-gazette.com/local/east/2017/12/11/Police-excessive-force-Allegheny-County-Port-Authority-Bruce-Kelley-K-9-lawsuit-federal-court/stories/201712110160.

40 Id.

41 Paula Reed Ward, "Officers Weren't Knifed by Man Who Was Eventually Shot, County Police Say," Pittsburgh Post-Gazette, February 5, 2016, accessed at https://www.post-gazette.com/local/city/2016/02/05/Officials-clarify-no-officers-cut-in-East-Busway-scuffle-that-killed-police-K-9-man/stories/201602050246.

42 Linda Hayes-Freeland, "Bond Reduced for Father of Man Who Killed Police K-9," KDKA TV, February 18, 2016, accessed at https://pittsburgh.cbslocal.com/2016/02/18/bond-reduced-for-father-of-man-who-killed-police-k-9/ (bond, set at $300,000, reduced after three weeks to $25,000).

43 Torsten Ove, supra note 39.

44 For example, Lisa Washington, "Hundreds Attend Memorial Service for K-9 Aren," KDKA TV, accessed at https://pittsburgh.cbslocal.com/2016/02/04/k9-aren-to-be-laid-to-rest-today-after-funeral-procession/.

45 Interview with Willie West, June 16, 2017 (notes and recording on file with the author).

46 East Pittsburgh, "Demographics," accessed at http://eastpittsburghboro.com/about/demographics/ (2016 census estimates pegged the population at 1,844, of whom 55 percent were African American).

47 Adeel Hassan, "Antwon Rose Shooting: White Police Officer Acquitted in Death of Black Teenager," New York Times, March 22, 2019, accessed at https://www.nytimes.com/2019/03/22/us/antwon-rose-shooting.html.

48 Id.

49 Lauren del Valle and Ralph Ellis, "Former East Pittsburgh Officer Found Not Guilty in Fatal Shooting of Unarmed Teenager." CNN, March 23, 2019, accessed at https://www.cnn.com/2019/03/22/us/officer-michael-rosfeld-antwon-rose-pittburgh-testimony/index.html.

50 Brentin Mock, "In Police Violence, the Fates of Cities and Suburbs Are Intertwined," CityLab, March 26, 2019, accessed at https://www.citylab.com/equity/2019/03/cities-suburbs-police-violence-antwon-rose-pittsburgh/585676/.

GLOSSARY

Abuse of process Abuse of process may be either a crime or a civil claim. In either context, it means that the police or a person used the legal system to bring a criminal charge or civil claim against another person for improper purposes. For example, in a criminal context, a police officer who charged a person with a crime not because the person violated the law but for purposes of harassment would have committed an abuse of process.

Allegations A statement of fact, claimed to be true, by a person involved in a criminal or civil case. Until a fact is proven, it remains an allegation. The term is used outside of legal settings as well, as when a person makes some kind of charge or factual assertion about a public issue or public figure.

Bench The bench is the place in the courtroom where the judge sits, which usually takes the form of a large raised desk. More often, "bench" refers to a trial in which a judge, not a jury, determines the outcome: "In a bench trial, the judge gives the verdict."

Civil case Civil cases contain no accusation of crime, but rather allegations of injury to the person or entity brining the case. Civil cases are brought by private individuals or entities; criminal cases (see definition) are brought by the local, state, or federal government, depending on the offense.

Complaint In a civil case in which a lawsuit is filed, the complaint is the document which begins the lawsuit. It is filed by the plaintiff, the party bringing the case (see definition). It contains the allegations that the plaintiff makes against the other side, the defendant.

Contingency fee In the American civil legal system, each side pays for its own legal representation, usually through hourly fees or through a full upfront fee. In lawsuits involving torts (see definition), lawyers may take on cases for plaintiffs without payment, but with a promise that any money eventually received by the plaintiff will be used to pay the lawyer, usually with one-third of the funds received. This fee is contingent; if, in the end, the plaintiff receives nothing, the lawyer receives nothing.

Criminal case In a criminal case, the government—not a private party— brings charges that a person (or sometimes an entity, such as a business) has committed an act that violates the criminal law. Criminal laws forbid certain kinds of conduct widely agreed upon to be offenses against the entire community and that put public or personal safety or property in jeopardy. Some criminal laws forbid certain acts always: For example, theft—to take someone else's property without permission and with the intention of permanently depriving the owner of it—is always a crime. Other criminal laws forbid acts only in certain circumstances: For example, it is not a crime to have sex with another person, but it is a crime—rape—to have sex with a person who does not consent. Criminal acts are considered harms not just to the victim but to everyone; therefore, unlike civil cases (in which one person alleges a private harm to herself by another), criminal cases are charged and brought to court only by the state. Criminal cases result in verdicts (see definition) of guilty or not guilty; in civil cases (see definition), verdicts declare whether or not the defendant (see definition) is at fault. If the defendant in a civil case is found liable (see definition of liability), he or she may have to pay money damages or take other actions; if a defendant in a criminal case is found guilty, he or she will carry the stigma of being a criminal and will also suffer punishment by the state: imprisonment, supervision outside of prison (e.g., probation), and/or fines (monetary penalties paid to the state).

Cross-examination Testimony (see definition) in courts by witnesses comes in response to questions asked by lawyers. After direct examination (see definition) of a witness by the lawyer who called the witness is completed, the other side's lawyer engages in cross-examination: asking leading questions— questions that suggest the answer—with the goal of exposing weaknesses in the witness's testimony, such as the witness's inability to perceive or remember things correctly, biases, failure to tell the truth, or criminal convictions.

Damages In most civil cases (see definition) the jury (or the judge, in a bench trial) is asked to find whether the defendant (see definition) is liable (i.e., responsible) for the injury, and if so, how much the defendant must pay the plaintiff (see definition) to compensate for the injury; the amount of compensation is called damages, or compensatory damages. In some cases, damages can also be assessed to deter bad conduct in the future; these are called punitive damages.

Defendant In a criminal case (see definition), the defendant is the person accused of a crime or crimes by the prosecution. In a civil case, the lawsuit is brought by the plaintiff (see definition), and the party against whom the suit is brought is called the defendant.

Defense The defendant or the defendant's case in either criminal or civil cases may be referred to as the defense.

Deliberations When a case is to be decided by a jury, the jurors hear the evidence (see definition) in court but are told not to discuss the case with each other or with anyone else while the case proceeds. When the trial has finished, the judge tells the jurors what the law is and then sends them to discuss the case between themselves to see if they can agree on a verdict (see definition); these discussions are called deliberations.

Deposition Used almost exclusively in civil cases, depositions are the taking of witness testimony (see definition), under oath, but outside court and before the trial begins. Depositions usually take place in a law office; lawyers for both sides are present and ask the witness questions in modified direct examination and cross-examination format (see definitions). A court stenographer is present and creates a word-for-word record of the proceedings. The pretrial period during which depositions take place is called discovery (see definition).

Direct examination Testimony (see definition) in courts by witnesses comes in response to questions asked by lawyers. When lawyers present the witnesses for the party they represent, they ask direct examination questions: typically, who, what, where, when, and why questions, but in any event questions that do not suggest any answer. For example, they may ask, "What happened?" or "Then what did you do?" Direct examination is followed by cross-examination (see definition).

Discovery The period during a civil case that follows the filing of the plaintiff's complaint, the defendant's formal written answer to the complaint, and any pretrial motion to dismiss the case and that precedes the trial itself. Discovery is used to flesh out the facts in the case by taking depositions (see definition), using written questions and answers, and other tools. The idea is to bring all of the facts to light prior to trial. The facts may bring about a settlement (see definition) before trial. If not, the facts become the basis upon which to try the case.

Evidence Any information gathered outside of court that is offered in court in order to prove the claims in the case. The term is used in both criminal and civil cases. The most common type of evidence is the testimony (see definition) of witnesses. The term also includes objects (e.g., in Jordan Miles's case, the Mountain Dew bottle, if retained by the officers, would have been a piece of evidence), results of forensic tests, and the opinions of experts.

Excessive force Police officers have the right, and sometimes the duty, to use force to achieve their lawful objectives, such as arresting a person. However, officers may only use an amount of force that is objectively reasonable under the circumstances—that is, enough to overcome any resistance they face, but not more than that amount. When more force is used than is objectively reasonable, a police officer may be alleged to have used excessive force. This was one of the claims that Jordan Miles brought against the three police officers: the force used against him exceeded what was objectively reasonable in the circumstances.

False arrest In order to make a lawful arrest, police must have probable cause (see definition) to believe the suspect committed a crime. A claim of false arrest, such as the one Jordan Miles brought against the three officers, is an allegation that the officers arrested him without probable cause and thus without sufficient legal justification.

Federal law The United States has two main levels of legal regulation: the systems of the 50 states and the District of Columbia, called state law, and the system of the national government, called federal law. These systems have their own spheres and exist in parallel; both of them cover criminal law and civil law, with different statutes. Federal law covers matters involving the U.S. Constitution and constitutional rights of Americans, and federal statutes are laws that govern national interests and topics such as interstate crimes and federal regulation of industries and activities.

Hearing A court proceeding that is not a full trial is called a hearing. Hearings can take place at a variety of points in a case, both before and after a trial; they can have a set purpose, such as the preliminary hearing in the criminal case against Jordan Miles, which was held to determine whether or not there was probable cause (see definition) to proceed with a criminal case. Other hearings may be held on request of one of the parties, to have the court consider a request or a motion.

Hearsay Assertions in statements made out of court, offered as evidence in a court, in order to prove what the statements assert, are called hearsay. For evidence of any kind to be accepted in court, it may not contain hearsay. For example, in a court case, Witness A may not answer a question by saying, "I was at the scene, and B told me that ...." Witness A may say what *she* perceived or did, but not what *someone else* said. This is because the person making the statement is not in court to be cross-examined. There are many exceptions to the rules against hearsay, but if a lawyer for one side objects to evidence as hearsay, and no exception applies, the hearsay testimony will not be allowed.

Implicit bias Implicit bias is the term used by psychologists to denote unconscious preferences for or against a social group, such as a race, ethnic or religious group, or gender. Implicit biases exist below the level of conscious awareness, but nevertheless may influence the person's behavior in ways that may have a negative impact on members of nonpreferred groups.

Liability In a civil case, the first legal question is whether the party accused of doing something wrong is actually responsible for that wrong. This question of responsibility in the legal system is usually called liability. (A person found guilty of a crime can also be called criminally liable, but that term is not as common.) Once a party is found liable, the second question is whether the party bringing the lawsuit suffered damages (see definition). But without a finding of liability, the question of damages need not be faced.

Litigate To litigate is to bring a claim in court and to do the work necessary to move the case through the court system to some kind of conclusion. It is usually used in the context of civil cases.

Motion Any request made to a court in the course of a civil or criminal trial may be called a motion. The term refers to the fact that the party (see definition) making the motion is said to be "moving" the court to take a certain action. Motions often come prior to trial and ask that the court dismiss all or part of the case, or that the court allow or disallow the use of certain evidence. Motions can also come during the trial.

Negligence The failure to exercise due and customary care in one's conduct or other actions is called negligence. Negligence is the basis for tort claims (see definition) in which another person or entity is damaged through the negligent party's lack of ordinary care—for example, leaving one's city sidewalk crusted with ice, resulting in a fall and injury to another.

Party The people or institutions that bring charges or claims in court, or those who are named in cases as committing the crime or harm and must therefore defend themselves in a case, are all called the parties to the case. In a civil case (see definition), the plaintiff (see definition) brings claims into court in a lawsuit, contending that she suffered harm because of the defendant (see definition). Both plaintiff and defendant are referred to as the parties to the case. In criminal cases, the prosecution (see definition) brings criminal charges against the defendant (see definition), the person accused of criminal conduct. Both prosecution and defense are referred to as the parties to the case.

Plaintiff In a civil lawsuit, the party who brings or starts the lawsuit is called the plaintiff. The term is not used in criminal cases (see definition). The plaintiff has the burden of proving the case; a failure to bring enough evidence to prove it results in a verdict against the plaintiff and for the defendant.

Pretrial motions In both criminal and civil cases, both parties can bring motions (see definition) before trial begins, asking the judge to do something with the case. Many such motions ask the court to dismiss the case altogether or in part; others ask for certain pieces of evidence to be excluded from testimony (see definition).

Prima facie This Latin phrase, translated as "on its face" or "at first look," is used to denote a minimum amount of evidence necessary for a criminal charge or a civil claim to go forward to the next step in the process. Presenting a prima facie case falls to the party attempting to prove the case—usually the prosecution in a criminal case and the plaintiff in a civil case. If a prima facie case is presented, the case moves on to the next phase.

Probable cause Probable cause is a standard used to describe the amount of evidence necessary for police to arrest a person, or for a judge to grant a search warrant. It is also the standard used to determine if a criminal case (see definition) should move from the preliminary stage—charges by the prosecution—to the trial stage. For probable cause for arrest to exist, there must be evidence that a crime has been committed and that it is probable that the suspect is involved. The U.S. Supreme Court has refused to describe how much evidence probable cause requires with any kind of precision, but it is far less than the amount necessary to convict in a criminal case—"beyond a reasonable doubt"—and less than the amount of evidence necessary to win a civil case—"more probable than not."

Prosecution The prosecution is the term for the state or the federal government in a criminal case (see definition); the prosecution brings the charges to court and institutes the criminal case against the defendant (see definition). The person conducting the case in court for the state or federal government is called the prosecutor.

Settlement In a civil case, the parties—plaintiff and defendant—may reach an agreement on what should happen, instead of going through a full trial and letting the jury or judge decide the outcome. A settlement will almost always include the formal dropping of the plaintiff's lawsuit in exchange for some combination of payment of money and certain actions (e.g., the rehiring of an employee or the acknowledgment of a mistake or wrong), as part of the agreement between the parties. The term can also refer to the amount of money paid in a settlement agreement.

Stop and frisk The case of *Terry v. Ohio*, decided by the U.S. Supreme Court in 1968, gives a police officer the right to order a person to stop, usually so the police officer can get an explanation for behavior the officer feels is suspicious. To have this authority, the officer must have reasonable suspicion—an amount of evidence that is less than probable cause, but more than a mere hunch or gut instinct—to believe that a crime is or has been committed, and the suspect is involved. The suspicion must consist of facts and inference the officer can articulate. In addition, if the officer has reasonable suspicion that the suspect is armed—either because the officer sees evidence of a gun under or in the suspect's clothing, or because the suspected crime includes armed violence—she may frisk the suspect, which means to perform a pat down of the suspect and his outer clothing in a search for weapons.

Testimony When a witness in court gives evidence (see definition) by answering questions posed by the lawyers, that evidence is called testimony. A witness who speaks in court is said to testify. Almost always, testimony in court is given under an oath to tell the truth. Sometimes, testimony may be given outside courts; one such circumstance is a deposition (see definition), in which testimony is given prior to the trial or hearing in the case and in a neutral place such as a law office.

Tort A legal claim usually asserting that the plaintiff (see definition) has been damaged by the negligence (see definition) of the defendant (see definition) is a tort.

"Under color of" This phrase occurs in various federal laws that require proof of action by a person acting under the authority that person has by virtue of state law. For example, a police officer making an arrest is acting "under color of" the laws of his state.

Unlawful seizure Any seizure of an object or a person by a police officer requires probable cause (or in the case of a stop and frisk, reasonable suspicion) to be lawful. Seizures include arrests. Any arrest without probable cause is considered unlawful seizure.

Use of force When a police officer must use any degree of physical force—from taking a person's arm to lead them away for arrest, to using a firearm to stop a deadly threat—this is considered a use of force.

Verdict A verdict is a decision made by either a judge or a jury that decides the ultimate question in a case. In a criminal case (see definition), the verdict is the guilty or not guilty decision on each crime charged. In a civil case, the verdict is the decision on whether or not the plaintiff (see definition) proved each claim.

Witness Any person who gives testimony (see definition) in a matter is called a witness. The testimony can come in court, or in any other setting, such as a deposition (see definition). The common definition of a witness is a person who observes something; for example, a person might be called an eyewitness, if he sees something. An eyewitness may give testimony in court about the thing, person, or event seen. But anyone who gives testimony is called a witness, regardless of the subject of the testimony.

INDEX

335